20,000 LEAGUES UNDER THE SEA

This supernatural apparition

Jules Verne

20,000 Leagues Under the Sea

ILLUSTRATED BY THE DILLONS

TRANSLATED BY ANTHONY BONNER

Books of Wonder

HARPERCOLLINS*PUBLISHERS*

Twenty Thousand Leagues Under the Sea by Jules Verne, translated by Anthony Bonner
Translation copyright © 1962 by Bantam Books, a division of Bantam Doubleday Dell Publishing Group, Inc.
Reprinted by permission of Bantam Doubleday Dell Publishing Group, Inc.
Illustrations copyright © 2000 by Leo and Diane Dillon
Afterword copyright © 2000 by Peter Glassman
Printed in the United States of America. For information address HarperCollins Children's Books,
a division of HarperCollins Publishers, 1350 Avenue of the Americas, New York, NY 10019.
www.harperchildrens.com
Books of Wonder
16 West Eighteenth Street, New York, NY 10011

Library of Congress Cataloging-in-Publication Data
Verne, Jules, 1828–1905.
 [Vingt mille lieues sous les mers. English]
 20,000 leagues under the sea / Jules Verne ; illustrated by the Dillons ; translated by Anthony Bonner.
  p.   cm. — (Books of wonder)
 Summary: Retells the adventures of a French professor and his two companions as they sail above and below
the world's oceans as prisoners of the fabulous electric submarine of the deranged Captain Nemo.
 ISBN 0-688-10535-1
 [1. Science fiction. 2. Submarines—Fiction. 3. Sea stories.] I. Title: Twenty thousand leagues under the
sea. II. Dillon, Diane, ill. III. Dillon, Leo, ill. IV. Bonner, Anthony. V. Title. VI. Series.
PZ7.V597 Tw8   2000   00-24336
[Fic]—dc21

1 2 3 4 5 6 7 8 9 10
❖
First HarperCollins Edition, 2000
Books of Wonder is a registered trademark of Ozma, Inc.

Contents

PART TWO

List of Illustrations

PART ONE

CHAPTER I
A Shifting Reef

The year 1866 was marked by a strange event, an unexplainable occurrence which is undoubtedly still fresh in everyone's memory. Those living in coastal towns or in the interior of continents were aroused by all sorts of rumors; but it was seafaring people who were particularly excited. Merchants, shipowners, skippers and masters of Europe and America, naval officers of all countries and the various governments of both continents were deeply concerned over the matter.

Several ships had recently met at sea "an enormous thing," a long slender object which was sometimes phosphorescent and which was infinitely larger and faster than a whale.

The facts concerning this apparition, entered in various logbooks, agreed closely with one another as to the structure of the object or creature in question, the incredible speed of its movements, the surprising power of its locomotion and the strange life with which it seemed endowed. If it was a member of the whale family, it was larger than any so far classified by scientists. Neither Cuvier, Lacépède, Dumeril nor Quatrefages would have admitted that such a monster could exist—unless they had seen it with their own scientists' eyes.

Taking an average of observations made at different times—and rejecting those timid evaluations which said the object was only two hundred feet long, and also putting aside those exaggerated opinions which said it was a mile wide and three miles long—one could nevertheless conclude that this phenomenal creature was considerably larger than anything at that time recognized by ichthyologists—if it existed at all.

But it did exist—there was no denying this fact any longer—and considering the natural inclination of the human brain toward objects of wonder, one can understand the excitement produced throughout the world by this supernatural apparition. In any case, the idea of putting it into the realm of fiction had to be abandoned.

On July 20, 1866, the steamer *Governor Higginson* of the Calcutta and Burnach Steam Navigation Company had encountered this moving mass five miles east of the Australian coast. Captain Baker first thought he had sighted an unknown reef; he was even getting ready to plot its exact position when two columns of water spurted out of the inexplicable object and rose with a loud whistling noise to a height of a hundred and fifty feet. So, unless the reef contained a geyser, the *Governor Higginson* was quite simply in the presence of an unknown aquatic mammal, spurting columns of water mixed with air and vapor out of its blowholes.

A similar thing was observed on July 23 of the same year in Pacific waters, by the *Christopher Columbus* of the West India and Pacific Steam Navigation Company. This extraordinary creature could therefore move from one place to another with surprising speed, since within a space of only three days, the *Governor Higginson* and the *Christopher Columbus* had sighted it at two points on the globe separated by more than 2100 nautical miles.

Two weeks later and six thousand miles from this last spot, the *Helvetia* of the Compagnie Nationale and the *Shannon* of the Royal Mail Steamship Company, passing on opposite courses in that part of the Atlantic lying between the United States and Europe, signaled one another that they had sighted the monster at 42° 15' N. Lat. and 60° 35' W. Long. In this simultaneous observation they felt able to judge the creature's minimum length at more than 350 feet, since it was larger than both ships each of which measured 330 feet over-all. But the largest whales, the Kulammak and Umgullick that live in the waters around the Aleutian Islands, never exceed 180 feet in length, if that much.

These reports arriving one after the other, with fresh observations made on board the liner *Le Pereire*, a collision between the *Etna* of the Inman Line and the monster, an official report drawn up by the officers of the French frigate *Normandie*, and a very reliable sighting made by Commodore Fitz-James' staff on board the *Lord Clyde*, greatly stirred public opinion. In lighthearted countries, people made jokes about it, but in serious practical-minded countries, such as England, America and Germany, it was a matter of grave concern.

In every big city the monster became the fashion: it was sung in cafés, derided in newspapers and discussed on the stage. Scandal sheets had a marvelous opportunity to print all kinds of wild stories. Even ordinary newspapers—always short of copy—printed articles about every huge, imaginary monster one could think of, from the white whale, the terrible "Moby Dick" of the far north, to the legendary Norse kraken whose tentacles could entwine a five-hundred-ton ship and drag it to the bottom. Reports of ancient times were mentioned, the opinions of Aristotle and Pliny who admitted to the existence of such monsters, along with those of the Norwegian bishop, Pontoppidan, Paul Heggede and finally Mr. Harrington, whose good faith no one can question when he claims to have seen, while on board the *Castillan* in 1857, that enormous serpent which until then had been seen in no waters but those of the old Paris newspaper, the *Constitutionnel*.

It was then that in scientific societies and journals an interminable argument broke out between those who believed in the monster and those who did not. The "question of the monster" had everyone aroused. Newspapermen, who always pretend to be on the side of scientists and against those who live by their imagination, spilled gallons of ink during this memorable campaign; and some even spilled two or three drops of blood, after arguments that had started over sea serpents and ended in the most violent personal insults.

For six months this war was waged with varying fortune. Serious, weighty articles were published by the Brazilian Geographical Institute, the Royal Scientific Academy of Berlin, the British Association and the Smithsonian Institute in Washington; others appeared in the *Indian Archipelago*, in Abbé Moigno's *Cosmos*, in Petermann's *Mittheilungen* and in the science sections of all the important newspapers of France and other countries. The smaller newspapers replied with inexhaustible energy. Their writers, cleverly parodying a saying of Linnaeus which had been quoted by the adversaries of the monster, stated that "nature does not make fools"* and called on their contemporaries

---

*This is a pun on the two French words *saut* ("jump, leap" as in the original saying of Linnaeus) and *sot* ("fool"), which are pronounced the same. (Translator's note.)

not to contradict nature by seriously discussing krakens, sea serpents, "Moby Dicks" and other reports of delirious sailors. Finally, in a much-dreaded satirical newspaper, its favorite writer took care of the whole matter by attacking the monster, dealing it a death blow and finishing it off in the midst of universal laughter. Wit had conquered science.

During the first months of the year 1867 the whole question seemed buried never to be revived, when new facts were brought before the public. It was no longer a question of a scientific problem to be solved, but of a real danger seriously to be avoided. The whole matter took on another aspect. The monster now became a small island, rock or reef, but a reef that was vague, shifting and indeterminate.

On March 5, 1867, the *Moravian* of the Montreal Ocean Company, sailing at night in 27° 30' Lat. and 72° 15' Long., struck on its starboard side a rock indicated on no chart. It had been cruising at thirteen knots, under the combined force of the wind and its 400-horsepower engines. Had it not been for the superior quality of its hull, the *Moravian* undoubtedly would have been split open by the blow and sunk with the 237 passengers it was bringing back from Canada.

The accident took place at about five in the morning, toward daybreak. The officers on watch rushed to the after part of the ship. They examined the sea carefully and saw nothing but an area of swirling water about a third of a mile away, as if the surface had been violently agitated. Their position was noted, and the *Moravian* continued on its way, apparently without any serious damage. Had it struck a submerged rock, or the enormous wreck of some sunken ship? There was no way of knowing, but an inspection of its hull in drydock showed that part of the keel had been broken.

Even this, although extremely serious in itself, might perhaps have been forgotten, like so many other occurrences, if three weeks later it had not been re-enacted under similar circumstances. But because of the nationality of the ship involved in this new collision and the reputation of the company to which it belonged, this event caused a tremendous stir.

There is no one who has not heard of the famous English shipowner, Cunard. In 1840 this shrewd businessman started a postal service between Liverpool and

Halifax with three wooden side-wheel ships of 1162 tons each and equipped with engines capable of developing 400 horsepower. Eight years later the company's fleet was increased by four ships of 1820 tons each and with 650-horsepower engines, and then two years after this, by two other vessels with yet greater tonnage and power. In 1853 the Cunard Line, whose mail-carrying privileges had just been renewed, successively added to its fleet the *Arabia*, the *Persia*, the *China*, the *Scotia*, the *Java* and the *Russia*, all of them very fast and larger than any ships which had ever plied the seas, except for the *Great Eastern*. Thus in 1867 the company owned twelve ships, eight with side-wheels and four with propellers.

If I give these brief details, it is so that everyone might know the importance of this ship company, known the world over for the intelligent way in which it is run. No transoceanic venture has been more cleverly organized, and none crowned with such success. In twenty-six years Cunard ships have crossed the Atlantic two thousand times, without missing a single voyage, with never a delay and without ever losing a single letter, man or ship. This is why passengers, in spite of strong competition from French liners, still choose the Cunard Line in preference to all others, as would appear from a survey of official documents of the last few years. No one, therefore, will be surprised at the stir caused by an accident involving one of its finest steamers.

On April 13, 1867, the *Scotia* was sailing at 15° 12' Long. and 45° 37' Lat. on a clear sea with a moderate breeze. It was traveling at a speed of 13.43 knots, propelled by its thousand-horsepower engines. Its side-wheels were striking the water in regular rhythm. It was then drawing 22 feet of water, with a displacement of 221,900 cubic feet.

At 4:17 in the afternoon, while the passengers were gathered in the big lounge having their tea, a slight blow was felt against the hull of the *Scotia*, on the quarter slightly behind the port wheel.

The *Scotia* had not struck something; it had been struck, and by some object which was more cutting or perforating than blunt. The blow had seemed so slight that nobody on board would have given it a second thought, had not the men working below rushed up onto the bridge and shouted: "We're sinking! We're sinking!"

At first the passengers were very frightened; but Captain Anderson quickly reassured them. For there was no real danger; the *Scotia* was divided into seven watertight compartments and could therefore face any leak with impunity.

Captain Anderson immediately went down into the hold. He found the fifth compartment flooded, and the speed with which this had happened proved that the leak was considerable. Fortunately this compartment did not contain the boilers, for then the fires would have gone out immediately.

Captain Anderson ordered the engines stopped at once, and one of the sailors dove to find out the extent of the damage. He soon discovered that there was a hole six feet across in the hull of the steamer. But such a hole could not be plugged up, and so the *Scotia* had to continue its voyage with its side-wheels half submerged. She was then three hundred miles from Cape Clear; and finally, three days behind schedule—a delay which caused great uneasiness in Liverpool—she came alongside the company docks.

After putting her in drydock, engineers inspected the *Scotia*. They could not believe their eyes. Eight feet below her waterline there was a neat hole in the form of an isosceles triangle. It was so perfectly shaped that it could scarcely have been done better with a precision instrument. The object which had made this hole must have been extremely unusual—and after being driven into the ship with prodigious force, enough to pierce a hull $1^{1}/_{2}$ inches thick, it must have withdrawn by itself in a manner completely unexplainable.

This new event once again stirred up public opinion. From then on, all unexplained losses at sea were attributed to the monster. This fantastic animal bore the responsibility for all such shipwrecks, which unfortunately are not few in number; for of the three thousand ships reported sunk each year by the *Bureau Veritas*, the number of steam or sailing ships assumed to be lost with all hands through absence of any news amounts to no less than two hundred!

And it was the "monster" who, rightly or wrongly, was held responsible for their disappearance and for the increasing danger of traveling between various continents, to the point where the public came out with a categoric demand that the seas be rid of this formidable creature, at any price.

CHAPTER II

The Pros and Cons

When these events took place, I was on my way back from a scientific expedition to the Badlands of Nebraska in the United States. The French Government had asked me to join this expedition because of my position as assistant professor at the Museum of Natural History in Paris. After spending six months in Nebraska, I finally arrived in New York toward the end of March, laden down with the many precious things I had collected there. I was to leave for France in the beginning of May. In the meanwhile, I was busy classifying my mineralogical, botanical and zoological treasures; it was then that the incident of the *Scotia* took place.

I was well informed on this much discussed subject—and in fact, how could I not have been? I had read and reread all the American and European newspapers without getting any nearer to a conclusion. This mystery intrigued me. I was unable to form any opinion about it, and drifted from one extreme to the other. That something had actually taken place, there could be no question; doubting Thomases were invited to touch the *Scotia*'s wound.

During my stay in New York, the question was at its height. The theory that it was a floating island or an elusive reef, upheld by people not competent to judge, had been completely abandoned. For unless this reef contained a motor, how could it move from one place to another with such prodigious speed?

Likewise the theory of the floating wreckage of some huge ship was rejected, also because of its rapidity of movement.

There therefore remained only two possible solutions to the problem, and each one developed its own group of partisans: on the one hand there were those who claimed it must be a monster of colossal strength, and on the other

hand there were those who held it to be a "submarine" with extremely powerful engines.

But this second theory, perhaps the most plausible, could not stand up against
the inquiries being carried out both in Europe and America. It seemed highly
improbable that a private individual could have such a mechanical device at his
disposition. How and when could he have built it? And how could he have kept
its construction a secret?

Only a government could possess such a weapon of destruction, and in these
disastrous times when man's genius is being put to work increasing the power of
weapons, some country might have tried to build such a formidable device.
After the chassepot rifles, torpedoes; after the torpedoes, underwater battering-
rams; and then—the reaction. At least, so I hope.

But the theory that it was some war machine fell through before the statements of various governments. Since it was a matter of public interest, with the
safety of transoceanic communications in question, there was no reason to
doubt the honesty of their statements. And in addition, how could anyone imagine that the construction of such a submarine could have escaped public notice?
To keep a secret under such circumstances is very difficult for an individual, and
surely impossible for a country whose every act is constantly watched by powerful rivals.

Therefore, after inquiries made in England, France, Russia, Prussia, Spain,
Italy, America and even Turkey, the theory of an underwater *Monitor* was defin-
itively rejected.

So once again, and in spite of the incessant jokes in lesser newspapers, everyone was talking about the monster, and people were soon inventing creatures
more absurd than the wildest dreams of some mad ichthyologist.

During my stay in New York, several people had done me the honor of consulting me on this matter. In France I had published a two-volume work in quarto called *The Mysteries of the Ocean Depths*. This book had been especially well
received by scientists, and had therefore made me a specialist in this rather obscure
branch of natural history. People wanted to know my opinion. As long as the facts
could still be denied, I confined myself to complete skepticism. But I soon found

myself driven into a corner and forced to explain in no uncertain terms. And finally, "the honorable Pierre Aronnax, Professor of the Paris Museum" was called upon by the New York *Herald* to formulate some sort of opinion.

I complied. I spoke because I could not remain silent. I discussed the problem from every angle, both political and scientific, and I give here an extract of my carefully written article, published in that newspaper on April 30. After examining one by one all the various solutions that had been proposed, I said:

Therefore, since all other theories must be rejected, one is forced to admit the existence of some marine animal of extraordinary power.

We know nothing about the great ocean depths. Soundings have been unable to reach them. What takes place in those remote canyons? What creatures live or can live twelve or fifteen miles below the surface? How are such animals built? We can scarcely even guess.

These questions go hand in hand with the problem under discussion. For either we know all the varieties of creatures which inhabit our planet, or we do not.

If we do not know them all, if nature still holds some secrets for us where life in the sea is concerned, then nothing could be more reasonable than to admit the existence of fish or whales of a kind unknown to us, especially built to inhabit the unfathomable depths of the ocean, and which some event, whim or desire brings to the surface at long intervals of time.

If, on the contrary, we know all species of living things, we must try to find the animal in question among the marine creatures already classified, and in this case I would favor admitting the existence of a giant narwhal.

The ordinary narwhal, or unicorn-fish, is a kind of whale which grows to a length of sixty feet. Multiply this five or ten times, give this fish strength in proportion to its size and you will have the animal under discussion. It would have the proportions observed by the officers of the *Shannon*, the weapon required to explain the hole in the *Scotia* and the strength needed to penetrate the hull of a steamer.

For the narwhal is armed with a kind of ivory sword, or halberd as some naturalists put it. It is a tusk as hard as steel. Occasionally these tusks are found imbedded in the bodies of other kinds of whales, against which the narwhal always wins. Others have been removed, not without difficulty, from the hulls of ships which they had pierced clean through as easily as a drill pierces a barrel. The museum in the Faculty of Medicine in Paris owns one of these tusks 7 feet 4 1/2 inches long and 19 inches thick at the base!

Now imagine this weapon ten times larger, and the fish ten times stronger, imagine it traveling at a speed of twenty miles an hour, multiply this speed by its mass and you will have a blow capable of producing the required catastrophe.

Therefore, until I receive fuller information, I shall be of the opinion that it is a unicorn-fish of colossal proportions, armed not with a halberd but with a real battering-ram like a warship, which it could equal in both size and strength.

This might be the explanation of this unexplainable phenomenon, unless it is all an illusion in spite of what has been glimpsed, seen, felt and experienced—which is still possible!

These last words were cowardice on my part; but to a certain degree I wanted to protect my scholarly reputation and not be the laughingstock of America, where people enjoy a hearty laugh. I left myself a way out. But in effect, I admitted to the existence of the "monster."

My article was hotly discussed and therefore became widely known. The solution it proposed, moreover, gave free rein to people's imaginations. The human mind enjoys grandiose ideas about supernatural creatures. And the sea is the proper medium for such ideas, for only there can giants arise and develop, giants alongside which earthly animals such as elephants or rhinoceros are nothing but dwarfs. The seas support the largest known species of mammals, and they perhaps conceal mollusks of incredible size, or terrifying crustaceans such as lobsters a hundred yards long or crabs weighing two tons! Why not? Long ago in geological times earthbound animals, quadrupeds, quadrumana, reptiles and birds all produced species of gigantic size. The Creator had formed them in a colossal mold which time has reduced little by little. Why could the sea with its unknown depths not have kept some vast specimens of life in another age, since, unlike the earth's shell which is constantly being altered, it is unchanging? Why could it not hide in its bosom the last survivors of titanic species, for whom years are centuries and centuries millennia?

But I am letting myself be carried away by reveries which I must now put aside. Enough of these fantasies which time has changed for me into terrible realities. But back then, people had already made up their minds about this matter, and the public wholeheartedly believed in the existence of some prodigious creature which had nothing in common with fabled sea serpents.

But although some saw it as a purely scientific problem, others, especially the more practical-minded people in America and England, thought it best to clear the ocean of this terrible monster in order to make transatlantic travel safe again. Industrial and commercial newspapers considered the question principally from this point of view. *The Shipping and Mercantile Gazette*, the *Lloyd*, the *Paquebot*, the *Revue Maritime et Coloniale* and all the periodicals concerned with insurance companies who threatened to raise their rates were unanimous on this point.

Once public opinion had made itself felt, the United States was the first country to go into action. A very fast frigate, the *Abraham Lincoln*, got ready to put to sea as soon as possible. The shipyards were thrown open to Commander Farragut, who had his ship fitted out with great speed and efficiency.

But then, as always happens, just when it had been decided to chase the monster, it did not reappear. For two months it was not heard of. No ship sighted it. It seemed as if this unicorn-fish knew about the plots being hatched against it. There had been so much discussion about it, and even over the transatlantic cable! Some jokers pretended that this sly creature had intercepted some telegram and was making use of the information it contained.

The frigate was therefore prepared for a long campaign and equipped with formidable fishing gear, but nobody knew where to send it. And everyone was growing more impatient when, on July 2, it was learned that a steamer of the line that plies between San Francisco and Shanghai had seen the animal three weeks earlier in northern Pacific waters.

This piece of news caused great excitement. Commander Farragut was ordered to set sail within twenty-four hours. The ship was stocked with food and its coal bunkers filled to the brim. Not a single man was missing for the ship's roll call. All that remained to be done was to light its furnaces, heat its boilers and weigh anchor! Another half day's delay would have been unforgivable! But then Commander Farragut asked nothing better than to be under way.

Three hours before the *Abraham Lincoln* was due to leave its pier in Brooklyn, I received the following letter:

Mr. Aronnax
Professor of the Paris Museum
Fifth Avenue Hotel, New York

Dear Sir:

If you would like to join the expedition of the *Abraham Lincoln,* the government of the Union would take great pleasure in having you represent France on this enterprise. Commander Farragut has a cabin at your disposal.

Very cordially yours,
J. B. Hobson,
Secretary of the Navy

CHAPTER III
As Monsieur Wishes

Three seconds before the arrival of J. B. Hobson's letter, I had no more thought about chasing the unicorn-fish than I had about trying to find the Northwest Passage. Three seconds after reading a letter from the honorable Secretary of the Navy, I realized that my true vocation, my sole aspiration was to chase this disturbing monster and rid the world of it.

But I had just come back from a long trip; I was tired and longing for rest. I had had only one desire: to return to my country, my friends, my little apartment near the Botanical Gardens and my precious collections! But nothing could keep me back. I forgot everything—weariness, friends and collections, and without a second thought I accepted the American Government's offer.

"Besides," I thought, "all roads lead back to Europe, and maybe the unicornfish will be kind enough to lure me toward the coasts of France! This worthy animal will let himself be caught in European waters—as a personal favor to me—and then I'll bring back no less than a foot and a half of his ivory tusk for the Museum of Natural History."

But in the meantime we had to look for this narwhal in the north Pacific, which meant going to France by way of the antipodes.

"Conseil!" I cried impatiently.

Conseil was my servant. A devoted young man who followed me on all my trips; a brave Belgian whom I liked and who liked me. He was impassive by nature, of regular habits as a matter of principle, eager out of habit, scarcely ever taken aback by life's surprises, very clever with his hands, fit for any kind of service and the sort of person who, in spite of having a name meaning "Advice," never gave any even when asked.

As a result of rubbing elbows with the little group of scientists attached to the Botanical Gardens, Conseil had picked up quite a bit of knowledge. In him I had a well-informed specialist in natural-history classification, who could, with an acrobat's ease, rush up and down the ladder of phyla, divisions, classes, subclasses, orders, families, genera, subgenera, species and varieties. But his knowledge ended there. His whole life was classification and he knew nothing else. He was very well read in the theory of classification, but knew little about the practical side, to the point where I don't think he could have told the difference between a sperm whale and an ordinary whale! But in spite of this, he was a fine young man.

For ten years now, Conseil had followed me everywhere science had led me. Never a murmur about the length or weariness of a trip. Never an objection to packing his suitcase for some new country, China or the Congo, no matter how far off it was. He would go anywhere without a question. Moreover his strong constitution defied all illness; he had powerful muscles, but no nerves, or at least he gave no appearance of having any.

He was thirty, and his age was to his master's as fifteen is to twenty. Please excuse me for thus stating that I was forty years old.

But Conseil had one defect. Being of a very formal nature, he only addressed me in the third person—to the point where it was annoying.

"Conseil!" I repeated, as I feverishly began my preparations for leaving.

I felt completely sure of this young man's devotion. I usually never asked him whether or not he would like to accompany me on my travels; but this time it was a question of an expedition that could go on indefinitely, of a dangerous enterprise in pursuit of an animal capable of sinking a frigate as if it were a nutshell! This was food for thought, even for the most impassive man in the world! What would he say?

"Conseil!" I shouted a third time.

Conseil appeared.

"Monsieur was calling?" he said as he entered.

"Yes, my boy. Get our things together, mine and yours. We're leaving in two hours."

"As Monsieur wishes," Conseil answered calmly.

"There's not a moment to lose. Pack all my traveling equipment, and as many suits, shirts and socks as you can—and hurry!"

"And Monsieur's collection?"

"We'll take care of that later."

"What! The archiotherium, hyracotherium, creodons, cheopotamus and the other specimens Monsieur collected?"

"They'll keep them for us at the hotel."

"And Monsieur's live babirusa?"

"They'll feed it while we're away. Besides, I'll have our menagerie sent to France after we leave."

"That means we're not going back to Paris?" Conseil asked.

"Yes . . . don't worry . . ." I answered evasively, "only by a rather roundabout way."

"Whatever roundabout way Monsieur wishes."

"Oh, it won't be too long! Just not quite as direct, that's all. We're taking passage on the *Abraham Lincoln*."

"Whatever suits Monsieur," replied Conseil calmly.

"You know, my friend, that it has to do with the monster . . . the famous narwhal. . . . We're going to rid the seas of this animal! The author of a two-volume work in quarto on *The Mysteries of the Ocean Depths* cannot turn down an invitation to go with Commander Farragut! It is a glorious mission, but . . . also dangerous! No one knows where it will take us! These creatures can be full of strange whims! But we'll go all the same! We have a commander who'll stop at nothing . . . !"

"Wherever Monsieur goes, I'll go too," answered Conseil.

"But think it over! I want to be completely frank with you. People don't always come back from expeditions such as these!"

"As Monsieur wishes."

A quarter of an hour later our trunks were ready. Conseil had done everything in the twinkling of an eye, and I could be sure nothing was missing, for he classified shirts and suits just as carefully as he did birds and mammals.

The elevator left us in the big mezzanine lounge. I went down the stairs leading to the lobby. I paid my bill at the huge reception desk which was always crowded with people. I left orders to have my cases of stuffed animals and dried plants sent to Paris. I opened an account large enough to take care of the babirusa, and with Conseil right behind, jumped into a carriage.

This cab, which charged four dollars a trip, went down Broadway to Union Square, followed Fourth Avenue to its junction with the Bowery, then took Katrin Street and stopped, at Pier 34. There, the Katrin Ferry took everything, men, horses and carriage, to Brooklyn, that great annex of New York situated on the other side of the East River, and in several minutes we arrived on the wharf alongside which the *Abraham Lincoln* was belching forth columns of black smoke through its two funnels.

Our baggage was immediately transferred to the deck of the frigate. I rushed aboard and asked for Commander Farragut. One of the sailors led me to the poop where I found myself in the presence of a handsome officer who stretched out his hand to me.

"Mr. Pierre Aronnax?" he said.

"Yes," I answered. "Commander Farragut?"

"In person. Welcome aboard, Professor. Your cabin is ready."

I bowed, and leaving the commander to take care of his preparations, I had myself taken to my cabin.

The *Abraham Lincoln* had been perfectly chosen and fitted out for its new task. It was a very fast frigate with superheating equipment permitting it to build up as much as seven atmospheres of steam pressure. Under these conditions the *Abraham Lincoln* could attain a speed of 18.3 knots, which although considerable was nevertheless not enough to grapple with the gigantic creature we were after.

The way it was fitted out inside corresponded favorably with its nautical qualities. I was very pleased with my cabin, which had a door leading to the officers' mess.

"We'll be very comfortable here," I said to Conseil.

"If Monsieur doesn't mind my saying so," answered Conseil, "as comfortable as a hermit crab in the shell of a whelk."

I left Conseil to secure our trunks and went back on deck to watch the preparations for departure.

Just then, Commander Farragut was ordering to cast off the last rope mooring the *Abraham Lincoln* to its Brooklyn pier. That meant that if I had been a quarter of an hour late, or even less, the frigate would have left without me, and I would have missed out on this extraordinary, strange and improbable expedition, a true account of which might well meet with some skepticism.

But Commander Farragut did not want to lose a single moment setting out for those waters where the animal had been sighted. He called for his engineer.

"Is the pressure up?" he asked.

"Yes, sir," answered the engineer.

"Go ahead," cried Commander Farragut.

At this order, transmitted to the engine room by means of a compressed-air device, the mechanics put the starting wheel into motion. The steam whistled through the half-open valves. The long horizontal pistons groaned and pushed the rods and drive-shaft. The blades of the propeller struck the water with increasing speed, and the *Abraham Lincoln* pushed forward amid an escort of a hundred ferryboats and tenders filled with spectators.

The Brooklyn and Manhattan wharves lining the East River were filled with people. Three hurrahs, rising from five hundred thousand chests, burst out one after the other. Thousands of handkerchiefs waved above the compact mass of the crowd, saluting the *Abraham Lincoln* till it reached the waters of the Hudson, at the tip of that elongated peninsula which contains the city of New York.

Then the frigate followed the New Jersey shore lined with villas and passed by the forts which saluted it with their largest cannon. The *Abraham Lincoln* answered by three times lowering and raising the American flag, whose thirty-nine stars shone on the mizzenmast. Then, slowing down in order to pass through the channel marked by buoys, it passed Sandy Hook where thousands of spectators cheered it once again.

The escort of boats and tenders did not leave the frigate until she reached the lightship whose two beacons mark the entrance to New York Harbor.

It was then three o'clock. The pilot got into his dinghy and rowed over to the little schooner waiting for him to leeward. The fires were stoked up and the propeller churned faster in the water; the frigate skirted the long, yellow coast of Long Island, and at eight in the evening, after losing sight of Fire Island to the northwest, it ran at full steam toward the dark waters of the Atlantic.

CHAPTER IV
Ned Land

Commander Farragut was a good sailor, worthy of the frigate he commanded. His vessel and he were one; he was the soul of the ship. As for the whale we were after, he had no doubts about it, and he would not let the men on board even discuss whatever doubts they may have had. He believed in it as some old women believe in the Leviathan—for him it was an act of faith, not logic. The monster existed and he would rid the seas of it—he had sworn he would. He was a kind of knight of Rhodes, a Dieudonné de Gozon going off to meet the dragon laying waste to his island. Either Commander Farragut would kill the narwhal or the narwhal would kill Commander Farragut. There was no middle course.

The officers on board shared their leader's feelings. One had to hear them talk, discuss, argue and calculate the various chances of an encounter, and see them watch the wide expanse of ocean. More than one voluntarily stood watch in the crosstrees, a duty he would have cursed under any other circumstances. As long as the sun was in the sky overhead, the masts were full of sailors so impatient that they could not bear just staying on deck, even though the *Abraham Lincoln* was not yet furrowing the suspect waters of the Pacific.

As for the crew, they asked nothing better than to meet the unicorn-fish, harpoon it and bring it on board to cut it up. They surveyed the sea tirelessly. Besides, Commander Farragut had mentioned a certain sum of two thousand dollars reserved for whoever, cabin boy or sailor, master or officer, sighted the animal first. I leave the reader to imagine how eyes were strained on board the *Abraham Lincoln.*

As for me, I did not lag far behind the others, and personally did my share of daily watching. The frigate was like the mythological Argus with its hundred eyes. Only Conseil appeared indifferent to what so interested us; he alone was out of step with the general enthusiasm on board.

As I said before, Commander Farragut had carefully equipped his boat with various devices for hunting this gigantic creature. A whaling ship could not have been better armed. We had every known device, from hand-thrown harpoons to blunderbusses which shot out barbed arrows and swivel guns with exploding shells. On the forecastle stood a special breech-loading cannon, with a thick barrel and narrow bore, just like the one which was to appear in the Exposition of 1867. This precious gun, invented by the Americans, could, without the slightest difficulty, send a conical projectile weighing nine pounds to a distance of ten miles.

The *Abraham Lincoln,* therefore, lacked no weapons of destruction. But it had something even better. It had Ned Land, the king of harpooners.

Ned Land was a Canadian gifted with extraordinary coordination, and he had no rival in his dangerous profession. He possessed qualities of skill and coolness, courage and cunning, to an extraordinary degree, and it was only the cleverest of whales that could escape the blow of his harpoon.

Ned Land was about forty. He was more than six feet tall and powerfully built, uncommunicative, sometimes violent and very hot-tempered when thwarted. He attracted one's attention, mostly because of his piercing eyes.

I think that Commander Farragut did wisely in taking this man on board. He alone was worth the whole crew, because of his eye and arm. He was like a powerful telescope, and at the same time like a cannon always ready to go off.

To say Canadian is the same as saying French, and as untalkative as Ned Land was, I must admit that he took a certain liking to me. My nationality undoubtedly attracted him. For him it was a chance to converse, and for me an opportunity to hear that old language of Rabelais which is still spoken in some

provinces of Canada. The harpooner's family came from Quebec, and in the days when this town belonged to France, they already constituted a large clan of hardy fishermen.

Little by little Ned began to take pleasure in talking, and I enjoyed listening to him tell of his adventures in Arctic waters. He would recount his fishing exploits and combats with a great natural sense of poetry. His recitals took on epic form, and I felt as if I were listening to some Canadian Homer, singing the Iliad of the far north.

Since then, I have gotten to know Ned Land well, and thus I feel I can describe him accurately. We have become old friends, united by that unalterable bond which is born and cemented amid the gravest dangers. Ah, brave Ned! I only ask to live another hundred years so that your memory will remain with me that much longer!

And now, what was his opinion about the sea monster? I am forced to admit that he did not believe in the unicorn-fish, and that he was the only one on board who did not share the general feeling of conviction. He even avoided talking about it, although I once got him to discuss the creature.

One magnificent evening, on July 30—that is to say three weeks after we had set sail—the frigate was off Cabo Blanco, thirty miles to the leeward of the Patagonian coast. We had crossed the Tropic of Capricorn, and the Straits of Magellan were less than seven hundred miles to the south. Within a week, the *Abraham Lincoln* would be sailing in Pacific waters.

Ned Land and I were sitting on the poop talking about one thing and another and looking at the mysterious sea whose depths have, till now, remained inaccessible to the eyes of man. In a natural way I brought the conversation around to the giant sea unicorn, and discussed our chances of failing or succeeding. Then, seeing that Ned let me talk on without saying much himself, I pressed him more closely.

"Why is it, Ned," I asked, "that you're not convinced this creature we're chasing really exists? Do you have some special reasons for being so skeptical?"

Before answering, the harpooner looked at me for several moments, then struck his broad forehead with his hand—as he often did—closed his eyes as if

The *Abraham Lincoln* was belching forth columns of black smoke.

to gather his thoughts and finally said:

"Maybe I have, Monsieur Aronnax."

"But a man like you, Ned, who's a professional whaler, who knows about large marine mammals, whose imagination could easily accept the idea of huge sea creatures, you should be the last to be skeptical under such circumstances!"

"That's where you're wrong, Professor," Ned answered. "It's all right for ordinary people to believe in fabulous comets that streak across the sky, or in prehistoric monsters living inside the earth, but to an astronomer or geologist these are nothing but a bunch of fantasies. It's the same with a whaler. I've hunted hundreds of them, harpooned many and killed a lot, but no matter how powerful or well armed they were, neither their tails nor their tusks were strong enough to crack the steel plates of a steamer."

"But Ned, they tell of ships that have been pierced right through by a narwhal's tusk."

"Maybe wooden ships," answered the Canadian, "but I've never seen it. And until I get some proof to the contrary, I won't admit that ordinary whales, sperm whales or unicorn-fish could do such a thing."

"But listen, Ned . . ."

"No, Professor, no. You can make it anything you want, but not that. A giant octopus maybe . . ."

"Even less likely, Ned. An octopus is a mollusk, a name that indicates the flabby nature of its flesh. Even if there were such a thing as an octopus five hundred feet long, they don't have any bone structure and therefore could never do the slightest damage to ships such as the *Scotia* or the *Abraham Lincoln*. So we're forced to admit that stories about krakens or other monsters like that are nothing but pure fables."

"But you, even though you're a professor of natural history," continued Ned Land in a sly tone of voice, "you still believe in the possibility of an enormous whale? . . ."

"Yes, Ned, and my conviction is based on logic and facts. I believe it to be a powerfully built mammal, belonging to the subkingdom of the vertebrates, like whales, cachalots and dolphins, and armed with a tusk of great penetrating power."

"Hm!" said the harpooner, shaking his head with the look of a man who did not want to be convinced.

"But you must remember," I replied, "that if such an animal exists, if it inhabits the ocean depths and if it lives in those layers of water situated several miles below the surface, then it must be built in some incredibly powerful way."

"Why?" Ned asked.

"Because incalculable strength is needed to stay at great depths and withstand the pressure there."

"Really?" said Ned, blinking.

"Yes, and I could give you some figures to prove it easily."

"Oh, figures!" answered Ned. "You can make figures do whatever you want."

"Perhaps in business, Ned, but not in mathematics. Now listen. The pressure of one atmosphere is represented by a column of water thirty-two feet high. In actual fact, the column of water would not be that high, because here we're dealing with sea water which has a greater density than fresh water. Well now, Ned, when you dive down into the sea, for every thirty-two feet of water between you and the surface, your body is supporting an additional pressure of one atmosphere, or in other words of 14.7 pounds per square inch of surface. It follows that at 320 feet this pressure is equal to ten atmospheres, a hundred atmospheres at 3200 feet, and a thousand atmospheres at 32,000 feet or about six miles. This is the same as saying that if you could reach such a depth in the ocean, your body would undergo a pressure of 14,700 pounds per square inch. Now, Ned, do you know how many square inches there are on the surface of your body?"

"I have no idea, Monsieur Aronnax."

"About two thousand six hundred."

"That many?"

"And right now those twenty-six hundred square inches of yours are supporting a pressure of 38,220 pounds."

"Without my noticing it?"

"Without your noticing it. And the reason you're not squashed by such a pressure is that air at exactly the same pressure penetrates inside your body, and thus there's a perfect equilibrium between the inside and outside pressure, which allows you to bear up under it painlessly. But in the water, things are quite different."

"Yes, I see," answered Ned who had become more attentive, "because the water surrounds you but doesn't get inside."

"That's right, Ned. And this means that at 32 feet below the surface you would be under an extra pressure of 38,220 pounds; at 320 feet, ten times that pressure, or 382,200 pounds; at 3200 feet, a hundred times that pressure, or 3,822,000 pounds; at 32,000 feet, a thousand times that pressure, or 38,220,000 pounds; or in other words you'd be flattened out as if they had pulled you from between the plates of a hydraulic press!"

"Good Lord!" Ned exclaimed.

"Well then, if vertebrates several hundred yards long and with bodies built to scale live at such depths, they must have a surface area equal to millions of square inches, then the pressure they undergo must be measured in the hundreds of billions of pounds. So you can see how strong their bone structure and body would have to be in order to resist such pressure!"

"They must be built," answered Ned Land, "with steel plates eight inches thick, like armored frigates."

"That's right, Ned, and then think of what damage could be produced by such an object traveling at high speed and striking the hull of a ship."

"Yes . . . you're right . . . maybe," answered the Canadian, bowled over by these figures but still unwilling to give in.

"Well, have I convinced you?"

"You've convinced me of one thing, Professor, and that is that if such animals exist in the ocean depths, they would have to be as strong as you say."

"But if they don't exist, you stubborn harpooner, how do you explain what happened to the *Scotia*?"

"Maybe it was . . ." said Ned hesitantly.

"Come, come!"

"Because . . . no, it couldn't be true!" replied the Canadian.

But this answer only proved how obstinate the harpooner was, nothing else.

That day I pushed him no further. No one could deny what had happened to the *Scotia*. The hole in its hull was so real that it had to be stopped up, and I don't think there can be any surer proof of a hole than this. But this hole hadn't just developed all by itself, and since it hadn't been produced by underwater rocks or machinery, it must necessarily be ascribed to the weapon of some animal.

Moreover, to my way of thinking—for all the reasons stated above—this animal belonged to the subkingdom of the vertebrates, the class of mammals, the group of pisciforms, and finally the order of cetaceans. As to what family it belonged, whale, cachalot or dolphin, as to its genus or species, that was a question to be cleared up later. But in order to solve this problem, one would have to dissect the unknown monster, in order to dissect it one would have to capture it, in order to capture it, harpoon it—which was Ned Land's job—in order to harpoon it, see it—which was the crew's job—and in order to see it, meet up with it—which was a matter of chance.

CHAPTER V
A Random Search

For a while, little happened on board the *Abraham Lincoln*, except for one event which displayed Ned Land's extraordinary skill, and showed what confidence we could have in him.

Off the Falkland Islands, on June 30, we communicated with some American whaling ships, and we learned that they had seen nothing of the narwhal. But one of them, the captain of the *Monroe*, knowing that Ned Land had shipped on board the *Abraham Lincoln*, asked for his help in hunting a whale they had sighted. Commander Farragut was eager to see Ned Land perform, and therefore authorized him to go aboard the *Monroe*. And our Canadian's luck was such that instead of one whale, he harpooned two in succession, striking one straight to the heart and capturing the other after a pursuit lasting only several minutes.

"There's no doubt about it," I thought; "if the monster gets a taste of Ned Land's harpoon, I won't put my money on the monster."

The frigate skirted the southeast coast of South America at great speed. On the third of July we were at the mouth of the Straits of Magellan, off the Cape of the Virgins. But Commander Farragut did not want to attempt this dangerous passage and set out on a course around Cape Horn.

The crew agreed with him to a man. And in point of fact, was there any chance of meeting the narwhal in these narrow straits? Many of the sailors stated that this creature could not get through them, that "it was too big"!

On July 6, toward three in the afternoon and about fifteen miles yet further south, the *Abraham Lincoln* went around that solitary island, that lost rock at the tip of South America to which Dutch sailors gave the name of their home town, Cape Horn. The course was then changed toward the northwest, and on the next day, the frigate's propeller was finally churning Pacific waters.

"Keep your eyes open!" cried the sailors of the *Abraham Lincoln*.

And they opened them wide. Their eyes and telescopes, undoubtedly a bit dazzled by the prospect of two thousand dollars, did not rest for a moment. Night and day people watched the surface of the ocean, and those who had special gifts for seeing in the dark had a 50 percent better chance of winning the prize money.

As for me, even though I cared little about the money, I was no less watchful than the others. Taking only several minutes for my meals, and sleeping only several hours, completely indifferent to sun or rain, I scarcely ever left the deck. Whether leaning over the forecastle rails or holding on to the taffrail, my eyes eagerly devoured the cotton foam turning the sea white out to the horizon. And how often did I share the excitement of officers and crew when some capricious whale lifted its black back above the surface of the water. The frigate's deck would immediately fill with people. The hatches would vomit forth a torrent of sailors and officers. Each one, with his chest heaving and an anxious look in his eyes, would watch the whale's progress. I would stare till I was nearly blind, while

Conseil, as impassive as ever, would say calmly: "If Monsieur would be kind enough to not keep his eyes so wide open, Monsieur would see much better!"

But all the excitement would be for nothing! The *Abraham Lincoln* would alter its course and race toward the creature—nothing more than an ordinary whale or common sperm whale, which would soon disappear amid a storm of curses!

Nevertheless the weather held good. The voyage was progressing under the best of conditions. It was the bad season in the Southern Hemisphere, for July in that region corresponds to our European January; but the sea remained calm and the air clear.

Ned Land continued to show the greatest skepticism; he even refused to look at the ocean except during his turn on watch—or at least when no whale was in sight. This was a pity, for his extraordinary eyesight would have been very useful. But eight hours out of twelve this stubborn Canadian stayed in his cabin, reading or sleeping. A hundred times I reproached him for his indifference.

"Bah!" he would answer, "it's all nonsense, Monsieur Aronnax, and even if it was some animal, what chance would we have of seeing it? Why we're just wandering about aimlessly. They say this creature nobody can find was last seen in mid-Pacific—all right, but that was two months ago, and according to what they say about your narwhal's character, he doesn't like to stay in one spot very long! He can move very fast. And you know better than I, Professor, that nature doesn't do things without reason, and she wouldn't give a sluggish animal like that the ability to move fast if it didn't need to use this ability. So if this creature does exist, it's already far away!"

I had no answer to this. Obviously we were wandering about blindly. What else could we do? Our chances were undoubtedly very limited. Nevertheless, as yet nobody had any doubts that we would succeed, and there was not a single sailor on board who would have bet against our sighting the narwhal soon.

On July 20, we crossed the Tropic of Capricorn at 105° W. Long., and on the twenty-seventh of the same month we crossed the equator at the 110th meridian. Once there, the frigate took a more definite westerly course, and entered the waters of the mid-Pacific. Commander Farragut was right in thinking it was best to remain in deep water and stay away from land, which the creature always seemed to avoid, "probably because there isn't enough water there for him," as the boatswain put it. The frigate therefore gave a wide berth to the Tuamotu Islands, the Marquesas and the Hawaiian Islands, crossed the Tropic of Cancer at 132° W. Long. and headed for the China Seas.

We were finally in the area of the monster's last little tricks! And, in a word, normal life on board came to an end. Hearts began beating madly, so much so that they would never be the same again. I cannot describe the nervous tension the crew was under. No one ate or slept anymore. Twenty times a day, an error in judgment or a mirage seen by some sailor perched in the crosstrees would cause intolerable feelings of anguish, and with these emotions repeated twenty times a day we all became so violently irritable that some reaction was bound to set in soon.

And in fact, it wasn't long before it did set in. For three months, each day of which seemed like a century, the *Abraham Lincoln* cruised all over the north Pacific, chasing whales that had been sighted, making quick changes in course, veering suddenly from one tack to another, stopping abruptly, putting on steam or reversing its engines so quickly as to risk harming them, and leaving no corner unexplored between the coast of Japan and America. And it found nothing! Nothing but vast deserted waters! Nothing even vaguely resembling a giant narwhal, or an underwater island, or the wreck of a sunken ship, or a shifting reef, or anything even slightly out of the ordinary!

So a reaction finally set in. Everybody became discouraged, and this led to skepticism. The men on board were gripped by a new feeling, composed of three-tenths shame and seven-tenths anger. They felt they had been a "bunch of fools" to let themselves get involved in such a pipe dream, and this feeling made them furious! All the emotions stored up for a year poured forth at once, and everyone thought only of catching up on the hours of eating and sleeping they had missed.

The human mind being as changeable as it is, people went from one excess to another. The warmest partisans of the enterprise were destined to become its most ardent critics. The reaction rose from the bowels of the ship, from the coal trimmers' quarters to the officers' mess, and surely without Commander Farragut's special stubbornness, the frigate would have turned south once and for all.

In any case, this useless search could not go on much longer, and the *Abraham*

Lincoln had no reason to feel ashamed, for it had made every possible effort to succeed. No crew in the American Navy has ever shown greater patience or willingness. They could not be blamed for their failure; there was nothing else to do but return.

A petition to this effect was made to the commander, but he refused to change his plans. The sailors no longer hid their discontent, and the work on board suffered as a result. I don't mean to say there was a mutiny, but after a reasonable period of refusing to consider their wishes, Commander Farragut, as Columbus had once done, asked for three more days. If during this time, the monster put in no appearance, the men at the helm could give it three turns and the *Abraham Lincoln* would head for European waters.

This promise was made on November 2. Its first effect was to rally the ship's crew. Once again the ocean was carefully scanned. Each man wanted to give it one last look in which he could sum up his memory of the trip. Telescopes were put to use feverishly. It was the last challenge thrown to the giant narwhal, and he could scarcely fail to answer this summons to appear!

Two days passed by. The *Abraham Lincoln* was cruising under low boiler pressure. A thousand methods were tried for attracting the animal's attention or arousing him from his apathy should he be in these waters. Huge chunks of lard were dragged behind the ship—to the great satisfaction of the sharks, I must admit. The ship's boats spread out in all directions around the *Abraham Lincoln* while it hove to, and they left no corner of the sea unexplored. But the evening of November 4 arrived without this underwater mystery having been unveiled.

On the next day, November 5, at noon, the allotted three-day period expired. After that, Commander Farragut, faithful to his promise, was to steer a course to the southeast and definitely abandon northern Pacific waters.

The frigate was then at 31° 15' N. Lat. and 136° 42' E. Long. Japan lay less than two hundred miles to leeward. Night was coming on. Eight o'clock had just struck. Thick clouds hid the new moon and the sea was rolling gently under the bow of the ship.

At that moment I was leaning on the forward starboard railing. Conseil was stationed next to me and looking at the sea off the bow. The crew, perched in the rigging, was examining the horizon as it slowly grew narrower and darker. The officers, equipped with their night binoculars, scoured the increasing gloom. Occasionally the ocean would sparkle with light from the moon as it peeped out from between two clouds. Then all trace of light would disappear into darkness.

I looked at Conseil and could see he was feeling little of the emotion gripping everyone else. Or at least, so I thought. But perhaps, for the first time, his nerves were atingle with a feeling of curiosity.

"All right now, Conseil," I said, "this is your last chance to pocket two thousand dollars."

"If Monsieur will permit my saying so," Conseil answered, "I have never given a thought to this prize money, and I think that even if the Government of the Union had promised a hundred thousand dollars, it would be none the poorer."

"You're right, Conseil. This was a foolish venture after all, and we jumped at it too quickly. Think how much time we've lost, and how much useless excitement we've undergone! We could have been back in France six months ago . . ."

"In Monsieur's little apartment," continued Conseil, "in Monsieur's museum! And I would have already classified Monsieur's fossils! And Monsieur's babirusa would already be installed in his cage in the Botanical Gardens attracting all the city's curiosity seekers!"

"Right, Conseil, but even that doesn't take into account that people will laugh at us when we get back!"

"Yes," Conseil answered calmly, "people will laugh at Monsieur. And I must say . . ."

"Yes, go ahead, Conseil."

". . . that Monsieur will be getting what he deserves!"

"Really?"

"When one has the honor to be a scientist like Monsieur, one doesn't get mixed up in . . ."

But Conseil was unable to finish his compliment, for in the midst of a general silence, a voice was suddenly heard. It was Ned Land's voice, and he was shouting: "Ahoy! There it is, abeam to leeward!"

CHAPTER VI
Full Steam Ahead

At this shout, the entire crew rushed toward the harpooner—commander, officers, boatswains, sailors and cabin boys. Even the engineers and coal stokers left their posts. The order to stop had been given, and the frigate was now merely coasting.

A great darkness reigned on the water, and no matter how good the Canadian's eyes might be, I wondered how he had been able to see what he had. My heart was beating so fast I thought it would burst.

But Ned Land had made no mistake, and all of us soon saw the object he was pointing to.

At a distance of about four hundred yards off the *Abraham Lincoln*'s starboard quarter, the sea seemed to be lit up from below. It wasn't merely a matter of some kind of phosphorescence—there could be no mistake about that. The monster was several fathoms below the surface and gave off that same intense and yet unexplainable glow that several ship captains had already mentioned. Such magnificent radiance could only come from some source of great power. The area of light covered an immense, very elongated oval-shaped area in the water, and in the middle this light was so intense that its brilliance was unbearable.

"It's nothing more than a mass of tiny phosphorescent particles," cried one of the officers.

"No," I answered with conviction, "small sea organisms can never produce such strong light. It must have some basically electrical source. . . . Besides, look, look! It's moving! It's going forward, backward! It's heading for us!"

A shout rose from the crew of the frigate.

"Silence!" said Commander Farragut. "Helm to leeward! Reverse engines!"

Sailors rushed to the helm and engineers to the engine room. The ship's direction was immediately reversed, and the *Abraham Lincoln* cast to port and went around in a semicircle.

"Right helm! Engines forward!" cried Commander Farragut.

These orders were carried out and the frigate moved rapidly away from the source of light.

Or rather, it *tried* to move away; but the supernatural animal approached at a speed double that of the ship.

We were all gasping for breath. Stupefied rather than afraid, we remained silent and stock-still. The animal was gaining on us effortlessly. Even though the frigate was then traveling at fourteen knots, this creature did a complete circle around us and enveloped our ship in its electric sheets as if in some luminous dust. Then it went two or three miles off, leaving a phosphorescent trail like the swirling smoke left by the locomotive of an express train. Suddenly, from the dark edge of the horizon where it had gone to get up momentum, it rushed headlong toward the *Abraham Lincoln* with terrifying speed, stopped abruptly twenty feet from her hull and then disappeared—not by diving down, for its light did not diminish gradually, but suddenly and as if the source of this brilliance had been abruptly turned off! It then reappeared on the other side of the ship, having either gone around it or under it. At any moment, a fatal collision could have taken place.

Nevertheless, I was astonished at the frigate's maneuvers. It was fleeing, not attacking. It was being chased instead of chasing as it should, and I mentioned this to Commander Farragut. His face, ordinarily so impassive, became covered with an indescribable look of astonishment.

"Mr. Aronnax," he replied, "I have no idea what kind of a formidable creature I'm dealing with, and I don't want to risk my frigate foolishly in such darkness. Besides, how can you attack or defend yourself against something when you don't even know what it is? We'll wait for daylight, and then the roles will be reversed."

"Do you have any more doubts, Commander, as to the nature of the animal?"

"No, it's obviously a gigantic narwhal and one that can produce electricity."

"It might perhaps be," I added, "some type of animal closer to an electric eel or ray."

"Perhaps," answered the commander, "and if it possesses such dreadful power, it must surely be the most terrible creature God ever created. That is why, sir, I want to be on my guard."

The crew stayed up all night; no one thought of sleeping. The *Abraham Lincoln,* unable to compete with the animal's speed, had slowed down and was cruising at half speed. The narwhal also slowed down, allowing itself to be gently rocked by the waves; it seemed to have made up its mind not to leave the field of combat.

Toward midnight, however, it disappeared, or to put it more accurately, it "went out" like a large glow-worm. Had it fled? This was more to be feared than hoped for. But at seven minutes to one in the morning, a deafening whistling sound was heard, like that produced by a violently expelled spout of water.

Commander Farragut, Ned Land and I were on the poop, anxiously peering through the dark night.

"Ned Land," asked the commander, "you've often heard whales roar, haven't you?"

"Often, sir, but never a whale like this that brought me two thousand dollars."

"Don't worry, the prize money's yours. But tell me, wasn't that the same noise whales make when they spurt out water?"

"It was the same noise, sir, but this one was infinitely louder. No, there's no mistake about it—it's some kind of a whale lying out there in the water. With your permission, sir," added the harpooner, "we'll have a few words with him at dawn."

"If he's in a mood to listen," I answered in a skeptical tone of voice.

"Just let me get within four harpoon lengths of him," replied the Canadian, "and he'll darned well have to listen!"

"But if you want to get near it," said the commander, "that means I'll have to put a whaleboat at your disposal!"

"Naturally, sir."

"But wouldn't that be endangering the lives of my men?"

"Along with mine!" answered the harpooner unaffectedly.

Toward two in the morning, the source of light reappeared as intense as before five miles to windward of the *Abraham Lincoln*. In spite of the distance, and in spite of the noise of wind and sea, we could clearly hear the powerful swishings of the animal's tail, and even its panting breath. It seemed as if, when coming up for breath, air was sucked into the enormous narwhal's lungs just as steam would be sucked into the cylinders of a two-thousand-horsepower engine.

"Hmm!" I thought. "A whale with the strength of a cavalry regiment, that ought to be a fine specimen of a whale!"

Till daybreak we remained on the alert and ready for combat. The various devices for hunting the creature were placed along the railings. The first mate saw to the loading of the blunderbusses that could send harpoons for a mile, and of those long swivel guns which fired explosive shells whose wound was fatal even to the most powerful animals. Ned Land spent his time sharpening a harpoon—a terrible weapon in his hands.

At six o'clock day began to break, and with the first glimmer of dawn the electric light of the narwhal disappeared. At seven the day was well along, but a very thick morning mist obscured our view to the point where the best telescopes could not pierce it. This caused disappointment and anger.

I climbed up to the spars of the mizzenmast. Some officers were already perched on the mastheads.

At eight o'clock the mist began to move slowly across the water, and its huge swirls rose little by little. The horizon grew both wider and clearer.

Suddenly, just as on the day before, we could hear Ned Land's voice:

"There it is, astern on the port side!" cried the harpooner.

Every eye turned toward the place he had indicated.

There, a mile and a half away from the frigate, a long blackish body was sticking about three feet above the surface. Its tail was moving violently and producing considerable foam. Never had a fish's tail churned the sea with such power. An immense wake of a dazzling white color marked the long curved course in which the animal had traveled.

The frigate approached the whale and I examined it for myself. The reports of the *Shannon* and the *Helvetia* had somewhat exaggerated its size, and I estimated it to be no more than 250 feet in length. Its width and depth were difficult to judge, but as far as I could see the animal was perfectly proportioned in all its dimensions.

While I was observing this phenomenal creature, two jets of vapor and water rushed out of its blowholes and rose to a height of a hundred and twenty feet, thus permitting me to judge its method of breathing. I came to the definite conclusion that it belonged to the subkingdom of the vertebrates, the class of mammals, subclass of monodelphians, division of pisciforms, order of cetaceans, family of . . . Here I could not decide. The order of cetaceans includes three families: whales, cachalots and dolphins, and it is in this last that narwhals are grouped. Each of these families is divided into several genera, each genus into species, and each species into varieties. I was still missing variety, species, genus and family, but with the help of Heaven and Commander Farragut I would undoubtedly be able to complete my classification before too long.

The crew was impatiently awaiting their leader's orders. After he had carefully observed the animal for a while, the commander called for his chief engineer. The engineer ran over.

"Is your pressure up?" asked Commander Farragut.

"Yes, sir," answered the engineer.

"Good. Stoke the fires even more, and then full steam ahead!"

This order was greeted with three cheers. The hour of combat had struck. A few moments later, the frigate's two funnels belched forth torrents of black smoke, and the deck shook with the trembling of the boilers.

The *Abraham Lincoln,* pushed by its powerful propeller, headed straight for the animal. The latter allowed the ship to approach to within a hundred yards; then, not bothering to dive, it started slowly off, maintaining its distance.

This chase went on for about three-quarters of an hour, without the frigate being able to gain an inch on the whale. It became obvious that at this rate we would never reach it.

Commander Farragut was angrily twisting the thick tuft of hair on his chin. "Ned Land!" he cried.

The Canadian came over to him.

"Tell me now, Master Land," the commander asked, "would you still advise me to put out the longboats?"

"No, sir," Ned replied, "because we're not going to catch that animal until it decides to let us get near."

"So what do we do?"

"Get up more steam if you can, sir. As for me, with your permission of course, I'll take up my position in the bobstays of the bowsprit, and if we get near enough, I'll harpoon it."

"Go ahead, Ned," replied Commander Farragut. "Engineer!" he shouted. "Build up more pressure!"

Ned Land took up his post. The fires were stoked even more; the propeller was turning at forty-three revolutions per minute and steam poured out of the valves. The log was thrown, and it was calculated that the *Abraham Lincoln* was traveling at a speed of 18.5 knots.

But the cursed animal was also running off at a speed of 18.5 knots.

For an hour the frigate maintained this speed without gaining an inch! It was humiliating for one of the fastest ships in the American Navy. A mute anger spread among the crew. The sailors swore at the monster, but it did not deign to answer them. Commander Farragut was no longer merely twisting his beard, he was biting it.

The engineer was once again called up.

"Have you reached your maximum pressure?" asked the commander.

"Yes, sir," replied the engineer.

"Are the valves up to pressure?"

"Six and a half atmospheres."

"Get them up to ten."

This was an American order if there ever was one. It made me feel as if we were in one of those famous races on the Mississippi.

"Conseil," I said to my faithful servant standing next to me, "do you know that we'll probably all be blown sky high?"

"As Monsieur wishes!" replied Conseil.

And I'll admit that I was not unhappy at the thought of running this risk.

The valves were charged. Coal was poured into the furnaces. The ventilators sent torrents of air across the live coals. The *Abraham Lincoln*'s speed increased. The masts trembled down to their very foundations, and the swirling smoke scarcely had room to make its way up the narrow chimneys.

The log was heaved once again.

"Well?" Commander Farragut asked the helmsman.

"Nineteen point three knots, sir."

"Lay on more coal."

The engineer obeyed. The pressure gauge showed ten atmospheres. But the whale had undoubtedly also "laid on more coal," for without seeming in the least disturbed, it also cruised at 19.3 knots.

What a chase! I couldn't possibly describe the emotions that made me tremble from head to foot. Ned Land was standing at his post with the harpoon in his hand. Several times the animal let us get near.

"We're gaining on it! We're gaining on it!" the Canadian would cry.

Then, just as he was getting ready to strike, the whale would dash off at a speed which I guessed to be no less than thirty knots. And even while we were traveling at top speed, it decided to make fun of the frigate by swimming around us! A cry of rage rose from every breast!

By noon we had gotten no nearer than we had been at eight in the morning.

Commander Farragut then decided to use more direct methods.

"Well," he said, "this animal may be able to go faster than the *Abraham Lincoln*, but I doubt if it can outdistance our conical shells. Boatswain, man the forward gun!"

The cannon in the forecastle was immediately loaded and aimed. It was fired, but the shell passed several feet above the whale, who was half a mile off.

"Let someone else try who's got better aim," cried the commander, "and there's five hundred dollars in it for whoever can pierce that infernal creature's skin!"

An old gray-bearded gunner—I can still see him—with a calm eye and impassive face, walked up to the cannon, put it in position and took a long time sighting it. There was a loud explosion, and then cheers from the crew.

The shell had reached its target and struck the animal, but not in the usual way; instead it glanced off and splashed into the water two miles away.

"That's too much!" cried the old gunner in a rage. "That critter's covered with six-inch armor plate!"

"Curses!" cried Commander Farragut.

The chase began again, and Commander Farragut, leaning toward me, said, "I'll track down that animal until my frigate bursts!"

"Good!" I said, agreeing with his decision.

We at least hoped that the animal would get tired, or at least that it would tire more quickly than a steam engine. But no such luck. Hours passed without its giving any sign of exhaustion.

Nevertheless it must be said in praise of the *Abraham Lincoln* that it absolutely refused to give up. According to my estimate, we covered at least three hundred miles on that unlucky sixth of November! But then night came on and wrapped the rolling sea in its darkness.

Now I thought our expedition had ended, and that we would never see this fantastic animal again. But I was wrong.

At 10:50, the electric light reappeared, three miles to windward of the frigate, as intense and pure as on the previous night.

The narwhal seemed immobile. Maybe it was tired out from its exertions during the day and was sleeping, letting itself be gently rocked by the rolling waves. Now was our chance, and Commander Farragut resolved to take advantage of it.

He gave orders. The *Abraham Lincoln* was kept at half speed, and went forward cautiously so as not to wake its adversary. It is not at all unusual to meet up with whales sound asleep in mid-ocean, and to be able to attack them successfully. Ned Land had harpooned more than one while it lay sleeping. The

Canadian once again took up his post in the bobstays of the bowsprit.

The frigate approached silently, stopped its engines four hundred yards from the animal and then just coasted. No one dared breathe on board. The deck was wrapped in a deep silence. As we got within a hundred feet from the source of light, it became so intense and brilliant as to dazzle us.

Just then I leaned over the forward rail and could see Ned Land below me, hanging on to the rigging with one hand and brandishing his terrible harpoon in the other. Scarcely twenty feet remained between him and the immobile animal.

Suddenly his arm snapped forward with a violent jerk, and the harpoon was thrown. I heard a ringing noise as the weapon seemed to hit something hard.

The electric light suddenly went out, and two enormous streams of water broke over the deck of the frigate, rushing in a torrent from stem to stern, knocking over men and breaking the lashings of the spars.

Then there was a terrible crash. I did not even have time to reach for something to hold on to, but was hurled over the railing and into the sea.

CHAPTER VII
An Unknown Species of Whale

Even though I was surprised by this unexpected fall, I still have a very clear memory of my sensations at the time.

I was first of all dragged down to a depth of about twenty feet. I am a good swimmer, although I couldn't pretend to equal Byron or Edgar Allan Poe who are masters of the art, and this dive did not make me lose my head. Two strong kicks brought me back to the surface.

My first thought was to try to find the frigate. Had the crew noticed my disappearance? Had the *Abraham Lincoln* come about? Was Commander Farragut putting a lifeboat to sea? Did I have any chance of being saved?

I was surrounded by total darkness. But I could make out a vague black shape disappearing toward the east, its riding lights slowly fading as it got farther away. I felt I was done for.

"Help! Help!" I cried, as I swam desperately toward the *Abraham Lincoln*.

My clothes began to get in the way. The water was making them stick to my body, paralyzing my movements. I was sinking! I was drowning! . . .

"Help!"

It was my last shout. My mouth filled with water. I struggled against being dragged down to the depths . . .

Suddenly a powerful hand grabbed my clothes. I felt myself violently brought back to the surface and then heard, yes, heard the following words spoken in my ear: "If Monsieur would be so extremely kind as to lean on my shoulder, Monsieur would be able to swim much more comfortably."

I seized the arm of my faithful Conseil. "You!" I said. "It's you!"

"Yes," answered Conseil, "awaiting Monsieur's orders."

"Did the crash throw you into the water along with me?"

"Not at all. But being in Monsieur's service, I followed Monsieur!"

This worthy fellow seemed to think this was all perfectly natural!

"And the frigate?" I asked.

"The frigate?" replied Conseil, rolling over on his back. "I think Monsieur would be wise not to count on that too much!"

"What do you mean?"

"I mean that when I was getting ready to jump into the water, I heard the men at the helm shouting, 'The propeller and the rudder are broken' . . ."

"Broken?"

"Yes, broken by the monster's tusk. As far as I could make out, this was the only damage sustained by the *Abraham Lincoln*. But what's unpleasant for us is that she no longer answers her helm."

"That means we're done for!"

"Perhaps," Conseil answered calmly. "Nevertheless, we still have several hours, and one can do a lot of things in several hours!"

Conseil's unshakable coolness gave me courage.

I was swimming more vigorously now, but I was still hampered by the clothes clinging to me like a lead cloak, and I found it very difficult to stay afloat. Conseil noticed this.

"With Monsieur's permission, I will make an incision," he said.

With this, he slipped a knife inside my clothes and split them open from top to bottom with one fast sweep. Then he quickly took them off me, while I swam for both of us.

Then I in turn did the same for Conseil, and we continued to "navigate" next to one another.

But the situation was still just as terrifying. Perhaps our disappearance had not been noticed, and even if it had, the frigate could not maneuver to leeward toward us, since it had no rudder. So our only hope was lifeboats.

Conseil reasoned all this out coolly and laid his plans accordingly. What an extraordinary character! This impassive fellow was acting no differently than if he were sitting in the living room of his house.

We decided that since our only chance of rescue lay in being picked up by the lifeboats of the *Abraham Lincoln*, we ought to manage so as to be able to wait for them as long as possible. I resolved to divide our forces so we would not both become exhausted at the same time, and this is what we decided to do. While one of us would stretch out on his back with his arms crossed and his legs extended, the other would push him forward. But this was to last no longer than ten minutes, after which we would change roles; and alternating thus we could remain afloat for several hours, and perhaps until daybreak.

Our chances seemed slim, but hope springs eternal in the human breast! Besides, there were two of us. And—as improbable as it may seem—I must admit that even though I tried to destroy all illusion and give myself over to despair, I could not!

The collision between the frigate and the whale had taken place at about eleven at night. I therefore estimated we would have to swim eight hours before sunrise. This was just barely possible, taking turns as we did. The sea was calm and tired us little. Occasionally I would try to peer through the thick darkness, which was broken only by the phosphorescence produced by our movements in the water. I would look at the luminous waves as they splashed over my hand, their glistening surface broken only by pale splotches. It was as if we had dived into a bath of mercury.

Toward one in the morning, a dreadful tiredness came over me. Violent cramps seized my legs. Conseil had to hold me up, and the responsibility of keeping us alive rested with him alone. I soon heard the poor fellow panting. I realized he could not hold out much longer.

"Let me go! Let me go!" I said.

"Abandon Monsieur? Never!" he answered. "I would prefer to drown first!"

Just then the moon appeared over the edge of a large cloud being blown toward the east. The surface of the sea sparkled beneath its rays. This bountiful light restored our strength. I once more held up my head. I looked around at every corner of the horizon. I caught sight of the frigate. She was five miles away, and we could make out little more than a vague shape. But there were no lifeboats!

I tried to shout even though it would have done no good at that distance! My swollen lips allowed no sound to come out. Conseil was able to articulate several words, and I heard him repeat several times: "Help! Help!"

We lay still in the water for a moment and listened. It might only have been a ringing in my ear, but it seemed as if I heard someone answer Conseil's shout.

"Did you hear that?" I murmured.

"Yes! Yes!"

And Conseil gave one more desperate shout.

This time there could be no doubt about it. A human voice was answering ours! Was it the voice of some other poor soul abandoned in mid-ocean, some other victim of the collision? Or was it a lifeboat from the frigate hailing us in the darkness?

Conseil made a supreme effort, and leaning on my shoulder while I stayed afloat with my last ounce of strength, he raised himself half out of the water and then fell back exhausted.

"What did you see?"

"I saw . . ." he murmured, "I saw . . . better not talk . . . got to keep our strength . . ."

What had he seen? Then—I don't know why—the thought of the monster crossed my mind for the first time! . . . But what about the voice? . . . In this day and age there were no longer any Jonahs taking refuge in the bellies of whales!

Meanwhile, Conseil was still pushing me along. He would occasionally lift up his head, look out in front and let out a shout. He would be answered by a voice getting nearer and nearer. But I could scarcely hear it. I was at the end of my tether. My fingers became stiff; I could no longer use my hand for support; my mouth began opening convulsively and filling with salt water. A chill crept through my body. I lifted my head one last time, and then I began to sink . . .

Just then something hard knocked against me. I grabbed on to it. I felt something dragging me, bringing me back to the surface—but my chest was collapsing and I passed out . . .

I must have regained consciousness quickly, thanks to someone giving me a strong massage. I half opened my eyes . . .

"Conseil!" I murmured.

"Did Monsieur call for me?" replied Conseil.

Just then, by the fading light of the moon sinking down toward the horizon, I made out a face which wasn't Conseil's but which I immediately recognized.

"Ned!" I cried.

"Yes, it's me, still chasing my prize!" answered the Canadian.

"Were you also thrown into the sea by the collision?"

"Yes, Professor, but I was a little luckier than you and was able to stand on a floating island right away."

"A floating island?"

"Or, to put it another way, on our giant narwhal."

"What do you mean, Ned?"

"Only I soon saw why my harpoon hadn't been able to penetrate, and why it had only been blunted on its skin."

"Why, Ned? Why?"

"Because the critter's covered with steel plates!"

At this point in my story, I must gather myself together, clarify my memory and make doubly sure of my statements.

The Canadian's last words had produced a turmoil in my mind. I quickly climbed to the top of the half-submerged creature or object which was serving as our place of refuge. I felt it with my foot. It was obviously something hard and impenetrable, and not made out of the soft flesh which covers marine mammals.

But this hard exterior could be no more than a bony shell like that of pre-historic animals, and I could then easily class the monster among amphibious reptiles, such as turtles or alligators.

But no! The blackish back supporting me was smooth and polished rather than rough. When struck it gave off a metallic noise, and as unbelievable as it seemed, it was made of bolted-down plates.

There was no longer any room for doubt! The animal, the monster, the phe-nomenon of nature that had intrigued the whole scientific world, confused and misled seamen of both hemispheres, I now had to admit was something even more astounding—it was the work of man.

Had I discovered some truly fabulous, mythological creature, it would not have come as a greater shock to me. It was quite easy to believe that God had created something prodigious. But suddenly to find, before one's very eyes, the impossi-ble realized by mysterious human means, that truly was a staggering thought!

But there was no question about it! We were stretched out on the back of some sort of underwater boat, built, as far as I could make out, in the form of a huge steel fish. Ned Land had already made up his mind about this. Conseil and I could only agree with him.

"So," I said, "this thing must contain some means of locomotion and a crew to guide it."

"Obviously," replied the harpooner, "but all the same, in the three hours I've spent on this floating island, it hasn't given a single sign of life."

"It hasn't moved?"

"No, Monsieur Aronnax. It's just laid here rocked by the waves, without budging."

"We know, however—and there can be no doubt about it—that it's capable of great speed. Therefore, since such a speed must be produced by an engine, and an engine requires a mechanic to run it, I conclude . . . that we've been saved."

"Hmm!" said Ned Land reservedly.

Just then, as if to prove me right, there was a swirling in the water to the rear of this strange thing—undoubtedly produced by a propeller—and it began moving. We barely had time to take a good hold on its topside, which was only about two and a half feet above water level.

"As long as it cruises on the surface," Ned Land murmured, "we'll be all right. But if it takes it into its head to dive, I wouldn't give two dollars for my life!"

He could have made the price even lower. It had therefore become urgent to communicate with whatever creatures were inside this machine. I tried to find some opening or hatch; but I could only see steel plates fastened by even, unbroken lines of bolts.

Moreover, the moon then disappeared, leaving us in total darkness. We were forced to wait until daybreak to find some means of getting inside the submarine.

Thus our lives depended completely on the whims of the men at the helm of this machine, and if they decided to dive, we were lost! Unless this happened, I was sure we would eventually be able to communicate with them. Moreover, unless they manufactured their own air, they were forced to return to the surface from time to time to renew their supply of oxygen. There must therefore be some opening between the inside of the submarine and the outside atmosphere.

As for the hope of being saved by Commander Farragut, we had to give up all thought of that. We were being taken off to the west, and I estimated we were traveling at the relatively moderate speed of twelve knots. The propeller was churning the water in an absolutely regular rhythm, occasionally rising above the surface and sending columns of phosphorescent water to great heights.

Toward four in the morning, it started to go faster. We were soon traveling at a headlong speed, and it became difficult to hang on with the waves crashing into us. Luckily, Ned found a large mooring ring attached to the upper part of its steel-plated back, and we were able to get a firm hold on it.

Finally this long night came to an end. My incomplete memory of it does not permit me to recount all my impressions. Only one detail comes to mind.

During certain moments when the sea was calm, I occasionally thought I could hear vague sounds of music, a sort of fleeting harmony produced by far-off chords. What mystery lay behind this underwater boat, about which the entire world had been vainly seeking an explanation? What sort of creatures lived inside this strange ship? What sort of an engine permitted it to travel so fast?

Then dawn came. For a while we were wrapped in morning mists, but it was not long before they began breaking up. I was about to start a careful examination of the submarine's topside—which formed a kind of horizontal platform—when I felt it starting to go down little by little.

"Confound it!" cried Ned Land, striking the steel plates with his foot. "Open up! Show us a little hospitality!"

But it was difficult to make ourselves heard in the midst of the deafening beat of the propeller. Luckily, the ship stopped diving.

Suddenly there was a loud clanking noise from inside the submarine. One of the plates rose up, a man appeared, uttered a strange cry and quickly disappeared.

Several moments later, eight solidly built young men with masked faces came silently out on deck and brought us inside their formidable machine.

CHAPTER VIII
"Mobilis in Mobile"

This operation of taking us below was carried out roughly and at the speed of lightning. Neither my friends nor I had time to realize what was happening. I don't know how they felt as they were being brought into that floating prison, but as for me, a chill went down my spine. What sort of people were we dealing with? Undoubtedly with some new kind of pirates roaming the sea in their own fashion.

The hatch had barely closed behind me when I was surrounded by total darkness. My eyes, still under the influence of strong daylight, could make out nothing. I could feel my feet clinging to the rungs of an iron ladder. Behind me were Ned and Conseil, also held firmly by masked men. At the bottom of the ladder, a door opened and immediately closed behind us with a loud clang.

We were alone. Where? I couldn't say, or scarcely imagine. The darkness surrounding us was so total that after several minutes I could only make out some vague glow floating about in the blackest of nights.

Ned Land, however, was furious with having been treated this way, and he gave free rein to his indignation.

"Confound them!" he cried. "These people are as hospitable as a bunch of Caledonians! They're probably nothing better than cannibals! It wouldn't surprise me a bit! But let me tell you—I'll give them some trouble before they eat me!"

"Calm down, Ned, calm down," Conseil said quietly. "Don't get carried away beforehand. We're not stewing in a pot yet!"

"Maybe not," replied the Canadian, "but it certainly looks like it! It's black enough in here to be the inside of a pot. But I've still got my bowie knife with me and I can still see well enough to use it. The first bandit that lays a hand on me . . ."

"Don't get so excited, Ned," I said to the harpooner, "and don't make our situation worse with useless violence. How do we know somebody isn't listening to us? Instead let's try and find out where we are!"

I walked with my arms stretched out before me. After five steps I bumped into an iron wall, made of plates bolted together. I then turned around and knocked against a wooden table with several stools next to it. The floor of this prison was covered with a thick linen mat which muffled the noise of our steps. The bare walls revealed no trace of a door or window. Conseil, going around the room in the opposite direction, finally met me and we came back to the middle of the cabin. It must have been about twenty feet long and ten feet wide. As for its height, Ned Land, in spite of his great size, could not touch the ceiling.

A half an hour went by without event when suddenly, from nearly total darkness, we were subjected to blinding light. Our prison was suddenly lit up, or that is to say, it became filled with a light so bright that at first I could not stand it. By its whiteness and intensity, I recognized it as being the same electric light that had produced that magnificent effect of phosphorescence around the submarine. After being forced to close my eyes for a while, I opened them again and could see that the light was coming from a frosted half-globe in the ceiling of the cabin.

"Finally we can see!" cried Ned Land, who was standing with his knife in hand, ready for anything.

"Yes," I said, "but we're still just as much in the dark about our situation."

"Monsieur must be patient," said the imperturbable Conseil.

The sudden lighting up of the cabin had permitted me to examine it carefully. It contained nothing but the table and five stools. The door was invisible and probably hermetically sealed. No sound reached our ears. Everything seemed dead inside the boat. Was it going forward, staying on the surface or diving down into the ocean depths? There was no way of knowing.

But there must have been some reason for the light being turned on. This seemed to indicate that some of the crew would turn up soon. For if you want to forget about people, you don't light up their cells.

I turned out not to be wrong. There was a noise of bolts, the door opened and two men appeared.

One of them was short but powerfully built, with broad shoulders, strong arms and legs, a large head, thick black hair, a big mustache and lively, penetrating eyes; his whole personality seemed full of that vitality which characterizes the people of southern France. One felt too, that his speech must have been colorful and spicy. But I was never able to verify this, for in front of me he always spoke in a strange and completely incomprehensible language.

The other person deserves a more detailed description. A disciple of Gratiolet or Engel would have been able to read his face like an open book. I could easily make out his dominant characteristics: self-confidence—from the fine way his head was set on his shoulders, and from his look of cold assurance; calm—because his rather pale skin showed his coolness of blood; energy—evinced by the rapid way he would contract his eyebrows; and finally courage—for his deep breathing indicated an expansive, vital nature.

In addition this man was proud. His firm calm look seemed to reflect thoughts of high nature, and one could see in everything, in his bodily and facial movements, an undeniable openness of manner.

I felt myself "involuntarily" reassured in his presence, and I predicted that our interview would have a favorable outcome.

Whether he was thirty-five or fifty, I could not tell. He was tall with a broad forehead, a straight nose, firm mouth, splendid teeth and delicate hands, slender and long—eminently "psychical" to use a term from palmistry, or in other words worthy of serving a high-minded, passionate soul. This man seemed one of the most admirable I had ever met. One strange detail: his eyes, which were rather far apart, had an almost ninety-degree range of vision. This ability—I was later able to verify it—was backed by eyesight even better than Ned Land's. When this man fixed his look upon some object, he would frown and squint in such a way as to limit his range of vision; and then he would look. And what a look! How he could magnify objects made smaller by distance! How he could penetrate to your very soul! How he could pierce the surface of the water, so impenetrable to our eyes, and read the ocean depths! . . .

These two strangers wore otter-skin caps, sealskin boots and clothes made out of some special material which hung loosely from their bodies, giving them great freedom of movement.

The taller of the two—obviously the captain of the ship—examined us very carefully without saying a word. He then turned to his companion and said something in a language I didn't recognize. It was a sonorous, harmonious, supple language, the vowels of which seemed to undergo a wide variety of accentuation.

The other answered with a nod, and added two or three totally incomprehensible words. He then looked at me as if he were questioning me directly.

I replied in French that I didn't understand his language; but he did not seem to understand me, and the situation became awkward.

"Monsieur might try to tell our story anyhow," Conseil said to me. "These gentlemen will perhaps understand a few words of it."

I began reciting our adventure, pronouncing each word very carefully and without omitting a single detail. I told them our names and positions, then formally presented us to them: Professor Aronnax, his servant Conseil and Ned Land, master harpooner.

The man with the calm, gentle eyes listened to me silently, politely and with remarkable attention. But nothing in his facial expression showed that he had understood my story. When I had finished he didn't say a word.

I could still try talking English. Perhaps I could make myself understood in this almost universal language. I knew English as well as I knew German, that is to say well enough to read it fluently, but not well enough to speak it correctly. But in this situation, we above all had to make ourselves understood.

"All right, it's your turn," I told the harpooner. "Whip out your best English and see if you have better luck than I did."

Ned, without hesitating, began our story all over again, and I could understand almost every word. It was basically the same, but differed in details. Being more emotional, the Canadian told it in much livelier fashion. He complained bitterly of being imprisoned without regard to people's rights, asked what they thought they were doing in locking us up like this, invoked the law of habeas corpus, threatened to bring them to court, flailed about, gesticulated, shouted and finally, with a very expressive gesture, made it clear that we were dying of hunger.

And this was perfectly true, even though we had almost completely forgotten about it.

To his great amazement, the harpooner seemed to have been no better understood than I. Our visitors did not bat an eyelid. It was obvious they understood neither the language of Arago nor that of Faraday.

Having thus exhausted our resources of language in vain, we were very puzzled. I no longer knew what to do, when suddenly Conseil said to me: "With Monsieur's permission, I could tell our story in German."

"What! You know German?" I cried.

"No better than most Belgians, by Monsieur's leave."

"Fine. Go ahead, my boy."

And then Conseil, in a calm voice, recounted for the third time the various details of our story. But in spite of his elegant turns of phrase and good accent, German proved equally unsuccessful.

Finally, at my wit's end, I gathered together the remains of my early school-
ing and started out narrating our adventure in Latin. Cicero would have blocked
his ears and sent me off to the kitchen, but I managed to get through it. The
result was the same.

After this last attempt had come to nothing, the two strangers exchanged
a few words in their strange language and went out, without even making one
of those reassuring gestures known the world over. The door closed behind
them.

"This is disgraceful!" cried Ned Land, bursting out for the twentieth time.
"We talked to those idiots in French, English, German and Latin, and neither of
them had the good grace to answer us!"

"Calm down, Ned," I told the raging harpooner. "Anger will get you nowhere."

"But can't you see, Professor," said our irascible companion, "that we're
going to die of starvation in this iron cage?"

"Nonsense!" said Conseil philosophically. "We can still hold out for a long
time!"

"We mustn't despair, my friends," I said. "We've been in worse situations
than this. So please do me the favor of waiting a while before you form an opinion of the captain and crew of this boat."

"My mind's completely made up," replied Ned Land. "They're nothing but
a bunch of scoundrels . . ."

"All right, then, what country are they from?"

"Scoundrelland!"

"That's all very well and good, Ned, but that country hasn't yet been very
clearly marked on maps, and I must admit that it's very difficult to try and figure out just where they are from. They're neither English, French or German—
that's all we can say for sure. All the same, I'd be tempted to say they're from
some southern region. But whether they're Spaniards, Turks, Arabs or Indians,
it's impossible to tell from their appearance. As for their language, I can't understand a word of it."

"That's the disadvantage of not knowing every language," answered
Conseil, "or of not having a world language!"

"Even that wouldn't do any good!" replied Ned Land. "Can't you see that these people have made up their own private language, just to annoy perfectly decent people who want a bite to eat? But in every country of the world, when you open your mouth, move your jaw up and down, click your teeth together and smack your lips, isn't that something everybody can understand? Whether you're in Quebec, Tuamotu, Paris or the North Pole, doesn't that mean: I'm hungry—give me something to eat! . . ."

"Yes," said Conseil, "but some people are so stupid that they . . ."

In the middle of his sentence, the door opened. A steward entered. He brought us underwear, coats and sailor's pants, all made out of a cloth I did not recognize. I got into them quickly, and my companions did the same.

Meanwhile, the steward—who was mute, or perhaps deaf—had set the table for three.

"This is more like it," said Conseil.

"Bah!" retorted the begrudging harpooner. "What kind of stuff do you think we'll get? Probably turtle liver, shark fillet or dogfish steaks!"

"We'll see," said Conseil.

The dishes with their silver covers were placed symmetrically on the table-cloth and we sat down to eat. There was no doubt about it, we were in the hands of civilized people, and except for the electric light, I would have thought myself in the Adelphi Hotel in Liverpool or the Grand Hotel in Paris.

I must admit, however, that there was no bread or wine. The water was fresh and clear, but it was only water—which wasn't much to Ned's liking. Among the things offered us, I could recognize various delicately prepared fish; but there were certain dishes which, although excellent, were completely unfamiliar to me, and I could not even have said to what kingdom, animal or vegetable, their contents belonged. As for the dinner service, it was elegant and in perfect taste. Each utensil—spoons, forks, knives and plates—had engraved on it a letter surrounded by a motto, which looked like this:

Mobile in mobile element! This motto corresponded perfectly to the submarine itself, on the condition that one translated the preposition *in* by *"in"* and not *"on."* The letter *N* was undoubtedly the initial of the enigmatic person who commanded this ship as it sailed through the ocean depths!

Ned and Conseil spent little time worrying about such things. They devoured their food, and I soon did the same. Moreover, I felt reassured about our fate, and it seemed obvious that our hosts did not want to let us die of starvation.

Nevertheless, everything in this world passes and comes to an end, even the hunger of people who have not eaten for fifteen hours. Once we had had our fill, we felt a great urge to sleep. But this was quite natural, considering we had spent an entire night struggling against death.

"It certainly is going to be a pleasure to sleep," said Conseil.

"Me too," replied Ned Land.

My two companions stretched out on the floor of the cabin, and soon they were sound asleep.

As for me, I felt the same strong need to rest, but I gave in to it less easily. Too many thoughts crowded into my mind, too many insoluble questions occupied my brain, too many ideas kept my eyelids half open! Where were we? What strange power carried us forward? I felt—or rather I thought I felt—the ship dive into the deepest layers of the ocean. I was beset by dreadful nightmares. In mysterious sanctuaries I saw whole worlds of unknown animals, of species seemingly related to the submarine, living, moving and terrifying! . . . Then my brain grew calmer, my imagination became lost in a vague drowsiness and I soon fell into a deep sleep.

I felt something dragging me, bringing me back to the surface.

CHAPTER IX
Ned Land's Temper

I have no idea how long we slept, but it must have been a long time, for afterward we felt completely rested. I woke up first. My companions had not yet moved, and were still stretched out in their corners like inert objects.

I had scarcely gotten up from this somewhat hard bed when I felt my mind clearing, my brain returning to normal. So I once again began carefully examining our cell.

Nothing had been changed in the cabin itself. The prison was still a prison and the prisoners still prisoners. The steward, however, had cleared off the table while we were asleep. There was therefore nothing to indicate that our situation would change in the near future, and in all seriousness I asked myself if we were destined to live indefinitely in this cage.

This thought seemed all the more painful, for although my mind was free from the obsessions of the day before, I felt as if there were a weight on my chest. I found it difficult to breathe. The air felt heavy and insufficient for my lungs. Even though our cell was enormous, it was obvious that we had used up a large part of the oxygen it contained. For it is a known fact that in one hour a man uses up the oxygen contained in $3\frac{1}{2}$ cubic feet of air, and that this air, which then holds an almost equal quantity of carbon dioxide, becomes unbreathable.

It was therefore urgent that the air in our prison be renewed, along with, undoubtedly, all the air in the submarine.

This gave rise to a question in my mind. How did the commander of the submarine solve this problem? Did he obtain his air chemically, releasing the oxygen contained in potassium chlorate by means of heat, and absorbing the carbon dioxide with potassium lye? In this case he must have kept up some contact with dry land, in order to get the chemicals needed for this operation. Or did he merely store air under pressure in reservoirs, and then feed it out according to the needs of his crew? Perhaps. Or—and this process would be the easiest, cheapest and therefore the most likely—did he merely come to the surface to breathe like whales, and thus replenish his air supply every twenty-four hours? In any case, whatever method he used, it seemed to me the time had come to put it into operation without delay.

In fact I was already obliged to speed up my breathing in order to make use of the little oxygen remaining in the room, when suddenly I felt refreshed by a current of pure air containing a strong smell of salt. It was sea air, revivifying and full of iodine! I opened my mouth wide and allowed my lungs to soak it up. At the same time, I felt a movement, a slight but undeniable rolling. The steel-plated monster of a ship had evidently come to the surface to breathe, just like a whale. Its method of respiration was therefore now a matter of certainty.

When my lungs had soaked up enough of this pure air, I tried to find the "aer-iferous" conduit, if you will, which had brought us this life-giving oxygen, and I soon found it. Above the door there was a ventilating hole through which passed a column of fresh air, thus renewing the impoverished atmosphere of our cell.

I had gotten to this point in my investigations when Ned and Conseil woke up almost at the same time, undoubtedly because of the fresh air that had entered the room. They rubbed their eyes, stretched and were on their feet in an instant.

"Did Monsieur sleep well?" Conseil asked with his usual politeness.

"Very well, thank you," I answered. "And you, Ned?"

"Very soundly, Professor. I may be wrong, but it seems to me as if I'm breathing sea air."

Sailors don't make mistakes about such things, and I told the Canadian what had happened while he was asleep.

"Good!" he said. "That accounts for the roaring we heard when the so-called narwhal was in sight of the *Abraham Lincoln.*"

"Right, Ned. It was breathing."

"The only trouble, Monsieur Aronnax, is that I have no idea what time it is, unless maybe it's lunch time."

"Lunch time, Ned? Breakfast time would be more accurate, for I'm sure this is already the following day."

"That would mean," said Conseil, "that we've slept for twenty-four hours."

"I think so," I answered.

"I won't argue with you," retorted Ned Land. "Whether it's lunch or breakfast, the steward'll be more than welcome, whichever he wants to bring."

"Perhaps he'll bring both!" said Conseil.

"Fine," replied the Canadian, "we have a right to two meals, and as for me, I could polish them both off without any trouble at all."

"In any case, Ned, let's wait," I answered. "It's obvious these people don't intend to let us die of starvation, otherwise that last meal wouldn't make any sense."

"Unless it was just to fatten us up!" exclaimed Ned.

"Come, come," I said. "We haven't fallen into the hands of cannibals!"

"One time doesn't make it a custom," the Canadian answered seriously. "Who knows whether these people haven't gone a long time without fresh meat, and as a result, three healthy well-built individuals like the professor, his servant and myself . . ."

"Put such ideas out of your mind, Ned," I replied, "and above all don't let such ideas make you lose your temper against our hosts, and thus make our situation that much worse."

"Anyway," said the harpooner, "I'm so hungry I could eat a horse, and I don't see either lunch or breakfast turning up!"

"Ned," I said, "we have to conform to the rules on board, and I imagine our appetites are running faster than the cook's watch."

"Well, then, we'll have to set ours by his," said Conseil calmly.

"That's you all over, Conseil my friend," retorted the impatient Canadian. "You never get riled up. Always calm. You'd be capable of thanking God before saying grace, and then dying of starvation rather than complaining!"

"What good would it do?" asked Conseil.

"Complaining doesn't have to do any good—it's enough all by itself. And if these pirates—I say pirates out of respect to the professor, and so as not to annoy him since he won't allow me to call them cannibals—if these pirates think they're going to keep me in this stifling cage without hearing me let loose with some of my swearing, they're making a big mistake! Come now, Monsieur Aronnax, tell me frankly. Do you think they're going to keep us cooped up for long in this iron box?"

"To tell the truth, Ned, I don't know any more than you."

"But what would be your guess?"

"My guess is that quite by chance we've stumbled on a very important secret. Now if the crew of the submarine wants to keep this secret, and if this is more important to them than the lives of three men, I think our chances of survival are slim. If this is not the case, the monster which has swallowed us up will, at the first opportunity, return us to the world inhabited by our fellow men."

"Unless they enroll us in the crew," said Conseil, "and thus keep us . . ."

"Until some frigate," interrupted Ned Land, "that's faster and more maneuverable than the *Abraham Lincoln* captures this pirates' den and makes its crew, and us along with it, walk the plank."

"Perhaps you're right, Ned," I replied, "but as far as I know, nobody has yet made us any propositions along this line. So it's useless discussing what we should do in such and such a situation. I repeat, let's wait and see what happens, and in the meanwhile just sit still, for there's nothing we can do anyway."

"No, Professor!" replied the harpooner, refusing to give up. "We have to do something."

"Do what, Ned?"

"Escape."

"Escaping from prisons on land is difficult enough, but from an underwater prison it would seem to me completely out of the question."

"All right, Ned," asked Conseil, "what do you have to say to that? I can't imagine an American ever at a loss for something to say!"

The harpooner, visibly embarrassed, remained silent. Under the conditions in which fate had placed us, escape was absolutely impossible. But a Canadian is partly a Frenchman, and one could see this clearly in his answer.

"Well, Monsieur Aronnax," he said after several moments' thought, "do you know what people do when there's no way out of a jail?"

"No, Ned."

"It's simple—they just make sure they stay there."

"Good for you!" cried Conseil. "It's better being inside one than above or below it!"

"But only after tossing out the jailers, wardens and guards," added Ned Land.

"What, Ned! You're thinking seriously of taking over this ship?"

"Very seriously," answered the Canadian.

"But that would be impossible."

"Why, Professor? If we get the opportunity, I don't see why we shouldn't take advantage of it. If there are only about twenty men on board this ship, that shouldn't frighten two Frenchmen and a Canadian, should it?"

It was best to agree with the harpooner rather than start another discussion. So I only answered: "Let's see what happens, Ned, and then decide. But until such time, please try and be a little more patient. Our only chance lies in some kind of a ruse, and if you keep losing your temper we'll never have the slightest chance of fooling them. So promise me you'll try to accept our situation without getting so angry."

"I promise, Professor," replied Ned in a not too reassuring tone. "I won't do or say a thing to show them how I feel, even when meals aren't served up as regularly as we'd like."

"So I have your word of honor, Ned," I answered the Canadian.

Then the conversation stopped and each one of us became lost in his own thoughts. I must admit that as far as I was concerned, in spite of the harpooner's confidence, I held out little hope. I could not see where we would get the opportunity Ned Land mentioned. In order to be operated as it was, this submarine needed a large crew, and this meant that if we had to fight it out, we would be too strongly outnumbered. Moreover, first of all we had to be free, and we weren't. I could see no means of escaping from a cell so hermetically sealed as the one we were in. And whatever secrets the strange captain of this ship wanted to keep—and this was undoubtedly the case—he would never let us wander about freely on board. Now, would he get rid of us by some violent means, or would he just let us off on some bit of land? That was what we didn't know. Either of these theories seemed plausible, and one had to be a harpooner to entertain ideas of gaining our freedom by force.

Moreover, I realized that Ned Land was becoming more and more embittered as he brooded over his situation. I began to hear him mumbling swear-words, and his gestures once again became menacing. He would get up, pace about like a wild animal in a cage and strike the wall with his fists and feet. Besides, after such a long wait we were beginning to feel violent pangs of hunger, and this time the steward did not appear. And for people with good intentions, the crew seemed to be taking a very long time supplying our needs.

Ned Land, tormented by the gnawing sensation in his stomach, was getting more and more worked up, and in spite of having given me his word, I was afraid he might not be able to restrain himself if some member of the crew came in.

For two more hours, Ned Land's temper got worse and worse. He shouted and yelled, but all in vain. The steel-plated walls were deaf. I could not even hear any noise inside the boat; it seemed dead. It wasn't moving, for I would obviously have felt it vibrate beneath the pulse of the propeller. It was undoubtedly lying deep in the ocean, and no longer belonged to life on earth. All this dreary silence was frightening.

As for our being abandoned and isolated in our cell, I had no idea how long it would last. The hopes I had felt after our interview with the captain were slowly vanishing. His gentle look, generous face and noble bearing were all beginning to disappear from my memory. I now saw this mysterious person as he really must have been—pitiless and cruel. I saw him as being a stranger to all human feelings, inaccessible to emotions of pity and the implacable enemy of his fellow men, toward whom he had sworn an everlasting hatred!

But was this man going to let us die of starvation, locked up in this narrow prison, exposed to those horrible temptations brought on by fierce hunger? This awful thought took ahold of my mind and imagination, and I felt myself overcome by a terrible feeling of horror. Conseil remained calm. Ned Land was roaring.

Just then we heard a noise outside. There was a sound of footsteps on the metal floor. Bolts were pulled, the door opened and the steward appeared.

Before I could do anything to stop him, the Canadian rushed at the poor man and knocked him over, clutching his throat. The steward was choking in his powerful grip.

Conseil was trying to loosen the harpooner's hands from his half-unconscious victim, and I was about to help him, when suddenly I was nailed to the spot by the following words spoken in French: "Calm down, Mr. Land; and you, Professor, please listen to me!"

CHAPTER X
The Man of the Seas

It was the captain who had spoken.

At these words, Ned Land quickly got up.

At a sign from his master, the steward, nearly strangled, left reeling; but such was the captain's power over his crew that this man did not give a single sign of the resentment he must have felt against the Canadian. Conseil, curious in spite of himself, and I, stunned by what had happened, waited in silence for the outcome of this scene.

The captain leaned against the corner of the table, crossed his arms and looked at us intently. Why did he hesitate? Did he regret having spoken in French? Perhaps.

After several moments' silence, which none of us dreamed of interrupting, he said in a calm, penetrating voice:

"Gentlemen, I also speak French, English, German and Latin. I could therefore have answered you at our first meeting, but I wanted to get to know you first and then think the matter over. Your four versions, almost exactly the same, made me certain of your identities. I now know that fate has put me in the presence of Monsieur Pierre Aronnax, professor of natural history at the Paris Museum and lately entrusted with a scientific mission abroad, Conseil, his servant, and Ned Land, of Canadian origin, harpooner on board the frigate *Abraham Lincoln* of the United States Navy."

I nodded in agreement. The captain's words were not a question but a statement, and no answer was therefore expected. This man expressed himself with complete ease and without accent. His sentences were correct, his words well chosen and his fluency remarkable. And yet I did not "feel" him to be a compatriot.

He then continued: "You have undoubtedly felt, Monsieur, that I took too long to make my second visit. It was because once I knew who you were, I wanted to consider carefully what to do with you. For a long time I could not make up my mind. It is most unfortunate that circumstances have put you in the presence of a man who has broken all ties with humanity. You came and disturbed my life . . ."

"Involuntarily," I said.

"Involuntarily!" the stranger answered, raising his voice a bit. "Was the *Abraham Lincoln* involuntarily hunting me throughout the ocean? Did you take passage aboard that ship involuntarily? Did your shells bounce involuntarily off the hull of my submarine? Did Ned Land's harpoon strike me involuntarily?"

I felt as if there were pent-up anger in these words. But I had a completely logical answer to his accusations, and I gave it. "Monsieur," I said, "you undoubtedly have no idea of the discussions you have provoked in America and Europe. You don't know how much the various accidents produced by collisions with your submarine have stirred up public opinion in both continents. I won't bore you with the innumerable theories which have been put forward to try and explain the unexplainable phenomenon to which only you had the secret. But you must understand that in pursuing you throughout the Pacific, the *Abraham Lincoln* thought it was hunting some powerful sea monster which must at all costs be cleared from the ocean."

A half smile played about the captain's lips, then in a calmer voice he said: "Monsieur Aronnax, would you dare state that your frigate would not have pursued and shot at a submarine as well as a monster?"

This question embarrassed me, for Commander Farragut would certainly not have felt a moment's hesitation. He would have thought it his duty to destroy a ship of this kind just as well as a giant narwhal.

"You can therefore understand, Monsieur," the stranger went on, "why I have the right to treat you as enemies."

I didn't answer, and with good reason. What use are the best of arguments when they can be destroyed by force?

"I have given the matter considerable thought," the captain went on. "Nothing forced me to show you any hospitality. If I were forced to leave you, I wouldn't have the slightest interest in seeing you again. I would just put you on the ship's platform on which you took refuge, dive down beneath the surface and then forget that you ever existed. Wouldn't I be within my rights?"

"Within the rights, perhaps, of a savage," I replied, "but not those of a civilized man."

"Professor," the captain retorted sharply, "I'm not what you would call a civilized man! I've broken with all of society for reasons which I alone can appreciate. I therefore don't obey its rules, and I advise you never to refer to them again in front of me!"

This was said in no uncertain terms. A flash of anger and disdain had lit up his eyes, and I felt this must be a man with a terrible past. Not only had he put himself outside the realm of human law, but he had made himself independent and free in the strictest sense of the word, and placed himself beyond the reach of such laws! Who would dare pursue him into the ocean depths, when even on the surface he could defy all attempts to harm his ship? What boat could withstand the impact of this underwater *Monitor*? What armored ship, no matter how thick its hull, could resist a blow of its lance? No man could ask him to account for his actions. God, if he believed in Him, and his conscience, if he had one, were the only judges to whom he was answerable.

While these thoughts crossed my mind in rapid succession, this strange person was silent, absorbed and as if wrapped up in himself. I looked at him with mixed feelings of horror and curiosity, just as Oedipus undoubtedly looked at the sphinx.

After a long silence, the captain once again started speaking. "So for a long time I could not make up my mind," he said, "but finally I thought that my own interests could be reconciled with the natural sense of pity found in every man. Since fate has put you here, you will remain on board. You will be free, and in exchange for this liberty, I shall impose on you only one condition. If you give me your word that you will accept it, that will be enough."

"Go on, Monsieur," I replied; "I imagine your condition will be acceptable to a man of honor."

"Yes, Monsieur, and here it is. It is quite possible that certain unforeseen events might oblige me to order you to stay in your cabins for several hours or days, depending on the situation. Since I prefer never to use force, I will expect from you, under such circumstances more than any other, total obedience. In this way, I will clear you of any responsibility, for I will be the one who has made it impossible for you to see what you should not see. Do you accept this condition?"

This meant that strange things happened on board, things that shouldn't be seen by people who had not put themselves outside the law! Of all the surprises the future had held in store for me, this proved not to be the least.

"We accept," I answered. "Only, with your permission, Monsieur, I would like to ask one question—only one."

"Go ahead."

"You said we were free on board."

"Completely."

"I would like to know, then, what this freedom involves."

"The freedom to walk about, to look, and even to examine everything that goes on here—except in some rare circumstances—in short, the same freedom enjoyed by all of us on board."

It was obvious we didn't understand each other.

"Excuse me, Monsieur," I replied, "but this freedom is no more than that of a prisoner who is allowed to move around in his cell! That isn't enough for us."

"It will have to do!"

"What! We have to give up forever the idea of seeing our country, our friends and our families?"

"Yes, Monsieur. But giving up the insupportable yoke of life on earth, which men mistake for liberty, will perhaps not be so unpleasant as you imagine!"

"One thing's certain," cried Ned Land, "I'll never give my word not to try to escape!"

"I'm not asking for your word on that score, Master Land," the captain answered coldly.

"Monsieur," I said, becoming angry in spite of myself, "you're taking advantage of our situation! This is cruelty!"

"No, Monsieur, it's kindness! You're my prisoners of war! I'm keeping you, when at a word I could have you plunged into the ocean depths! You attacked me! You have come upon a secret which no man in the whole world was to know—the secret of my existence! And you think I'm going to send you back to that world which must know me no more? Never! By keeping you, it's not you that I'm guarding, but myself!"

These words showed clearly that the captain's mind was made up, and that no arguments would be of any use against him.

"So," I said, "you're quite simply letting us choose between life and death?"

"That's right."

"My friends," I said, "when the problem's put like this, we have no choice. But we've made no promises to the captain of this ship."

"None, Monsieur," replied the stranger.

Then in a gentler tone, he continued. "Now please permit me to finish what I wanted to tell you. I know you, Monsieur Aronnax. You, if not your companions, will find that the stroke of fate which brought you here will not give you much cause for complaint. Among my favorite books for studying you'll find your own work on the great ocean depths. I have often read it. You have carried your knowledge as far as earthbound science will permit. But you don't know everything; you haven't seen everything. Therefore let me tell you, Professor, that you won't regret the time spent on board my ship. You will travel through a land of marvels. Your mind will be in a continual state of astonishment and stupefaction. It will be difficult for you to get bored with the continual spectacle that will pass before your eyes. I am starting out on another underwater trip around the world—who knows, perhaps my last—and once more I shall see everything I have been able to study beneath these seas through which I have traveled so many times, and you will accompany me in my studies. Starting today, you will enter a new element, and you will see what no man has yet seen—for I and my crew don't count anymore—and thanks to me, you will be able to penetrate the last secrets of our planet."

I cannot deny that these words had a great effect on me. He had hit me in my weakest spot, and for a moment I forgot that contemplating sublime things is never worth losing one's freedom. But I trusted to the future to solve this problem. I therefore merely answered: "Monsieur, although you have broken with humanity, I would like to think that you have not abandoned all humanitarian feelings. We are castaways who have been charitably taken aboard your ship, and we won't forget it. And as for me, I won't deny that if my interest in science could be even greater than my desire for freedom, this promised voyage would offer me great compensations."

I thought the captain was going to stretch out his hand to seal our bargain, but he didn't. I felt sorry for him.

"One last question," I said just as this mysterious person seemed about to withdraw.

"Go ahead, Professor."

"By what name should I address you?"

"Monsieur," he answered, "for you I shall be merely Captain Nemo, and you and your companions will be for me merely passengers on the *Nautilus*."

Captain Nemo called out. A steward appeared. The captain gave him orders in that strange language I could not recognize. Then turning to the Canadian and Conseil, he said: "A meal is waiting for you in your cabin. Please follow this man."

"You won't catch me refusing!" answered the harpooner.

Conseil and he finally left the cell in which they had been locked up for more than thirty hours.

"And now, Monsieur Aronnax, our lunch is ready. Allow me to go first."

"At your orders, Captain."

I followed Captain Nemo, and after crossing the threshold of our cell, I went down a sort of electrically lit corridor, similar to the gangways on ordinary ships. After walking thirty or so feet, a second door opened in front of us.

We then entered an austerely decorated dining room. At each end of this room stood two high oak sideboards inlaid with ebony. On their shelves lay china, porcelain and glass of incalculable value, and also a silver dinner service sparkling beneath the lights set in the painted ceiling.

In the center of the room was a richly set table. Captain Nemo pointed out the seat I was to occupy.

"Sit down," he said. "You must be dying of hunger."

The lunch consisted of a variety of dishes supplied from the ocean, and several others unknown to me. These last were very good, and I quickly became accustomed to their peculiar flavor. They seemed rich in phosphorus, and I thought they too must come from the sea.

Captain Nemo looked at me. Even though I said nothing, he guessed what I was thinking and answered the questions I was dying to ask.

"Although most of this food might be unknown to you," he said, "you can eat it without worrying. It's both healthy and nourishing. For a long time now I've given up ordinary land food, and I'm none the worse for it. And my crew, who are all fit and strong, eat no differently than I do."

"Does that mean," I said, "that all these dishes come from the sea?"

"Yes, Professor, the sea furnishes me with everything I need. Sometimes I drag nets behind the ship and haul them in when they're full to the bursting point, or sometimes I go out hunting in this element which seems inaccessible to men and stalk the game that lives in underwater forests. And my flocks, like those of Neptune's old shepherd, graze without fear over the immense prairies of the ocean. I have there vast properties which I alone exploit, and which are continually sown with all kinds of crops by the Creator's hand."

I looked at Captain Nemo somewhat astonished, and replied: "I can perfectly understand, Monsieur, that your nets furnish your table with excellent fish; I understand less well how you hunt aquatic game in your underwater forests; but

I don't understand at all how a slice of meat, no matter how small, could be included on your menu."

"In spite of which," replied Captain Nemo, "I never eat the flesh of land animals."

"But then what is this?" I asked, pointing to a plate on which remained several slices of steak.

"What you think is meat, Professor, is nothing but sea-turtle steak. Here also are some dolphin livers which you would think were stewed pork. I have an excellent cook, whose specialty is preparing seafood. Take a taste of all these dishes. Here are sea cucumbers we put up in jars and which a Malayan would declare unrivaled in the whole world, here is cream made from whale's milk, and sugar extracted from rockweed in the North Sea, and lastly permit me to offer you anemone jam, which is as good as that made from the most delicious fruit."

I tasted all these things more out of curiosity than as a connoisseur, while Captain Nemo regaled me with his unlikely stories.

"But the ocean, Monsieur Aronnax—that prodigious and inexhaustible provider, does not only nourish me; it also clothes me. The cloth you are now wearing was made from the filaments of certain shellfish; it was colored with the same purple dye used by ancient Greeks and Romans, and then tinted with some violet shades I extract from Mediterranean sea hares. The perfumes you will find on the shelf in your bathroom are produced by distilling certain marine plants. Your bed is made out of the softest eel grass. The pen you will use is made out of whalebone, and your ink is the secretion of the cuttlefish. I receive everything from the sea, just as one day all will return to it!"

"You love the sea, don't you, Captain?"

"Yes, I love it! The sea is everything. It covers seven-tenths of the globe. Its breath is pure and healthy. It is an immense desert where a man is never alone, for he can feel life quivering all about him. The sea is only a receptacle for all the prodigious, supernatural things that exist inside it; it is only movement and love; it is the living infinite, as one of your poets has said. And in fact, Professor, it contains the three kingdoms of nature—mineral, vegetable and animal. This last is well represented by the four groups of zoophytes, by the three classes of articulata, by the five classes of mollusks, by the three classes of vertebrates, mammals and reptiles, and those innumerable legions of fish, that infinite order of animals which includes more than thirteen thousand species, only one-tenth of which live in fresh water. The sea is a vast reservoir of nature. The world, so to speak, began with the sea, and who knows but that it will also end in the sea! There lies supreme tranquillity. The sea docs not belong to tyrants. On its surface, they can still exercise their iniquitous rights, fighting, destroying one another and indulging in their other earthly horrors. But thirty feet below its surface their power ceases, their influence dies out and their domination disappears! Ah, Monsieur, one must live—live within the ocean! Only there can one be independent! Only there do I have no master! There I am free!"

Captain Nemo suddenly fell silent in the midst of this burst of enthusiasm. Had he let himself be carried beyond the bounds of his usual reserve? Had he said too much? For several moments he paced up and down, seeming very disturbed. Then his nerves calmed down, his face took on its usual cold expression, and turning toward me, he said: "Now, Professor, if you would like to look over the *Nautilus*, I am at your disposal."

CHAPTER XI
The *Nautilus*

Captain Nemo got up and I followed him. A double door in the back of the dining room opened, and we entered another room the same size as the one we had just left.

It was a library. A large collection of uniformly bound books was set in high bookcases of black Brazilian rosewood inlaid with brass. They followed the shape of the room, and at their base were huge couches covered in brown leather and curved so as to give greater comfort. In front of them stood small movable desks on which one could rest the book one was reading, and which could be drawn up or pushed away at will. In the middle of the room there was a huge table covered with pamphlets and a few old newspapers. This whole ensemble was bathed in electric light coming from four frosted-glass globes in the ceiling. I stood in wonder before this room so ingeniously fitted out, and I could not believe my eyes.

"Captain Nemo," I said to my host who had just stretched out on a divan, "this library would do honor to more than one palace on land, and I am really astounded to think that it travels with you into the ocean depths."

"Where could one find greater solitude or silence, Professor?" replied Captain Nemo. "Can you boast of greater tranquillity in your office in the museum?"

"No, Monsieur, and I must admit that it is very shabby alongside yours. Why, you have six or seven thousand books . . ."

"Twelve thousand, Monsieur Aronnax. These are my only ties with life on dry land—a life which ended for me the day my *Nautilus* first dove beneath the surface of the ocean. That day I bought my last books, pamphlets and newspapers, and since then I have preferred to think that humanity has neither thought nor written anything. Moreover, Professor, you may feel free to use these books whenever you wish."

I thanked Captain Nemo and went over to the bookshelves. There were all sorts of works on science, morality and literature written in every known language; but I did not see a single book on politics or economy. It seemed as if such works were completely forbidden on board. There was, however, one odd thing about the library: all the books were arranged without thought for the language in which they were written, and this mixture proved that the captain of the *Nautilus* could read effortlessly whatever book came to hand.

Among them I noticed all the masterpieces of ancient and modern writers, that is to say, the most beautiful works history has produced—poetry, fiction and science from Homer to Victor Hugo, from Xenophon to Michelet, from Rabelais to George Sand. But this library leaned heavily toward science; books on mechanics, ballistics, hydrography, meteorology, geography, geology, etc., took up no less space than works on natural history, and I understood that all this formed the captain's principal source of study. I saw there all of Humboldt's works, all of Arago, Foucault, Henry Sainte-Claire Deville, Chasles, Milne-Edwards, Quatrefages, Tyndall, Faraday, Berthelot, Secchi, Petermann, Commander Maury, Agassiz, etc., the memoirs of the Academy of Science, the bulletins of various geographical societies, etc., and, in a conspicuous place, the two volumes which had perhaps won me this relatively warm reception on the part of Captain Nemo. Among the works of Joseph Bertrand, his book called *The Founders of Astronomy* furnished me with a date. Since I knew that it had appeared during the year 1865, I could conclude that the *Nautilus* could not have been launched before this date. Thus it was no more than three years, at the most, since Captain Nemo had begun his underwater existence. I hoped that more recent works would allow me to arrive at a more exact date, but I had plenty of time to undertake this project later, and I did not want to further delay our tour through the wonders of the *Nautilus*.

"Monsieur," I said, "I would like to thank you for allowing me to use this library. It contains many scientific treasures that will be very useful to me."

"This room is not only a library," said Captain Nemo, "but also a smoking room."

"A smoking room!" I cried. "Do you smoke on board?"

"Certainly."

"I am therefore forced to believe, Monsieur, that you still maintain relations with Havana."

"Not at all," answered the captain. "Try this cigar, Monsieur Aronnax, and even though it doesn't come from Havana, you will appreciate it if you are a connoisseur."

I took the cigar he offered me; in form it resembled those from Cuba, but it seemed to be made of gold leaf. I lit it with a little brazier set in an elegant bronze stand, and I took my first puffs with all the delight of a habitual smoker who had not had a cigar in two days.

"It's excellent," I said, "but it isn't made of tobacco."

"No," replied the captain, "this tobacco comes neither from Havana nor the Orient. It's made from a kind of seaweed rich in nicotine which I get from the sea—not without some difficulty. Do you still miss your Havana cigars, Monsieur?"

"Captain, from now on I wouldn't even look at one."

"Then please feel free to take one whenever you want, and without worrying about where they come from. Even though there's no label to guarantee their quality, they're still not bad."

"On the contrary."

Just then Captain Nemo opened another door, opposite the one through which we had entered, and I was led into a huge, splendidly lit room.

It had four walls with the corners cut off at angles; it was thirty-three feet long, twenty feet wide and sixteen feet high. A luminous ceiling decorated with small arabesques gave off a soft, clear light on the wonders brought together in this museum. For it was a veritable museum, in which an intelligent, prodigal hand had brought together all the treasures of nature and art and placed them about in a slightly helter-skelter fashion, giving somewhat the impression of an artist's studio.

Thirty or so paintings by famous masters, uniformly framed and separated by trophies, decorated the walls hung with tapestries of severe design. There I saw works of the greatest value, and which, for the most part, I had already admired in private European collections or art exhibits. The various schools of the earlier masters were represented by a Madonna of Raphael, a Virgin of Leonardo da Vinci, a nymph by Correggio, a woman by Titian, an Adoration of the Magi by Veronese, an Assumption by Murillo, a portrait by Holbein, a monk by Velázquez, a martyr by Ribera, a village fair by Rubens, two Flemish landscapes by Teniers, three little genre paintings by Gerard Douw, Metsu and Paul Potter, two works by Géricault and Prudhon, several seascapes by Backhuysen and Vernet. Among the works of modern painters, there were pictures signed by Delacroix, Ingres, Decamps, Troyon, Meissonier, Daubigny, etc., and small models of marble and bronze statues copied from the loveliest works of antiquity stood on pedestals in the corners of this magnificent museum. That state of stupefaction which the commander of the *Nautilus* had predicted was beginning to take hold of my mind.

"Professor," this strange man then said, "I hope you will excuse the informal way I have received you, and also the disorder reigning in this room."

"Monsieur," I replied, "without trying to find out who you are, I hope you will permit me to recognize you as an artist."

"Merely an amateur, Monsieur, nothing more. I used to enjoy collecting beautiful works created by the hand of man. I used to search and hunt for them avidly, and I have been able to collect some objects of great value. These are my last memories of life on earth, which is dead as far as I am concerned. In my eyes, your modern artists are already ancient, with two or three thousand years of existence, and I confuse them all in my mind. Great artists are ageless."

"And musicians," I said, pointing to scores by Weber, Rossini, Mozart, Beethoven, Haydn, Meyerbeer, Hérold, Wagner, Auber, Gounod and many others, all spread out on the large organ against one of the walls of the room.

"These musicians," answered Captain Nemo, "are all the contemporaries of Orpheus, for differences in time disappear in dead men's memories—and I am dead, professor, as dead as whatever friends of yours lie six feet under!"

Captain Nemo stopped talking and seemed lost in a deep reverie. I contemplated him with great interest and silently analyzed the strange expression on his face. He was leaning on the corner of a precious inlaid table; he no longer saw me—he forgot I was in the room.

Not wanting to disturb him in his withdrawal, I continued looking over the objects collected in this room.

Next to works of art, rarities of nature held an important place. They consisted mainly of plants, shells and other products of the ocean, all of which had undoubtedly been personally collected by Captain Nemo. In the middle of the room, an electrically illuminated jet of water fell back into a bowl made from a single giant clam. This shell, furnished by the largest of acephalous mollusks, measured about thirty-three feet around its delicately scalloped rim. It was even larger than those lovely giant clams given to Francis I by the Republic of Venice, and which the church of Saint-Sulpice in Paris has made into two huge holy-water basins.

Around this fountain, beneath elegant glass cases framed in brass, the most precious products of the sea ever beheld by a naturalist were carefully arranged and labeled.

The subkingdom of the zoophytes was represented by very curious specimens of its two divisions of polyps and echinoderms. From the first division there were organ-pipe corals, sea fans, soft Syrian sponges, isidae from the Moluccas, sea pens, marvelous virgularia from Norwegian waters, various umbella, alcyonaria, a whole series of madrepores which my teacher Milne-Edwards so wisely classed in sections, and among which I noticed flabella, ocullinae from Reunion Island, a "Neptune's chariot" from the West Indies, some superb types of corals, and all known species of those strange polyparies which gather together to form entire coral islands which some day will become continents. Among the echinoderms, notable for their spiny covering, there were star fish, pentracrini, feather stars, asterophons, sea urchins, sea cucumbers, etc.—thus forming a complete collection of this division.

A rather high-strung specialist in seashells would certainly have fainted before other and even more numerous glass cases in which specimens of mollusks were displayed. I saw there a collection of inestimable value, and which lack of time will not permit me to describe in its entirety. Among other things, I will only mention as a reminder, the royal hammer shell of the Indian Ocean, whose even white spots stood out clearly against a red and brown background; a brightly colored imperial spondylus covered with spines and only rarely found in European museums (I guessed it to be worth four thousand dollars); a common hammer shell from Australian waters, which is very difficult to obtain; exotic cockles from Senegal with their fragile white shells and double valves which a breath could shatter like a soap bubble; several varieties of watering pot shells from Java, looking like limestone tubes edged with leaflike pleats and very highly prized by collectors; a whole series of top shells, some colored greenish yellow and fished near the American continent, the others reddish brown and found in Australian waters—the former, which had come from the Gulf of Mexico, had remarkable shells in overlapping layers, the latter, captured in southern waters, were more star-shaped, and in addition, and rarest of all, there was the magnificent spur shell of New Zealand; then remarkable sulfurized tellinae; precious species of Venus shells; the trellized solarium from the coasts of Tranquebar; the marbled turban shell with its gleaming mother-of-pearl; the green parrot shell from the China Sea; the almost unknown conical shell of the genus Coenodulli; all the varieties of cowries used as money in India and Africa; the "Glory of the Sea," the most precious shell of the East Indies; and in addition, littorinae, delphinulae, turritellae, ianthinae, ovulae, volutes, olivae, mitrae, helmet shells, purpurae, whelks, harpae, murices, trumpet shells, cerithia, spindle shells, wing shells, pteroceras, limpets, hyalimaces, cleodorae and all sorts of delicate, fragile shells which science has baptized with the most charming names.

In separate special cases there were incomparably beautiful strings of pearls, which gleamed with fiery sparks beneath the electric light: there were pink pearls, taken from the pinnae of the Red Sea; green pearls from the haliotis iris; yellow, blue and black pearls, strange products of various mollusks from the world's oceans; and lastly several specimens of incalculable value produced by the rarest of pearl oysters. Some of these pearls were larger than a pigeon egg; they were as valuable, if not more so, than those the traveler Tavernier sold to the Shah of Persia for six hundred thousand dollars, and they seemed finer than that other pearl belonging to the Imam of Muscat, which I had believed unequaled in the whole world.

It was therefore impossible to estimate the value of this collection. Captain Nemo must have spent millions acquiring these various specimens, and I wondered where he got the money to indulge his collector's whims to such a degree. Suddenly my thoughts were interrupted by the following words: "You've been examining my shells, Professor. I can see why they might interest a naturalist; but to me they have a greater charm, for I have gathered them all with my own hands, and there is no corner of the sea I have left unexplored."

"I can easily understand, Captain, what a joy it must be to travel about amid such wealth. You are one of those rare men who have accumulated their treasure themselves. No museum in Europe has such a collection of marine products. But if I use up all my admiration for this, what will be left for the boat that carries it! I don't want to delve into your secrets, but I must admit that this *Nautilus,* the motor power it contains, the devices by which it is maneuvered, the powerful agent used to drive it—all this excites my curiosity to the highest degree. For instance, hanging over there on the wall, I see some instruments, and I haven't the vaguest idea what they're for. Could you tell me . . . ?"

"Monsieur Aronnax," Captain Nemo replied, "I have already said that you are free on board, and consequently no part of the *Nautilus* will be closed to you. You can visit the entire ship, and I would consider it a pleasure to act as your guide."

"I don't know how to thank you, Monsieur, but I would not like to abuse your kindness. I would merely like to know what these instruments . . ."

"Professor, you will see these instruments in my room, and it is there that I will have the pleasure of explaining their purpose. But first, come and look at the cabin I have reserved for you. I want you to see how you will be accommodated on board the *Nautilus.*"

I followed Captain Nemo as he led me through a door in the corner of the room and into one of the ship's passageways. After a few steps we turned into not a cabin but an elegant room, with a bed, dressing table and various other pieces of furniture.

I could only thank my host.

"Your room is next to mine," he said, opening a door, "and my cabin gives onto the room we have just left."

I entered the captain's cabin. It had a severe, almost monastic look about it. There was an iron cot, a work table and several dressers, all somewhat dimly lit. No comforts; just the strict necessities.

Captain Nemo pointed to a chair. "Please sit down," he said.

I sat down, and he began talking.

CHAPTER XII
All by Electricity

"Monsieur," said Captain Nemo, pointing to the instruments hanging on the walls of his room, "these are the devices needed to navigate the *Nautilus*. Here, as in the lounge, I have them always in sight, and they tell me my exact position and direction in the middle of the ocean. Some of them you already know, such as the thermometer, which gives the inside temperature of the *Nautilus;* the barometer, which indicates atmospheric pressure and predicts changes of weather; the hygrometer, which shows the dryness of the air; the storm glass, whose contents decompose and announce the arrival of storms; the compass, which gives me my course; the sextant which by determining the height of the sun, gives me my latitude; my chronometers, which permit me to find out my longitude; and lastly my telescopes, one for the day and the other for nighttime use, with which I examine every corner of the horizon when the *Nautilus* is on the surface."

"These are the usual nautical instruments," I answered, "and I know how they are used. But I see others which undoubtedly answer the *Nautilus'* special needs. Isn't that dial with a moving needle a pressure gauge?"

"Yes, it's a pressure gauge. It's in contact with the water outside, and by giving me its pressure tells me at what depth I'm traveling."

"And are these some new kind of sounding lines?"

"They're thermometrical sounding lines, to give me the temperature of the various layers of water."

"And what are these other instruments which are completely unfamiliar to me?"

"Before going any further, Professor, I must explain a few things," said Captain Nemo. "So please listen."

After a few moments of silence, he said: "There is one source of power which is obedient and rapid, easy and pliable, and which reigns supreme on board my ship. It does everything. It gives me light, heat and is the soul of all my machinery. This source is electricity."

"Electricity!" I cried, somewhat surprised.

"Yes, Monsieur."

"But Captain, the great speed with which your ship can move would seem to have little to do with electric power. Until now, its dynamic force has remained very limited and able to produce no more than a very small amount of energy!"

"Professor," answered Captain Nemo, "my electricity is not the usual kind, but I hope you will permit me not to go into it further."

"I won't insist on the matter, Monsieur, and I will be quite satisfied to be astounded at the results you have obtained with it. There is one question I would like to ask, however, but you need not answer if it is indiscreet. The materials you use to produce this marvelous source of power must get quickly used up. How, for instance, do you replace your zinc without going on shore?"

"I will answer your questions in a moment," Captain Nemo replied. "First, however, I would like to mention that in the ocean depths there exist mines of zinc, iron, silver and gold which would be quite easy to exploit. But I have used none of these earthly metals; I wanted to take only from the sea itself the means of producing my electricity."

"The sea?"

"Yes, Professor, and it was not difficult. In fact, by establishing a circuit between two wires at different depths, I could have obtained electricity through the resultant differences in temperature; but I preferred to use a more practical system."

"What was that?"

"You know the composition of sea water, don't you? Every thousand grams contain 96$1/2$ percent of water and about 2$2/3$ percent of sodium chloride; and then small quantities of magnesium chloride, potassium, magnesium bromide, magnesium sulfate, and sulfate and carbonate of lime. So you see that it contains a relatively large proportion of sodium chloride. And it is this sodium that I extract from sea water and use as a basic element."

"Sodium?"

"Yes, Monsieur. When mixed with mercury, it forms an amalgam which can replace zinc in batteries. The mercury never gets used up. Only the sodium is consumed, and the sea itself furnishes me with a steady supply of it. And besides, let me tell you that sodium batteries are the most powerful of all, their electromotive force being double that of zinc batteries."

"I can well understand, Captain, the excellence of such sodium. The sea contains it. Fine. But you still have to manufacture it, extract it. How do you manage that? Your batteries could obviously be used in this process, but if I'm not mistaken, the amount of sodium used up in this process would be greater than the amount extracted. You would therefore be using it up faster than you could produce it!"

"No, Professor, I don't extract it by means of batteries; I merely heat it by means of coal."

"Coal?" I said.

"Yes, but gotten from the sea," replied Captain Nemo.

"Can you dig coal from underwater mines?"

"Later you will see me do it. I only ask you to be a bit patient—you'll have plenty of time for patience. But keep this in mind: I get everything from the ocean—it produces my electricity, and electricity gives the *Nautilus* its heat, light and movement—in short, its life."

"But not the air you breathe?"

"Oh, I could make the air I need, but I could see no use in it since I can surface any time I want. But if electricity doesn't supply me with air, it at least operates the powerful pumps which store it in special tanks, thus allowing me to remain in the ocean depths as long as I want."

"Captain," I said, "I can only admire what you've done. You have obviously discovered something which other men will one day find out: the true dynamic force of electricity."

"I'm not so sure they will find it," Captain Nemo answered coldly. "But in any case, you already know one use I've made of this precious source of energy.

It gives us a light that is more uniform and continuous than that of the sun. Now look at this clock; it's electric and works with an accuracy that surpasses the finest chronometers. I've had it divided into twenty-four hours, like Italian clocks, because for me there exists no night or day, sun or moon, but only this artificial light that I bring with me to the ocean depths! As you can see, it is now ten o'clock."

"Precisely."

"Another use of electricity: this dial in front of us indicates the speed of the *Nautilus*. It is connected by an electric wire to the patent log, and its needle tells me the ship's actual speed. Right now, in fact, we're cruising at fifteen knots."

"Marvelous!" I replied. "How right you were, Captain, to use such a source of power—it can replace wind, water and steam!"

"We're not through, Monsieur Aronnax," said Captain Nemo, getting up. "If you will be kind enough to follow me, we'll visit the after part of the *Nautilus*."

I was by now familiar with the entire forward part of the submarine, and here is an exact description of how it was divided up, starting amidships and going forward to the spur on its prow: first there was the dining room, 16 1/2 feet long and separated from the library by a watertight bulkhead; then the library, also 16 1/2 feet long. Afterward came the big lounge, 33 feet long, separated from the captain's room, which was 16 1/2 feet long; then my cabin, 8 feet long; and lastly an air reservoir, which was 24 1/2 feet long and extended up to the bow. That made a total of 115 feet. The watertight bulkheads had doors that could be hermetically closed by means of a kind of rubber gasket around the edge, and these doors made the *Nautilus* safe even if it should spring a leak.

I followed Captain Nemo down the gangway to the center of the ship. There I saw a kind of well between two watertight bulkheads. An iron ladder against the wall led to its upper end. I asked the captain where it led.

"To the dinghy," he replied.

"What! You have a dinghy on board?" I exclaimed in surprise.

"Certainly. And it's a splendid little boat, light and unsinkable. We use it when we want to go fishing or out for a stroll."

"But that means you have to surface in order to use it."

"Not at all. This dinghy is lashed to the upper part of the *Nautilus'* hull, and set in a hollow place especially designed for it. It's completely covered by its own deck and thus absolutely watertight. It's held down with strong bolts. This ladder leads to a hatch in the *Nautilus'* hull which corresponds to a similar hatch in the side of the dinghy. This allows me to go straight up into the dinghy. The crew closes one hatch, the one on the *Nautilus,* and I close the other by means of press screws; I then undo the bolts and the boat shoots up to the surface. Once there I open the hatch cover, which till now has been kept tightly closed, set up the mast and sails or take out my oars, and I'm off."

"But then how do you come back on board?"

"I don't come back, Monsieur Aronnax; the *Nautilus* comes to me."

"At a command from you, I suppose!"

"Yes, at a command from me. I remain attached to it by an electric wire. I send them a message, and that's that."

"Right," I said, intoxicated with all these wonders, "nothing could be simpler!"

After passing the stairs which led to the platform, I saw a cabin about 6 1/2 feet long in which Conseil and Ned Land were busy devouring their lunch. From there a door opened onto a 10-foot kitchen situated between the ship's vast storerooms.

There all the cooking was done by electricity, which for this purpose was even more powerful and obedient than gas. Platinum sponges, connected to electric wires and placed beneath the top of the stoves, gave off an even heat over a large area. Electricity was also used to heat a still, which, by means of evaporation, supplied excellent drinking water. Next to the kitchen there was a well-laid-out bathroom, complete with hot and cold running water.

Beyond the kitchen was the crew's quarters, about 16 1/2 feet long. But the door was closed, and I could not see how it was furnished and hence perhaps get an idea of the number of men needed to operate the *Nautilus.*

Then came a fourth watertight bulkhead separating this room from the engine room. A door opened and I found myself in the compartment where Captain Nemo—undoubtedly a first-class engineer himself—had placed the machinery which drove his vessel.

This well-lit room was at least 65 feet long. It was divided into two sections: the first contained the apparatus for producing electricity, and the second the mechanism for transmitting this power to the propeller.

I was first of all surprised by a rather peculiar odor which filled the compartment. Captain Nemo guessed my thoughts. "It comes from the gas given off in using sodium," he said, "but it produces nothing more than a slight discomfort. And besides, every morning we purify the ship by ventilating it with fresh air."

In the meanwhile I was examining the *Nautilus'* machinery with the greatest curiosity.

"As you can see," said Captain Nemo, "I use Bunsen cells instead of those developed by Ruhmkorff, which would have been useless. The Bunsen cells are few, but large and powerful, which in my experience is an advantage. The electricity passes back through big electromagnets, actuating a set of rods and gears which in turn transmit the power to the propeller shaft. The propeller is twenty feet in diameter and can do up to twenty revolutions per second."

"What speed does that give you?"

"Fifty knots."

There was a mystery behind all this, but I did not want to ask too many questions. How could electricity be made to produce such power? Where did this almost limitless force originate? Was it in some high tension developed by a new kind of coil? Was there something about its transmission that an unknown system of levers* could increase infinitely? There was no way of knowing.

"Captain Nemo," I said, "I'm fully aware of the results, and I don't expect any explanations. I saw the *Nautilus* maneuver around the *Abraham Lincoln* and so I'm well acquainted with its speed. But that isn't enough. You have to be able to see where you're going! You have to be able to steer the ship to the right, to the left, up and down! How do you reach the great ocean depths, where the water pressure has to be counted in the hundreds of atmospheres? How do you

---

*And it so happens that people are now talking about just such a discovery, in which a new system of levers produces considerable power. Did the inventor meet Captain Nemo?

come back to the surface? And lastly, how do you stay at a desired depth? I hope I'm not being too inquisitive."

"Not at all, Professor," replied the captain after a moment's hesitation, "in view of the fact that you're destined never to leave this submarine. Come into the lounge. That is our real workroom, and there I'll tell you everything you want to know about the *Nautilus*."

CHAPTER XIII
Some Figures

A moment later we were seated on a sofa in the lounge smoking cigars. The captain handed me a diagram of the *Nautilus* showing cross sections and side views. He then began to describe the ship as follows: "Now, Monsieur Aronnax, here are the various dimensions of the ship you're on. It's in the shape of a very elongated cylinder with conical ends—rather like a cigar. This shape has already been used in London in several ships of the same sort. This cylinder is exactly 230 feet long from stem to stern, and its beam, at the widest point, is 26 feet. It is therefore not built exactly in the ratio of ten to one, as with your fast steamers, but its lines are sufficiently long and curved so that the displaced water moves away easily and acts as no obstacle.

"These two dimensions will enable you, by a simple calculation, to obtain the surface and volume of the *Nautilus*. It has a surface area of 10,885 square feet, and a volume of 52,980 cubic feet—which means that when it is entirely submerged it displaces 52,980 cubic feet of water, or in other words 1657.9 tons.

"When I laid my plans for a ship destined to sail beneath the surface, I wanted it, when at a state of equilibrium in the water, to be nine-tenths submerged and ɑly one-tenth above the surface. Consequently its ratio of weight to volume ɑd to be nine to ten, or in other words it had to weigh 1492.13 tons. I therefore ɑd to be careful not to exceed this weight while having it built to the afore-mentioned dimensions.

"The *Nautilus* has two hulls, one inside the other and joined together by T-shaped irons, thus giving the ship great strength. And thanks to this cellular arrangement, it has the resistance of a solid mass. Its sides cannot give way; they adhere to the ship by themselves, without rivets, and the homogeneity of its construction, achieved by the perfect union of the materials involved, permits it to defy the most violent seas.

"These two hulls are made out of steel plates whose density is between seven- and eight-tenths that of water. The first of these is no less than two inches thick and weighs 434.46 tons. The second hull, along with the keel which is twenty inches high and ten inches long and alone weighs 68 tons, the engine, the ballast, the various accessories and furnishings, the bulkheads and inside braces, all weigh 1057.67 tons, which added to the 434.46 of the first hull make the required total of 1492.13 tons. Do you follow me?"

"Yes," I answered.

"Therefore," continued the captain, "when the *Nautilus* is floating, one-tenth of it is above water. Now if I have reservoirs with a capacity equal to this tenth, or in other words of 165.79 tons, and fill them with water, the boat would then weigh 1657.9 tons and would be completely submerged. And this is exactly what happens, Professor. I have just such reservoirs aboard, in the lower parts of the *Nautilus*. I open some cocks, water enters and the boat sinks just below the surface."

"Yes, Captain, but now we come to the real problem. I understand how you can go just below the surface. But as you go deeper, below this point, won't your submarine encounter a pressure and therefore a force pushing it upward equal to one atmosphere for every thirty-two feet of water, or almost fifteen pounds per square inch?"

"That's right, Monsieur."

"So unless you fill the *Nautilus* completely, I don't see how you can make it dive down to great depths."

"Professor," replied Captain Nemo, "you must not confuse static and dynamic situations, or you will fall into serious errors. It requires very little effort to attain the great depths of the ocean, for an object develops a 'sinking' tendency. Please follow my reasoning."

"I'm listening, Captain."

"When I wanted to calculate the increase in weight I had to give the *Nautilus* in order to dive, I only had to concern myself with the greater density of water at increasingly lower depths."

"That much is evident," I said.

"Now although water is not absolutely incompressible, it is at least compressible only to a very small degree. As a matter of fact, according to the latest calculations, this reduction in volume amounts to no more than a proportion of .0000436 per atmosphere, or for each thirty-two feet of depth. So if I want to go down to a depth of thirty-two hundred feet, I take into account the reduction in volume at a pressure equivalent to that of a column of water thirty-two hundred feet high, or in other words a pressure of a hundred atmospheres. The reduction in volume would therefore be .00436. Hence I must increase the weight of the ship to 1665.14 tons instead of 1657.9 tons. Or in other words, an increase of 7.24 tons."

"No more than that?"

"No more than that, Monsieur Aronnax, and these figures are easy to check. But I have supplementary reservoirs capable of taking on a hundred tons. I can therefore go down to considerable depths. When I want to come back to the surface, I have only to get rid of this water and empty all the reservoirs, and then the *Nautilus* will again emerge by one-tenth of its total height."

To these arguments, based on figures, I could raise no objection.

"I cannot argue with your calculations, Captain," I answered, "and moreover it would be rather ridiculous to do so, since daily experience has proved you right. But I foresee one very real problem."

"And what is that, Monsieur?"

"When you go down to a depth of thirty-two hundred feet, the *Nautilus*' hull sustains a pressure of a hundred atmospheres. If at that moment you want to empty the supplementary reservoirs in order to lighten your ship and permit it to rise to the surface, your pumps must overcome this pressure of a hundred atmospheres, which is equal to 1470 pounds per square inch. That would require a force . . ."

". . . that could only be supplied by electricity," Captain Nemo quickly interjected. "I repeat, Monsieur, that the dynamic power of my engines is almost infinite. The *Nautilus'* pumps have prodigious force, as you were able to see when they threw torrents of water over the *Abraham Lincoln*. Besides, I only use these supplementary reservoirs to attain depths between fifty hundred and sixty-five hundred feet, and that with a view to sparing my machinery. But when I decide to visit the deepest parts of the ocean, six or eight miles below the surface, I use slower but no less infallible means."

"What are they, Captain?"

"But this brings me naturally to an explanation of how the *Nautilus* is maneuvered."

"I'm very anxious to learn how this is done."

"In order to steer this ship to starboard or to port—in order to maneuver, in a word, horizontally—I use an ordinary rudder with a large afterpiece fixed to the rear of the sternpost, operated by a wheel and pulley-tackle. But I can also move the *Nautilus* up and down by means of two fins attached to the side of the ship at its center of gravity. They are completely movable and are operated from inside by means of powerful levers. As long as these fins are held parallel to the boat, it moves horizontally. When they are placed at an angle, the *Nautilus,* according to the degree of this angle and the speed at which it is traveling, dives or rises as steeply or gently as I wish. And if I want to rise even more quickly, I merely disengage the propeller, and water pressure makes the *Nautilus* rise vertically like a hydrogen balloon going straight up into the air."

"Bravo, Captain!" I cried. "But now how can the helmsman follow the course you have given him underwater?"

"The helmsman is inside a special compartment that juts out on the top of the hull and which is equipped with lenslike windows."

"You have glass that can stand up under such pressures?"

"Absolutely. It's fragile when it's hit, but it's nevertheless very strong. In

The machinery which drove his vessel

some experiments made with fishing by electric light in 1864 in the middle of the North Sea, glass plates only 9/32 of an inch thick were found capable of withstanding a pressure of sixteen atmospheres and at the same time permitting powerful heat rays to penetrate them. Now the lenses I use are more than eight inches thick at their centers, or in other words about thirty times thicker."

"Granted, Captain Nemo; but in order to see, some light has to pierce the darkness, and I wonder how in the midst of the black depths . . ."

"Behind the helmsman's compartment there is a powerful electric light whose rays illuminate the water for half a mile around."

"Bravo, bravo, Captain! That explains the so-called narwhal's phosphorescence which so intrigued scientists! While we're on this subject, I would like to ask you if the collision of the *Nautilus* with the *Scotia*, which caused such a stir, was accidental."

"Completely accidental, Monsieur. I was cruising six feet below the surface when the collision took place. Besides, I was able to see that the damage was not really serious."

"No, Monsieur, it wasn't. But as for your encounter with the *Abraham Lincoln* . . ."

"Professor, I'm sorry for one of the finest ships in the American Navy, but I was being attacked and I had to defend myself! Even then, all I did was put the frigate in a position where it could do me no more harm—she will have little trouble repairing her damages in the nearest port."

"Ah, Commander," I cried enthusiastically, "your *Nautilus* is truly an extraordinary ship!"

"Yes," Captain Nemo replied with genuine emotion, "and I love it as if it were my own flesh and blood! In one of your ships sailing amid the hazards of the ocean, everything seems fraught with danger. In traveling on the surface of the sea, one's first thoughts are about the abyss below, as the Dutchman Jansen so well put it. But on the *Nautilus* one has nothing to fear. The hull itself is untouchable, for it has the rigidity of iron; there is no rigging to be harmed by rolling or pitching; no sails to be carried off by the wind; no boilers to be torn open by steam; no fear of fire since the ship is made of steel not wood; no coal supply which can run short, since I run the ship on electricity; no chance encounter to fear, since I am alone in sailing in deep water; no storms to ride out since several yards below the surface reigns absolute peace! There, Monsieur—a ship to end all ships! And if it's true that the designer has more confidence in a boat than the builder, and the builder more than the captain, then you can understand how great is my trust in the *Nautilus*, since I am its captain, builder and designer all in one!"

Captain Nemo spoke with an infectious eloquence. He seemed transformed by the fire in his eyes and his impassioned gestures. Yes, he loved his ship as a father loves his child!

But one perhaps indiscreet question naturally came to mind, and I could not help asking him: "Are you, then, also a nautical engineer, Captain Nemo?"

"Yes, Professor," he answered. "I studied in London, Paris and New York when I was still an inhabitant of dry land."

"But how were you able to construct this marvelous *Nautilus* in secret?"

"Every part of it, Monsieur Aronnax, was sent to me from a different part of the globe, and to a disguised address. Its keel was forged by Creusot, its propeller shaft by Pen and Company in London, the steel plates of the hull by Leard in Liverpool, its propeller by Scott in Glasgow. Its reservoirs were built by Cail and Company in Paris, its engines by Krupp in Prussia, the spur on its bow in the Motala workshops in Sweden, its precision instruments by Hart Brothers in New York, et cetera, and each of these companies received my plans under different names."

"But after these various sections were made," I answered, "they had to be assembled and put in place."

"Professor, I set up a workshop on a desert island in midocean. There, my workers, or rather my companions, whom I taught and educated, helped me complete the *Nautilus*. Then when it was finished, fire destroyed all trace of our stay on the island, which I would have blown up had it been possible."

"But this boat must have cost a fortune."

"An iron ship costs $225 per ton, Monsieur Aronnax. Now, the *Nautilus* weighs almost fifteen hundred tons. It therefore cost $337,500, or $400,000 with all its furnishings, or close to a million dollars counting the works of art and other collections it contains."

"One last question, Captain Nemo."

"Go ahead, Professor."

"You must therefore be a very rich man."

"Infinitely rich, Monsieur, and I could easily pay France's two-billion-dollar debt!"

I stared fixedly at the strange person telling me these things. Was he taking advantage of my credulity? The future would tell me.

CHAPTER XIV
The Black Stream

That part of the earth's surface occupied by water is evaluated at more than 147,959,620 square miles, or over 94 billion acres. This liquid mass has a volume of 2,250,000,000 cubic miles and would form a sphere with a diameter of over 2000 miles which would weigh 3 quintillion tons. And in order to understand this number, one must realize that a quintillion is to a billion what a billion is to one, or in other words that there are as many billions in a quintillion as there are units in a billion. And this mass of liquid is more or less equal to the quantity of water that all the rivers of the earth would pour forth in forty million years.

In early geological times, a period of fire was followed by a period of water. At first the ocean covered everything. Then little by little, during the Silurian period, mountaintops appeared forming islands, disappeared beneath the floods and then rose again, joined together to form continents, and finally the land became fixed as we now know it. The solid element had won 37,657,000 square miles from the liquid element, or slightly over 24 billion acres.

The shape of the continents makes it possible to divide these waters into five great areas: the Arctic, Antarctic, Indian, Atlantic and Pacific Oceans.

The Pacific Ocean extends from north to south between the two polar circles and from west to east between Asia and America through 145 degrees of longitude. It is the calmest of all the oceans; its currents are wide and slow, its tides moderate and its rainfall abundant. Such was the ocean I was destined to first see under the strangest of conditions.

"Professor," said Captain Nemo, "if you would like to accompany me, I am going to take our bearings and determine our point of departure for the voyage. It's a quarter to twelve. I am going to surface."

The captain pressed a button three times. The pumps began to expel the water from the reservoirs; the pressure gauge showed that the *Nautilus* was rising, and then it stopped.

"We're there," said the captain.

I walked to the companionway leading up to the platform. I climbed the iron steps, passed through an open hatch and arrived on the topside of the *Nautilus*.

The platform was only 2 1/2 feet above water level. The bow and stern of the *Nautilus* had that spindle shape which gave it the form of a long cigar. I noticed that its steel plates overlapped somewhat, making them look like the scales of large land reptiles. I could therefore easily understand how even with the finest binoculars this vessel had always been taken for a marine animal.

Toward the middle of the platform, the dinghy, half-buried in the hull of the ship, protruded slightly. Fore and aft, there were two small compartments with inclined sides and containing windows of thick lenslike glass: one contained the helmsman who steered the *Nautilus* and the other held the powerful electric light which guided him on his route.

The sea was splendid, the sky serene. The long ship scarcely felt the broad ocean swell. A light easterly breeze rippled the surface of the water. The horizon was free from any trace of mist and could be clearly seen for purposes of observation.

Nothing was in sight. No reef, no island. No *Abraham Lincoln*. A vast desert. Captain Nemo measured the height of the sun with his sextant, thus getting his latitude. He waited for several minutes until, through the eyepiece, he could see the sun touching the horizon. During this operation not one of his muscles moved, and the instrument would not have been more immobile in a marble hand.

"It's noon, Professor," he said. "Whenever you want . . ."

I took one last look at the sea, slightly yellow as it always is near the coast of Japan, and I went back down to the lounge.

There the captain determined his bearings and chronometrically calculated his longitude. He then said: "Monsieur Aronnax, we're at 137° 15' West . . ."

"Of what meridian?" I asked anxiously, hoping his answer would indicate his nationality.

"Monsieur," he replied, "I have chronometers set according to the meridians of Paris, Greenwich and Washington. But in your honor, I shall use the one set according to Paris."

This answer told me nothing. I bowed and the commander went on.

"137° 15' West of the Paris meridian, and 30° 7' North Latitude, or in other words about three hundred miles from the coast of Japan. And today, the eighth of November, at noon, begins our voyage of underwater exploration."

"May God be with us!" I replied.

"And now, Professor," the captain added, "I leave you to your studies. I have given orders for our course to be set for east-northeast and at a depth of 165 feet. Here are some large-scale charts on which you may follow our journey. This room is at your disposal; and now, with your permission, I shall retire."

Captain Nemo bowed. I remained alone, lost in thoughts about the commander of the *Nautilus*. Would I ever find out to what country this strange man belonged, he who boasted that he belonged to none? What had brought on this hatred he felt for the human race, a hatred which was perhaps seeking some terrible revenge? Was he one of those unrecognized scientists, one of those geniuses whom "the world had humiliated," as Conseil put it, a modern Galileo, or one of those scientists like the American, Maury, whose career had been shattered by political revolutions? I could not yet say. As for me, whom fate had thrown aboard this ship, and whose life Captain Nemo held in his hands, he had received me coldly but nonetheless hospitably. Except for one detail: he had never shaken my hand when I had stretched it out to him, nor had he ever stretched his out to me.

For a whole hour I remained lost in these thoughts, trying to penetrate this mystery which so fascinated me. Then my glance fell on the vast map of the world laid out on the table, and I placed a finger on our present position.

The sea, like land, also has rivers. They are special currents that can be easily recognized by their temperature and color, and the most remarkable of these is called the Gulf Stream. Science has been able to determine the place of five such currents: one in the north Atlantic, a second in the south Atlantic, a third in the north Pacific, a fourth in the south Pacific and a fifth in the southern Indian Ocean. It seems likely that once upon a time a sixth existed in the northern Indian Ocean, when the Caspian and Aral Seas were united to the great Asian lakes and formed a single expanse of water.

Now the point on the map indicated by my finger was in one of these great currents, the Black Stream, or as the Japanese call it, the Kuro Siwo. It starts in the Bay of Bengal where it is heated by the tropical sun, crosses the Straits of Malacca, flows along the coast of Asia, curves along the north Pacific to the Aleutian Islands, carrying along with it the trunks of camphor trees and other objects it has picked up on its way and cutting a clear path through the ocean with the deep blue of its warm waters. It was this current the *Nautilus* was going to cross. I looked at it on the map. I could see it lose itself in the vast expanse of the Pacific, and I felt as if I were being carried off with it, when Ned Land and Conseil appeared at the door of the lounge.

My two friends were thunderstruck by all the marvels spread before their eyes.

"Where are we? Where are we?" cried the Canadian. "In the Quebec museum?"

"With Monsieur's permission," Conseil interjected, "it seems more like the Sommerard Palace!"

"My friends," I answered, motioning for them to enter, "you're neither in Canada nor in France, but on board the *Nautilus*, 165 feet below the surface of the ocean."

"If Monsieur says so, we must believe him," said Conseil; "but this room is enough to astonish even a Belgian like myself."

"Don't worry about your astonishment, my friend. Look around. For a good classifier like you, there's enough here to keep you busy for a good while."

I didn't have to encourage Conseil. He was already leaning over the cases and mumbling the naturalist's language: class of Gastropods, family of Buccinoids, genus of cowries, species of *Cyproea madagascariensis*, etc.

Meanwhile Ned Land, who cared little for shells and mollusks, questioned me about my interview with Captain Nemo. Had I found out who he was, where he came from, where he was going, how deep he would take us? In short, a thousand questions which I didn't have time to answer.

I told him all I knew—or rather didn't know—and asked him what he had heard or seen.

"I haven't heard or seen a thing," answered the Canadian. "I haven't even seen any of the crew of this ship. Could that be electrical too?"

"Electrical!"

"I swear I'm almost ready to believe it. But you, Monsieur Aronnax," asked Ned Land, still clinging to his ideas, "can't you tell me how many men there are on board? Ten, twenty, fifty, a hundred?"

"I have no way of knowing, Ned. And besides, for the moment anyhow, please give up your ideas of seizing control of the *Nautilus*, or of escaping. This boat is a masterpiece of modern industry, and I feel lucky to have seen it. Many people would jump at the chance we've had, if only to stroll in a land of wonders. So be calm, and let's try and see what goes on around us."

"See what goes on around us!" cried the harpooner. "We can't and never will see a thing from inside this steel-plated prison! This boat travels and navigates like a blind man . . ."

Just as Ned Land uttered these last words, the room was plunged into darkness, total darkness. The ceiling lights had gone out so quickly that it made my eyes hurt, just as if we had gone abruptly from utter darkness to brilliant light.

We all remained silent, without moving, not knowing what pleasant or unpleasant surprise awaited us. But then there was a noise of something sliding. It seemed as if panels were moving along the sides of the *Nautilus*.

"This is the end!" said Ned Land.

"Order of hydromedusae!" murmured Conseil.

Suddenly light entered from each side of the room, through two oblong openings. The surrounding water appeared brilliantly lit up by the electric light atop the *Nautilus*. Two glass panels separated us from the sea. At first I shuddered at the thought that this fragile partition would break; but it was held in by strong copper frames which gave it an almost limitless resistance.

The sea was distinctly visible within a radius of a mile around the *Nautilus*. What a sight! What pen could describe it? Who could paint the effects of light penetrating these transparent layers of water and growing dimmer as it reached into the distant corners of the ocean?

The clarity of sea water is well known. It is clearer than spring water. The mineral and organic substances it holds in suspension actually increase its transparency. In certain parts of the ocean, in the West Indies for example, a sandy bottom almost five hundred feet down can be seen with surprising clarity, and the sun's rays are apparently able to penetrate to depths of a thousand feet. But the *Nautilus* could produce its own light in the ocean depths. It was no longer illuminated water, but liquid light.

If one admits Ehremberg's theory that the great ocean depths are illuminated by phosphorescence, then nature has reserved one of her most extraordinary spectacles for its inhabitants, as I could see by the thousand different ways the light played about before my eyes. On each side of the room I had a window open to unexplored depths. The darkness within the room made it easier to see out, and we looked through this clear glass as if through the window of an immense aquarium.

The *Nautilus* did not seem to be moving, but this was an illusion due to the fact that there were no points of reference. Occasionally, however, lines of water divided by the spur on the submarine's prow would stream by us at great speed.

We stood leaning against the windows in a state of stupefaction, and no one broke the silence until Conseil finally said: "You wanted to see something, Ned, and now you've got it!"

"Unbelievable!" mumbled the Canadian, who had forgotten his rage and his plans for escape, and now felt irresistibly attracted to the spectacle before him. "It's worth coming a long way to see something like this!"

"Ah!" I said to myself, "now I understand the life Captain Nemo leads. He's created a private world for himself, full of the most astounding marvels!"

"But where are the fish?" observed the Canadian. "I don't see any fish."

"What difference does it make, Ned," replied Conseil, "since you couldn't tell them apart anyway?"

"Me! A fisherman!"

This started an argument between the two friends, for they were both knowledgeable on the subject of fish, but in different ways.

Everyone knows that fish form the fourth and last class of the subkingdom of the vertebrates. They have been very accurately described as "vertebrates with a double circulatory system and cold blood, breathing through gills and living in the water." They form two distinct groups: those with true bone structure and those which are cartilaginous, that is to say whose spinal column is made of cartilage.

Perhaps the Canadian had a vague idea of this distinction, but Conseil knew it only too well. And now that he had become such good friends with Ned, he felt he had to show off his knowledge. He therefore said: "Ned, you're a killer of fish, a first-class fisherman. You've caught a great number of these interesting creatures. But I'll bet you don't know how to classify them."

"Yes I do," answered the harpooner in all seriousness. "They're classified into those you can eat and those you can't."

"That's a glutton's way of classifying them," replied Conseil. "But let's see if you know the difference between fish with true bone structure and those which are cartilaginous."

"A little bit, Conseil."

"And the subdivisions of these two big classes?"

"I haven't a clue," answered the Canadian.

"Well, Ned, listen and concentrate. Fish with true bone structure are divided into six orders: first, the Acanthopterygii, whose upper jaw is complete and mobile and whose gills are shaped like a comb. This order comprises fifteen families, that is to say three-quarters of all known fish. Type: the common perch."

"Not bad eating," answered Ned Land.

"Second," Conseil continued, "the Abdominales, whose ventral fins are underneath behind the pectorals, without being attached to the shoulder bone. This order is divided into five families and includes most freshwater fish. Type: the carp and the pike."

"Phew!" said the Canadian with an air of disdain. "Freshwater fish!"

"Third," said Conseil, "the Subbrachii, whose ventral fins are attached beneath the pectoral fins and directly onto the shoulder bone. This order comprises four families. Type: plaice, dabs, turbots, brills, sole, et cetera."

"Marvelous!" cried the harpooner, who refused to consider fish from any other point of view but that of how good they were to eat.

"Fourth," continued Conseil, unconcerned, "the Apods, with elongated bodies, lacking ventral fins, and covered with thick and often sticky skin. This order contains only one family. Type: eels."

"Not so good," replied Ned Land.

"Fifth," said Conseil, "the Lophobranchii, whose jaws are complete and free-moving, but whose gills are made of little tufts grouped in pairs along their branchial arches. This order comprises only one family. Type: sea horses and pipefishes."

"Terrible, terrible!" said the harpooner.

"Sixth," said Conseil, "the Plectognathi, whose maxillary bone is attached to the side of the intermaxillary which forms the jaw, and whose post-temporal bone is united with the skull, thus making it immobile. The fish of this order lack true ventral fins, and they comprise two families. Types: the globefish and the sunfish."

"They're enough to dishonor the pot they're cooked in!" cried the Canadian.

"Did you understand all that, Ned?" Conseil asked.

"Not in the least, my friend," replied the harpooner. "But go on anyhow— it's very interesting."

"As for cartilaginous fish," continued the imperturbable Conseil, "they only comprise three orders."

"The fewer the better," said Ned.

"First, the Cyclostomi, whose jaws are welded into a kind of mobile ring and whose gills consist of a large number of holes. This order comprises only one family. Type: the lamprey."

"You can't help but like them," said Ned Land.

"Second, the Selachii, whose gills are like those of the Cyclostomi, but whose lower jaw is mobile. This order, the most important of the class, comprises two families. Types: rays and sharks."

"What!" cried Ned, "rays and sharks in the same order! But let me tell you, my friend, that in the interest of the rayfish it would be best not to put them together in a tank!"

"Third," continued Conseil, "the Sturiones, whose gills usually consist of only one slit with a gill cover. This order includes four genera. Type: the sturgeon."

"Ah, Conseil, you've kept the best for the last—or at least in my opinion. Is that all?"

"Yes, Ned," said Conseil, "but even when you know that much you still know nothing, for these families are divided into genera, subgenera, species, varieties . . ."

"Well then, Conseil," said the harpooner, leaning against one of the windows, "here are your varieties passing by now."

"Look, fish!" cried Conseil. "It's as if we were in front of an aquarium!"

"No," I answered, "for an aquarium is a cage, and these fish here are as free as birds in the air."

"Come on, Conseil, tell us their names!" said Ned Land.

"I can't," answered Conseil. "'That's my master's job!'"

And to tell the truth, although this fine young man was an enthusiastic classifier, he was not a naturalist, and I don't know if he could have distinguished a tuna from a bonito. In a word, he was the opposite of Ned Land, who could name all these fish without a moment's hesitation.

"A triggerfish," I said.

"A Chinese triggerfish!" answered Ned Land.

"Genus of Balistes, family of Sclerodermi, order of Plectognathi," murmured Conseil.

There was no doubt about it, between the two of them, Ned and Conseil would have made a distinguished naturalist.

The Canadian had made no mistake. A school of triggerfish with their flat bodies and grainy skin, and with the spike on their top fin, were playing around the *Nautilus,* waving the four rows of spines on each side of their tails. Their coloring was marvelous: white underneath and gray on top, with gold spots which glistened in the somber, swirling water. Some rays were undulating around them like a piece of cloth flapping in the wind, and among them I noticed, to my great joy, a Chinese ray, yellowish on top and a delicate pink underneath, and armed with three spikes behind his eye; a rare species, and one that was even doubtful in Lacépède's day, for he had never seen one except in a collection of Japanese drawings.

For two hours, a whole aquatic army escorted the *Nautilus.* Among these fish, as they played and leaped, rivaling each other in beauty, brilliance and speed, I could make out a green wrasse, a red mullet with a double black stripe, a type of goby with a rounded caudal fin, white in color and with violet spots on his back, a Japanese scomber, a beautiful mackerel of the type that inhabits these waters, with a blue body and silver head, some blue-gold azurors, whose name alone is better than any description, some striped giltheads with blue and yellow fins, another type of gilthead with a black band across its caudal fin, yet another type with an elegant corset of six stripes, some aulostoma, well described by their popular name of flutemouth or snipefish, some specimens of which grow to be a yard long, some giant salamanders, and spiny morays, six-foot-long serpents with small, lively eyes and with a huge mouth bristling with teeth, etc.

Our admiration didn't diminish for a moment. We kept up an incessant commentary. Ned would name the fish, Conseil would classify them and I would go into ecstasies over their movements and the beauties of their forms. Never before had I been able to observe these creatures alive and free in their natural element.

I won't cite all the varieties of fish which passed before our dazzled eyes—an entire collection of those living in Japanese and Chinese waters. These fish would gather around the ship thicker than birds in the sky, undoubtedly attracted by the gleam of the electric light.

But suddenly the lounge itself was bathed in light. The iron panels closed. The enchanting vision disappeared. But I kept on dreaming until my eyes fell on the instruments hanging on the wall. The compass still pointed to north-by-northeast, the pressure gauge showed a pressure of five atmospheres, corresponding to a depth of 160 feet, and the electric log showed us to be traveling at fifteen knots.

I waited for Captain Nemo, but he did not appear. It was five o'clock.

Ned Land and Conseil returned to their cabin, and I to mine. My dinner was waiting for me. It consisted of turtle soup made from the most delicate hawkbills, a surmullet whose white flesh had been rolled and folded and whose liver had been prepared as an excellent side dish, and then some fillets of emperor fish, which seemed to me even better than salmon.

I spent the evening reading, writing and thinking. Then I was overtaken by drowsiness. I stretched out on my eelgrass bed and fell sound asleep while the *Nautilus* glided through the strong current of the Black Stream.

CHAPTER XV
A Letter of Invitation

On the next day, November 9, I awoke after a long twelve-hour sleep. As usual, Conseil came in to ask "how Monsieur had slept" and to offer his services. He had left his Canadian friend sleeping like a man who spent his life doing nothing else.

I let him chatter on as he pleased, without giving much thought to answering him. I was preoccupied with Captain Nemo's absence during our reunion of the previous afternoon, but I hoped to see him again soon.

I quickly got into my clothes made of byssus fabric. Conseil made several comments on them, and I told him they were made from the shiny, silky threads with which the pinna, a kind of oysterlike creature very common near the shores of the Mediterranean, attaches itself to rocks. In olden days, people used it to make beautiful cloth, stockings and gloves, for it is both very soft and warm. The crew of the *Nautilus* could therefore dress at little cost and without having to take anything from cotton plants, sheep or silkworms on land.

Once dressed, I went to the big lounge. It was empty.

I plunged into a study of the valuable shellfish gathered in the glass cases. I also went through the vast collection of rare marine plants, which, although dried out, still conserved their marvelous colors. Among these precious hydrophytes, I noticed some whorled cladostephae, peacocklike padinae, caulerpae shaped like vine leaves, graniferous callithamnion, delicate scarlet-tinted ceramiacea, fan-shaped agars, acetabularia looking like the tops of mushrooms and which for a long time were classed among zoophytes, and finally many different kinds of sea wrack.

The entire day went by without my being honored by a visit from Captain Nemo. The panels of the lounge never opened. Perhaps he did not want us to become bored with these beautiful things.

The *Nautilus* kept heading ENE at a speed of twelve knots and at a depth varying between 165 and 200 feet.

On the next day, November 10, the same neglect and solitude. I saw none of the crew. Ned and Conseil spent most of the day with me. They were astonished at the captain's mysterious absence. Was this strange man sick? Had he changed his mind about what to do with us?

But, as Conseil pointed out, we were enjoying complete freedom and good food. Our host was keeping his side of the bargain. We could not complain, and the strangeness of our fate held such fine compensations that we had no right to blame him.

That day I started a diary of our adventures, which has since permitted me to recount them with the greatest accuracy. However, there was one peculiar thing about this diary: it was written on paper made from eelgrass.

Early in the morning of November 11, fresh air spreading throughout the inside of the *Nautilus* told me that we had surfaced in order to renew the oxygen supply. I went to the central companionway and up onto the platform.

It was six o'clock. The sky was clouded and the sea gray but calm. There was hardly any swell. I was hoping to meet Captain Nemo there, but I had no idea whether or not he would come out on deck. I saw only the helmsman imprisoned in his glass cage. I sat down on the ledge formed by the dinghy's hull and took deep breaths of the delicious salt air.

Little by little, the mist began to lift beneath the sun's rays as it rose over the eastern horizon. The sea flamed like a powder trail under its light. The high, scattered clouds took on bright, delicately shaded colors, and numerous "mares' tails"* showed that it would be windy all day long. But what was wind to the *Nautilus*, which could brave any storm?

I was admiring this joyous sunrise, so gay and invigorating, when I heard someone climbing up the companionway.

I got ready to greet Captain Nemo, but it was the first mate who appeared. I recognized him as being the man who had accompanied the captain when he had first visited us in our cell. He walked forward on the platform without seeming to notice my presence. With a powerful telescope he very carefully scanned the entire horizon. Then, when this examination was over, he went to the hatch and pronounced the following words. I remember them well, for each morning they were repeated under the same conditions. They were: "Nautron respoc lorni virch."

As to what they meant, I have no idea.

After uttering these words, the first mate went back inside the ship. I thought that the *Nautilus* would probably once again dive below the surface, and I therefore went down the hatch and along the gangways to my cabin.

Five days went by like this, without the slightest change in the routine of our lives. Every morning I went up on the platform. The same sentence was uttered by the same man. Captain Nemo did not appear.

I had given up hope of seeing him when, on November 16, as I entered my room along with Ned and Conseil, I found a note lying on my table.

I opened it impatiently. The handwriting was clear and neat, but somewhat ornate and Germanic in style. The note read as follows:

*Little, light white clouds with scalloped edges.

November 16, 1867

Professor Aronnax, on board the *Nautilus*:

Captain Nemo has the pleasure of inviting Professor Aronnax on a hunting expedition tomorrow morning in his forests of Crespo Island. He hopes no previous engagements will prevent the Professor from accepting, and he would also be very pleased if his companions would care to join him.

Captain Nemo
Commander of the Nautilus

"A hunting expedition!" cried Ned.

"In his forests of Crespo Island!" added Conseil.

"Does that mean he sometimes goes on shore?" asked Ned Land.

"There seems to be little doubt about it," I said as I reread the letter.

"Well then, there's nothing to do but accept," said the Canadian. "Once we're on dry land we'll see what we can do. Besides, I wouldn't mind eating a few fresh pieces of venison."

I did not even try to understand the contradiction between Captain Nemo's obvious distaste for dry land, even islands, and his invitation to hunt in a forest. I merely answered: "Let's first see what this Crespo Island is like."

I consulted a map and at 32° 40' N. Lat. and 167° 50' W. Long. I found a little island which had been first sighted in 1801 by Captain Crespo and which on old Spanish maps was called Roca de Plata—"Silver Rock." We were therefore about eighteen hundred miles from our point of departure, and the *Nautilus'* slightly altered course was bringing us toward the southwest.

I pointed to this little rock lost in the middle of the north Pacific. "If Captain Nemo does occasionally go on dry land," I said, "he at least chooses islands that are completely deserted!"

Ned Land shrugged his shoulders without answering, and then he and

Conseil left. After supper, served by the same mute, impassive steward, I went to sleep, not without some anxiety.

When I awoke on the morning of the next day—November 17—I could feel that the *Nautilus* was completely immobile. I got dressed quickly and entered the big lounge.

Captain Nemo was there waiting for me. He got up, bowed and asked if I would like to accompany him.

"But Monsieur," I said, "first allow me to ask you one question."

"Go ahead, Monsieur Aronnax, and I'll answer it if I can."

"Well then, Captain, how is it that you, who have broken off all relations with dry land, own forests on Crespo Island?"

"Professor," replied the captain, "these forests of mine ask neither light nor heat from the sun. They are inhabited by no lions, tigers, panthers or any quadruped. They are known only to me. They grow only for me. These forests are not on land, but under water."

"Underwater forests!" I cried.

"Yes, Professor."

"And you're offering to take me there?"

"That's right."

"On foot?"

"Without your feet even getting damp."

"And we're going to hunt?"

"We're going to hunt."

"With guns?"

"With guns."

I looked at the commander of the *Nautilus* in a way that was not exactly flattering.

"He's gone out of his mind," I thought. "He must have had some sort of an attack that lasted for a week; and he's still under the effects of it. Too bad! I liked him better peculiar than crazy!"

These thoughts could be clearly read on my face, but Captain Nemo merely invited me to follow him, which I did resignedly.

We entered the dining room, where breakfast was laid out on the table.

"Monsieur Aronnax," said the captain, "I would like you to have breakfast with me. We can talk while we eat. I promised you a walk through a forest, but I didn't promise I'd find you a restaurant there. So please eat like a man who won't do so again until late in the day."

I did honor to the meal. It was made up of various fish and slices of sea cucumber seasoned with very appetizing varieties of seaweed, such as *Porphyra laciniata* and *Laurentia primafetida*. As a drink we had clear water to which, following the captain's example, I added several drops of a fermented liquor extracted, according to the Kamchatkian method, from a kind of seaweed called *Rhodomenia palmata*.

At first Captain Nemo ate without saying a word, but then after a while he said: "Professor, when I invited you to go hunting in my forests of Crespo Island, you thought I was contradicting myself. When I told you these forests were under water, you thought I was mad. Professor, you should never make hasty judgments about people."

"But, Captain, believe me . . ."

"Please listen to what I have to say, and then you'll see whether you were right in accusing me of contradictions or madness."

"I'm listening."

"Professor, you know as well as I that a man can live under water as long as he takes with him a supply of air to breathe. Usually when men work under water, they wear a waterproof suit, have their head enclosed in a metal helmet and receive their air from above by means of force pumps and outlet regulators."

"That's the normal diving apparatus," I said.

"Right, but under those conditions the man isn't free. He's attached by a rubber pipe to the pump sending him air, and this pipe is like a chain binding him to one spot; if he were bound like this to the *Nautilus* he could certainly not go very far."

"But then how can you be free?" I asked.

"By using a device invented by two of your compatriots, Rouquayrol and

Denayrouze, which I have perfected for my own use and which will permit a man to venture into new physiological conditions without suffering from any bodily harm. It's composed of a tank with thick steel walls in which I store air at a pressure of fifty atmospheres. This tank is carried on the back by means of straps, like a soldier's pack. At the top there is a compartment from which the air, held back by a kind of bellows, is released under normal pressure. In the usual Rouquayrol apparatus two rubber tubes go from this compartment to a mask covering the mouth and nose of the man using it; one is for breathing in fresh air and the other for exhaling, and the tongue is used to close off one or the other depending on the user's needs. But for me, since I have to move around under considerable pressure in the ocean depths, I had to have my head enclosed in a copper sphere, somewhat like that of divers, and it is to this helmet that the inhaling and exhaling tubes are connected."

"Right, Captain, but the air you can take with you must get used up quickly, and once it contains no more than fifteen percent of oxygen it's no longer any good for breathing."

"That's right, but as I have said, Monsieur Aronnax, the *Nautilus'* pumps allow me to store air under considerable pressure, and thus I can put enough air in the tanks to last for nine or ten hours."

"I have no further objections to make," I answered; "I would only like to know, Captain, how you light your way along the ocean floor."

"With a Ruhmkorff device, Monsieur Aronnax. The breathing apparatus is carried on the back, whereas this is attached to the belt. It's composed of a Bunsen battery which is activated not with potassium bichromate, but with sodium. An induction coil gathers the electricity produced and sends it along to a special kind of lantern. Within this lantern there is a glass tube in the form of a coil which contains only a residue of carbonic gas. When the apparatus is turned on, this gas becomes luminous, giving off a whitish continuous light. Thus equipped, I breathe and see perfectly well."

"Captain Nemo, you have given me such overwhelmingly convincing answers to all my objections that I hardly dare have any doubts left. But even though I'm forced to believe in your Rouquayrol and Ruhmkorff devices, I still have reservations about the gun I'm going to use."

"But it's not a gun that uses powder," replied the Captain.

"What is it then, an air gun?"

"Of course. How do you expect me to manufacture powder on board, when I have neither saltpeter, sulfur, nor charcoal?"

"Besides," I said, "in order to shoot under water, in a medium 855 times denser than air, you have to overcome a considerable resistance."

"That presents no difficulty. There are certain cannons, perfected after Fulton's time by the Englishmen Philip Coles and Burley, by the Frenchman Furcy and by the Italian Landi, which have a device for closing out water, thus making it possible to shoot under such conditions. But let me say again that since I have no powder, I use air instead under high pressure, abundantly furnished by the *Nautilus'* pumps."

"But this air must get used up in no time at all."

"Yes, but more can be supplied from the tanks on our backs if we need it. All I have to do is add a special little spigot. Besides, you'll see, Monsieur Aronnax: in these underwater hunting expeditions we use little air or bullets."

"But it still seems to me that in this semidarkness and in the midst of this liquid so much denser than air, you can't fire far and the shells must spend themselves very quickly."

"Monsieur, with these guns every shot is fatal, and as soon as an animal is touched, no matter how lightly, he falls down dead."

"Why?"

"Because these guns don't shoot ordinary bullets, but little glass capsules invented by the Austrian chemist Leniebroek, and I have a large stock of them. These glass capsules are covered with a steel case and weighted with lead; thus they are veritable little Leyden jars into which electricity has been forced under very high tension. At the slightest blow they discharge, and the animal, however large he may be, falls dead. In addition, these capsules are no larger than size four shot, and an ordinary gun could be loaded with ten of them."

"I'll argue no more," I replied, getting up from the table. "There's nothing left for me but to take up my gun. Wherever you go, I'll go too."

Captain Nemo led me to the stern of the *Nautilus*. As we passed Ned and Conseil's cabin, I called them and they immediately fell in behind us.

We then came to a kind of cell up against the ship's side near the engine room. It was there that we put on our hunting costumes.

CHAPTER XVI
A Walk Across the Plains

This cell was both the arsenal and the dressing room of the *Nautilus*. A dozen diving outfits were hanging on the wall waiting for us.

When Ned Land saw them, he showed an obvious distaste at the idea of putting them on.

"But Ned," I said, "these forests of Crespo Island are under water!"

"Yes, I know," said the harpooner, disappointed at seeing his dreams of fresh meat vanish. "But you, Monsieur Aronnax—are you going to put on that outfit?"

"I've got to, Ned."

"Do whatever you want, Monsieur," replied the harpooner, shrugging his shoulders, "but as for me, I'll never get into clothes like that unless they force me to."

"Nobody's going to force you, Ned," said Captain Nemo.

"Is Conseil going to try it?" asked Ned.

"I follow Monsieur wherever he goes," answered Conseil.

At a call from the captain, two men from the crew came over to help us put on these heavy, waterproof suits, made of seamless rubber and constructed in such a way as to be able to bear up under considerable pressure. It was like strong yet supple armor. The suit consisted of trousers and a jacket. The trousers ended in thick shoes equipped with heavy lead soles. The fabric of the jacket was held firm by copper plates which protected the chest against the water pressure and allowed the lungs to function freely; its sleeves ended in gloves that were supple enough for the wearer to perform any normal operations with his hands.

As one can see, these highly perfected diving costumes were a far cry from the bulky outfits such as the cork breastplates, the special sea clothes, the boxes, etc., which were invented and praised during the eighteenth century.

Captain Nemo, one of his companions—a kind of Hercules who must have had incredible strength—Conseil and I had soon finished putting on our diving suits. We were completely outfitted except for our metal helmets. But before putting these on, I asked Captain Nemo's permission to examine one of the guns we were going to use.

A member of the *Nautilus'* crew handed me a rather ordinary-looking rifle with a steel butt which was hollow inside and fairly large. This was the reservoir containing the compressed air which a trigger-operated valve released into the chamber. A magazine hollowed out in the side walls of the butt contained some twenty electric bullets which were automatically placed in the chamber by means of a spring. As soon as one shot had been fired, a second was ready to go off.

"Captain Nemo," I said, "this weapon seems both perfect and easy to operate. I ask only to try it out. But how are we going to get out onto the ocean floor?"

"Right now the *Nautilus* is sitting on the bottom at a depth of thirty feet, and we have only to be on our way."

"But how are we going to get out?"

"You'll see."

Captain Nemo put on his spherical helmet. Conseil and I did the same, not without first hearing the Canadian sarcastically wish us "good hunting." The top part of our jackets ended in a threaded copper collar, onto which the metal helmet could be screwed. Three holes covered by thick glass permitted us to see in any direction, merely by turning our heads inside the helmet. As soon as we were completely dressed, the Rouquayrol devices were placed on our backs;

they began to work at once, and, as for me, I found breathing very easy.

Then, with the Ruhmkorff lamp at my belt and the gun in my hand, I was ready to leave. But I felt imprisoned in these heavy clothes and nailed to the deck by my lead soles; I was unable to take a single step.

But they had foreseen this difficulty, and I felt myself being helped into a little compartment adjoining the dressing room. My companions were also helped along and entered right behind me. I heard a watertight door close behind us, and we were enveloped in total darkness.

After several minutes a loud whistling noise reached my ears. I could feel something cold rising from my feet to my chest. Evidently someone inside the submarine had opened a spigot, allowing the outside water to flood the room we were in. It was soon filled and a second door in the hull of the *Nautilus* opened. A dim light entered. A moment later we were walking on the ocean floor.

And now, how can I describe my impressions of this walk beneath the surface of the ocean? Words are powerless to recount such marvels! When the painter's brush cannot even reproduce the effects produced by water, how can the pen hope to succeed?

Captain Nemo walked out in front, and his companion followed several paces behind us. Conseil and I stayed near one another, as if it might have been possible to talk through the metal around our heads. I no longer felt the weight of my clothing, shoes and air tank, nor of the thick helmet inside which my head bobbed around like an almond inside its shell. All these objects, once in the water, lost a part of their weight equal to the amount of water displaced, and I found I was profiting greatly by the law Archimedes discovered. I was no longer an inert mass, but had a relatively great freedom of movement.

I was astounded to see how much light reached the ocean floor thirty feet below the surface. The sun's rays easily penetrated this liquid mass, and they made it seem transparent. I could see objects clearly at a distance of a hundred yards. Beyond that, the ocean depths were tinted with delicate shades of ultramarine which turned to a purer blue as the distance got greater, and then disappeared in the midst of a vague shadowiness. Indeed, this water surrounding me was no more than another kind of air, denser than the atmosphere but almost as transparent. Above me I could see the calm surface of the sea.

We walked over fine-grained sand, without the ripples one finds on beaches where the tide has left its mark. This dazzling carpet acted as a reflector, sending back the sun's rays with surprising intensity. As a result, there was an immense reverberation of light which penetrated each liquid molecule. Will the reader believe me if I state that at this depth of thirty feet I could see as well as if I were in broad daylight?

For a quarter of an hour I walked over this blazing sand, strewn with an almost imperceptible dust from shells. The hull of the *Nautilus,* looking like a long reef, disappeared little by little, but its searchlight, once night had come over the ocean floor, would facilitate our return by throwing out its strong, clear beams. This phenomenon is difficult to understand for someone who has only seen a searchlight's clearly outlined, whitish rays on land. There, the dust saturating the air gives them the appearance of a luminous mist; but on water, as well as under water, their electric gleam is transmitted with incomparable purity.

But we kept on walking, and the vast sandy plain seemed unending. With my hand I parted liquid curtains, which closed in again behind me, and the trace of my footsteps was quickly erased by the pressure of the water.

Soon, some objects looming up in the distance became visible. I recognized a magnificent foreground of rocks covered with splendid specimens of zoophytes, and I was mainly struck with a very special effect produced by the medium we were in.

It was then ten in the morning. The sun's rays struck the surface at a rather oblique angle, and, refracted by this contact as if passing through a prism, they tinted the edges of flowers, rocks, plants, shells and corals with the seven colors of the solar spectrum. It was a marvelous feast for the eyes; colors crisscrossed one another in a veritable kaleidoscope of green, yellow, orange, violet, indigo and blue—the entire palette of an enthusiastic colorist! How I would have liked to describe to Conseil the impression this made on me, and compete with him in uttering phrases of wonder! How I would have enjoyed, like Captain Nemo and his companion, being able to exchange thoughts by means of previously arranged signals! So, for lack of anything better, I talked to myself, shouting inside my copper helmet and perhaps wasting more air than I should have with these vain words.

Conseil and I both stopped to admire this marvelous spectacle. Confronted by so many specimens of zoophytes and mollusks, he was obviously classifying, classifying, classifying. The ground was covered with polyps and echinoderms. Different kinds of isidae, cornularia which live in isolation, tufts of virgin oculinae formerly called "white coral," bristling fungi shaped like mushrooms, and sea anemones holding on to rocks with their muscular disks all formed a flower bed dotted with porpitae dressed in their collars of azure tentacles, starfish studding the sand, verrucose asterophytons which looked like delicate lace embroidered by the hands of water nymphs and whose borders moved gently in the eddies produced by our walking. I hated the thought of squashing beneath my feet the brilliant specimens of mollusks which were strewn over the ground by the thousands: concentric combshells, hammer shells, wedge shells (which can actually jump), top shells, red helmet shells, wing shells and so many other products of the inexhaustible ocean. But we had to keep going, and as we walked, we could see swimming overhead schools of Portuguese men-of-war with their ultramarine-blue tentacles trailing along behind them, jellyfish with their milky white or delicate pink bodies edged around with blue, all shading us from the sun's rays, and panopyrae pelagiae which in the darkness would have strewn our path with their phosphorescence.

For a quarter of a mile these wonders continued; whenever I stopped to admire them, Captain Nemo would motion for me to keep moving, and I would have to set out again. But soon the ground changed. The plain of sand was followed by an area of slimy mud, which in America is called "ooze," entirely composed of siliceous and calcareous shells. We then crossed a prairie of seaweed, oceanic plants which had not yet been uprooted by the force of the water and which were growing in wild profusion. This thick, soft lawn would have rivaled the most velvety carpet woven by the hand of man. However, there were plants not only underfoot, but also overhead. A light arbor of marine plants, classified in the luxuriant family of the algae in which there are more than two thousand species, crisscrossed the surface. I could make out long ribbons of sea wrack, some globular and others tubular, laurenciae, cladostephae with their slender foliage, and some dulse which looked like cactus fans. I noticed that the green plants remained nearer the surface, while those colored red occupied a medium depth, leaving the black or brown hydrophytes to form the gardens and flower beds on the deeper parts of the ocean floor.

These algae are a real prodigy of creation, one of the marvels of universal plant life. This family produces both the smallest and the largest plants on earth. Of the smallest kinds, as many as forty thousand have been counted within the space of $1/25$ square inch; whereas sea wrack has been found measuring almost a third of a mile in length.

It was about an hour and a half since we had left the *Nautilus*. It was now almost noon. I could see this by the right angle at which the sun's rays entered the water and by the fact that they were no longer refracted. The magical colors had disappeared little by little, and the emerald- and sapphirelike nuances had vanished from our world. We walked with a steady step which resounded on the ocean floor with surprising intensity. The slightest noises were transmitted with a speed to which our land-trained ears were unaccustomed. Water, in fact, is a better conductor of sound than air, and carries it four times as fast.

Just then, the ground began to slope sharply downward. The light became uniformly shaded. We reached a depth of three hundred feet and a pressure of ten atmospheres. But my diving suit was so constructed that this pressure caused me no discomfort. The only unpleasant sensation I experienced was in trying to bend my fingers, but even this soon disappeared. As for the fatigue I should have felt after walking two hours in such an unaccustomed costume, I felt nothing. The water helped me to move with surprising ease.

At this depth, I could still make out the sun's rays, but only feebly. Their brilliant intensity had given way to a kind of reddish dusk, halfway between day and night. Nevertheless, we could still see our way clearly, and it was not yet necessary to start using our Ruhmkorff lamps.

Just then, Captain Nemo stopped. After waiting for me to catch up to him, he pointed to several dark masses outlined in the shadows a short way off.

"That must be the forest of Crespo Island," I thought. And I was right.

CHAPTER XVII
An Underwater Forest

We had finally arrived at the edge of this forest, undoubtedly one of the most beautiful in all of Captain Nemo's vast domain. He considered it his own, and claimed the same rights over it as had the first men at the beginning of time. Moreover, who was going to dispute his ownership of this underwater property? What braver pioneer was going to come with an ax and clear away these dark groves?

This forest was composed of large, treelike plants, and as soon as we had gone under its vast arches, I was struck by the strange shape of their branches— a shape I had never seen before.

None of the grass covering the ground nor any of the branches attached to the trees was inclined, bent or in any way horizontal. Everything rose toward the surface. There were no filaments or ribbons, no matter how thin, which weren't standing as straight as ramrods. Due to the density of the element which had produced them, sea wrack and creepers grew in a rigid, vertical line. They were normally motionless, but when I pushed them aside with my hand, they immediately went back to their original position. This was the reign of the vertical.

I soon became accustomed to this peculiar arrangement of things, as well as to the relative darkness which surrounded us. The forest floor was strewn with sharp rocks which were difficult to avoid. The plant life here seemed quite complete, richer than it would have been in the Arctic or tropical zones where such products are less numerous. But for several minutes I involuntarily confused the two kingdoms, mistaking zoophytes for hydrophytes, animals for plants. But who would not have made the same mistake? Fauna and flora are so closely related to one another in this underwater world!

I noticed that all the specimens of the vegetable kingdom were only lightly held to the ground. Without roots and not caring whether they are fixed to something solid, sand, shells or pebbles, they only ask of the ground for something to hang on to, not for their life's blood. These plants are self-propagating, and derive their existence from the water which sustains and nourishes them. Most of them had, instead of leaves, whimsically shaped blades in a narrow range of colors, comprising only pink, carmine, green, olive, tan and brown. I now saw, but no longer dried out like the specimens in the *Nautilus,* some padinae spread out fan-shaped like a peacock's tail as if to catch the breeze, scarlet-colored ceramiaceae, laminaria stretching out their edible shoots, slender wavy nereocystes growing to a height of fifty feet, bunches of acetabula whose stems grew thicker at the top, and many other deep-sea plants, all without flowers. "What a strange and peculiar world," as one clever naturalist put it, "where the animal kingdom flowers and the vegetable kingdom doesn't!"

Among these various shrubs, as big as the trees of temperate zones, and beneath their damp shadows, were massed together real bushes of living flowers, hedges of zoophytes on which blossomed striped maeandrinae with their twisting furrows, yellowish caryophylliae with transparent tentacles, and tufts of zoantharia. And, to complete the illusion, fish flies flew from branch to branch like a flock of hummingbirds, while yellow lepisacanthae with bristling jaws and pointed scales, dactylopteridae and monocentridae rose at our feet like a flock of snipe.

Toward one in the afternoon Captain Nemo gave the signal to halt. I was rather pleased to stop, and we stretched out under a bower of alariae with their long ribbons shooting out as straight as arrows.

This short rest delighted me. Nothing was lacking but the charm of conversation. But it was impossible to talk. I brought my large copper helmet near Conseil's. I saw his eyes shining with joy, and to show his satisfaction, he bobbed his head around inside his helmet in the most comical way imaginable.

I was very surprised not to feel very hungry after walking for four hours. I had no idea what caused my stomach to react this way. But on the other hand, as happens with all divers, I felt an uncontrollable desire to sleep. Soon my eyes closed behind their thick glass windows and I fell into a deep slumber, which till then I had been able to fight off merely by walking. I was thus merely following the example of Captain Nemo and his powerful companion, who had already stretched out and gone to sleep.

There was no way of knowing how long I dozed, but when I awoke it seemed as if the sun were sinking toward the horizon. Captain Nemo had already gotten up, and I was beginning to stretch my limbs, when an unexpected sight brought me quickly to my feet.

Only a few steps away, a monstrous spider crab, three feet high, was eying me ready to jump. Although my diving suit was thick enough to protect me from his bite, I could not help shuddering with horror. Just then Conseil and the sailor from the *Nautilus* awoke. Captain Nemo pointed out the hideous crab to his companion, who knocked it down with one blow of his rifle butt, and I watched the monster's claws writhe in horrible convulsions.

This encounter made me think that even more fearful animals must inhabit these dark depths, animals against which my suit would not be thick enough to protect me. Until now this had not occurred to me, and I resolved to be on my guard. Moreover, I supposed that this halt had marked the end of our walk; but I was wrong, and instead of returning to the *Nautilus*, Captain Nemo continued his daring excursion.

The ground continued falling off, but at an even greater angle, taking us deeper and deeper. It must have been around three o'clock when we reached a depth of about five hundred feet in a narrow valley between high, vertical walls. Thanks to the perfection of our diving equipment, we were thus going three hundred feet deeper than men had ever gone before.

I say five hundred feet, even though no instrument permitted me to calculate this depth. But I knew that even in the clearest water the sun's rays penetrate no deeper. And just then the darkness had become almost complete. Ten steps away I could see nothing. I was therefore walking, groping my way along, when I suddenly saw a bright white light shining ahead. Captain Nemo had just turned on his electric lamp. His companion did the same. Conseil and I followed their example. By turning a screw, I connected the coil to the glass spiral; and the sea, lit by our four lanterns, was illuminated within a radius of eighty feet.

Captain Nemo continued on into the obscure depths of the forest, whose shrubs were getting scarcer and scarcer. I noticed that vegetable life disappeared quicker than animal life. Deep-sea plants were already abandoning the soil which was becoming increasingly arid; but it was still swarming with animals—zoophytes, articulata, mollusks and fish.

As we walked I thought that the light from our Ruhmkorff lamps would necessarily attract some inhabitants of these dark depths. But if they did approach, it was never near enough for us to shoot them. Several times I saw Captain Nemo stop, put his gun to his shoulder and then, after a moment, bring it down again and continue on his way.

Finally at about four o'clock, this marvelous excursion came to an end. A huge, magnificent wall of rock rose before us, a heap of gigantic blocks, an enormous, unclimbable granite cliff hollowed out with dark caves. This was the edge of Crespo Island. This was land.

Captain Nemo stopped suddenly. He motioned for us to halt, and as much as I would have liked to try and climb this wall, I too had to stop. Here ended Captain Nemo's domains. He did not want to go farther. Beyond lay that part of the globe on which he was never again to set foot.

We began the return trip. Captain Nemo had again taken the lead, and continued walking forward without hesitation. It seemed to me that we were not returning to the *Nautilus* by the same path. This new route, very steep and difficult, brought us quickly up toward the surface. Nevertheless this return to the upper layers of the ocean was not so sudden as to bring about too quick a decompression, which would have done us serious injury and produced those internal lesions so fatal to divers. Very soon the light reappeared and grew stronger, and, since the sun was already low on the horizon, the refraction again edged every object with a rainbowlike border.

At a depth of thirty feet we walked amid a swarm of little fish of all kinds, more numerous than birds in the air and also more agile. But no underwater game worthy of a shot had yet met our gaze.

Just then I saw the captain quickly shoulder his gun and follow something moving among the shrubbery. He fired, I heard a faint hissing sound, and an animal fell dead several feet away.

It was a magnificent sea otter, an *enhydris*, the only quadruped that lives entirely in the ocean. This one was five feet long and must have been very valuable. Its fur, chestnut brown on top and silver underneath, was of the kind so sought after on the Russian and Chinese market. Its quality and luster would have made it worth at least four hundred dollars. I looked admiringly at this strange animal with its round head and short ears, its large eyes and catlike whiskers, its clawed, webbed feet and tufted tail. This precious carnivore, hunted and tracked by fishermen, is becoming extremely rare, and it has taken refuge mainly in the north Pacific, from which it will probably soon disappear completely.

Captain Nemo's companion came over to take the animal. He put it on his shoulder, and once again we started on our way.

For an hour a sandy plain stretched out before us. Often it rose to within six feet of the surface. I could then see our image clearly reflected on the surface, but in reverse; above us there was an identical band of men, exactly reproducing our movements and gestures, with the only difference that it was walking upside down, with its feet in the air.

I also noticed another strange effect. Thick clouds passed by, forming and disappearing rapidly; but when I thought it over, I realized that these so-called clouds were merely due to the varying height of the water in the midst of a ground swell, and when I looked carefully I could see the foam breaking on its crests and spreading over the surface. I could even see the shadows of large birds overhead as they came down and skimmed the water.

It was then that I witnessed one of the finest shots that has ever thrilled a hunter. We could clearly make out a large bird with broad wingspread soaring in our direction. Captain Nemo's companion raised his gun and fired when it was only several feet above the surface. The animal fell dead, and the force of its fall brought it within the hunter's grasp. It was a magnificent albatross—a splendid specimen of these oceangoing birds.

But this incident did not interrupt our march. For two hours we crossed sandy plains alternating with prairies of seaweed in which it was very difficult to walk.

I was at the end of my strength when we finally saw a vague glimmer piercing the darkness of the water a half a mile away. It was the *Nautilus'* light. We would be on board within twenty minutes and once there I could again breathe comfortably, for I felt that the air now furnished by my tank was very low in oxygen. But I had not reckoned with an encounter which somewhat delayed our arrival.

I was some twenty paces behind, when I saw Captain Nemo turn and run toward me. With his powerful arms he pushed me down, while his companion did the same to Conseil. At first I did not know what to make of this sudden attack, but I was reassured by seeing the captain lie down next to me and remain immobile.

I was therefore stretched out on the ground, sheltered by a shrub of seaweed, when I raised my head and saw some huge shapes swirl past leaving streams of phosphorescence behind them.

The blood froze in my veins! I saw we were being threatened by two formidable dogfish, those terrible sharks with enormous tails and dull glassy eyes, who secrete a phosphorescent substance through holes around their snouts. They are like monstrous fireflies who can crush an entire man in their jaws of iron! I don't know if Conseil was busy classifying them, but as for me, I was observing their silver bellies and huge mouths bristling with teeth from a not altogether scientific point of view—rather as a prospective victim than as a naturalist.

Very fortunately, these voracious animals have bad eyesight. They passed by without seeing us, letting their brownish tails brush against us, and as if by a miracle, we escaped a danger surely greater than that of meeting a tiger in the jungle.

A half an hour later, guided by the electric light, we reached the *Nautilus*. The outside door had been left open, and once we were inside the first compartment, Captain Nemo closed this door behind us. He then pressed a button. I could hear pumps working inside the submarine, I felt the water level lowering around me, and in a few moments the compartment was entirely empty. The inside door was opened and we stepped into the dressing room.

There our diving suits were taken off, although not without some difficulty; and I, exhausted and dying of hunger, went to my room in a state of wonder at our extraordinary excursion in the ocean depths.

Walking on the ocean floor

CHAPTER XVIII

Four Thousand Leagues Under the Pacific

The next morning, November 18, I had completely recovered from my exhaustion of the day before, and I went up onto the platform just as the first mate was uttering his usual daily phrase. It then struck me that it referred to the condition of the ocean, or rather that it meant "nothing in sight."

And as a matter of fact, the ocean was deserted. There was not a sail on the horizon. The hills of Crespo Island had disappeared during the night. The ocean absorbed all the colors of the spectrum except blue, which it threw off in all directions and turned the water a magnificent indigo color. The sea looked like silk printed with large wavy patterns.

I was admiring this splendid sight when Captain Nemo appeared. He did not seem to notice my presence and began a series of astronomic observations. When he was through, he went over and leaned on the searchlight housing and gazed abstractedly at the surface of the ocean.

In the meanwhile, twenty or so sailors from the *Nautilus*, all strong and well built, had come up on the platform. They had come to take in the nets that had been trailed behind the ship all night. These sailors obviously came from different countries, even though they were all European in type. I could clearly see that there were Irishmen, Frenchmen, a few Slavs and a Greek or Cretan. But these men spoke little, and when they did, it was in that strange language whose origin I could not even guess. I therefore had to give up any hope of questioning them.

The nets were hauled in. They were a kind of dragnet similar to those used on the coast of Normandy. They were like huge pockets held open by a floating rod and a chain interwoven in the lower meshes. Thus arranged, they would drag along the ocean floor and gather everything in their path. That day they had brought up many curious specimens from these waters so rich in sea life: there were angler fish, whose peculiar movements made them look like comedians on stage, black commersons with their antennae, triggerfish with red stripes running around their bodies, globefish with their poisoned flesh, several olive-colored lampreys, macrorhynchi with their silvery scales, cutlass fish who can give as strong a shock as an electric eel or an electric ray, scaly notopteri with brown cross-stripes, a greenish variety of cod, several kinds of gobies, etc. Finally there were several larger kinds of fish: a caranx with a prominent head and a body about three feet long, several lovely bonitos decked in blue and silver, and three magnificent tuna whose great speed had not been enough to save them from the dragnets.

I reckoned that this haul had brought in more than a thousand pounds of fish. It was a good catch, but not exceptional. Since these nets were always left trailing for several hours, they always picked up a whole world of underwater creatures. We would therefore not be short of excellent provisions, which the *Nautilus'* speed and the attraction of its electric light could renew endlessly.

These various products of the sea were immediately lowered through the hatch and brought to the storeroom, some to be eaten fresh and others to be preserved.

Now that the fishing was ended and the air supply renewed, I thought that the *Nautilus* would once again be off on its underwater journey. I was therefore about to go back to my room, when Captain Nemo, without any sort of preamble, turned toward me and said: "Look at the ocean, Professor! Can you say it isn't alive? Doesn't it also have its moments of anger and tenderness? Yesterday it went to sleep just as we did, and now it's awakening after a peaceful night!"

The captain hadn't even bothered to say "good morning"! It was as if this strange man were continuing some conversation he had begun earlier.

"Look!" he said. "It's awakening beneath the sun's caresses! Once again it's going to relive its daily life! How fascinating it is to study its functions! It has a pulse, arteries and occasional spasms; and I agree with the scientist, Maury, who discovered that it has a circulation as real as that of blood in animals."

I felt sure that Captain Nemo expected no answer on my part, and it seemed senseless for me to utter phrases such as "of course," "certainly" and "you're quite right." He was talking more to himself, with long pauses between each sentence. He was thinking out loud.

"Yes," he said, "the ocean indeed has circulation, and to set it in motion the Creator of all things has only to alter its temperature or content of salts or of microscopic animals. Changes in temperature bring about varying densities which cause currents and counter-currents. Evaporation, which is nonexistent in polar regions and very active in equatorial zones, makes for a permanent exchange of polar and tropical waters. Moreover, I've come across vertical currents which make it really seem as if the ocean is breathing. I have observed how molecules of water are heated on the surface, go down to the ocean depths, attain their maximum density at 36° Fahrenheit, then lose their heat, thereby becoming lighter, and once again rise to the surface. At the Pole you'll see the consequences of this phenomenon, and you'll understand why, by this law of all-foreseeing nature, ice can only form on the surface of the water!"

While Captain Nemo was finishing this sentence, I said to myself, "The Pole! Does this madman intend to take us there too!"

In the meanwhile the captain had stopped talking. For a while he merely gazed at this sea which he had so thoroughly and incessantly studied. Then he started in again.

"Salts," he said, "exist in large quantities in the ocean, and if you removed all those it contained you would have a mass of 121,500,000 cubic miles, which if it were spread out over the earth would form a layer about thirty-five feet thick. And don't think that the presence of these salts is merely due to some whim of nature. No, they make the waters of the sea less susceptible to evaporation and prevent the winds from taking off too much of this water vapor, which upon turning back into water would submerge the temperate zones of the earth. These salts play an immense, stabilizing role in the general functioning of the globe!"

Captain Nemo stopped, straightened up and took several steps on the platform; and then, coming back to me, he said: "And as for those countless microscopic organisms, millions of which exist in one small drop of water and eight hundred thousand of which one would need to make up one milligram in weight, their role is just as important. They take in marine salts, absorb the solid elements in water; by their formation of corals and madrepores they are the true creators of calcareous continents! And then, the drop of water, deprived of its mineral content, becomes lighter and rises to the surface where it absorbs those salts left behind by evaporation, becomes heavier, and goes back down bringing new elements to be consumed by these organisms. Thus you have a double current, rising and falling—incessant movement and life! And this life is more intense, luxuriant and vast than that on land; it spreads out over all parts of that ocean which people have said is a place of death for men and of life for millions of animals—and for me!"

When Captain Nemo talked like this, he became transformed and I found myself very moved.

"There you have real life!" he added. "And I can imagine founding cities in the sea, agglomerations of underwater houses which, like the *Nautilus*, would come to the surface each morning to breathe, cities that would be free and independent! But even then, who knows but some despot might come along . . ."

Captain Nemo finished the sentence with a violent gesture. Then, addressing me directly and as if to dispel a morbid thought, he asked: "Monsieur Aronnax, do you know how deep the ocean is?"

"All I know, Captain, is what I've learned from the principal soundings people have made."

"Could you cite them, so I can check them as we go along?"

"I'll give you those I remember. If I'm not mistaken, the north Atlantic has been found to have an average depth of 27,000 feet, and the Mediterranean 8,000 feet. The most remarkable soundings have been taken in the south Atlantic, near the thirty-fifth parallel, and they've shown depths of up to 40,000, 46,230 and 49,700 feet. In short, it has been estimated that the average depth of the ocean is about four miles."

"Well, Professor," replied Captain Nemo, "I hope to be able to give you more accurate figures. As for the average depth in this part of the Pacific, let me tell you that it is only 13,000 feet."

Having said this, Captain Nemo went over to the hatch and climbed down the companionway. I followed him and went into the lounge. I could feel the propeller start up, and soon the log showed us to be traveling at twenty knots.

During the days and weeks that followed I saw Captain Nemo rarely. His first mate regularly marked the ship's position on the chart and I was thus able to follow its course with great accuracy.

Conseil and Ned Land spent many hours with me. Conseil had told his friend about the marvels of our underwater excursion, and the Canadian regretted not having accompanied us. But I hoped he would have another chance to visit these ocean forests.

Almost every day the panels of the lounge remained open for several hours, and we would never get tired watching the mysteries of underwater life.

The *Nautilus'* general course was to the southeast and it cruised at depths between three and five hundred feet. One day, however—and I never knew why—it dove at a steep angle by means of its side fins and reached a depth of 6,500 feet. The thermometer read 39.65° Fahrenheit, a temperature which at that depth was apparently constant in all latitudes.

On November 26, at three in the morning, the *Nautilus* crossed the Tropic of Cancer at 172° W. Long. On the twenty-seventh it passed within sight of the Hawaiian Islands, where the famous Captain Cook had met his death on February 14, 1779. We had by then traveled 4,860 leagues from our point of departure. When I came up on the platform that morning, I could see, about two miles off to leeward, Hawaii, the largest of the seven islands that form this archipelago. I could clearly make out the cultivated fields around its edge, the various mountain chains running parallel to the coast and the volcanoes domi-nated by Mauna Kea, which rises to 13,800 feet above sea level. Among other specimens from these waters, the nets brought up some peacocklike flabellaria, a flat, amusingly shaped polyp peculiar to this area.

The *Nautilus* continued on its southeasterly course. On the first of December it crossed the equator at 142° W. Long., and on the fourth of the same month, after a rapid and uneventful crossing, we sighted the Marquesas. Three miles off, at 8° 57' S. Lat. and 139° 32' W. Long., I saw Martin Point on Nukuhiva, the main island in this group belonging to France. I could only make out the wooded mountains outlined against the horizon, for Captain Nemo did not like to get too near land. Here, the nets brought up some lovely specimens of fish: there were coryphaenae with their azure fins and golden tails, whose flesh is unequalled in all the world; hologymnosae with almost no scales but which taste superb; ostorhincae with their bony jaws; yellowish thasards as good to eat as bonito—all worthy of being classified in the ship's kitchen.

After leaving these charming islands protected by the French flag, the *Nautilus* traveled about two thousand miles between the fourth and the eleventh of December. This journey was noteworthy for our encounter with an immense school of squid, a curious mollusk closely related to the cuttlefish. French fishermen call them *encornets*, and they belong to the class of Cephalopoda and the family of Dibranchiata, which also comprises the cuttlefish and the argo-naut. These animals were especially carefully studied by naturalists of classical times, and they not only furnished numerous metaphors to Greek orators, but also an excellent dish for the dinner tables of the rich, if we can believe Atanaeus, a Greek doctor who lived before Galen.

It was during the night of December 9 to 10 that the *Nautilus* encountered this army of mollusks, which are particularly nocturnal. We could count them by the millions. They were migrating from temperate to warmer regions, fol-lowing in the wake of herrings and sardines. Through the thick glass panels we could watch them swimming backward very fast, impelling themselves by means of their locomotor tube, chasing fish and other mollusks, eating the little ones and being eaten by the larger ones, and in indescribable confusion tossing around the ten arms nature had attached to their heads like a crest of pneumatic serpents. In spite of its speed, the *Nautilus* cruised for several hours in the midst of this swarm of animals, and its nets brought in great numbers of them, among which I could recognize all nine species that d'Orbigny had classified as living in the Pacific.

As the reader can easily see, during this trip the sea showed us its most mar-velous spectacles, and with continual variation. The scenery seemed to change for our own pleasure, and we were called upon not only to witness the works of the Creator in the midst of the waters, but also to penetrate the most fearful mysteries of the ocean.

On December 11 I was reading in the big lounge. Ned Land and Conseil were watching the luminous waters through the half-opened panels. The *Nautilus* lay motionless, with its reservoirs filled, at a depth of over three thousand feet, a relatively uninhabited region of the ocean in which only larger fish make an occasional appearance.

I was reading a delightful book by Jean Macé called *Servants of the Stomach* and savoring its ingenious lessons, when Conseil interrupted me.

"Would Monsieur please come here a moment?" he said in a strange tone of voice.

"What is it, Conseil?"

"I would like Monsieur to see for himself."

I got up, went over to the window and looked out.

Beneath the electric light an enormous, blackish, immobile mass was suspended in the water. I watched it attentively, trying to see if it was some kind of gigantic whale. But a thought suddenly crossed my mind.

"A ship!" I cried.

"Yes," answered the Canadian, "a disabled vessel that's sunk!"

Ned Land was right. It was a ship with its severed shrouds still hanging from its chainplates. Its hull seemed to be in good condition, and it had apparently sunk no more than several hours before. Three stumps of masts, cut off several feet above the deck, showed that this ship when already taking on water had tried sacrificing its masts. But it must have been lying on its side and filled with water, for it was still heeling over to port. It was a sad sight, this carcass lost beneath the waves, but its deck was an even sadder sight, for there were still several cadavers bound in ropes! I could count four—four men, one of whom was still standing at the helm—and then a woman, half out of a hatch on the poop deck and holding a child in her arms. By the brilliant light of the *Nautilus* I could make out her features, which had not yet been decomposed by the water. In a supreme effort she had raised the child over her head, and this poor little creature's arms were still entwined around its mother's neck. The positions of the four sailors were frightening: they were twisted in convulsive movements, making a last effort to tear off the ropes binding them to the ship. Only the helmsman, with his face clear and serious, his graying hair stuck to his forehead, his hand clutching the wheel, seemed still to be steering his sunken three-master through the ocean depths!

What a scene! We were all left speechless, our hearts beating fast, before the idea of actually witnessing a sinking and, in a sense, being able to photograph its final moments! And already I could see enormous sharks with fire in their eyes, moving in on the wreck, attracted by the human flesh!

In the meanwhile, the *Nautilus* circled around the sunken ship, and for an instant I could make out on its stern: *Florida, Sunderland.*

CHAPTER XIX
Vanikoro

This terrible sight was the first of a series of maritime disasters which the *Nautilus* was to meet on its way. When it sailed through more frequented waters, we often saw sunken hulls rotting in the ocean, and yet deeper we came across cannons, cannonballs, anchors, chains and a thousand other iron objects being devoured by rust.

But the *Nautilus* went on, carrying us with it in a life of isolation. Then on December 11 we sighted the Tuamotu Archipelago, which Bougainville had considered so dangerous, and which stretches out over thirteen hundred miles from east-southeast to west-northwest, between 13° 30' and 23° 50' S. Lat., and 125° 30' and 151° 30' W. Long., from Ducie to Lazareff Island. This archipelago covers an area of 330 square miles and consists of about sixty island groups, among which is the Gambier group over which France has imposed its rule. They are all coral islands. A slow but steady rising due to the work of polyps will one day connect them one to the other. Then this new island will later become welded to neighboring archipelagos and a fifth continent will stretch from New Zealand and New Caledonia all the way to the Marquesas.

Once, when I was presenting this theory to the captain, he answered coldly: "It isn't new continents the earth needs, but new men!"

Our course had taken us in the direction of Clermont-Tonnerre Island, one of the most peculiar of the whole group, which was discovered in 1822 by Captain Bell of the *Minerva*. I was therefore able to study the way in which these islands had been built up by madrepores.

Madrepores, which must not be confused with corals, are basically a fabric covered with a limestone crust, and their variations of structure led my illustrious teacher, Milne-Edwards, to class them in five sections. The tiny creatures which produce this polypary live by the millions inside their cells, and it is their limestone deposits which turn into rocks, reefs and islands. Sometimes they form a circular ring around a lagoon or lake which is kept in contact with the sea by gaps in the surrounding wall. Other times they form barrier reefs like those off the coast of New Caledonia and various of the Tuamotu Islands. In yet other places, like Réunion Island and Mauritius, they have formed steep, high fringing reefs next to which the ocean drops off to considerable depths.

As we cruised only several hundred yards off Clermont-Tonnerre Island I gazed in admiration at this huge edifice built by microscopic workers. These walls had been formed by several kinds of madrepores, principally millepores, astraea and maeandra. These polyparies grow mainly in the more agitated water near the surface and thus build their foundations from above, foundations which slowly sink along with the remains of secretions supporting them. This at least is Darwin's theory, one which I feel is superior to that which says that these madrepores are built up on the tops of mountains or volcanoes submerged only several feet below the surface of the sea.

I was able to observe these strange walls from very near, for where they dropped off into deep water our sound read more than a thousand feet. In addition our electric light made this brilliant limestone sparkle.

Conseil asked me how long it took these colossal reefs to form, and I astonished him greatly by telling him that scientists had calculated that they grew at the rate of one-eighth of an inch per century.

"So, in order for walls to grow this high," he said, "it must have taken . . ."

"A hundred and ninety-two thousand years, Conseil, and we would therefore have to stretch biblical times much further back into the past. Besides, the formation of coal, that is to say the mineralization of forests buried by floods, required an even longer period of time. But when they use the word 'day' in the Bible, they must mean whole epochs and not just the time from one sunrise to the next, for according to the Bible itself, the sun does not date from the first day of the creation."

When the *Nautilus* came back to the surface, I could make out the entire island of Clermont-Tonnerre with its low tree-covered outline. Its madreporic rocks had evidently been fertilized by waterspouts and storms. One day, a seed brought by a hurricane from nearby lands fell on its limestone surface covered with decomposed fish and marine plants which formed a kind of primitive soil. Then a coconut, brought by the waves, arrived on this new shore. It took root. As it grew, the tree prevented water from evaporating. A stream was born. Then little by little vegetation gained ground. Several small creatures, worms and insects, arrived on tree trunks which the wind had torn from neighboring islands. Turtles came to lay their eggs there. Birds nested in the young trees. Thus animal life developed, and finally man, attracted by its fertility, appeared. This is how microscopic animals built islands.

Towards evening, Clermont-Tonnerre melted into the distance, and the *Nautilus* then altered its course considerably. After touching the Tropic of Capricorn at 135° W. Long., it started off in a west-northwesterly direction, making its way through the intertropical zone. Even though the summer sun beat down fiercely, we felt no discomfort from its heat, for at depths of 100 to 150 feet below the surface, the temperature never rose above fifty or fifty-five.

On December 15 we passed to the west of the bewitching Society Islands and charming Tahiti, the queen of the Pacific. That morning I saw, several miles to leeward, the high mountains of this island. The waters near it furnished us with excellent fish for our menus: mackerel, bonito, albacore and several varieties of a sea serpent called munaephori.

The *Nautilus* had by then traveled 8,100 miles. 9,720 had been recorded on the log when it passed between the Tonga Islands (where the crews of the *Argo,* the *Port-au-Prince* and the *Duke of Portland* had perished) and the Samoan Archipelago (where Captain Langle, the friend of La Pérouse, was killed). We then passed near the Fiji Islands, where the savages had massacred the sailors of the *Union* and Captain Bureau from Nantes, commander of the *Aimable-Joséphine.*

This archipelago stretches 300 miles from north to south and 270 miles from east to west; it lies between 6° and 2° S. Lat., and 174° and 179° W. Long. It comprises a certain number of islands, islets and reefs, among which the most important are Viti Levu, Vanua Levu and Kandavu.

It was Tasman who discovered this group in 1643, the year Torricelli invented the barometer and Louis XIV mounted the throne. I leave the reader to decide which of these events has been more useful to the human race. Then came Cook in 1714, d'Entrecasteaux in 1793 and finally Dumont d'Urville in 1827 untangled the geographical web of this archipelago. The *Nautilus* headed for Wailea Bay where Captain Dillon, who first uncovered the mystery of La Pérouse's shipwreck, had such terrible adventures.

The bay was dragged several times and furnished a vast amount of excellent oysters. We ate an enormous amount, opening them right at the table as Seneca advised. These mollusks belonged to a species called *Ostrea Iamettosa* which is very common off Corsica. The Wailea oyster bed must have been enormous, and surely, without the many forces destroying them, these beds would end up filling the world's bays, for up to two million eggs have been counted within a single oyster.

And the only reason Ned Land did not regret his gluttony, is that the oyster is the only article of food that never causes indigestion. In fact, it takes at least sixteen dozen of these creatures to furnish the 315 grams of nitrogenous substance necessary for a man's daily sustenance.

On December 25, the *Nautilus* was navigating among the New Hebrides which were discovered by Quiros in 1606, explored by Bougainville in 1768 and given their present name by Cook in 1773. The main part of this group is

formed by nine large islands stretching out in a line 360 miles long from NNW
to SSE, situated between 15° and 2° S. Lat. and between 164° and 168° E. Long.
We passed fairly close to Auru Island, which seemed like a mass of green forests
dominated by a very high peak.

It was Christmas Day, and Ned Land seemed to feel very keenly the lack of any
celebration, for among Protestants it is the most important of all their holidays.

I had not seen Captain Nemo for a week when on the morning of the twenty-
seventh he entered the lounge, and as always he acted as if he had just left us five
minutes before. I was busy tracing the *Nautilus'* course on the map when the
captain came over, put his finger on a certain place on the chart and spoke only
one word: "Vanikoro."

It was a magic name. This was the island where La Pérouse's ships had
foundered. I got up brusquely.

"Is the *Nautilus* taking us to Vanikoro?" I asked.

"Yes, Professor," replied the captain.

"And will I be able to visit this famous island where the *Boussole* and *Astrolabe*
went aground?"

"If you would like to, Professor."

"When will we get to Vanikoro?"

"We're there now, Professor."

With Captain Nemo following me, I went up on the platform and anxiously
scanned the horizon.

To the northeast there emerged two volcanic islands of different heights and
surrounded by a coral reef measuring forty miles in circumference. We were in
front of Vanikoro itself, which Dumont d'Urville had named "*Recherche*," and
more precisely in front of the little harbor of Vanu, situated at 16° 4' S. Lat. and
164° 32' E. Long. The land seemed covered with greenery from the beach to the
peaks in the interior, dominated by Mount Kapogo, 2,856 feet high.

After crossing the outer fringe of rocks through a narrow strait, the *Nautilus*
found itself inside the reef, in waters that varied between 180 and 240 feet in depth.
Under the green shade of some mangrove trees, I could make out several natives
showing signs of extreme surprise at our arrival. To them, this long black object

moving forward and scarcely rising above the surface probably seemed like some giant whale. In any case, it apparently filled them with fear and distrust.

Just then Captain Nemo asked me what I knew about La Pérouse's shipwreck.

"Only what everyone knows, Captain," I answered.

"And could you please tell me what everyone knows?" he asked, in a somewhat sarcastic tone of voice.

"Certainly."

I told him what had been made known by Dumont d'Urville's last works, of which I will give a brief résumé.

In 1785, La Pérouse and his second in command, Captain Langle, were sent by Louis XVI on a trip around the world. They embarked in two corvettes, the *Boussole* and the *Astrolabe*, which were never seen again.

In 1791, the French Government, justifiably anxious about the fate of these two corvettes, fitted out two large store ships, the *Recherche* and the *Espérance*, which left Brest on September 28 under the command of Bruni d'Entrecasteaux. Two months later, it was learnt through the testimony of a certain Bowen, commander of the *Albermale*, that the wrecks of sunken ships had been seen on the coast of New Georgia. But d'Entrecasteaux paid no attention to this information—which seemed very dubious—and instead headed for the Admiralty Islands which a Captain Hunter had designated as the place of La Pérouse's shipwreck.

He searched in vain. The *Espérance* and the *Recherche* even passed right in front of Vanikoro without stopping. Moreover, the trip ended very badly, for it cost d'Entrecasteaux his life, as well as that of two of his first mates and several of the crew.

It was Captain Dillon, an old hand at sailing Pacific waters, who first found undeniable evidence of the shipwrecked men. On May 15, 1824, his ship, the *Saint Patrick*, was passing by Tikopia Island, one of the New Hebrides, where a native sailor in a dugout canoe came alongside and sold him an engraved silver sword hilt. This native, moreover, said that when he had been in Vanikoro six years before, he had seen two Europeans from some ships that had gone aground many years before on the reefs of the island.

Dillon guessed that these were La Pérouse's ships, whose disappearance had caused such a stir throughout the world. He tried to sail to Vanikoro where, according to this native, there were still numerous remains of the ships, but contrary winds and currents prevented him from doing so.

Dillon returned to Calcutta. There he was able to interest the Asiatic Society and the East India Company in his discovery. A ship, which he christened the *Recherche*, was put at his disposal and he left on January 23, 1827, accompanied by a French agent.

After stopping at several Pacific ports, the *Recherche* anchored off Vanikoro on July 7, 1827, in this same Vanu Harbor where the *Nautilus* was now floating.

There he found many remains of the wrecked ships: iron implements, anchors, grommets from pulley blocks, mortars, an eighteen-pound shot, fragments of astronomical instruments, a piece of taffrail and a bronze bell with the following inscription—"Bazin made me"—which was the mark of the foundry of the Brest arsenal around 1785. There could be no further doubt.

Dillon remained on the scene of the wreck until October to glean whatever additional information he could. He then left Vanikoro and headed for New Zealand. After putting in at Calcutta on April 7, 1828, he returned to France where he was very warmly received by Charles X.

But in the meanwhile, Dumont d'Urville, without knowing about Dillon's discovery, had already left to search for the wrecked ships elsewhere. For a whaler had reported finding some medals and a cross of Saint Louis in the hands of savages of the Louisiade Archipelago and New Caledonia.

Dumont d'Urville had therefore set out to sea in the *Astrolabe,* and two months after Dillon had left Vanikoro, d'Urville anchored off Hobart. There he found out about Dillon's work, and in addition he learned that a certain James Hobbs, first mate of the *Union* from Calcutta, had gone ashore on an island situated at 8° 18' S. Lat. and 156° 30' E. Long. and had seen some natives using iron bars and wearing red cloth.

Dumont d'Urville was somewhat perplexed and he did not know if he could believe the stories he had read in rather unreliable newspapers. He nevertheless decided to follow in Dillon's footsteps.

On February 10, 1828, the *Astrolabe* appeared off Tikopia, took a deserter living on that island as guide and interpreter, headed for Vanikoro and sighted it on February 12. D'Urville skirted its reefs till the fourteenth, and only on the twentieth did he anchor inside the barrier, in Vanu Harbor.

On the twenty-third, several ship's officers walked around the island and brought back some remains of no importance. The natives, adopting a system of denial and evasion, refused to show them where the accident had taken place. This shiftiness made them think that the natives had maltreated the shipwrecked men, and in fact they seemed to fear that Dumont d'Urville had come to avenge La Pérouse and his unfortunate companions.

Nevertheless, on the twenty-sixth, the natives, finally won over by presents and understanding they had no reason to fear reprisals, led the first mate, Monsieur Jacquinot, to the scene of the shipwreck.

There, in twenty or twenty-five feet of water, between the Pacu and Vanu reefs, lay anchors, cannons and iron and lead ballast all caked with limestone deposits. The longboat and the whaleboat of the *Astrolabe* were sent to the spot, and after long exhausting effort, their crew was able to haul up an anchor weighing eighteen hundred pounds, a cast-iron eight-pound cannon, a piece of lead ballast and two copper guns.

Dumont d'Urville questioned the natives and found out that La Pérouse, after having lost his two ships on the reefs, had built a smaller vessel only to go down a second time. . . . Where? Nobody knew.

Then, beneath a clump of mangrove trees, the commander of the *Astrolabe* erected a memorial to the famous navigator and his companions. It was a simple four-sided pyramid on a coral base, with no iron fittings to tempt the natives.

Then Dumont d'Urville wanted to leave; but since his crew had come down with a fever common in these unhealthy islands and since he himself was very sick, he was unable to weigh anchor till the seventeenth of March.

In the meanwhile, the French Government had become worried that Dumont d'Urville did not know about Dillon's discovery and had sent to Vanikoro a corvette stationed on the west coast of America called the *Bayonnaise*, under the command of Legoarant de Tromelin. The *Bayonnaise* anchored off Vanikoro several months after the departure of the *Astrolabe*. It found nothing new, but was able to report that the savages had not touched the memorial to La Pérouse.

This is essentially what I told Captain Nemo.

"So it's still not known," he said, "where the third ship constructed by the shipwrecked men perished?"

"No, no one knows."

Captain Nemo said nothing, but beckoned me to follow him into the lounge. The *Nautilus* sank several yards below the surface, and the panels opened.

I rushed to the window, and beneath encrustations of coral, fungi, syphonulae, alcyonia, cariophyllae and through myriads of lovely fish, girelles, glyphisidons, pompheridae, diacopae and holocentri, I could make out objects the dredges had been unable to bring up, iron stirrups of footropes, anchors, cannons, shot, capstan fittings, a stem-post—all of them from the sunken ships which were now covered with a carpet of living flowers.

While I was looking at these pitiful wrecks, Captain Nemo said gravely: "On December 7, 1785, Commander La Pérouse left with the *Boussole* and the *Astrolabe*. He first anchored at Botany Bay, afterward visited the Friendly Islands and New Caledonia, headed for the Santa Cruz archipelago and then put in at Nomuka in the Hapai Islands. Finally his ships arrived near the unknown reefs of Vanikoro. The *Boussole,* which was in the lead, ran aground on the southern shore. The *Astrolabe* came to its assistance and suffered the same fate. The first ship was destroyed almost immediately; but the second, stranded to leeward, held together for several days. The natives received the shipwrecked men quite warmly. They installed themselves on the island and built a smaller vessel from the remains of the other two. Several sailors chose to remain at Vanikoro. The others, weak and ill, left with La Pérouse. He headed for the Solomon Islands and there perished with all hands on the western coast of the main island of the group, between Cape Deception and Cape Satisfaction!"

"But how do you know all this?" I cried.

"Here is what I found on the spot of their last shipwreck!"

Captain Nemo showed me a tin box stamped with the French coat of arms and all corroded by salt water. He opened it and I saw a bundle of papers, all yellow but still legible.

They were the actual instructions of the Minister of the Navy to Commander La Pérouse, annotated along the margins in Louis XVI's own handwriting!

"Ah! What a fine death for a sailor!" said Captain Nemo. "How tranquil is a coral tomb, and may the heavens grant that my companions and I be buried in no other!"

CHAPTER XX
Torres Strait

During the night of December 27–28, the *Nautilus* left the shores of Vanikoro and cruised off at a high speed. We headed southwest, and in three days we had covered the two thousand miles separating La Pérouse's islands from the southeast tip of New Guinea.

Early on the morning of January 1, 1868, Conseil joined me on the platform. "With Monsieur's permission," he said, "I would like to wish Monsieur a happy new year."

"What, Conseil! You act just as if I were still in Paris in my office next to the Botanical Gardens! But I accept your good wishes and thank you. I would only like to know what you mean by a 'happy New Year' in our present situation. Will this year see the end of our imprisonment, or will it merely see us continuing our voyage?"

"To tell the truth," replied Conseil, "I really don't know how to answer Monsieur's question. There's no doubt about it—we've been seeing many strange things, and for two months now we haven't even had time to be bored. Besides, the last marvel is always the most astonishing one, and if things keep getting better this way, I can't imagine how they'll end. It's my opinion that we'll never see anything quite like this again."

"Never again, Conseil."

"And what's more, Captain Nemo really lives up to his name;* he could scarcely bother us less if he didn't exist at all."

"That's right."

"I therefore think—with Monsieur's permission—that a happy new year would be one which would allow us to see everything . . ."

"To see everything, Conseil? That would take a long time. But what does Ned Land think?"

"Ned Land completely disagrees with me," answered Conseil. "He has a positive mind and a very demanding stomach. He's getting tired of looking at fish and eating nothing else day after day. He feels the lack of meat, bread and wine; it's hard for a Saxon to go without his beefsteaks and his dash of brandy or gin!"

"As for me, Conseil, that isn't what bothers me, and I've found it easy to get accustomed to the diet on board."

"So have I," replied Conseil. "That's why I think as much about staying as Ned Land does about escaping. So if the coming year is bad for me, it will be good for him, and vice versa. This way one of us is sure to be happy. But as for Monsieur, I wish him whatever will make him happy."

"Thank you, Conseil. Only we'll have to put the New Year's presents off for some other time, and for now be content with a good handshake. That's all I have to give at the moment."

"Monsieur was never so generous," answered Conseil.

And with this, the fine young fellow was off.

On January 2, we had traveled 11,340 miles, or 5250 leagues from our point of departure in the Japan Sea. In front of the *Nautilus'* prow stretched the dangerous waters of the Coral Sea off the northeast coast of Australia. Our boat cruised several miles off this fearful shoal against which Cook's ships almost ran aground on June 10, 1770. Cook's vessel struck a rock, but it did not sink, thanks to the fact that the piece of coral it had hit came loose and stuck in the hull.

I would have liked very much to visit this thousand-mile-long reef against

---

* "Nemo" is a Latin word meaning "no man," "nobody." (Translator's note.)

which waves broke with the intensity of thunderclaps. But just then the *Nautilus'* side fins drew us down to a great depth, and I was able to see nothing of these high coral walls. I had to be content with the various specimens of fish brought up by our nets. Among others I noticed some albacore, a species of mackerel about the size of a tuna with bluish flanks and vertical stripes which disappear when it dies. Whole schools of these fish accompanied us and furnished our table with an excellent dish. We also brought in a large number of giltheads about a quarter of an inch long which tasted like dorado, and flying pyrapedes, veritable underwater swallows which on dark nights streak both air and water with their phosphorescent gleams. Among mollusks and zoophytes, I found in the meshes of the dragnet various species of alcyonaria, sea urchins, hammer shells, spur shells, solaria, cerithia and cavolinia. Plant life was represented by lovely floating seaweed, laminaria and macrocystes, impregnated with the gum that seeps through their pores, and among which I picked out a marvelous *Nemastoma geliniaroida* which was placed alongside the other curiosities of nature in the museum.

Two days after crossing the Coral Sea, on the fourth of January, we sighted the coast of New Guinea. It was then that Captain Nemo told me he intended to reach the Indian Ocean by passing through Torres Strait. But that was all he said. Ned was pleased to hear that we were drawing nearer to European waters.

Torres Strait, which separates Australia and New Guinea, is dangerous not only because of its reefs but also because of the savages who live along its coast.

To the north lies New Guinea, 1200 miles long and 400 miles wide and with an area of 300,000 square miles. It is situated between 0° 19' and 10° 2' S. Lat. and between 128° 23' and 146° 15' E. Long. At noon, while the first mate was shooting the sun, I could make out the summits of the Arfalx Mountains rising in terraces and then ending in sharp peaks.

This island was discovered in 1511 by the Portuguese Francisco Serrano, and was then visited successively by Don José de Meneses in 1526, by Grijalva in 1527, by the Spanish general Alvar de Saavedra in 1528, by Iñigo Ortez in 1545, by the Dutchman Shouten in 1616, by Nicholas Sruick in 1753, by Tasman, Dampier, Fumel, Carteret, Edwards, Bougainville, Cook, Forrest, MacCluer, by d'Entrecasteaux in 1792, by Duperrey in 1823 and by Dumont d'Urville in 1827. De Rienzi stated that this was the original home of the Negroes who occupy the Malay Archipelago, and I felt certain that our hazardous course would bring us face to face with the fearful Andamanese.

The *Nautilus* was therefore entering the most dangerous strait on earth, one which the bravest navigators had hardly dared approach, which Luis Paz de Torres had confronted coming back from the south seas in Melanesia and in which, in 1840, the grounded ships of Dumont d'Urville came near to going down with all hands. But the *Nautilus,* heedless of the sea's dangers, was about to navigate among these coral reefs.

Torres Strait is about a hundred miles wide, but it is obstructed by all kinds of islands, reefs and rocks which make it nearly impossible to sail through. As a result, Captain Nemo took all the necessary precautions before entering it. Then he started out, cruising slowly along the surface. The *Nautilus'* propeller struck the water in a slow rhythm, like the tail of a huge whale.

Taking advantage of this situation, my two companions and I stationed ourselves on the platform, which was, as always, deserted. Before us rose the helmsman's compartment, and I felt sure that Captain Nemo himself was inside guiding his *Nautilus.*

In my hands I held the splendid charts of Torres Strait made by the hydrographic engineer Vincendon Dumoulin with the assistance of Ensign Coupvent-Desbois—who was now an admiral—both of whom were part of Dumont d'Urville's staff during his last trip around the world. Along with those made by Captain King, these are the best charts with which to unravel the tangled web of this narrow passage, and I was following them closely.

Around the *Nautilus* the sea was boiling furiously. The current, traveling from southeast to northwest at a speed of $2^{1}/_{2}$ knots, broke over the corals emerging from the sea around us.

"What an awful stretch of water!" said Ned Land.

"Terrible," I said, "and hardly suitable for a ship like the *Nautilus.*"

"That darned captain must be very sure of his course, because I can see bunches of coral that would only have to graze this hull to knock it into a thousand pieces!"

It was indeed a dangerous situation, but the *Nautilus* slipped past these terrible reefs as if by magic. He did not follow the route of the *Astrolabe* and the *Zélée* which had proved fatal to Dumont d'Urville. He went farther to the north, ran along Murray Island and came back toward the southwest near Cumberland Passage. I thought he would surely run aground once and for all when he took the ship through a large number of almost unknown little islands near Tound Island and Evil Channel.

I was wondering whether Captain Nemo, rash almost to the point of madness, intended to sail his ship through the strait where Dumont d'Urville's two corvettes had gone aground, when once again he changed his course and headed due west toward Gueboroar Island.

It was then about three in the afternoon. The current was easing off—it was almost full tide. The *Nautilus* approached the island, which I can still see with its remarkable border of screw pines. We were less than two miles from its shore.

Suddenly a blow knocked me over. The *Nautilus* had just struck a reef. It remained immobile, listing slightly to port.

When I got up, I saw that Captain Nemo and his first mate were on the platform. They were examining the ship's position, exchanging several words in their incomprehensible language.

Here was our situation. Two miles to starboard rose Gueboroar Island, whose coast extended from north to west like an immense arm. Toward the south and east, we could already make out the tops of several coral formations which the ebb tide was beginning to uncover. We had gone aground at high tide, which would make it difficult to refloat the *Nautilus*. Nevertheless the ship had suffered no damage, for her hull was solidly joined. But even though it could never sink or spring a leak, there was a serious danger of its remaining grounded forever on these reefs, and that would be the end of Captain Nemo's submarine.

I was thinking about all this when the captain came over looking as cool and calm as ever. He seemed neither disturbed nor unhappy.

"An accident?" I asked.

"No, an incident," he replied.

"But an incident," I retorted, "that will force you once again to live on that land you have been fleeing!"

Captain Nemo gave me an odd look and made a gesture of denial. It was his way of stating that nothing would ever force him again to set foot on land. He then said: "No, Monsieur Aronnax, the *Nautilus* is not lost. It will still take you through the wonders of the ocean. Our voyage is only beginning, and I have no desire to deprive myself so quickly of the honor of your company."

"Nevertheless, Captain Nemo," I said, paying no attention to his irony, "the *Nautilus* went aground at high tide. Now in the Pacific the tides are not strong, and if you can't unballast the *Nautilus*—which seems to me impossible—I don't see how it can be refloated."

"You're right, Professor," replied Captain Nemo, "the tides in the Pacific aren't strong, but in Torres Strait there is all the same a difference of five feet between high and low tide. Today's the fourth of January, and in five days there'll be a full moon. Now I'll be very surprised if this obliging satellite doesn't raise these waters and do me a service for which I will be very grateful to her."

With this, Captain Nemo and the first mate went back inside the *Nautilus*. The ship no longer moved—it was immobile, as if embedded in a solid masonry of coral.

"Well, Monsieur?" said Ned Land, coming over to me after the captain left.

"Well, Ned, we're going to wait calmly for the high tide of the ninth; it seems that the moon is going to be obliging enough to float us again."

"Just like that?"

"Just like that."

"And the captain isn't even going to try putting anchors out and heaving the boat off the reef with winches?"

"Why, if the tide will do the trick?" said Conseil simply.

The Canadian looked at Conseil and shrugged his shoulders. The sailor in him could not accept such a situation.

"Monsieur," he said, "believe me when I say that this hunk of iron will never again sail on the water or under it. It's only fit to be sold by the ton. So I think the time's come to part company with Captain Nemo."

"Ned, my friend," I answered, "I don't think the *Nautilus'* situation is as bad as you make out. In four days we'll know how much faith we can put in these Pacific tides. Besides, it would be one thing to think about escaping if we were off the coast of England or southern France, but in New Guinea it's another matter, and what's more, we'll have plenty of time to think about escaping if the *Nautilus* doesn't manage to get free of these reefs. But then we'll be in an even worse situation."

"But couldn't we even look over the ground a bit?" Ned Land continued. "There's an island over there. On that island there are trees. Under those trees there are animals carrying around chops and roast beefs, and I wouldn't mind a bit sinking my teeth into a little good meat."

"This time Ned's right," said Conseil. "I agree with him. Couldn't Monsieur get his friend Captain Nemo to take us to that island, if only so we don't forget how it feels to be on dry land?"

"I can ask him," I said, "but he'll only refuse."

"We would appreciate it if Monsieur would give it a try," said Conseil, "and then we'll know just how good the captain's intentions are."

To my great surprise, Captain Nemo not only granted me the permission I asked, but did it with great willingness and readiness, without even making me promise to come back on board. But escaping across New Guinea would have been very dangerous, and I would never have advised Ned Land to try it. It was better to be a prisoner on board the *Nautilus* than fall into the hands of the natives on that island.

The dinghy was put at our disposal for the following morning. I did not ask whether or not Captain Nemo was going to come with us. I even felt sure that no member of the crew would accompany us, and that Ned Land would be left in charge of sailing the boat. Besides, it was less than two miles to shore, and the Canadian would have no trouble at all taking this light dinghy through the reefs so fatal to large ships.

The next day, January 5, the dinghy was unlashed, taken out of its compartment and launched from the platform. It only took two men to perform the entire operation. The oars were already in it, and we had only to take our places.

At eight o'clock, armed with guns and axes, we left the *Nautilus*. The sea was quite calm. A light breeze was coming from the land. Conseil and I were at the oars, rowing vigorously, and Ned steered us through the narrow passages between shoals. The dinghy proved easy to manage and scooted along at a brisk pace.

Ned Land couldn't contain his joy. He was like a convict who had broken out of jail, and he didn't give a thought to the fact that he would have to return.

"Meat!" he would keep on repeating. "We're going to eat meat, and what meat! Real game! And to think that we never get any bread! I'm not saying I don't like fish, but you mustn't overdo a good thing, and it'll be nice for a change to have a piece of fresh venison grilled over a charcoal fire."

"You glutton!" said Conseil. "Stop it; you're making my mouth water."

"We still don't know if there's game in these forests," I said, "nor if what game there is might not be so big that it could hunt the hunter."

"You may be right, Monsieur Aronnax," replied the Canadian, whose teeth seemed to have been whetted like an ax blade, "but I'd eat sirloin of tiger if there were no other four-legged animals on this island."

"Ned's beginning to make me nervous," said Conseil.

"I don't care what kind it is," continued Ned Land, "but the first animal I see with four feet and no feathers or with two feet and feathers will be greeted with a gunshot."

"There you go, Ned," I said, "flying off the handle again."

"Don't worry about me, Monsieur Aronnax," replied the Canadian, "and keep rowing! Before twenty-five minutes are up I'll be able to offer you some really tasty dish."

At eight-thirty the *Nautilus'* dinghy ran gently aground on a sandy beach, after safely passing through the coral reefs surrounding Gueboroar Island.

CHAPTER XXI
Several Days Ashore

I was quite excited to be on dry land again. Ned Land tested the ground with his foot, as if he wanted to take possession of it. It had nevertheless been only two months since we had become what Captain Nemo called "passengers aboard the *Nautilus*," but in reality, prisoners of its commander.

Within a few minutes we had walked several hundred yards inland. The ground was chiefly of coral formation, but several dried-out stream beds strewn with bits of granite showed that this island had been formed in an earlier geological epoch. Huge trees, sometimes reaching a height of two hundred feet, were bound together with garlands of tropical vines, natural hammocks rocked by a light breeze. There were mimosas, banyans, casuarinas, teak trees, hibiscus, pendanus and palm trees mingled together in wild profusion, and beneath the shade of their green vaulting and at the foot of their gigantic trunks grew orchids, leguminous plants and ferns.

But the Canadian did not even notice all these splendid specimens of New Guinea plant life; he preferred the useful to the attractive. He found a coconut tree, knocked down several coconuts, broke them open and we drank the milk and ate the meat with a satisfaction that was like a protest against the everyday fare of the *Nautilus*.

"Excellent!" said Ned Land.

"Exquisite!" replied Conseil.

"I shouldn't think Captain Nemo would object," said the Canadian, "to our taking a store of coconuts aboard."

"I shouldn't think so," I answered, "but he won't want to taste them himself!"

"Too bad for him!" said Conseil.

"And all the better for us!" retorted Ned Land. "That'll leave us more of them."

"But let me say one thing, Ned," I said to the harpooner as he was just about to put away another one; "coconuts are all very well and good, but before we fill the dinghy with them, it might be wise to find out if the island doesn't produce something more useful. It would be very nice to have fresh vegetables, for instance, on board the *Nautilus*."

"Monsieur's right," answered Conseil, "and I propose that we reserve three spaces in our boat: one for fruit, one for vegetables and the third for venison, of which so far I haven't seen a single sign."

"You must never give up, Conseil," replied the Canadian.

"Let's be on our way," I said, "and keep our eyes open. Even though this island appears to be uninhabited, we might still run into some individuals who aren't so fussy about what kind of game they hunt!"

"Ha, ha!" said Ned Land, moving his jaws significantly.

"Goodness, Ned!" cried Conseil.

"Yes," retorted the Canadian, "I'm beginning to understand the charms of cannibalism!"

"Ned! What are you saying!" cried Conseil. "You—a cannibal! Why, it won't be safe being near you—and to think we share a cabin! Am I going to wake up one morning and find myself half eaten?"

"Conseil, I like you a lot, but not enough to eat you unless I have to."

"I still don't know if I can trust you," replied Conseil. "But let's get on with our hunting. We absolutely must shoot some game to satisfy this cannibal, or else one of these mornings Monsieur will only find bits and pieces of a valet to serve him."

During this conversation we had entered the darker parts of the forest, and for two hours we explored it in every direction.

We were lucky in our search for edible vegetables, and one of the most useful products of the tropics provided us with a food very much lacking on board.

I am referring to the breadfruit tree which is very abundant on Gueboroar Island. I noticed mainly the seedless kind which in Malay is called "Rima."

This tree was easily distinguishable from the others by its straight, forty-foot trunk. Its top, gracefully rounded and crowned with large many-lobed leaves, was enough for a naturalist instantly to recognize the Artocarpus which has been so successfully introduced into the Mascarene Islands. From its mass of greenery stood out a large round fruit four inches in diameter and covered with a skin wrinkled into hexagonal shapes. And this useful plant has been bestowed by nature on regions lacking in wheat; it requires no care and bears fruit eight months of the year.

Ned Land knew this fruit well. He had already eaten it on some of his many voyages, and he knew how to prepare it. The mere sight of it excited him and he could no longer restrain himself.

"Monsieur," he said, "I'll die if I don't taste a bit of that breadfruit!"

"Go ahead, Ned, take as much as you want. We're here to try things out."

"It won't take long," replied the Canadian.

Using a lens, he started a fire of deadwood which was soon crackling joyously. While he was doing this, Conseil and I chose the best breadfruit we could find. Some of them were not yet ripe enough, and their thick skin covered a white pulp almost without fibers. Others, in great numbers, were yellowish and gelatinous, and only waiting to be picked.

These fruits were without pits. Conseil brought a dozen or so to Ned Land, who cut them in thick slices and put them on the hot coals. As he did this, he would say: "You'll see, Monsieur, how good this bread is!"

"Especially after you haven't had any for a long time," said Conseil.

"But it isn't really bread," added the Canadian; "it's more like delicate pastry. Haven't you ever eaten any, Monsieur?"

"No, Ned."

"Well then, get ready for a real treat. If you don't come back for more, then I'm no longer the king of harpooners!"

After several minutes, the part of the fruit exposed to the fire was completely toasted. Inside it had turned into a kind of white paste which tasted something like an artichoke.

This bread really was excellent, and I ate it with great relish.

"But unfortunately," I said, "bread like this can't be kept fresh, and so it seems useless to store it on board."

"Ah-hah, Monsieur!" cried Ned Land. "Maybe that's what naturalists think, but now that I'm the baker I've got other ideas. Conseil, gather up a bunch of this fruit and we'll take it with us when we go back."

"But how will you prepare it?" I asked the Canadian.

"By making a fermented paste out of its pulp which will then keep indefinitely without going bad. Then when I want some, I'll cook it in the kitchen on board, and in spite of a slightly acidy flavor, you'll still find it's very good."

"So, Master Land, I see that with this bread we'll have everything we want."

"No, Professor, we'll still need some fruit or at least a few vegetables."

"Well then, let's look for some fruit and vegetables."

We finished collecting the breadfruit, and then set out to complete this "onshore" dinner.

Our search did not prove to be in vain, for toward noon we had gathered a considerable stock of bananas. These delicious products of the Torrid Zone ripen throughout the year, and the Malays, who call them "pisang," eat them without cooking them. Along with these bananas, we also gathered some enormous jacks, a fruit with a very strong flavor, some delicious mangoes and some pineapples of unbelievable size. And even though it took us a long time to collect all this, we felt no regrets at having done so.

Conseil was always watching Ned. The harpooner walked in front, picking up more fruit along the way to complete our provisions.

"Now we have everything we need, don't we, Ned?" said Conseil.

"Hm!" remarked the Canadian.

"What is there to complain about?"

"All these vegetables and fruit don't make a meal," answered Ned. "They're just the end of a meal, the dessert. But what about the soup? What about the roast?"

"That's right," I said, "Ned promised us some chops, but I don't quite see where we're going to find them."

"Monsieur," answered the Canadian, "our hunting expedition hasn't even yet begun. Patience! We'll find some sort of animal, and if not here, then some other place . . ."

"And if not today, then tomorrow," added Conseil. "Besides, we shouldn't wander too far off. In fact, I propose we go back to the dinghy."

"What! Already!" cried Ned.

"We have to get back before nightfall," I said.

"What time is it then?" asked the Canadian.

"It's at least two," answered Conseil.

"How time flies on shore!" cried the Canadian with a sigh of regret.

"Let's go," replied Conseil.

So we went back through the forest. On the way we completed our harvest by picking up some palm cabbages which we had to get out of the tops of trees, some small beans which I recognized as being the kind the Malays call "abru," and yams of excellent quality.

We were heavily loaded down when we arrived at the dinghy, but Ned Land still felt he didn't have enough. But luck was with him. Just as he was about to get into the boat, he noticed several trees twenty-five or thirty feet high belonging to the palm family. These trees, as precious as the breadfruit, are justly considered among the most useful products of Malaysia.

They were sago palms, plants which grow wild and reproduce themselves, like mulberry trees, by means of both shoots and seeds.

Ned Land knew what to do with these trees. He took his ax and started chopping vigorously. He had soon felled two or three sago palms. We could tell they were full grown by the white dust covering their branches.

I watched him more as a naturalist than as a starving man. He began by removing from each trunk a band of bark about an inch thick which covered a network of elongated fibers forming inextricable knots cemented together by a kind of gummy flour. This flour was the sago itself, an edible substance which is the principal diet of the Melanesians.

For the moment, Ned Land did no more than cut these trunks up into pieces, as one would for firewood. Later he would take out the flour, pass it through a cloth to separate it from the fibrous ligaments, let it dry out in the sun and then put it in molds to harden.

Finally at five in the afternoon, loaded down with all our booty, we left the island, and a half an hour later we were alongside the *Nautilus*. No one came out to greet us. The enormous steel-plated cylinder seemed deserted. When we had brought our provisions on board, I went down to my room. I found my supper ready. I ate and then went to sleep.

On the next day, January 6, nothing had changed on board. There was not a sound inside the submarine, not a single sign of life. The dinghy was still alongside, exactly as we had left it. We resolved to go back to Gueboroar Island. Ned Land hoped to have more luck hunting than on the day before and he wanted to try another part of the forest.

We were off at dawn. The tidal current was with us, and in no time at all we arrived at the island.

We got out, and thinking it might be better to follow the Canadian's instincts, we let him be the leader, and he soon threatened to outdistance us with his long legs.

Ned Land headed westward from the coast, and then, after fording several streams, he reached a high plain bordered by splendid forests. We saw several kingfishers near the streams, but they wouldn't let us approach them. Their caution proved to me that these birds knew what to expect from two-legged creatures like us, and I concluded that if this island was not inhabited, it was at least frequently visited by human beings. After crossing a fairly rich prairie, we reached the edge of a little forest filled with the singing of birds as they flitted from tree to tree.

"They're only birds," said Conseil.

"You can still eat them!" answered the harpooner.

"But Ned," said Conseil, "I don't see anything but ordinary parrots."

"Conseil, my friend," Ned replied gravely, "a parrot is like pheasant to someone who has nothing else to eat."

"And what's more," I said, "if it's cooked right, it makes a very good dish."

And indeed, beneath the thick foliage of this forest, a whole world of parrots flitted from branch to branch, awaiting only a more careful education to speak the language of human beings. As it was, they chattered away, accompanied by many-colored parakeets, grave-looking cockatoos who seemed to be meditating some philosophical problem, while brilliant red lories passed by like pieces of bunting carried off by the wind, in the midst of kalaos with their noisy flight, papuas with their fine shadings of blue and all sorts of other birds that were charming but inedible.

Nevertheless, one kind, which is seen only in these regions and which never passes the limit of the Aru Islands and New Guinea, was lacking in this collection. But I was lucky enough to be able to see it before long.

After crossing a fairly thick copse, we came upon a plain covered with shrubs. There I saw rise a flock of magnificent birds whose long feathers were so arranged that they had to fly into the wind. Their undulating flight, the graceful curves they described in the air and their shimmering colors made one look at them in wonder. I had no difficulty recognizing them.

"Birds of paradise!"

"Order of Passeriformes, section of Clystomorae," replied Conseil.

"Family of the partridges?" asked Ned Land.

"I don't think so, Ned. But I'm counting on your skill to capture one of these charming specimens of the tropics."

"I'll try, Professor, even though I'm handier with a harpoon than with a gun."

The Malays, who carry on a brisk trade in these birds with the Chinese, have various methods for catching them, none of which we could use. Sometimes they put snares in the tops of the high trees where these birds perch, and sometimes they use a strong glue that paralyzes their movements. And they even go so far as to poison the springs where these birds go to drink. But all we could do was try shooting them in flight, which left us little chance of getting one. And in fact we used up a good part of our ammunition in vain.

By eleven in the morning we had reached the foothills of the mountains which cover the center of the island, and we had as yet killed nothing. We were beginning to feel terrible pangs of hunger. We had relied on what we would be able to kill, and we had made a mistake. But Conseil, very luckily and to his great surprise, brought down two birds and thus assured us our lunch. They were a white pigeon and a ringdove. We quickly removed their feathers, put them on a spit and roasted them over a fire. While they were cooking, Ned prepared some breadfruit. Then the pigeon and the ringdove were devoured right down to the bone and declared excellent. The nutmeg on which they had gorged themselves perfumed their flesh and made it delicious to eat.

"It's as if chickens were fed on truffles," said Conseil.

"And what do we lack now, Ned?" I asked.

"Four-legged game, Monsieur Aronnax," replied Ned Land. "All these pigeons are no better than an hors d'oeuvre, something to whet your appetite! I won't be happy until I've killed an animal with chops on it!"

"And I won't be happy, Ned, until I catch a bird of paradise."

"So let's keep on hunting," answered Conseil, "but heading back toward the coast. We've reached the foothills of the mountains, and I think it would be best if we returned toward the forest region."

This was a good piece of advice and we followed it. After walking for an hour, we reached a veritable forest of sago palms. Several harmless snakes scurried away beneath our feet. The birds of paradise fled at our approach, and I had given up hope of ever getting one when Conseil, who was out in front, suddenly bent down, let out a cry of victory and came back to me carrying a magnificent bird of paradise.

"Good work, Conseil!" I cried.

"Monsieur is too kind," replied Conseil.

"No, my boy. That was a stroke of genius taking one of these birds alive, and with your bare hands!"

"But if Monsieur would examine it closely, he would see that there was no great merit in what I did."

"Why not, Conseil?"

"Because this bird is as drunk as a lord."

"Drunk?"

"Yes, Monsieur, drunk from all the nutmeg he had eaten under the nutmeg tree where I caught him. Look, Ned, you see the terrible effects of drunkenness!"

"Good Lord!" retorted the Canadian. "Considering the amount of gin I've

We were heavily loaded down when we arrived at the dinghy.

had in the last two months, you haven't got much grounds for accusing me of drunkenness!"

In the meanwhile I examined this strange bird. Conseil was right. This bird of paradise had become drunk to the point of being powerless. It could not fly, and could scarcely walk. But this didn't disturb me, and I just let it sleep off the effects of the nutmeg.

This bird belonged to the loveliest of the eight species found on New Guinea and neighboring islands. It was the "great emerald" bird of paradise, one of the rarest kinds. It was about a foot long, with a relatively small head and tiny eyes placed near the base of its beak. But it displayed a marvelous range of colors, with its yellow beak, brown feet and claws, hazel wings with purple tips, pale yellow head, emerald throat, and chestnut-brown stomach and chest. Two long, slim, threadlike feathers shaped like downy horns rose above its tail and completed the ensemble of this marvelous bird which natives have poetically named the "sun bird."

I wanted very much to bring this superb specimen of a bird of paradise back to Paris and present it to the Botanical Gardens, which doesn't possess one alive.

"You mean to say they're very rare?" asked the Canadian, in the tone of voice of a hunter whose interest in game is not exactly artistic.

"Very rare, my friend, and above all very difficult to capture alive. And even when dead, these birds are the object of an important commerce, to the point where the natives have hit on the idea of fabricating them, just as others forge pearls or diamonds."

"What!" cried Conseil. "There are people who make fake birds of paradise?"

"Yes, Conseil."

"Does Monsieur know how the natives do it?"

"Yes. During the monsoon season, these birds of paradise lose their magnificent tail feathers, which naturalists call the subulary feathers. The bird counterfeiters pick up these feathers, which they then cleverly attach to some poor parakeet they have already altered to suit their purposes. They then dye the place where the feathers were joined on, varnish the entire bird and send it off to European museums or collectors."

"Yes," said Ned Land, "but even though you've got the wrong bird, you've at least got the right feathers, and once you don't intend to eat it, I don't see what difference it makes!"

Although my desires had been fulfilled by the capture of this bird of paradise, those of our Canadian hunter had not yet been satisfied. Fortunately, at about two o'clock, Ned Land brought down a splendid wild boar, of a kind the natives call "bari-utang." This creature seemed to have turned up especially to bring us real meat from a four-legged animal, and his arrival was very welcome. Ned Land was very proud of his shot. The boar had been hit with the electric bullet and had fallen down stone dead.

The Canadian skinned and cleaned it, and then removed a half dozen chops to be grilled for our evening meal. Then once again we set out hunting, for Ned and Conseil were to perform yet more exploits.

And in fact, these two friends, by beating the bushes, flushed a herd of kangaroos, which fled bounding along on their huge hind legs. But they did not flee so fast that our electric bullets could not stop them.

"Ah, Professor!" cried Ned Land, carried away by the excitement of hunting, "what marvelous meat, especially when it's braised! What a supply for the *Nautilus*! We've got two, three, five! And to think we'll have it all to ourselves, without those imbeciles on board having even one mouthful!"

I think that if Ned, in his overexcitement, had not talked so much, he would have massacred the entire herd! But he was content with a dozen of these—as Conseil put it—interesting marsupials which form the first order of aplacental mammals.

They were small, and belonged to a species of "rabbit kangaroo" which lives in hollowed-out trees and can travel at great speed. But although their size is not great, their meat is highly esteemed.

We were very satisfied with the results of our hunting. Ned was delighted and suggested coming back to this enchanted island the next day. He probably would have liked to depopulate it of all its edible quadrupeds. But he did not count on what was to happen.

At six in the afternoon we were back on the beach. Our dinghy was grounded in its usual spot. The *Nautilus* looked like a long reef two miles from shore.

Ned Land, without any further delay, set to work on the important matter of dinner. He was very expert in this kind of cooking. The chops from the "bari-utang," grilled over a charcoal fire, were soon filling the air with a delicious odor! . . .

But here I am talking like Ned Land, in ecstasy over freshly grilled pork! Please excuse me for the same reasons I excused Ned Land.

In short, the dinner was excellent. Two ringdoves rounded out this unusual menu. Some sago paste, a bit of breadfruit, several mangoes, a half a dozen pineapples and the fermented liquor from certain kinds of coconuts all helped to put us in a very joyous state. It even seems to me that my two companions' brains were perhaps a bit clouded.

"What if we don't go back to the *Nautilus* tonight?" said Conseil.

"What if we don't ever go back?" added Ned Land.

But just then a stone landed at our feet, cutting short the harpooner's proposition.

CHAPTER XXII
Captain Nemo's Thunderbolts

Without getting up we looked in the direction of the forest. My hand stopped halfway up to my mouth, but Ned's completed the trip.

"Stones don't fall from the sky," said Conseil, "unless perhaps it was a meteorite."

Another carefully polished stone knocked a ringdove leg out of Conseil's hand, thereby strengthening his argument.

We all three got up and shouldered our rifles, ready for an attack.

"Is it monkeys?" cried Ned Land.

"Almost," replied Conseil; "it's savages."

"Head for the dinghy!" I cried, going toward the water.

It had become necessary to beat a hasty retreat, for twenty or so natives, armed with bows and slings, had appeared at the edge of a copse over to the right, scarcely a hundred paces away.

Our dinghy was beached about sixty feet from us.

Even though the savages advanced slowly, without running, they were clearly in a very hostile frame of mind. Stones and arrows rained around us.

Ned Land did not want to abandon his provisions, and in spite of the fast-increasing danger, he tucked the boar under one arm and the kangaroos under the other and broke camp as fast as he could.

Within two minutes we were at the water's edge. It only took us a moment to put our provisions and arms in the dinghy, push it into the water and put our oars in place. We had not gone four hundred yards when a hundred savages, shouting and waving their arms about, entered the water up to their waists. I looked to see if their appearance had made anybody come out on the deck of the *Nautilus,* but it had not. The big vessel lay out in the open water, absolutely deserted.

Twenty minutes later we were climbing on board. The hatches were open. After making fast the dinghy, we went below.

As I drew near, I could hear music coming from the lounge. There was Captain Nemo bent over his organ, lost in a musical ecstasy.

"Captain!" I said.

He did not hear me.

"Captain!" I repeated, tapping him on the shoulder.

He gave a start and turned around.

"Ah! It's you, Professor!" he said. "How was your hunting expedition? Did you find any interesting botanical specimens?"

"Yes, Captain," I answered, "but we've unfortunately brought back with us a herd of two-legged creatures that make me a little nervous."

"What sort of two-legged creatures?"

"Savages."

"Savages!" replied Captain Nemo in an ironic tone of voice. "Does it surprise you, Professor, to set foot on land and find savages? Where won't you find savages? Besides, these creatures you call savages—are they any worse than others?"

"But Captain . . ."

"As for me, Monsieur, wherever I went I saw nothing but savages."

"But if you don't want them on board the *Nautilus*," I replied, "you would do well to take some precautions."

"Calm down, Professor, there's nothing to worry about."

"But there are a lot of them."

"How many did you count?"

"At least a hundred."

"Monsieur Aronnax," answered Captain Nemo, once again placing his fingers on the keyboard of the organ, "even if all the natives of New Guinea were gathered together on that beach, the *Nautilus* would have no reason to fear their attack!"

The captain's fingers started running over the keyboard, and I noticed that he played only on the black keys, which gave his melodies an essentially Scottish flavor. He had soon forgotten my presence and was once again deep in a reverie, and this time I made no effort to dispel it.

I went back up on the platform. It was already night, for in these latitudes the sun sets quickly without any period of twilight. I could just barely make out Gueboroar Island. But numerous fires on the beach told me that the natives had no intention of leaving.

I stayed alone on deck for several hours, sometimes thinking about these natives—but without being afraid, for I had been won over by the captain's imperturbable confidence—and sometimes forgetting them and admiring the splendor of the tropical night. My thoughts also drifted toward France, in the wake of stars which would be over it in several hours. The moon shone amid the constellations of the zenith. This led me to think that, the day after tomorrow, this faithful, obliging satellite would return and lift the *Nautilus* from its coral bed. Toward midnight, seeing that everything was calm on the dark ocean as well as beneath the trees on shore, I returned to my cabin and went peacefully to sleep.

The night passed without mishap. The Papuans were undoubtedly terrified by the sight of the monster grounded in the bay, for the open hatches would have given them easy access to the inside of the *Nautilus.*

At six o'clock on the following morning—it was the eighth of January—I went back up to the platform. Dawn was breaking. As the mist rose, the island slowly came into view, first its beaches, then its mountain peaks.

The natives were still there, but in far greater numbers than the day before— five or six hundred perhaps. Some of them had taken advantage of the low tide and had advanced along the tops of corals to less than four hundred yards from the *Nautilus.* I could see them clearly. They were true Papuans with handsome faces and athletic bodies, high, broad foreheads, noses that were wide but not flat, and white teeth. Their woolly hair was dyed red, and thus provided a sharp contrast to their black shining bodies. Bone earrings hung from their cut and distended earlobes. For the most part these savages were naked. But I could make out several women among them dressed in grass skirts held up by belts also made from some plant. Several of the chieftains wore necklaces made of crescent-shaped objects or of red and white beads. Almost all of them were armed with bows, arrows and shields, and around their shoulders hung a kind of net containing the stones they hurled from their slings with deadly accuracy.

One of the chieftains nearest the *Nautilus* was examining it carefully. He must have been a very high-ranking "mado," because he was dressed in banana leaves with scalloped edges and painted in bright colors.

I could have shot this native easily, for he was only a short distance away; but I thought it best to wait for really hostile demonstrations. In relations between Europeans and savages, it is best for Europeans not to attack first.

During the entire period of low tide, these natives prowled around the *Nautilus,* but without being in the least troublesome. I heard them repeat the word "assai" many times, and by their gestures I understood they were inviting me to come ashore with them—an invitation I felt I should decline.

So, for the entire day the dinghy did not leave the side of the *Nautilus,* to Ned

Land's great annoyance, for he had wanted to complete his supply of provisions. This clever Canadian spent his time preparing the food he had brought back from Gueboroar Island the day before. As for the savages, they headed back toward the beach at about eleven in the morning, as soon as the tops of the corals began to disappear beneath the rising tide. But I could see that more and more of them were congregating on the beach. They were probably coming from neighboring islands, or from New Guinea itself. Nevertheless, I could not see a single native dugout canoe.

With nothing better to do, I thought I would try dredging these lovely clear waters in which I could see masses of shells, zoophytes and marine plants. Moreover, it was the last day the *Nautilus* would be spending in these waters—that is, if it managed to get free during the next day's high tide, as Captain Nemo had predicted.

So I called Conseil and he brought me a small, light dredge, more or less like those employed by oyster fishermen.

"About those savages," he said, "if Monsieur doesn't mind my saying so, they don't seem to have very bad intentions."

"All the same, they're cannibals, my boy."

"A cannibal can still be an honorable man," replied Conseil, "just as a glutton can be honest. One doesn't exclude the other."

"That's all very well, Conseil. I'll even grant you that these cannibals are honorable and that they go about devouring their prisoners honorably. But since I don't like the idea of being devoured, even honorably, I'll stay on my guard, for the commander of the *Nautilus* seems to be taking no precautions whatsoever. Now to work."

We fished for two hours without bringing up anything of value. Our dredge would fill up with Midas' ears, harp shells, melaniae and the loveliest hammer shells I had ever seen. We also brought up several sea cucumbers, pearl oysters and a dozen small turtles which were reserved for the kitchen on board.

But then when I was least expecting it, I put my hand on something marvelous, or rather, I should say, a natural deformity that is very rare. Conseil had just brought up the dredge filled with various ordinary shells, when he suddenly saw me plunge my hand into the net, pull out a shell and utter the conchologist's cry—the most piercing noise the human throat can produce.

"What happened to Monsieur?" asked Conseil, very startled. "Has Monsieur been bitten?"

"No, my boy, even though I would have gladly given a finger for this discovery!"

"What discovery?"

"This shell," I said, holding up the object of my triumph.

"But it's nothing more than a porphyry olive shell, of the genus olive, order of pectinibranchia, class of gastropods, phylum of mollusks . . ."

"Yes, Conseil, but instead of having its spiral going from right to left, this olive shell has it going from left to right!"

"Is that possible!" cried Conseil.

"Yes, my boy, it's a left-handed shell!"

"A left-handed shell!" repeated Conseil excitedly.

"Look at its spire!"

"Ah, believe me, Monsieur," said Conseil as he took the precious shell in his trembling hands, "I've never felt such a thrill!"

And it was indeed something to be thrilled about! As naturalists have pointed out, right-handedness is one of the laws of nature. Stars and their planets move and rotate from right to left. Man usually employs his right hand rather than his left hand, and consequently the things around him, such as staircases, locks, watch springs, etc., are made to be used from right to left. Now nature generally follows this law for the spirals on its shells. They are all right-handed, with rare exceptions, and when one happens to find a specimen that is left-handed, collectors will pay you its weight in gold.

Conseil and I were absorbed in the contemplation of our treasure, and I was promising myself to give it to the museum, when, as luck would have it, a stone thrown by a native came and shattered this precious object in Conseil's hand.

I let out a cry of despair! Conseil grabbed my gun and aimed it at a savage waving his sling about thirty feet away. I tried to stop him, but he fired and broke the charm bracelet hanging on the native's arm.

"Conseil!" I cried, "Conseil!"

"What's wrong? Can't Monsieur see that this cannibal attacked first?"

"Yes, but a shell isn't worth a man's life!" I said.

"Ah, the scoundrel!" cried Conseil. "I would have been happier if he had broken my shoulder!"

Conseil was in earnest, but I could not agree with him. The situation, however, had changed in the last few moments without our having noticed it. There were twenty or so canoes around the *Nautilus*. They were the kind made from hollowed-out tree trunks—long, thin and very fast. They were kept upright by means of two bamboo pontoons floating on the water. The men paddling them were half naked, and their advance made me somewhat uneasy.

It was obvious that these Papuans had already come into contact with Europeans and were familiar with their ships. But what were they to make of this long iron cylinder stretched out in the bay, without masts or funnel? It undoubtedly made them nervous, for at first they had kept at a respectful distance. Nevertheless, seeing that it didn't move, they had gained confidence little by little, and were now trying to get more familiar with it. But it was precisely this familiarity that had to be prevented. Our guns, which made almost no sound when fired, would produce little effect on these natives, who only respected things which made a great deal of noise. Lightning without thunderclaps would scarcely have frightened them at all, even though the danger lay in the lightning itself, not in the noise.

The dugout canoes were drawing nearer the *Nautilus,* and suddenly a cloud of arrows landed on the ship.

"Good Lord! It's hailing!" cried Conseil. "And maybe the hail's poisoned!"

"We must warn Captain Nemo," I said as I went below.

I entered the lounge. No one was there. I gathered up my courage and knocked on the door of the captain's cabin.

A voice said, "Come in." I entered and found Captain Nemo deep in mathematical calculations, covering sheets of paper with x's and other algebraic signs.

"Am I disturbing you?" I said, trying to be polite.

"Yes, you are, Monsieur Aronnax," replied the captain, "but I can only imagine that you had serious reasons for doing so."

"Very serious. We're surrounded by native dugout canoes, and within several minutes we'll undoubtedly be attacked by a couple of hundred savages."

"Oh!" said Captain Nemo calmly, "have they come with their canoes?"

"Yes, Monsieur."

"Well then, Professor, all we have to do is close the hatches."

"Precisely, and I came to say that . . ."

"Nothing could be simpler," said Captain Nemo.

He pressed a button and transmitted an order to the ship's crew.

"Everything's been taken care of, Monsieur," he said after several moments. "The dinghy's in place and the hatches closed. You couldn't possibly be worried that these gentlemen might stave in a hull on which cannonballs from your frigate had no effect."

"No, Captain, but there's still another danger."

"And what's that, Monsieur?"

"It's that tomorrow, at about this time, the hatches will have to be opened again to replenish the *Nautilus'* air supply . . ."

"Unquestionably, Monsieur, since this vessel breathes like a whale."

"But if the Papuans are on the platform then, I can't see how you'll be able to prevent them from entering."

"Then, Monsieur, your guess is that they'll come on board?"

"I'm sure they will."

"Well then, Monsieur, let them come. I can't see any reason for preventing them. After all, they're nothing but a bunch of poor devils, and I don't want a single one of these wretched Papuans to lose his life because of my visit to Gueboroar Island!"

I was about to leave when Captain Nemo suggested I sit down next to him. He seemed very interested in knowing about our excursions on shore and about our hunting expeditions, but he did not seem to understand the Canadian's violent need for meat. Then the conversation touched on several other topics, and Captain Nemo, without being any more talkative than usual, seemed friendlier.

Among other things, we talked about the *Nautilus'* present situation, and its having run aground on exactly the same spot where Dumont d'Urville had almost lost his ships. Then the captain said: "D'Urville was one of your great sailors, one of your most gifted navigators! He was the Captain Cook of France. The poor man! To have confronted the ice floes of the South Pole, the coral reefs of Oceania and the cannibals of the Pacific, only to die miserably in a train wreck! If such a man had time to reflect during the last seconds of his life, imagine what his thoughts must have been!"

As he talked about d'Urville, Captain Nemo seemed deeply moved, and I can only put this to his credit.

Then, looking at a map, we went over what the French navigator had done, his trips around the world, his double attempt to reach the South Pole which had resulted in the discovery of Adélie Land and Louis Philippe Land, and finally his charting of the principal islands of Oceania.

"What your d'Urville did on the surface of the ocean," said Captain Nemo, "I have done beneath the surface, and more easily and completely. Whereas the *Astrolabe* and the *Zélée* were at the mercy of storms, the *Nautilus* is like a calm, stationary studio in the midst of the ocean!"

"Yes, Captain," I said, "but there's still one way in which the *Nautilus* resembles Dumont d'Urville's corvettes.

"How, Monsieur?"

"It's that the *Nautilus* has become stranded just as they did!"

"The *Nautilus* is not stranded, Monsieur," Captain Nemo answered coldly. "The *Nautilus* is built to rest on the ocean floor, and all the things d'Urville had to do to refloat his ships are unnecessary for me. The *Astrolabe* and the *Zélée* almost perished, but the *Nautilus* is in no danger at all. Tomorrow, at the exact time I told you, the tide will calmly lift up the ship and it will once again be on its way through the ocean."

"Captain," I said, "I don't doubt . . ."

"Tomorrow at two-forty P.M.," added Captain Nemo getting up, "the *Nautilus* will be afloat and leave Torres Strait without having suffered the slightest damage."

This was said in a dry tone of voice, and afterward he made a slight bow. He was asking me to leave, and I went to my cabin.

There I found Conseil, eager to know the results of my interview with the captain.

"When I suggested that the *Nautilus* was in danger from the Papuans, he answered me very sarcastically. So all I can say is to have confidence in him and go to sleep without worrying."

"Monsieur doesn't need me for anything?"

"No, my friend. What's Ned Land doing?"

"With Monsieur's permission," answered Conseil, "Ned is making a kangaroo pie which is going to be superb!"

I remained alone and went to bed, but I didn't sleep too well. I could hear the savages walking about on the platform and occasionally letting out blood-curdling yells. But the night passed by without the crew doing a thing. They seemed no more disturbed by the presence of these cannibals than soldiers inside a fort would worry about ants crawling over their fortifications.

At six in the morning I got up. The hatches had not been opened. The air inside had therefore not been renewed, but the reservoirs, always filled against any eventuality, were functioning and letting a little oxygen into the impoverished atmosphere of the *Nautilus*.

I worked in my room till noon, without seeing Captain Nemo even for a moment. No one on board seemed to be making the slightest preparations for departure.

I waited a while longer and then went to the lounge. It was two-thirty. In ten minutes the tide would reach its maximum height, and if Captain Nemo had not made a rash prediction, the *Nautilus* would be set free at once. If not, it would be many months before it would leave its coral bed.

Nevertheless I could feel the submarine making slight movements—forerunners of when the ship would be set free. I could hear the hull grating against the hard coral.

At 2:35 Captain Nemo appeared in the lounge.

"We're about to leave," he said.

"Oh!" I replied.

"I've given orders to open the hatches."

"What about the Papuans?"

"What about them?" answered the captain with a slight shrug of his shoulders.

"Won't they get inside the *Nautilus*?"

"How?"

"By going down the hatches you've opened."

"Monsieur Aronnax," Captain Nemo calmly replied, "you can't go down the *Nautilus'* hatches that easily, even when they're open."

I looked at the captain.

"You don't understand?" he said.

"No, not at all."

"Well then, come and see."

I went toward the companionway. There I found Ned Land and Conseil watching several members of the crew opening the hatches, while from the outside could be heard curses and cries of rage.

The hatch lids opened outward. Twenty horrible faces appeared in the opening. But the first of these natives to put his hand on the railing of the companionway was thrown back by some invisible force, and ran off shouting and jumping about wildly.

Ten of his companions followed him and suffered the same fate.

Conseil was ecstatic. Ned Land, carried away by his violent instincts, rushed for the companionway. But as soon as he grabbed the railing with his hands, he too was thrown back.

"Good Lord!" he cried. "I've been struck by lightning!"

This explained everything. It was no longer a mere railing, but an electrically charged cable stretching up to the platform. Anybody touching it would get a powerful shock—a shock that would have been fatal if Captain Nemo had charged this railing with all the electricity at his disposal! One could really say that between him and his assailants he had placed an electric barrier that no one could cross unharmed.

In the meanwhile the Papuans had retreated in terror. As for us, we laughingly consoled and massaged poor Ned Land, who was cursing like a man possessed by the devil.

But just then, at precisely the moment predicted by the captain, the *Nautilus* was raised up by the sea and left its coral bed. The blades of its propeller struck the water slowly and majestically. Little by little it increased its speed, and sailing along the surface of the ocean, it left the dangerous waters of Torres Strait safe and sound.

CHAPTER XXIII
Bitter Dreams

On the next day, January 10, the *Nautilus* once again began cruising under water, but at a remarkable speed which I estimated at no less than thirty-five knots. Its propeller was turning so fast that I could neither follow nor count its revolutions.

When I thought what electricity had been made to do aboard the *Nautilus*, not only giving it motion, heat and light, but also protecting it against attacks from the outside, my admiration became boundless, not only for the ship but also for the engineer who had designed it.

We were headed due west, and on January 11 we passed Cape Wessel, which is situated at 135° E. Long. and 10° N. Lat., and forms the eastern tip of the Gulf of Carpentaria. There were still many reefs, but they were no longer so close to one another, and here too they were very accurately marked on the chart. The *Nautilus* had no difficulty avoiding the Money Shoals on her port side and the Victoria Reefs on her starboard, situated at 130° W. Long. along the tenth parallel which it was following.

On January 13, Captain Nemo sighted Timor Island at 122° W. Long. This is a body of land covering 12,500 square miles and governed by rajahs. These monarchs consider themselves descendants of crocodiles, which they claim is the highest possible origin a human being can have. As a result the rivers of this island are full of their scaly ancestors, which the inhabitants worship. They are protected, spoilt, adulated, nourished and fed young girls, and woe to the outsider who touches one of these sacred creatures.

But the *Nautilus* had no desire to come into contact with these horrible animals. Timor was only visible for a moment, at noon, while the first mate was taking our position. In the same way, I only got a glimpse of Rotti Island, which is part of the same archipelago and whose women have a great reputation for beauty in the markets of Malaya.

From then on, the *Nautilus* altered its course toward the southwest. We were heading for the Indian Ocean. Where were Captain Nemo's whims taking us? Would he go back toward the coast of Asia? Would he head for European waters? This seemed unlikely for a man fleeing the inhabited parts of the globe. Would he therefore turn southward? Would he go around the Cape of Good Hope and Cape Horn, and then push on to the Antarctic? Would he finally return to the Pacific where his *Nautilus* could navigate easily and freely? The future would tell us.

On January 14, after going alongside the Cartier, Hibernia, Seringapatam and Scott Reefs—the land's last efforts against the water—we lost all sight of land. The *Nautilus* had considerably reduced its speed, and we would sail alternately under water or on the surface in the most capricious way imaginable.

During this part of the trip, Captain Nemo made interesting experiments on ocean temperatures at different depths. Such experiments usually are done with rather complicated instruments and the results are doubtful at best, whether they are obtained by thermometrical sounding gear which often breaks beneath the water pressure, or by devices which make use of the varying resistance of metals to electrical currents. But Captain Nemo could merely go down and take the temperature at whatever depth he wanted, and his thermometer, in contact with the surrounding water, would give him an instantaneous and reliable reading.

It was thus that the *Nautilus,* either by filling its reservoirs or diving by means of its side fins, reached successive depths of 10,000, 13,000, 17,000,

23,000, 30,000 and 33,000 feet. The final result of these experiments was that the ocean has a constant temperature of 40° Fahrenheit at a depth of 3000 feet in any latitude.

I followed these experiments with great interest. Captain Nemo seemed completely absorbed in them. I often asked myself what his aim was in making these observations. Was it for his fellow men? I doubted it, for one day or another his work would perish with him in some unknown sea! Unless of course he intended to give me the results of his experiments. But this would have meant admitting that my strange voyage was to end at some point. And this end was not yet in sight.

In any case, Captain Nemo also told me of other figures he had obtained, which established the relationship between varying densities of water in the world's principal oceans. From this information, I was able to draw a personal lesson which had nothing to do with science.

It was on the morning of January 15. The captain, with whom I was strolling on the platform, asked me if I knew the different densities of sea water. I said I didn't, and added that science was lacking accurate observations on this subject.

"I have made such observations," he said, "and I can answer for their accuracy."

"Yes," I said, "but the *Nautilus* is a world all of its own, and the secrets of its scientists don't reach men on shore."

"You're right, Professor," he said after several moments' silence. "It's a world all of its own. It is as foreign to life on land as those planets which accompany the earth around the sun, and we will never know what results might have been obtained by scientists on Saturn or Jupiter. But since fate has brought us together, I can tell you the results of my experiments."

"I'm listening, Captain."

"As you know, Professor, sea water is denser than fresh water, but this density is not uniform. In fact, if we represent the density of fresh water by 1, I have found the density of the water in the Atlantic to be 1.028, that in the Pacific 1.026, in the Mediterranean 1.030 . . ."

"Ah!" I thought. "He ventures into the Mediterranean!"

"1.018 for the Ionian Sea, and 1.029 for the Adriatic."

There was no doubt about it, the *Nautilus* did not avoid the more frequented seas near Europe, and I concluded that he would take us—perhaps fairly soon—toward more civilized lands. This news would make Ned Land very happy.

For several days our time was spent doing all sorts of experiments on the varying salinity of water at different depths, on its electrical content, its coloration and transparency, and in all this work Captain Nemo showed an ingenuity which was only equaled by his kindness toward me. Then for several days I saw him no more, and once again I lived aboard in isolation.

On January 16, the *Nautilus* seemed to be resting only several feet below the surface. Its electrical machinery was not functioning, and its stationary propeller allowed the ship to rock back and forth at the mercy of ocean currents. I guessed that the crew was busy repairing something inside the submarine which had given way under the strain of the machinery's violent mechanical movements.

My companions and I then witnessed a strange spectacle. The panels of the lounge were open, and since the *Nautilus*' light was not on, the water around us appeared like nothing more than an area of vague darkness. Overhead the sky was stormy and covered with thick clouds, therefore only dimly lighting the upper layers of the ocean.

I was observing the state of the sea under these conditions—in which the largest fish could only be seen as a dim shadow with scarcely any outline—when suddenly the *Nautilus* became surrounded with light. At first I thought the light on top of the submarine had been turned on and that its powerful rays were illuminating the waters. But I was wrong, and soon I was able to see how mistaken I had been.

The *Nautilus* was floating in the midst of a phosphorescent layer which, in the semidarkness, seemed extraordinarily bright. This effect was produced by myriads of tiny, luminous animals, whose glitter increased as they touched the submarine's metal hull. I also saw flashes of light in the midst of these waters, looking like streams of melted lead in a blazing furnace, or metal brought to a red-white heat; they were such that by contrast some of the other luminous areas were like shadows in the fiery waters, from which all shadows should have disappeared. No, this was no longer the calm gleam of normal light! It was full of an extraordinary intensity and movement! This light felt as if it were alive!

In reality, it was produced by an infinite number of tiny marine organisms, minute noctilucae, drops of transparent jelly with a threadlike tentacle, up to 25,000 of which have been counted within the space of thirty cubic centimeters. And their light was increased yet more by the peculiar gleam of jellyfish, starfish, aurelia, piddocks and other phosphorescent zoophytes impregnated with that sea foam made from organic matter decomposed by the ocean and perhaps with the mucus secreted by fish.

For several hours the *Nautilus* floated amid these brilliant waters, and our admiration increased at seeing large marine animals playing about in them as if they were fire-eating salamanders. There, surrounded by this fire which does not burn, I saw elegant fast porpoises—those tireless clowns of the sea—and ten-foot-long sailfishes—those heralds of hurricanes—whose formidable swords occasionally struck the window of the lounge. And we also saw smaller creatures: various kinds of triggerfish, jumping scombroidea, wolf fish and a hundred others who left dark streaks in the luminous water.

We were enchanted by this dazzling spectacle. Was some atmospheric condition increasing the intensity of this phenomenon? Was some storm raging on the surface? If so, the *Nautilus* felt none of its fury ten or twenty feet below; it merely rested peacefully in the midst of calm waters.

Thus our trip continued, continually producing new marvels to excite our wonder. Conseil would observe and classify his zoophytes, articulata, mollusks and fish. The days went by quickly; I no longer even counted them. Ned, as usual, tried to find ways to vary the diet on board. We were like snails—we had become adapted to our shells, and I can state from experience that it is easy to become a perfect snail.

So our existence seemed easy and natural, and we no longer thought about another kind of life on land. Then something took place which reminded us of the strange situation we were in.

On January 18, the *Nautilus* was at 105° E. Long. and 15° S. Lat. The weather was menacing, the sea rough and wavy. A strong east wind was blowing. The barometer had been dropping for several days, and it now told us that a struggle of the elements was soon to come.

I had gone up on the platform just as the first mate was taking our position. As usual, I waited to hear the daily phrase repeated. But that day it was replaced by another, no less incomprehensible. Captain Nemo appeared almost at once, and with a telescope began observing something on the horizon.

For several minutes the captain remained immobile. Then he lowered his telescope and exchanged a dozen or so words with the first mate. The latter seemed in the throes of some emotion he was vainly trying to contain. But Captain Nemo, having more self-control, remained cool. Moreover, he seemed to be making objections, while the first mate was trying to assure him of something. Or at least, that is what I gathered from the conversation, by their various tones and gestures.

As for me, I looked carefully in the same direction and saw nothing. The sky and sea met along the horizon in an absolutely clear, unbroken line.

Nevertheless, Captain Nemo paced up and down the platform without looking at me, perhaps without even seeing me. His step was firm, but less regular than usual. He would occasionally stop, cross his arms and look out to sea. What could he be looking for in that vast space? The *Nautilus* was several hundred miles from the nearest coast!

Then the first mate would take up his telescope again, look obstinately at the horizon and also pace up and down, stamping his foot, obviously much more nervous than his commander.

But I felt this mystery would soon be cleared up, for on Captain Nemo's orders the ship increased its speed.

Just then, the first mate again drew the captain's attention to something. The latter stopped his pacing and pointed his telescope at the place indicated. He looked through it for a long time. All this intrigued me immensely, and so I went down to the lounge to get a very powerful telescope I often used. Then, leaning it on the searchlight housing which rose up on the forward part of the platform, I got ready to scan the entire horizon.

But I had not yet gotten it up to my eye when the telescope was abruptly snatched out of my hands.

I turned around. Captain Nemo was standing before me, but I scarcely recognized him. He wore such a frown that I could scarcely see his sullenly flashing eyes. His set jaw, rigid body, clenched fists and bowed head showed that his entire frame was in the grip of violent anger. He did not move. My telescope had fallen from his hand and rolled toward his feet. Had I, without meaning to, provoked this anger? Did this strange person imagine I had uncovered some secret forbidden to passengers of the *Nautilus*?

No, I was not the object of his hatred, for he wasn't even looking at me. His gaze remained fixed on that invisible point on the horizon.

Then Captain Nemo once again regained his usual composure and calm. He spoke several words to the first mate in their strange language, and then turning toward me—"Monsieur Aronnax," he said in a commanding tone of voice, "I'm going to ask you to carry out part of our bargain."

"What do you want me to do, Captain?"

"You must allow yourself to be locked up along with your companions until I decide you can be set free again."

"I have no choice," I answered, looking at him fixedly. "But could I ask you just one question?"

"No, Monsieur."

After such an answer, arguing was out of the question. I could only obey. Resistance would have been impossible.

I went down to the cabin occupied by Ned Land and Conseil, and told them about the captain's decision. I leave the reader to imagine how the Canadian received this piece of news. But there was no time for explanations. Four members of the crew were waiting at the door, and they took us to the cell in which we had spent our first night on board the *Nautilus*.

Ned Land tried to protest, but the only answer he got was to have the door closed in his face.

"Could Monsieur tell us what this is all about?" asked Conseil.

I told my companions what had happened. They were as astonished as I, and knew just as little.

I became lost in thought, and could not forget the strange worried look on Captain Nemo's face. But I was unable to make two logical ideas follow one another, and I was getting involved in the most absurd thoughts, when I was pulled from my reverie by Ned Land.

"Look! Here's our lunch!"

And indeed the table was all set. It was obvious that Captain Nemo had ordered this to be done at the same time he had told the crew to increase the *Nautilus'* speed.

"With Monsieur's permission," said Conseil, "I would like to make a recommendation."

"Yes, my boy," I replied.

"Well, it would be best if Monsieur ate, for we don't know what might happen."

"You're right, Conseil."

"But this is the same food we get every day," complained Ned Land.

"Yes, but what would you have said, Ned," asked Conseil, "if they hadn't given us any lunch at all!"

There was nothing the harpooner could say to that.

We sat down and started in. The meal passed in comparative silence. I ate little. Conseil, with his usual prudence, forced himself to eat something. Ned Land was the only one who hadn't lost his appetite. After we had finished, each of us went to rest in a corner of the room.

Just then the light went out, leaving us in complete darkness. Ned Land was soon asleep, and surprisingly enough, it was not long before Conseil was also in a deep slumber. I was wondering what had brought on this extraordinary need to sleep, when I felt my brain becoming more and more drowsy. In spite of all my efforts to keep them open, my eyes slowly closed. A painful suspicion crossed my mind. Some sleeping powder had obviously been mixed with the food we had just eaten! Imprisonment was therefore not enough to keep us from knowing about Captain Nemo's doings—we had to be put to sleep too!

I could hear the hatches closing. The gentle rocking motion of the ship stopped. Had the *Nautilus* left the surface? Had it gone down to deeper, calmer waters?

I tried to fight off my drowsiness, but it was impossible. My breathing grew feebler, and I felt as if a mortal cold were creeping up my almost paralyzed limbs. My eyelids closed like lead weights. I fell into a morbid sleep, full of hallucinations. Then the visions disappeared and left me completely unconscious.

CHAPTER XXIV
The Coral Kingdom

The next day I awoke feeling surprisingly clearheaded. To my great astonishment, I was in my cabin. My companions had undoubtedly been brought back to theirs while they too were unconscious. They would know no more than I of what had gone on during the night, and I could only count on chance future events to unveil this mystery.

I thought of leaving my room. Was I free again or still a prisoner? I was completely free! I opened the door and went down the corridor to the central companionway. The hatches, which had been closed the day before, were now open. I went out onto the platform.

Ned Land and Conseil were waiting for me. I questioned them. They knew nothing. They too had slept soundly, and had been equally surprised to wake up in their cabin.

As for the *Nautilus,* it seemed to be as calm and mysterious as ever. It was cruising on the surface at a moderate speed. Nothing seemed to have changed on board.

Ned Land scanned the ocean with his sharp eyes. It was deserted. The Canadian could see nothing on the horizon, neither sail nor land. A strong west wind was blowing, and long whitecaps were making the ship roll considerably.

After renewing its air supply, the *Nautilus* dove and then cruised at a depth of about fifty feet, so that it could surface again quickly. And this was done several times during that day of January 19, completely contrary to the usual practice on board. The first mate would then go up to the platform, and the usual phrase would reverberate inside the ship.

As for Captain Nemo, he did not appear. Of the other people on board, I saw only the poker-faced steward, who served me with his usual efficiency and silence.

At about two o'clock I was in the lounge classifying my notes when the door opened and Captain Nemo entered. I bowed. He answered with an almost imperceptible bow, without saying a word. I went back to work, hoping he would give me some sort of explanation about what had happened the night before. But he did nothing of the kind. I looked at him. His face looked tired; I could tell from his red eyes that he had not slept; his whole countenance showed deep sorrow and regret. He paced back and forth, sat down, got up, took up a book, put it down, checked his instruments without taking his usual notes, and in short, seemed unable to stay in one place for a single moment.

Finally he came over to me and said: "Are you a doctor, Monsieur Aronnax?"

This question was so unexpected that I looked at him for a moment without answering.

"Are you a doctor?" he repeated. "Several of your colleagues have studied medicine—Gratiolet, Moquin-Tandon and others."

"Yes," I said, "I am a doctor. I practiced for several years before starting my work in the Paris museum."

"Good."

My answer had evidently satisfied Captain Nemo. But I had no idea what it was all about, and I waited for more questions before saying anything else.

"Monsieur Aronnax," said the captain, "would you mind treating one of my men?"

"Is somebody sick on board?"

"Yes."

"All right, I'll do it."

"Come."

I admit my heart was beating fast. I don't know why, but I felt there was a connection between the illness of a crew member and the events of the night before, and this mystery preoccupied me as much as the sick man himself.

Captain Nemo led me to the rear of the *Nautilus*, into a cabin next to the crew's quarters.

There, stretched out on a bed, lay a man of about forty with a strongly molded face—a true Anglo-Saxon type.

I leaned over him. It was not a disease he had—but a wound. His head, wrapped in bloodstained bandages, was resting on two pillows. I removed these bandages and the wounded man let me do it without uttering a single word of complaint, merely staring into space with a blank look in his eyes.

The wound was horrible. The skull had been smashed by a blunt instrument, and the brain, which was exposed, had suffered considerable abrasions. Within this dissolving mass, blood clots had formed and turned to the color of wine dregs. He had received both a concussion and contusion of the brain. His breathing was slow, and occasional spasmodic movements would contort the muscles of his face. His brain was working more and more sluggishly, bringing on paralysis of feeling and movement.

I took his pulse. It was intermittent. His limbs were already turning cold, and I saw that death was approaching without my being able to do a thing about it. I dressed the poor man's wound, readjusted the bandages on his head and turned to Captain Nemo.

"How did he get this wound?" I asked.

"What difference does it make!" he answered evasively. "A collision of the *Nautilus* broke one of the levers in the engine room, and it struck him on the head. But what do you think of his condition?"

I hesitated to say what I thought.

"You can talk freely," the captain said. "He doesn't understand French."

I looked once more at the wounded man, then answered: "He'll be dead within two hours."

"Nothing can save him?"

"Nothing."

Captain Nemo clenched his fists and several tears appeared in his eyes—eyes which I would have thought incapable of crying.

For several more minutes I observed the dying man as life left him little by little. He seemed even paler beneath the electric light bathing his deathbed. I looked at his intelligent face, prematurely lined probably through sorrow or misery. I hoped to discover the secret of his life in whatever last words might escape from his lips!

"You may go now, Monsieur Aronnax," said Captain Nemo.

I left the captain with the dying man and returned to my cabin very moved by the scene I had just witnessed. Throughout the entire day I felt sinister forebodings. That night I slept badly, and between frequently interrupted dreams, I thought I could hear far-off moans and a kind of funeral singing. Was it the prayer for the dead, murmured in that language I could not understand?

The next morning I went up on deck. Captain Nemo was already there. As soon as he saw me he came over and said:

"Professor, would you like to make another underwater excursion today?"

"With my companions?" I asked.

"If they would like to."

"We're at your orders, Captain."

"Then would you please go change into your diving suits."

There was no mention of the man who was dying or already dead. I went and rejoined Ned Land and Conseil. I told them about Captain Nemo's invitation. Conseil was eager to accept, and this time, the Canadian also seemed anxious to go along.

It was eight in the morning. At eight-thirty we were all dressed for this new excursion, and each of us had been given an air tank and an electric lamp. The double door was opened and we stepped out, along with Captain Nemo and a dozen members of the crew—at a depth of thirty feet—onto the solid bottom on which the *Nautilus* was resting.

A gentle slope led down to a rough bottom at a depth of about ninety feet. The terrain here was completely different from that I had seen during my first excursion beneath the Pacific. Here there was no fine sand, no underwater prairies, no marine forest. I immediately recognized this marvelous region into which Captain Nemo was leading us. It was the coral kingdom.

Within the phylum of zoophytes and the class of Alcyonaria, there is the order of Gorgonaria which contains the three divisions of Gorgoniae, Isidae and Coralliae. It is in this last group that coral belongs—that curious substance which was first classified in the mineral, then in the vegetable and finally in the animal kingdom. To the ancients it was a medicine, and to moderns it is jewelry; but it was only in 1694 that Peysonnel from Marseilles finally classified it within the animal kingdom.

Coral is a group of microscopic animals gathered on a brittle, rocklike poly-pary. These polyps—which produce these little creatures by a kind of sprout-ing process and therefore provide their sole means of growth—not only partake of this communal existence, but also have a life of their own. This is therefore a kind of natural socialism. I was familiar with the latest work that had been done on this strange zoophyte which, as naturalists have pointed out, slowly petrifies into treelike shapes. Nothing, therefore, could have been more inter-esting for me than to visit one of the petrified forests that nature had planted beneath the sea.

After turning on our Ruhmkorff lamps, we followed a coral bed which was in the process of formation and which, with the help of time, would one day close off this portion of the Indian Ocean. Our path was bordered with thickly tangled shrubs covered by little flowers with star-shaped white lines.

The light produced a thousand charming effects as it played about among these brightly colored branches. I thought I could see these tissuelike cylindri-cal tubes tremble beneath the wavy motion of the water. Small, fast fish would dart past like flocks of birds. I was tempted to pick the coral's fresh flowers and delicate tentacles, some of which had just blossomed and others scarcely yet opened. But if my hand drew near these living, sensitive flowers, an alarm would immediately spread throughout the colony. The white blossoms would dart inside their red cases and vanish from sight; the shrub would change into a block of stony bulges.

Quite by chance I came across the most precious of all corals. It was as valuable as the kind taken from the Mediterranean off the shores of France, Italy and North Africa. Its lively colors have justified the poetic names it has received in commerce: *red coral, blood coral* and *blood foam.* This kind of coral is sold for as much as fifty dollars a pound and here there was enough of it to make hundreds of coral fishermen rich. This precious substance, often mixed with other polyparies, formed compact inseparable groups called "macciota," and on them I noticed marvelous specimens of pink coral.

But soon the shrubs began to grow closer together and the treelike formations taller. Veritable petrified copses opened up before us covered with shapes like girders of some fantastic architecture. Captain Nemo entered a dark gallery which sloped gently down and brought us to a depth of three hundred feet. The light from our lamps would occasionally produce magical effects as it reflected off these sharp rugged natural arches and off the formations hanging down from above like chandeliers, making them sparkle like dots of fire. Between these coral shrubs I noticed other no less peculiar polyps: melites, iris and corallina, some green and others red, species of seaweed which become encrusted with calcareous salts and which naturalists, after long discussions, have finally classified in the vegetable kingdom. But as one scientist put it, this is perhaps the point where life rises from its stony sleep, without yet detaching itself from its crude point of departure.

Finally, after walking for two hours, we had reached a depth of around a thousand feet, that is to say, the extreme limit at which coral begins to form. But here there were no more isolated bushes or low clumps of trees; we were now in an immense forest made of enormous mineral plantlike formations—huge petrified trees connected by garlands of those elegant, magnificently colored underwater vines called plumularia. We passed freely beneath their high branches lost in the shadows of the deep, while beneath our feet organ-pipe corals, brain corals, star corals, fungiae and cariophylli formed a carpet of flowers studded with dazzling jewels.

What an indescribable spectacle! Oh, if we had only been able to talk to one another! Why did we have to be imprisoned beneath this mask of metal and glass! Why couldn't we be like fish, or better yet like amphibians who can live under and above water, according to where their fancy takes them.

In the meanwhile Captain Nemo had stopped. My companions and I also came to a halt, and as I turned around, I could see the crew forming a half circle around their commander. A closer look showed me that four of them were carrying an oblong object on their shoulders.

We were standing in the midst of a vast clearing surrounded by the high tree-like formations of the underwater forest. Our lamps gave off a kind of twilight, making long shadows on the ground. But at the edge of this clearing the darkness became almost total and was broken only by the tiny sparks given off from the live coral ridges.

Ned Land and Conseil were next to me. As we watched, it occurred to me that we were going to witness a strange scene. I looked at the ground and noticed that in certain places there were regularly shaped mounds that betrayed the hand of man.

In the middle of the clearing, on a pedestal of crudely piled-up rocks, stood a coral cross with its long arms looking as if they were made of petrified blood.

At a sign from Captain Nemo, one of the men stepped forward, took a pick from his belt and began digging a hole several feet from the cross.

Suddenly I understood! This clearing was a graveyard; this hole, a tomb; and that oblong object, the body of the man who had died in the night! Captain Nemo and his men were coming to bury their companion in this resting place on the inaccessible ocean floor!

My mind had never been so stirred! Never had such staggering thoughts invaded my brain! I did not want to see what my eyes could not help seeing!

Meanwhile the grave was slowly being dug. Fish scurried here and there as their retreat was disturbed. I could hear the pick resounding against the hard ground, occasionally shooting out a spark as it struck some piece of flint lost on the ocean floor. The hole became longer and wider, and soon it was deep enough to receive the body.

Then those carrying it drew near. The body, wrapped in a white byssus cloth, was laid in its watery grave. Captain Nemo and all the friends of the dead man knelt down in an attitude of prayer. . . . My two companions and I bowed our heads devoutly.

The grave was then covered with the rubble previously dug out, thus forming a small mound.

When this had been done, Captain Nemo and his men got up again; then, going over to the grave, they knelt once more and all stretched out their hands as a last farewell. . . .

Then the funeral procession started on its way back to the *Nautilus*, again passing beneath the forest arches, through thickets and next to coral shrubs.

Finally we could make out the lights on board. Their rays guided us to the ship itself. At one o'clock we were all back.

As soon as I had changed my clothes, I went up on the platform with my mind full of all sorts of obsessive ideas. I went and sat next to the searchlight housing.

Captain Nemo joined me. I got up and said: "So this man died during the night, as I had predicted?"

"Yes, Monsieur Aronnax," answered Captain Nemo.

"And now he's lying next to his companions in the coral graveyard?"

"Yes, forgotten by the rest of the world, but not by us! We have dug the grave, and now the polyps will take charge of sealing it for eternity!"

The captain buried his face in his hands, vainly trying to repress a sob. He then added: "That is our peaceful cemetery, several hundred feet beneath the surface of the ocean!"

"At least there, Captain, your dead can sleep quietly, beyond the reach of sharks!"

"Yes," Captain Nemo replied gravely, "beyond the reach of sharks and of men!"

PART TWO

What an indescribable spectacle!

CHAPTER XXV
The Indian Ocean

We now come to the second part of our journey under the sea. The first ended with that moving scene in the coral graveyard which made such a deep impression on me. It made me realize that not only did Captain Nemo spend his entire life within the world's vast oceans, but he had even prepared his grave in one of its most impenetrable depths. There, no sea monster would trouble the last sleep of the *Nautilus'* crew, of those friends bound together in death as well as in life! Nor would any men disturb them, as the captain had added.

He always showed this same fierce, implacable hatred of human society.

As for me, I was no longer satisfied by Conseil's theories. He still felt that the commander of the *Nautilus* was merely one of those unrecognized scientists full of contempt for a world which has treated them with such indifference. He still thought of him as a misunderstood genius who had been deceived by life on earth and therefore taken refuge in an inaccessible region where his instincts could have free play. But to my way of thinking, this theory only explained one side of Captain Nemo.

In fact, the mysterious events of the previous night—our being imprisoned and put to sleep, the violence with which the captain had snatched the telescope from my hands, and the man mortally wounded by some inexplicable collision of the *Nautilus*—all this made me look for other answers. No, Captain Nemo was not merely content to flee the company of men! His formidable ship was not only used to give him the freedom he wanted, but also to wreak some terrible revenge!

At the moment I could see nothing clearly, just vague glimmers of light in the darkness; but right now I must limit myself to describing my thoughts as they were slowly formed by succeeding events.

Nothing bound us to Captain Nemo. He knew it was impossible to escape from the *Nautilus*. We had not promised to remain on board. We were merely captives, prisoners whom he called guests just for the sake of politeness. All the same, Ned Land had not given up hope of regaining his freedom. He was certain to take advantage of the first opportunity presented him, and I would undoubtedly do the same. And yet, I could not have gone without a certain feeling of regret, for the captain had been so generous in letting me share the *Nautilus'* secrets! And in addition, was this man to be hated or admired? Was he a martyr or an executioner? Also, to be perfectly frank, before leaving him forever I wanted to finish this underwater journey around the world which had already begun so splendidly. I wanted to see all the marvels contained in the earth's oceans. I wanted to see what no man had seen before, even though I might have to pay with my life for my insatiable curiosity! What had I seen till then? Nothing, or almost nothing, for we had so far only traveled six thousand leagues across the Pacific.

But I knew only too well that the *Nautilus* was sailing toward inhabited lands, and that if some chance of escaping arose, it would be cruel to spoil things for my companions merely because of my passionate curiosity for the unknown. I would have to follow them, perhaps even lead them. But would we ever get this opportunity? The ordinary man in me, deprived of his free will, longed for such an occasion; but the scientist in me dreaded it.

At noon of that day—January 21, 1868—the first mate came out on deck to take our position. I went up on the platform, lit a cigar and watched him carry out his task. It seemed clear that he did not understand French, for I made several remarks which, if he had understood me, would have evoked some reaction; but he remained impassive and silent.

While he was looking through his sextant, one of the sailors of the *Nautilus*—that powerful man who had accompanied us on our first underwater excursion to Crespo Island—came to clean the windows around the compartment containing the light. I took this opportunity to examine it. It contained lenses which, as in lighthouses, increased its strength a hundredfold and sent its light out in the desired direction. This electrical device had been constructed so as to give every possible bit of light. It worked in a vacuum, which gave it both regularity and strength. This vacuum also saved the graphite points between which ran the electric arc, and this was an important economy for Captain Nemo, for he could not easily have replaced them. In this manner they scarcely suffered any wear at all.

When the *Nautilus* was about to dive again, I went back down to the lounge. The hatches were closed, and our course set due west.

We were then traveling through the Indian Ocean, that vast liquid plain which covers an area of 2,125,000 square miles and whose waters are so clear that anyone looking down through their surface gets a feeling of vertigo. The *Nautilus* generally cruised at a depth between three and six hundred feet. We went on like this for several days. For anybody but me, with my great love of the sea, the hours would have seemed long and monotonous; but my daily walks on the platform where I soaked up the bracing sea air, the spectacle of these rich waters through the glass panels of the lounge, the reading of the books in the library and the drawing up of my notes used all my time and left me not a single moment of boredom or weariness.

All of us remained in perfect health. The food on board seemed to agree with us marvelously, and as for me, I could easily have done without the variations Ned Land managed to bring on board in a spirit of protest. Moreover, living at such a constant temperature, we did not even have to worry about catching colds. Besides, that madreporaria Dendrophyllia, known in the south of France as "sea fennel" and of which there was a certain stock on board, would have made an excellent medicine against coughs.

For several days, we saw a great quantity of gulls. Some were very skillfully shot, and cooked in a special way, furnished a very agreeable dish of sea game. Among the birds which stay far from any land and rest on the surface of the ocean when they are tired from flying, I saw some magnificent albatross (which belong to the family of the Longipennes) with their harsh cry which sounds like a donkey braying. The family of the Totipalmatae was represented by fast-flying petrels, which are so quick at catching fish swimming near the surface, and by numerous phaethons or tropic birds, and especially the red-striped phaethon, which is about the size of a pigeon and whose white body feathers shaded with pink contrast sharply with its black wings.

The *Nautilus'* nets brought in several kinds of sea turtles, mainly hawkbills with their rounded backs and highly prized shells. These reptiles can dive easily and stay under water a long time merely by closing the valve situated at the end of their nasal passages. Several of these hawkbills were still asleep inside their shells when we captured them: this is the way they can rest and remain protected from attack by other ocean animals. The flesh of these turtles is not too good, but their eggs make an exquisite dish.

As for fish, they called forth our greatest admiration when the mystery of their underwater life was unveiled through the open panels of the lounge. I noticed several species which I had not yet been able to observe.

I will mention mainly the trunkfishes peculiar to the Red Sea, the Indian Ocean and the waters of equatorial South America. These fish—like turtles, armadillos, sea urchins and shellfish—have a covering which is neither chalky nor stony, but made of true bone. Sometimes it is shaped like a triangle and sometimes like a square. Among the triangular variety, I noted some about two inches long with a brown tail and yellow fins, whose flesh is not only exquisite but very healthy; I recommend that these fish be acclimatized to fresh water, a change which many salt-water fish can undergo with little difficulty. I also saw square trunkfish with four large bumps on their backs; trunkfish with white dots on the bellies, which can be tamed like birds; trigoniae armed with spines formed by an extension of their bony shell and whose strange grunting sound has earned them the name of "sea pigs"; and then dromedary fish, with their large conical humps, whose flesh is tough and leathery.

In Conseil's daily notes, I also noticed certain fish of the genus Tetraodon peculiar to these waters: spenglerians with a red back and white chest which can be recognized by their three longitudinal rows of filaments; and electric tetraodons seven inches long and very brightly colored. Then, among other genera, there were ovoids which looked like a brownish-black egg and had white stripes and no tail; porcupine fish covered with spines and capable of blowing themselves up till they formed a spiked ball; sea horses, common to all oceans; flying pegasi with their long snout, whose very large wing-shaped pectoral fins permit them, if not to fly, at least to jump up into the air; macrognathae with long jaws—splendid fish ten inches long and brilliantly colored; pale dragonets with their round heads; myriads of jumping blennies with black stripes and long pectoral fins, dashing along the surface at tremendous speed; delicious velifera, who can raise their fins and use them like sails to catch favorable currents; magnificent kurtidae, on whom nature has lavished yellow, sky blue, silver and gold; trichoptera with their wings made of filaments; miller's-thumbs with their lemon-colored spots, making slight hissing noises; gurnards, whose liver is considered poisonous; greenlings with mobile flaps over their eyes; and finally bellows fish with their long tubelike snouts, true flycatchers of the sea, armed as they are with a gun unequaled by Chassepots or Remingtons which kills insects merely by striking them with a drop of water.

In the eighty-ninth genus of fish (according to Lacépède's classification) and belonging to the second subclass of bony fish characterized by a gill cover and a bronchial membrane, I noticed a scorpion fish, whose head is armed with spines and which has only one dorsal fin; these are with or without scales depending on their subgenus. The second subgenus gave us specimens of didactyla twelve to sixteen inches long, with yellow stripes and a fantastically shaped head. As for the first subgenus, it furnished us with several specimens of that strange fish called the "anglerfish" which has a large head covered with ridges and bumps. It has spines all over its body along with two irregular and hideous horns, its body and tail are covered with calluses and its sting can inflict a serious wound; it is a repulsive and horrible fish.

From the twenty-first to the twenty-third of January the *Nautilus* traveled 250 leagues (540 miles), or in other words it averaged twenty-two knots. During this time we saw many kinds of fish which were attracted by the electric light and which tried to follow alongside; most of them, though, were soon outdistanced by the *Nautilus,* but some managed to remain next to us for quite a time.

On the morning of the twenty-fourth we sighted the Keeling Islands at 12° 5' S. Lat. and 94° 33' E. Long. These coral formations with their magnificent coconut trees had been visited by both Darwin and Captain Fitzroy. The *Nautilus* sailed in close to the reefs surrounding these deserted islands. Its dredges brought up many specimens of polyps and echinoderms along with strange shells from the subkingdom of the mollusks. Several precious shells of the species delphinula were added to Captain Nemo's collection, and I also added a spotted astraea, a kind of parasitical polypary often attached to a shell.

But soon the Keeling Islands disappeared beneath the horizon, and our course was set to the northwest, toward the tip of the Indian peninsula.

"Civilization!" Ned Land said to me one day. "It's certainly better than New Guinea where there are more savages than deer! In India, Professor, there are roads, railroads and towns with Englishmen, Frenchmen and Hindus. Why you wouldn't have to walk more than five miles to meet a fellow countryman. What do you say? Isn't it about time to part company with Captain Nemo?"

"No, Ned," I said in a firm tone of voice. "Let's let things ride. The *Nautilus* is going toward the inhabited parts of the globe. It's heading for Europe—why don't we let it take us there. Once we're in our own waters, then we'll see what we can do. Besides, I don't imagine that Captain Nemo will allow us to go hunting on the coasts of Malabar or Coromandel the way we did in New Guinea."

"Well then, Monsieur, why can't we do without his permission?"

I did not answer the Canadian. I wanted no arguments. Also, at heart I wanted to make full use of the stroke of fate which had thrown me aboard the *Nautilus*.

After leaving the Keeling Islands, we traveled at a slower speed and often very capriciously, often diving very deep for no apparent reason. Using the ship's side fins we occasionally reached depths of one or two miles, but without ever attaining the bottom of the Indian Ocean, which soundings of 42,500 feet have not been able to reach. As for the temperature at these lower depths, the thermometer read a constant 39°. I did however notice that the upper layers of the sea were always colder in shallow water than in the open ocean.

On January 25, the sea was completely deserted and the *Nautilus* spent the day on the surface, with its powerful propeller striking the water and making it shoot up to great heights. (This was undoubtedly one of the factors that made people think it was a giant whale.) I spent most of the day on the platform looking at the ocean. Nothing appeared on the horizon until about four o'clock when I saw a long steamer off to the west heading in the opposite direction. Its masts were visible for a moment, but it couldn't have seen the *Nautilus* which lay so flat in the water. I thought to myself that this steamship probably belonged to the Peninsular and Oriental Company, which runs between Ceylon and Sydney, touching at King George Sound and Melbourne.

At five in the afternoon, just before the rapid twilight which binds day to night in the tropics, Conseil and I witnessed a strange and marvelous sight.

There is a charming animal which the ancients said it was good luck to meet. Aristotle, Athenaeus, Pliny and Oppian studied its habits and described it with all the poetry of Greece and Rome. They called it the nautilus or the pompylius, whereas nowadays it is called the argonaut.

Anyone consulting Conseil would have learned from this worthy fellow that the subkingdom of the mollusks is divided into five classes; that the first of these classes, that of the cephalopods, which are sometimes naked and sometimes covered with a shell, comprises two families—the Dibranchiata and the Tetrabranchiata, distinguished by the number of gill plumes they have; that the family of the Dibranchiata includes three genera, the argonaut, the squid and the sepia, and that the family of the Tetrabranchiata only contains one, the nautilus. After this explanation, it would be inexcusable for anyone to confuse the argonaut, which is *acetabuliferous,* that is to say equipped with siphons, and the nautilus, which is *tentaculiferous,* or in other words equipped with tentacles.

It was a school of these argonauts which was just then traveling along the surface. We could make out several hundred, and they belonged to a species which only exists in the Indian Ocean.

These graceful mollusks move backward by breathing water in and then squirting it out through a tube. Of their eight tentacles, six, long and thin, were floating in the water, while the other two, rounded and palm-shaped, were held up in the wind like small sails. I could clearly make out their wavy, spiraled shells which Cuvier so justly compared to elegant longboats. And the shell really is like a boat, for the animal inside does not adhere to this shell he has made.

"An argonaut is free to leave his shell," I said to Conseil, "but he never does."

"Just like Captain Nemo," Conseil wisely answered. "Perhaps he would have done better to call his ship the *Argonaut*."

For about an hour the *Nautilus* cruised amid this school of mollusks. Then suddenly they were seized by some kind of fear. As if at a signal, all the sails were taken down, all the tentacles pulled in, the bodies contracted and the shells turned over to alter their center of gravity; then the entire flotilla disappeared beneath the surface. It was instantaneous, and no naval squadron could have maneuvered with greater precision.

Just then night came on, and the little waves brought on by the breeze died down peacefully around the *Nautilus*.

On the next day, January 26, we crossed the equator at the eighty-second meridian and re-entered the Northern Hemisphere.

During the entire day, a formidable school of sharks followed the ship. That part of the world abounds in these terrible animals which make the seas so dangerous. There were Port Jackson sharks with a brown back and whitish belly, armed with eleven rows of teeth; eyed sharks, whose neck has a large black spot encircled in white and resembling an eye; Isabelle sharks with a rounded snout covered with dark dots. Often these powerful animals would rush at the glass panels of the lounge with such violence as to make me very nervous. Ned Land was beside himself. He wanted the submarine to surface and give him a chance to harpoon these monsters. He was particularly excited by several dogfish whose mouths were lined with teeth arranged like a mosaic, and some large tiger sharks fifteen feet long. But soon the *Nautilus* increased its speed and quickly outdistanced the fastest of these sharks.

On January 27, off the entrance to the vast Bay of Bengal, we several times came across a very grim sight—cadavers floating on the surface. They were the dead from Indian villages who had been carried out to sea by the Ganges, and whom the vultures, the country's only morticians, had not finished devouring. But there was no lack of sharks to help them in their grisly task.

Toward seven in the evening, the *Nautilus* cruised half submerged through a whitish sea. As far as one could see the ocean seemed to be made of milk. Was it some effect of the moon's rays? No, for the new moon was still hidden from sight beneath the horizon. Although the sky was lit up by light from the stars, it seemed black by contrast with the whiteness of the water.

Conseil couldn't believe his eyes, and he asked me what caused this strange phenomenon. Fortunately I was able to give him an answer.

"That's what is called a milk sea," I said; "it takes place off the coasts of Amboina and in these waters."

"But could Monsieur tell me," asked Conseil, "what produces such an effect, for I can't imagine that the water's actually been changed into milk!"

"No, my boy, this whiteness is due to the presence of myriads of tiny creatures like little luminous worms with jellylike, colorless bodies about the thickness of a hair and less than a hundredth of an inch in length. These creatures sometimes attach themselves to one another over a distance of several miles."

"Several miles!" cried Conseil.

"Yes, my boy, and don't try and figure out how many that would take! You won't be able to, for if I'm not mistaken, some sailors have traveled over these milk seas for forty miles."

I don't know if Conseil paid any attention to my advice, but he became lost in thought, undoubtedly trying to calculate how many creatures a hundredth of an inch in length could be contained in a space forty miles square. As for me I continued observing the phenomenon. For several hours, the *Nautilus* sailed through this white expanse, and I noticed that it slipped through this soapy water without a sound, as if it were in the midst of one of those frothy eddies sometimes seen between the currents entering and leaving bays.

Toward midnight, the sea once again took on its ordinary color, but behind us, right out to the limits of the horizon, the sky reflected the whiteness of the water and for a long time seemed illuminated by the vague glimmers of an aurora borealis.

CHAPTER XXVI
A New Invitation from Captain Nemo

At noon on February 28, when the *Nautilus* surfaced at 9° 4' N. Lat., we sighted land lying eight miles off to the west. First I noticed a group of mountains rising in very peculiar shapes to a height of about two thousand feet. Once our position had been determined, I went back down to the lounge and looked at the chart. We were off Ceylon, that pearl which hangs below the Indian peninsula.

I went to the library looking for some book on this island (one of the most fertile on earth), and I found one by Sir H. C., Esq. called *Ceylon and the Cingalese*. I went back to the lounge and first of all learned that Ceylon was situated between 5° 55' and 9° 49' N. Lat., and 79° 42' and 82° 4' E. Long. It is 275 miles long and 150 miles wide at its largest point; it is 900 miles in circumference, and 24,448 square miles in area, or in other words, it is a little smaller than Ireland.

Just then Captain Nemo and the first mate appeared.

After taking a look at the chart, Captain Nemo turned toward me and said: "Ceylon is famous for its pearl fisheries. Would you enjoy visiting one of them, Monsieur Aronnax?"

"I certainly would, Captain."

"Fine. It will be easy. But even though we will see the fisheries, we will not see any fishermen. Their season has not begun yet. Never mind. I'll give the order to head for the Gulf of Manaar, where we'll arrive during the night."

The captain said several words to the first mate, who immediately left the room. Soon the *Nautilus* dove, and after a while we could see by the pressure gauge that it was maintaining a depth of a hundred feet.

I looked for the Gulf of Manaar on the chart. I found it along the ninth parallel, off the northwest coast of Ceylon. One side of it was formed by a prolongation of little Manaar Island. In order to get there, we had to travel up the whole western coast of Ceylon.

"Professor," said Captain Nemo, "there are pearl fisheries in the Bay of Bengal, in the Indian Ocean, in the China Sea and the Japan Sea, off America in the Gulf of Panama and the Gulf of California; but the finest pearl fishing is off the coast of Ceylon. However, we'll be arriving a bit early. The fishermen only come to the Gulf of Manaar during the month of March, and then for thirty days their three hundred boats ferret out this treasure of the sea. Each boat has ten men to row and ten to fish. The latter are divided into two groups who take turns diving. They go down as deep as forty feet using a heavy stone they grip with their feet and which is attached to the boat by means of a rope."

"You mean to say," I exclaimed, "that they still use such primitive methods?"

"Yes," answered Captain Nemo, "even though these fisheries belong to the world's most industrious people, the English, who got them by the Treaty of Amiens in eighteen-two."

"But I should think that a diving suit like the ones you have would be very useful for such work."

"Yes, these poor fishermen can't stay under water for long. The Englishman, Perceval, in describing his voyage to Ceylon, mentions a Kaffir who could stay down for five minutes before coming back up to the surface, but I find this hard to believe. I know that some divers can stay down for fifty-seven seconds, and the most skillful for eighty-seven seconds; but they're very rare, and when these poor creatures get back in the boat, bloodstained water pours out of their nose and ears. I think that they can stay down for an average of thirty seconds, and during this time they toss as many pearl oysters as they can grab into a little sack; but generally they don't live long. Their eyes grow weak or become ulcerated, their bodies become covered with sores and sometimes they die of a stroke under water."

"Yes," I said, "it's a sad way to earn a living, and especially when you think it's all done just to satisfy a few people's whims. But tell me, Captain, how many oysters can a boat take in during a day?"

"From forty to fifty thousand. I've even heard it said that in eighteen-fourteen, when the British Government sent out some of its own divers, they brought in seventy-six million oysters in twenty days."

"Do these fishermen at least make a fairly good living?"

"Hardly, Professor. At Panama they earn a dollar a week. Usually they earn a penny for each oyster containing a pearl, and then when you think how many oysters they bring up containing nothing . . ."

"They only make a penny but their employers get rich! That's awful."

"You and your companions will now be able to visit the Manaar beds, Professor," said Captain Nemo, "and if by chance some fisherman is operating out of season, we'll be able to watch him work."

"Fine, Captain."

"By the way, Monsieur Aronnax, are you afraid of sharks?"

"Sharks?" I exclaimed. It struck me as a rather ridiculous question.

"Well?" said Captain Nemo.

"I must admit, Captain, that I've had little experience with this species of fish."

"We on the *Nautilus* are quite accustomed to them," said Captain Nemo, "and after a while you'll get used to them too. Moreover, we'll be armed, and on the way we'll perhaps be able to do a little shark hunting. It's very interesting. We'll see you early tomorrow morning, then, Professor."

After saying this in an offhand manner, Captain Nemo left the room.

If someone invited you to go bear hunting in the Swiss mountains, you would say, "Fine! Tomorrow we'll go bear hunting." If someone invited you to go lion hunting in the Atlas plains or tiger hunting in the jungles of India, you would say, "Ah-hah! It looks as if we're going tiger (or lion) hunting!" But if someone asked you to go hunting sharks in their own element, you would perhaps want to think it over for a minute or two before accepting.

As for me, I passed my hand over my forehead and found I had broken out in a cold sweat.

"Let's take our time," I said to myself, "and give this matter a little thought. It was one thing hunting sea otters in underwater forests as we did off Crespo

Island. But it's something else again walking over the ocean floor when you're almost sure to meet sharks! I know perfectly well that in certain countries, particularly the Andaman Islands, the Negroes don't hesitate to attack sharks with a dagger in one hand and a noose in the other, but I also know that many of them don't come back alive! Besides, I'm not a Negro, and even if I were, I might be a bit nervous about doing something like this."

So there I was, daydreaming about sharks capable of cutting a man in two with their row upon row of teeth. I could already feel a pain in my side. In addition, I was disturbed by the offhand way the captain had invited me. He had said it as if we were going to hunt harmless foxes in some forest!

"Well," I thought, "Conseil wouldn't think of going, and that way I'll be able to get out of accompanying the captain."

As for Ned Land, I wasn't as sure how he would take the news. However great a danger might be, it always appealed to his combative nature.

I again took up the book on Ceylon, but I could not concentrate on it. Between the lines I kept seeing terrifying, wide-open jaws.

Just then, Conseil and the Canadian entered looking calm and happy. They didn't know what was waiting for them.

"Goodness me, Monsieur," said Ned Land, "that darned Captain Nemo of yours just made us a very pleasant proposition."

"Oh!" I said. "So you know . . ."

"With Monsieur's permission," answered Conseil, "the commander of the *Nautilus* has invited us to visit, along with Monsieur, the magnificent Ceylonese pearl fisheries. He asked us very politely and acted like a true gentleman."

"Did he tell you anything else?"

"No, Monsieur," answered the Canadian, "except that he had already spoken to you about this little excursion."

"That's right," I said. "But he didn't go into the matter of . . ."

"No, Professor. You'll be coming with us, won't you?"

"Me . . . oh yes! I see you like the idea, Ned."

"Yes, it might be very interesting."

"And maybe dangerous," I said in an insinuating tone of voice.

"Dangerous!" replied Ned Land, "a mere excursion in an oyster bed!"

Obviously Captain Nemo had not felt it was necessary to tell my companions about the sharks. As for me, I couldn't help feeling worried as I looked at them, as if they were already missing some limb. Should I warn them? Undoubtedly I should have, but I didn't know how to go about it.

"Would Monsieur," said Conseil, "give us some information on pearl fishing?"

"On the fishing itself," I asked, "or on the incidents which. . . ?"

"On the fishing itself," replied the Canadian. "It's always best not to be completely ignorant of something you're about to do."

"Well then, sit down, my friends, and I'll tell you everything I've just learned from a book on Ceylon and the Cingalese."

Ned and Conseil sat down on a couch, and the first thing the Canadian asked was: "Monsieur, just what is a pearl?"

"Ned," I answered, "to the poet, a pearl is an ocean tear; to Orientals it is a drop of hardened dew; to women it is an oblong jewel with a glassy sheen which they wear on their finger, around their neck or on their ear; to the chemist it is a mixture of calcium phosphate and calcium carbonate with a bit of gelatin; and finally to the naturalist it is merely an abnormal secretion from the same organ which produces mother-of-pearl in certain bivalves."

"Subkingdom of mollusks," said Conseil, "class of Acephala, order of Testacea."

"That's right, Conseil. Now among these Testacea, the abalones, turbos, tridacnae and pinnae marinae—or in other words all those which secrete mother-of-pearl, that blue, violet or white substance which coats the inside of their valves—are capable of producing pearls."

"Can mussels produce them too?" asked the Canadian.

"Yes, the mussels of certain rivers in Scotland, Wales, Ireland, Saxony, Bohemia and France sometimes produce pearls."

"I see," replied the Canadian.

"But," I continued, "the mollusk that produces the vast majority of the world's pearls is the pearl oyster, *Meleagrina margaritifera*. And a pearl is nothing but mother-of-pearl that has formed into the shape of a ball. It either sticks to the oyster's shell or becomes loosely embedded in his flesh. It always starts from some tiny hard object, a sterile egg or a grain of sand, over which a coating of mother-of-pearl is built up in thin, concentric layers over a period of several years."

"Is more than one pearl ever found in an oyster?" asked Conseil.

"Yes, my boy. Some oysters are veritable jewel boxes. I've even read of an oyster—but I can hardly believe it—which contained no less than a hundred and fifty sharks."

"A hundred and fifty sharks!" cried Ned Land.

"Did I say sharks?" I cried. "I meant to say a hundred and fifty pearls. It wouldn't make any sense to say sharks."

"It certainly wouldn't," said Conseil. "But would Monsieur now tell us how these pearls are removed from the oysters?"

"There are several ways of doing it, and often, if they are stuck to the valves, the fishermen have to take them out with pliers. But usually the oysters are spread out on mats of esparto grass covering the banks. They soon die in the open air, and after ten days, when they have rotted sufficiently, they are dumped into huge tanks of sea water. After this, they are opened and washed. Then begins the double task of the extractors. First they remove the layers of mother-of-pearl known in the business as 'true silver,' 'bastard white' and 'bastard black,' which are sent off in cases weighing between 250 and 300 pounds. Then they remove the flesh of the oyster, boil it and finally put it through a strainer so as not to lose even the tiniest pearls."

"Doesn't the price of pearls vary according to their size?" asked Conseil.

"It not only varies according to their size," I replied, "but also according to their shape, their 'water' or color, and their 'orient' or that luster which makes them so attractive to the eye. The loveliest pearls are called 'virgin pearls' or 'paragons'; they grow isolated in the mollusk's flesh; they are white, often opaque but sometimes of an opallike transparency, and usually spherical or pear-shaped. The spherical ones are used to make bracelets, whereas the pear-shaped ones are reserved for pendants, and since they are the most valuable, these last are sold individually. The other pearls which stick to the shell are less regular in shape and are therefore sold by weight. Finally, even further down the scale, there are the little pearls known as seed pearls; they are sold in bulk and are mainly used for the embroideries on church vestments."

"But it must be a very long hard job separating pearls according to their size," said the Canadian.

"No, my friend. This work is done with eleven sieves or strainers pierced with a varying number of holes. Pearls too large to pass through sieves with twenty to eighty holes are considered as being of the first category. Those which cannot get through strainers with a hundred to eight hundred holes are second-category pearls. And finally, those for which they have to use sieves with nine hundred to a thousand holes are the seed pearls."

"That's very clever," said Conseil; "they do the whole thing mechanically. And now could Monsieur tell us how much money is made from pearl fishing?"

"According to the book I have just read," I answered, "the Ceylon fisheries are rented out each year for the sum of six hundred thousand sharks."

"You mean dollars!" said Conseil.

"Yes, dollars! Six hundred thousand dollars," I continued. "But I don't think the fisheries bring in as much nowadays as they used to. And it's the same with American fisheries. During the reign of Charles V they brought in eight hundred thousand dollars a year, but now it's only about two-thirds of that. In short, I think the annual income from pearl fishing is about one million eight hundred thousand dollars."

"And haven't there been some famous pearls of great value?" asked Conseil.

"Yes, my boy. They say that Caesar offered Servillia a pearl estimated at four thousand dollars in terms of today's currency."

"I have even heard people claim," said the Canadian, "that there was a certain lady in the olden days who drank pearls in her vinegar."

"That was Cleopatra," answered Conseil.

"It must have tasted awful," commented Ned Land.

"Terrible," said Conseil. "But it's not everybody who can claim to have drunk a little glass of vinegar worth three thousand dollars."

"It's too bad I didn't marry that lady," said the Canadian, making a rather disquieting gesture.

"Ned Land married to Cleopatra!" cried Conseil.

"I was all set to get married," the Canadian answered seriously, "and it isn't my fault if it all fell through. I even bought my fiancée, Kate Tender, a pearl necklace, and then she went off and married someone else. And that necklace cost me no more than a dollar and a half, even though—and you'll just have to take my word for it, Professor—the pearls in it were about the largest I've ever seen."

"Ned, my boy," I answered laughingly, "those were artificial pearls, little glass balls coated inside with a substance called *'essence d'Orient.'*"

"Really!" replied Ned. "But that stuff they used to coat them with must cost a lot of money."

"No, Ned. It's nothing more than a silvery substance gotten from the scales of a fish called the bleak, and preserved in ammonia. It's almost worthless."

"Maybe that's why Kate Tender married someone else," Ned Land said philosophically.

"But to come back to real pearls," I said, "I don't think any king has ever owned a finer one than Captain Nemo."

"This one here?" said Conseil, pointing to the magnificent pearl in its glass case.

"Yes, it must be worth four hundred thousand . . ."

"Dollars!" said Conseil emphatically.

"Yes," I said, "four hundred thousand dollars, and it undoubtedly didn't cost the captain more than the effort of picking it up."

"Well," said Ned Land, "who's to say that tomorrow, on our excursion, we won't come across another one like it!"

"Nonsense!" exclaimed Conseil.

"Why not?"

"What good would all that money do us on board the *Nautilus*?"

"On board, maybe not," said Ned Land, "but . . . somewhere else."

"Where else?" said Conseil, shaking his head.

"Yes," I said, "Ned's right. If we ever brought a pearl like that back to Europe or America, it would help a lot toward making people believe the story of our adventures."

"I should say so," said the Canadian.

"But," said Conseil, always coming back to the practical side of things, "is pearl fishing dangerous?"

"No," I answered quickly, "and especially if you take certain precautions."

"What do you risk in this business?" said Ned Land. "Swallowing several mouthfuls of water?"

"That's about it, Ned. By the way," I said, trying to adopt Captain Nemo's offhand tone of voice, "are you afraid of sharks?"

"Me?" answered the Canadian. "A professional harpooner? It's part of my job to laugh at them!"

"It's not a question of fishing for them with a swivel hook," I said, "hauling them up on deck, cutting off their tail with an ax, opening up their bellies, tearing out their heart and throwing it in the sea!"

"Then you mean we're going to . . . ?"

"That's right."

"Under water?"

"Under water."

"As for me, just give me a good harpoon! Besides, Monsieur, you probably already know that sharks are built in a kind of odd way. They have to turn over in order to grab you, and that gives you time to . . ."

Ned Land had a way of saying the word "grab" that made a chill run down my spine.

"Well, Conseil, what about you? What do you think of sharks?"

"In all frankness . . ." said Conseil.

"Thank heavens," I thought.

"If Monsieur is willing to face sharks," said Conseil, "I don't see why his faithful servant shouldn't be willing to face them too."

CHAPTER XXVII
A Two-Million-Dollar Pearl

Night fell, and I went to bed. I slept rather badly. Sharks played an important role in my dreams.

The next morning at four o'clock, I was awakened by the steward Captain Nemo had placed at my service. I quickly got up, dressed and went to the lounge.

Captain Nemo was waiting for me. "Are you ready, Monsieur Aronnax?" he asked.

"I'm ready."

"Please follow me."

"What about my companions, Captain?"

"They've already been awakened, and they're waiting for us."

"Aren't we going to put on our diving suits?" I asked.

"Not yet. I haven't allowed the *Nautilus* to get too near shore, and we're still fairly far from the Manaar bank; but I've had the dinghy prepared. It will take us there and save us a long walk. Our diving suits are in it, and we'll put them on when we're about to start our underwater exploration."

Captain Nemo led me toward the central companionway leading up to the platform. Ned and Conseil were there, delighted by the "pleasure trip" they were about to take. The dinghy was tied alongside the *Nautilus*, and five sailors were in it with their oars in place, waiting for us.

It was still night. Patches of clouds covered the sky and I could only make out a few stars. I looked toward the land, but I saw only a vague line running along three-quarters of the horizon from the southwest to the northwest. During the night, the *Nautilus* had sailed up the western coast of Ceylon, and was now on the other side of the bay, or rather gulf, formed by this island and Manaar Island. It was in these dark waters that lay the oyster beds, that inexhaustible field of pearls that stretched for more than twenty miles.

Captain Nemo, Conseil, Ned Land and I took our places in the stern of the dinghy. The coxswain held the tiller and his four companions took up their oars. The ropes mooring us were released, and we were off.

The dinghy headed south. The oarsmen did not hurry. I noticed that although they pulled vigorously, they waited ten seconds between strokes, according to the system used in most navies. When their oars were in the air, drops of water would fall off and crackle on the dark surface of the ocean like bits of molten lead. A light swell coming from the open sea made the dinghy roll slightly, and several wave crests slapped against its bow.

We were silent. What was Captain Nemo thinking? Perhaps about the shore we were approaching, and which he felt to be too near, unlike the Canadian who felt it was still too far away. As for Conseil, he had come along merely out of curiosity.

Toward five-thirty, the first glimmers of dawn outlined the horizon more clearly. Toward the east it was rather flat, and then toward the south it rose a bit. The island was five miles away, and its shore still blended with the misty waters. Between us and the land, the sea was deserted. Not a single boat or diver was in sight. A profound silence reigned in this meeting place of pearl fishermen. As Captain Nemo had said, we had arrived in these waters a month too soon. At six, daylight was suddenly upon us, with that rapidity peculiar to tropical regions where there is no real dawn or twilight. The sun's rays pierced the cloud banks piled up on the horizon, and the sun itself rose rapidly.

I could now clearly make out the shore with a few trees spread out here and there.

The dinghy continued on toward Manaar Island rising up to the south. Captain Nemo stood up and looked at the sea. He then gave the order to drop anchor. But scarcely any chain had to be let out, for this was one of the shallowest spots in the entire oyster bed and the water was little more than three feet deep. The dinghy immediately swung around in the ebb tide.

"Here we are, Monsieur Aronnax," said Captain Nemo. "You see this narrow bay. In a month it will be filled with fishermen and their boats, and it is in these waters they will so bravely dive. This bay is well situated for such fishing. It's sheltered from strong winds, and there's never much of a swell, all of which is very helpful to the divers. Now let's put on our suits and begin our excursion."

I did not answer, and while the sailors helped me put on my diving suit, I looked at these questionable waters. Captain Nemo and my two companions were also getting dressed. None of the men from the *Nautilus* were going to accompany us on this new excursion.

Soon we were imprisoned up to our necks in our rubber suits and our air tanks were fixed on our backs. As for the Ruhmkorff lamps, they were not in sight. I mentioned this to Captain Nemo before my head was encased in its copper helmet.

"We won't need them," he answered. "We won't be going very deep and therefore the sun's rays will be enough to light our way. Besides it wouldn't be wise to take an electric lamp along with us. Its light might have the unfortunate effect of attracting some of the more dangerous inhabitants of these waters."

As Captain Nemo said this, I turned to Conseil and Ned Land. But their heads were already inside their helmets, and they could neither hear nor answer.

I had one last question to ask Captain Nemo. "What about our guns?"

"Guns! What good would they do? Don't your mountaineers attack bears with a dagger? Isn't steel safer than lead? Here's a sturdy knife. Put it in your belt, and let's be off."

I looked at my companions. They were armed like us, and moreover Ned Land was wielding an enormous harpoon he had put in the dinghy before leaving the *Nautilus*.

I then followed the captain's example and allowed my heavy copper helmet to be put on; our air reservoirs immediately started functioning.

A moment later, the sailors helped us overboard one after another, and we found ourselves standing on a sandy bottom in about five feet of water. Captain Nemo motioned for us to follow him; we went down a gentle slope and disappeared below the surface.

Once I was under water, my fears vanished. I became astonishingly calm.
The ease with which I could move increased my confidence, and the strangeness
of the spectacle captivated my imagination.

The sun was already lighting up the water enough to make the tiniest objects
visible. After walking for ten minutes we found ourselves at a depth of sixteen
feet, and the terrain leveled off almost completely.

Schools of strange fish of the genus Monopteridae, whose tail is their only
fin, flew up from beneath our feet like flocks of snipe in a marsh. I also recognized a Java fish, a veritable two-and-a-half-foot serpent with a pale belly
which, except for the golden stripes on its sides, would be easy to mistake for a
conger. Among the genus Stromateidae, characterized by a short, compressed,
oval-shaped body, I noticed some species decked in gorgeous colors, carrying
their dorsal fin like a scythe. These fish are edible, and when dried and mari-
nated they make an excellent dish known as *karawade*. I also saw some
Tranquebar fish, belonging to the genus Apsiphoroidae, whose bodies were
covered with a scaly armor in eight longitudinal sections.

The sun lit up the waters more and more as it slowly rose in the sky. The
terrain changed little by little. The fine-grained sand had given way to a veritable paving of smooth rocks covered with a carpet of mollusks and
zoophytes. Among other specimens of these two subkingdoms, I noticed some
placenae with their thin, unequal valves—a kind of oyster found only in the
Red Sea and the Indian Ocean; orange-colored lucinae with their round shells;
awl-shaped terebellum; several of those Persian purpura which furnished a
marvelous dye for the *Nautilus;* horned murices six inches long, erect in the
water like hands ready to seize us; cornigerous turbinellae bristling with
spines; lingulae; anatinae—an edible mollusk found in the markets of
Hindustan; somewhat luminous pelagian panopyrae; and finally superb flabel-
liform oculinae—marvelous fans which form one of the most remarkable
treelike growths in the ocean.

In the midst of these living plants, and beneath these arbors of hydrophytes,
ran legions of clumsy articulata, mainly frog crabs, whose shell is shaped like a
somewhat rounded triangle, birgi, found only in these waters, and horrible,

repulsive-looking parthenopes. Another no less hideous animal which I met several times was that enormous crab Darwin saw, a creature which nature has given the instinct and necessary strength to live off coconuts. It climbs up trees next to the shore, knocks down a coconut which breaks open upon hitting the ground, and then opens it with its powerful claws. Here, beneath the clear water, this crab scampered about with unbelievable agility, while green turtles of a species commonly found off the coasts of Malabar moved slowly among the tumbled-down rocks.

Toward seven o'clock we finally reached the area where pearl oysters reproduce by the millions. These precious mollusks were clinging to rocks, stuck by the brown byssus which prevents them from moving about. In this they are inferior to mussels, who can move around to a small extent.

The pearl oyster, the Meleagrina, whose valves are more or less equal, has a round, thick shell with a gnarled exterior. Several of these shells were marked with green bands radiating down from the top; these were the young oysters. But those that were black and rough were almost ten years old and measured as much as six inches in diameter.

Captain Nemo pointed to an enormous mass of pearl oysters, and I realized that here there was a literally inexhaustible supply, for nature's creative force was stronger than man's destructive instinct. But Ned Land, faithful to this instinct, was quickly filling a sack with the finest oysters.

However, we could not stop. We had to follow the captain, who seemed to be taking paths known only to him. The ocean floor rose considerably, and sometimes I could raise my arm above the surface. Then it would get deeper again. Often we would go around high rocks shaped like pyramids. In the darker hollows of their craggy surface large crustaceans were perched on their legs like war machines, looking at us with their set eyes, and about our feet crawled myrianidae, ariciae and annelidae stretching out their antennae and tentacles.

Just then a vast cave appeared before us, hollowed out in a picturesque pile of rock covered with all the lovely tapestry work of underwater vegetation. At first it seemed to me very dark inside this cave. The sun's rays appeared to lose their strength little by little. Their vague transparency became only a dim, blurred light.

Captain Nemo entered and we followed. My eyes soon became accustomed to the relative darkness. I could make out natural pillars supporting a whimsically shaped vaulting and resting on a granite base, like the heavy columns of Tuscan architecture. Why was our strange guide taking us into the depths of this underwater crypt? I was soon to know.

After going down a rather steep slope, we found ourselves standing at the bottom of a sort of circular pit. There Captain Nemo stopped and pointed to something I had not noticed.

It was an oyster of amazing size, a giant clam which could have made a holy-water basin big enough to hold a lake. It was seven feet wide, and therefore even bigger than the one in the *Nautilus'* lounge.

I went over to this phenomenal mollusk. He was fastened to a slab of granite, living all alone in the calm waters of the grotto. I calculated that this giant clam must have weighed about 650 pounds. Such an oyster must have contained 35 pounds of flesh, and it would have taken the stomach of a Gargantua to digest several dozen of these.

It was obvious Captain Nemo already knew this creature was here. It wasn't the first time he had paid it a visit. But I was wrong in thinking he had brought us here just to show us a wonder of nature. Captain Nemo had a particular reason for wanting to see how this giant clam was getting along.

The creature's two valves were partly open. The captain inserted his dagger to prevent them from closing again; then with his hand he lifted up the fringed membranes which formed the animal's cloak.

There, among the leaflike folds, I saw a loose pearl the size of a coconut. Its roundness, perfect clarity and marvelous sheen made it a jewel of incalculable value. I was carried away by my curiosity and stretched out my hand to take it, weigh it and feel it! But the captain stopped me and indicated he did not want me to touch it. He then removed his dagger with one swift motion and the two valves of the clam suddenly closed.

I then realized what Captain Nemo had in mind. By allowing this pearl to remain inside the giant clam, he could let it grow as much as he wanted. Each year the creature would add new layers to it. Only the captain knew where this marvelous fruit of nature was "ripening"; he alone was bringing it up, one might say, so that one day he might take it to his precious museum. He might even have started the growth of this pearl (as they do in China and India) by placing some piece of glass or metal inside the giant clam, and allowing this object to become covered with the creature's pearl-forming secretions. In any case, by comparing this pearl with others I knew and with those in the captain's collection, I estimated it to be worth at least two million dollars. But it was more a wonder of nature than a piece of jewelry, for I can't imagine what woman's ear could support such a weight.

The visit to the giant clam was over. Captain Nemo left the cave and we went back up to the oyster beds, in the midst of clear waters not yet disturbed by the work of divers.

We walked alone like people out for a stroll, each one stopping or wandering off whenever he wished. As for me, I was no longer a bit troubled by the dangers which my imagination had so ridiculously exaggerated. The ocean floor rose up, and soon I was walking in a depth of four feet with my head out of water. Conseil joined me, and putting his helmet alongside mine, made a friendly gesture with his eyes. But this raised plateau lasted only for several yards, and soon we were back in our element, for I feel I could now call it "our element."

Ten minutes later, Captain Nemo stopped suddenly. I thought we were going to start back. But no. He motioned for us to squat down beside him in a crevasse. He pointed to a place in the water, and I looked hard to try and discover what it was he saw.

About fifteen feet away, a shadow appeared and descended to the ocean floor. The disturbing idea that it might be a shark crossed my mind. But I was wrong, and as yet we were not face to face with one of these monsters of the deep.

It was a man, a live man, an Indian Negro, a poor devil of a fisherman who had undoubtedly come to gather what he could before harvest time. I could make out the bottom of his rowboat anchored several feet above his head. He would dive and then go back up time after time. A round stone which he clutched with his feet and which was tied to the boat by a rope helped him to get to the bottom more quickly. This was his only implement. Once down, in about fifteen feet of water, he would drop to his knees and fill his sack with whatever oysters lay at hand. Then he would go back up, empty his sack, bring the stone up and then start the process—which lasted about thirty seconds—all over again.

This diver did not see us. We were hidden in the shadow of a rock. And besides, how could this poor Indian ever have imagined that men, creatures like himself, were there beneath the surface, spying on him and observing every detail of his work!

Every time he dove he would only bring back ten or twelve oysters, for they had to be torn from the rocks to which they were so strongly fastened. And then how many of these oysters were completely lacking in those pearls for which he was risking his life!

I watched him very closely. He went up and down in a regular rhythm, and for half an hour no danger seemed to threaten him. I was therefore becoming very familiar with this interesting mode of fishing, when suddenly while the Indian was kneeling down, I saw him make a gesture of fright, get up and start back to the surface.

I then understood his terror. A gigantic shadow appeared above him. It was a huge shark moving in with fire in his eyes and his jaws open!

I was paralyzed with horror, incapable of moving.

With one powerful movement of its fins, this voracious creature shot toward the Indian, who jumped to one side and avoided the animal's bite. But he did not manage to avoid the tail, which struck him on the chest and knocked him flat on the ocean floor.

This scene had lasted no more than several seconds. Then the shark came back, turned over and was getting ready to cut the Indian in two, when the captain suddenly jumped up next to me. With his dagger in hand, he made straight for the monster, ready to fight it hand to hand.

Just as the shark was about to seize the unfortunate diver, he saw his new adversary, righted himself and swam rapidly toward him.

I can still see Captain Nemo's stance. Bracing himself for the struggle, he coolly awaited the formidable shark, and just as this creature was almost on him, he sidestepped with incredible speed, thus avoiding the jaws, and buried his dagger in the animal's belly. But it did not end there. A terrible struggle began.

The shark almost seemed as if it were bellowing. Blood poured from its wounds. The sea turned red, and through this murkiness I could see nothing.

Nothing, until through a clear spot in the water, I made out the brave captain clutching one of the animal's fins, fighting with it, riddling its belly with blows from his dagger, but without being able to finish it off, that is to say, strike it in the heart. The shark churned the water so furiously that it came close to knocking me over.

I would have liked to help the captain, but I was rooted to the spot by horror and could not move.

I merely looked on with dread. I saw the struggle take a new turn. The captain fell to the ground, knocked over by the enormous creature's weight. Then the shark's jaws opened like some huge shearing machine, and the captain would have been done for if Ned Land had not rushed forward as quick as lightning, and hurled his harpoon at the fish.

Masses of blood darkened the water. The shark thrashed about with indescribable fury. Ned Land had struck home; this was the monster's death rattle. However, it struggled on, and in one of its horrifying convulsions it knocked Conseil down.

But Ned Land had freed the captain. The latter, unharmed, immediately got up and went over to the Indian, cut the rope tying him to the rock, took him in his arms and with one strong kick brought him back to the surface.

All three of us followed, and in a moment, feeling as if we had been saved by a miracle, we reached the fisherman's boat.

Captain Nemo's first preoccupation was to bring the poor fellow back to life. I did not know if he would succeed. I was hopeful in any case, for the Indian had not been under long. But the blow from the shark's tail could have been fatal.

But fortunately, with Conseil and the captain giving him artificial respiration, he soon regained consciousness and opened his eyes. How surprised he must have been to see four copper helmets bending over him!

But above all, what must he have thought when Captain Nemo pulled a bag of pearls from the pocket of his diving suit and put them in his hand? The poor Indian accepted these alms from the man of the sea with a trembling hand. We could see by his startled eyes that he did not know to what kind of superman he owed both his life and his good fortune.

At a sign from the captain, we returned to the oyster bed and retraced our steps. Within half an hour we had found the anchor holding the *Nautilus'* dinghy.

Once we were in the boat, the sailors helped us take off our heavy copper helmets.

Captain Nemo's first words were spoken to the Canadian. "Thank you, Master Land," he said.

"I was just repaying a debt," Ned answered.

A vague smile played on the captain's lips, and that was all.

"To the *Nautilus*," he said.

The little boat sped over the water. Several minutes later we came across the floating carcass of the shark.

By the black coloring on the tips of its fins I could see that it belonged to the terrible melanopteron species of the Indian Ocean. It was more than twenty-five feet long, and its enormous mouth occupied a third of its body. By its six rows of teeth I could tell that it was an adult.

Conseil was looking at it in a purely scientific way, and I am sure he was classifying it, quite correctly, among the class of cartilaginous fish, order of Chondropterygii with fixed gills, family of Selachii and genus of Squali.

While I was looking at this inert mass, a dozen other sharks of the same species suddenly appeared around the boat. They threw themselves on the carcass and fought over the pieces without even giving us a thought.

At eight-thirty we were back on board the *Nautilus*.

Once we were there, I reflected on our excursion to the Manaar beds. Two thoughts inevitably came to mind. One concerned the captain's unparalleled courage, and the other his devotion for a human being, a representative of that race from which he was fleeing beneath the ocean. Whatever one might say, this strange man had not succeeded in entirely burying his heart.

When I mentioned this, he answered in a somewhat trembling voice: "This Indian, Professor, lives in the land of the oppressed, and to that land I still belong and shall till the day I die!"

CHAPTER XXVIII
The Red Sea

During the day of January 29, the island of Ceylon disappeared beneath the horizon, and the *Nautilus*, traveling at a speed of twenty knots, entered the winding channels separating the Maldive and Laccadive Islands. It even cruised near Kiltan Island, which is of coral origin, and which was discovered by Vasco da Gama in 1499. It is one of the nineteen principal islands of the Laccadive archipelago, which is situated between 10° and 14° 30' N. Lat., and 69° and 50° 72' E. Long.

We had then traveled 16,220 miles, or in other words, 7,500 leagues from our point of departure in the Sea of Japan.

The next day, January 30, there was no longer any land in sight when the *Nautilus* surfaced. It was heading north by northwest, toward the Gulf of Oman, which lies between Arabia and the Indian peninsula, and through which one enters the Persian Gulf.

This was obviously a dead end without any possible way out. Where was Captain Nemo taking us? I had no idea. But this did not satisfy the Canadian when he asked me where we were going.

"Ned, we're going wherever the captain takes it into his head to go."

"But he can't go far," replied the Canadian. "There's no other way out of the

Persian Gulf, and if we enter it, we'll soon have to come back the way we went."

"Well, then we'll come back, Ned, and if the *Nautilus* after that wants to visit the Red Sea, the Straits of Bab el Mandeb are always there for it to pass through."

"I don't think I need to tell you, Monsieur," replied Ned Land, "that the Red Sea is just as much of a dead end as the Persian Gulf. The Suez Canal isn't finished yet, and even if it were, a mysterious boat like ours wouldn't dare travel through it. So that means we won't get back to Europe by means of the Red Sea either."

"But I didn't say we were heading for Europe."

"Where do you suppose we're going then?"

"My guess is that after visiting the waters off Arabia and Egypt, the *Nautilus* will go back to the Indian Ocean, travel either through the Mozambique Channel or off the Mascarene Islands, and then head for the Cape of Good Hope."

"And what will happen once we get to the Cape of Good Hope?" asked the Canadian stubbornly.

"We'll enter the Atlantic which we haven't yet visited. But what's the matter, Ned? Are you getting tired of this undersea voyage? Are you getting bored with the continually varying spectacle of underwater wonders? As for me, I'll be sorry to see the end of a voyage like this which so few men have had the opportunity to make."

"But don't you realize, Monsieur Aronnax," replied the Canadian, "that soon it'll be three months since we became prisoners on board the *Nautilus*?"

"No, Ned, I don't, and what's more, I don't even want to think about it. I don't want to count the days and hours."

"But when will it all end?"

"When the time has come for it to end. Besides there's nothing we can do about it, and it's useless even to discuss the matter. If you came to me and said, 'Now's our chance to escape,' I wouldn't argue with you. But this isn't the case, and to tell you the truth, I don't think Captain Nemo will ever venture into European waters."

One can see by this short dialogue that I had become a fanatic on the subject of the *Nautilus* and had begun to identify with its captain.

Ned Land ended the conversation muttering to himself, "That's all fine and good, but the way I look at it, a man can't live without his freedom."

For four days—till February 3—the *Nautilus* visited the Gulf of Oman, at various speeds and depths. It seemed to be cruising at random, as if it couldn't decide what route to take. But it never crossed the Tropic of Cancer.

As we left the gulf, we sighted Muscat for a moment, the most important town in this area. I looked admiringly at its strange appearance, its white houses and fortifications contrasting with the black rocks surrounding it. I could make out the round domes of its mosques, the elegant spires of its minarets and its fresh, green terraces. But I got only a glimpse, for the *Nautilus* soon dove beneath the dark waters.

It then cruised six miles off the Arabian coast, near the regions of Mahra and Hadramut, with their line of mountains dotted here and there with ancient ruins. On February 5, we finally entered the Gulf of Aden, a perfect funnel stuck in the Straits of Bab el Mandeb, through which the waters of the Indian Ocean pass into the Red Sea.

On February 6, the *Nautilus* was within sight of Aden, perched on its promontory and joined to the mainland by a narrow isthmus, a kind of inaccessible Gibraltar, whose fortifications the English rebuilt after capturing it in 1839. I could make out the eight-sided minarets of this town, which according to the historian Idrisi used to be one of the richest commercial centers along the entire coast.

I was sure that Captain Nemo would now turn back; but I was wrong, and to my great surprise he did quite the opposite.

On the next day, February 7, we entered the Straits of Bab el Mandeb, whose name in Arabic means: "The Gate of Tears." They are twenty miles wide and thirty-two miles long, and it took the *Nautilus,* traveling at top speed, scarcely an hour to pass through them. But I saw nothing—not even Perim Island, which the British Government used to help defend Aden. Too many English or French steamers of the lines going from Suez to Bombay, Calcutta, Melbourne, Réunion and Mauritius plied this narrow passage for the *Nautilus* to dare show itself. We therefore cruised under water.

Finally, at noon, we were in the Red Sea.

The Red Sea, so famous from biblical times, is hardly ever refreshed by rains and is replenished by no important rivers. In addition, it is continually drained by a high rate of evaporation which causes it to lose five feet of water a year! A strange gulf, which, if it were closed off like a lake, would probably have dried up completely; unlike its neighbors the Caspian and Dead Seas whose water levels have dropped precisely to the point where their evaporation equals the amount of water entering them.

The Red Sea is 1600 miles long and has an average width of 150 miles. In the days of the Ptolemies and the Roman Emperors, it was the great commercial artery of the world, and when the canal is completed it will once again regain its former importance, which has already been partly restored by the Suez railway.

I did not even try to understand why Captain Nemo had taken us into this gulf. But I approved wholeheartedly of the *Nautilus'* having entered. It traveled at a slow speed, sometimes on the surface and sometimes under water to avoid ships. I was therefore able to observe this sea inside and out.

On February 8, during the first moments of daylight, we sighted Mokha, a town now in ruins, whose walls would collapse at the mere sound of a cannon, but in which there are still some scattered green date palms. Once upon a time it was a city of considerable importance, containing six public markets, twenty-six mosques, and its walls, defended by fourteen forts, were two miles in circumference.

Then the *Nautilus* drew nearer the shores of Africa, where the sea is considerably deeper. There, as the ship traveled through crystal-clear water, we could see through the open panels in the lounge marvelous shrubs of dazzling coral and huge chunks of rock covered with a splendid green fur of seaweed and sea wrack. What an indescribable spectacle, and what a variety of beautiful landscapes at the edge of these reefs and volcanic islands off the coast of Libya! But the *Nautilus* soon went back to the eastern shores where we could see these tree-like formations in all their glory. It was near the coast of Tehama, for there not only did masses of zoophytes flower below the surface, but they also formed

Perched on its promontory

picturesque networks to heights of sixty feet above water level; the latter were more whimsical in shape but less rich in color than the former, whose hues were kept vivid by the surrounding water.

How many delightful hours I passed looking through the window of the lounge! How many new specimens of underwater flora and fauna I was able to admire beneath the rays of our electric light! I saw mushroom-shaped fungi, slate-colored sea anemones—among others the *Thalassianthus aster*—organ-pipe corals shaped like flutes and awaiting only to be played by the god Pan, shells, found only in these waters, which were spiral-shaped at the base and which lay in hollows in the madreporic formations, and finally thousands of specimens of a polypary which I had not yet seen, the ordinary sponge.

The class of Spongiaria, the first within the division of the polyps, is constituted by this curious and useful product. The sponge is not a plant, as some naturalists still claim, but an animal of the lowest order, inferior even to the coral. There can be no doubt about its animal nature, and one cannot even go along with scientists of ancient times who said it was halfway between a plant and an animal. I must say, however, that naturalists do not agree as to the structures of sponges. For some it is a polypary, and for others, like Milne-Edwards, it is in a category all by itself.

The class of Spongiaria contains about three hundred species. They are found in most seas, and even in certain rivers, in which case they are called "fluviatile." But mainly they are found in the Mediterranean around the Greek Islands and off the coast of Syria, and in the Red Sea. There one encounters the "fine" sponges which are worth up to thirty dollars apiece, the blond Syrian sponges, the hard sponge of Barbary, etc. But since I had no hope of studying these zoophytes in the Mediterranean, I was content to observe them in the Red Sea.

I therefore told Conseil to join me while the *Nautilus*, at a depth of twenty-five to thirty feet, cruised slowly past all the beautiful rocks near the eastern coast.

There were sponges growing in all sorts of shapes—pediculate, leaflike, round and finger-shaped. They well justified the names given them by fishermen, who are better poets than scientists: basket sponges, chalice sponges, cat's tails, elk's horns, lion's feet, peacock's tails and Neptune's gloves. From their fibrous tissues, impregnated with a semifluid gelatinous substance, there escaped a steady little stream of water which, after bringing life-giving matter to each cell, was expelled by a contracting movement. This gelatinous substance disappears after the polyp dies, letting forth ammonia as it rots. Then nothing is left but the horny or soft reddish-brown fibers which make up the household sponge, and which are put to various uses according to their degree of elasticity or permeability.

These polyparies were stuck to rocks, to the shells of mollusks and even to the stems of hydrophytes. They decorated every twist and turn of the rocks, some spreading out, some standing up straight and others hanging like outgrowths of coral. I told Conseil that there were two ways of fishing for sponges: dredging or diving, and that the latter was preferable because it did not harm the fibers of the polypary, thereby reducing its value.

The other zoophytes swarming around the Spongiaria consisted principally of a very elegant kind of jellyfish; mollusks were represented by a species of squid which, according to d'Orbigny, are found only in the Red Sea; and reptiles were represented by virgata turtles of the genus Chelonia which furnished us with a healthy and excellent food.

As for fish, they were numerous and often remarkable. Here are those which the *Nautilus'* nets most frequently hauled in: among rays, I noticed some oval-shaped, brick-colored limmae, their bodies covered with different-sized blue spots, recognizable by their jagged double stingers, silver-backed arnacks, whip-tailed sting rays, and six-foot-long bockats which looked like huge overcoats flapping about in the water. I also saw aodons without a single tooth, even though they are a distant relative of the shark; eighteen-inch-long trunkfishes whose camellike hump ends in a bent spine; phidions looking like morays with their silver tails, bluish backs and brown pectoral fins edged in gray; fiatolae—a species of stromateidae striped with narrow gold bands and decked in the colors of the French flag; blennies sixteen inches long; superb caranxes decorated with seven black cross-stripes, blue and yellow fins, and scales of gold and silver; centropods, a kind of mullet with a yellow head; parrot fish, wrasse, triggerfish, gobies, etc., and thousands of other fish I had already seen in other waters.

On February 9, the *Nautilus* cruised through the widest part of the Red Sea lying between Suakin on the west coast and Kanfuda on the east coast, a distance of 190 miles.

At noon of that day, after our position had been taken, Captain Nemo came up on the platform. I promised myself not to let him go back down without at least having sounded him out on his plans. He came over as soon as he saw me, graciously offered me a cigar and said: "Well, Professor, how do you like the Red Sea? Have you seen enough of the wonders it contains, its fish, zoophytes, sponges and coral forests? Have you had a look at the towns spread out on its shores?"

"Yes, Captain Nemo," I replied, "and the *Nautilus* is marvelously fit for such a study. What a remarkable boat!"

"Yes, Monsieur; it is completely invulnerable! It has nothing to fear from the terrible storms, currents or reefs of the Red Sea."

"As a matter of fact," I said, "the Red Sea is supposed to be one of the worst seas on earth; in ancient times it had a terrible reputation."

"Terrible, Monsieur Aronnax. Greek and Latin historians have little good to say for it, and Strabo states that it is particularly rough when the Etesian winds are blowing and during the rainy season. The Arab Idrisi, who refers to it as the Gulf of Colzum, says that many ships perished on its sandbanks and that no one dared to sail on it at night. He says it is a sea subject to terrible storms, strewn with forbidding islands and 'with nothing to offer' either below or above the surface. One finds the same opinion in Arrian, Agatharchides and Artemidorus."

"One can easily see," I said, "that these historians hadn't sailed on the *Nautilus*."

"Yes," replied the captain with a smile, "but as far as that is concerned, modern men are no further along than the ancients. It took many centuries to discover the mechanical power of steam! Who knows if we will see a second *Nautilus* within a hundred years! Progress is a slow thing, Monsieur Aronnax."

"You're right," I replied, "your boat is one or maybe several centuries ahead of its time. What a pity that such a secret should die with its inventor!"

Captain Nemo did not answer. After several minutes of silence, he said: "We were discussing, I think, what ancient historians said about the dangers of navigation in the Red Sea."

"Oh yes," I replied, "but weren't their fears a bit exaggerated?"

"Yes and no, Monsieur Aronnax," said Captain Nemo, who seemed to know "his Red Sea" by heart. "What is no longer a danger for a modern ship that is well rigged, solidly built and in control of its direction thanks to steam power, offered all kinds of perils to olden vessels. You must realize that these first navigators went out in boats made of planks lashed together with palm ropes, calked with ground resin and coated with dogfish grease. They didn't even have instruments to tell them what direction they were going in, and they navigated by guesswork amid currents they hardly knew. Under such conditions, there were necessarily many shipwrecks. But nowadays, steamers plying between Suez and the South Seas have nothing to fear from the fury of this gulf, in spite of the monsoons which blow up from the south. Their captains and passengers no longer make sacrifices to appease the gods before leaving, nor do they dress in garlands and gold headbands to thank the gods upon returning."

"Yes," I said, "steam navigation seems to have killed the gratitude in sailors' hearts. But Captain, since you seem to have made a special study of this sea, could you tell me the origin of its name?"

"There are many explanations for it, Monsieur Aronnax. Would you like to know the opinion of a fourteenth-century chronicler?"

"Yes."

"This writer tries to maintain that it got its name after the passage of the Israelites, when Pharaoh perished in the waters which closed in at Moses' command:

> *'As a token of this wonder*
> *When the sea was rent asunder,*
> *Turning red, it then was known*
> *By the color it had shown.'"*

"That's very poetic, Captain Nemo," I answered, "but it is not a very satisfactory explanation. What is your own opinion?"

"My opinion, Monsieur Aronnax, is that its name is a translation of the Hebrew word 'Edrem,' and that the ancients gave it this name because of the peculiar color of its waters."

"But until now at least, I haven't seen anything but clear, colorless water."

"Undoubtedly, but as you go toward the head of the gulf, you'll see this strange phenomenon. I can remember having seen the Bay of Tor completely red, like a lake of blood."

"Do you attribute this color to the presence of some microscopic plant?"

"Yes, it's a purple sticky substance produced by tiny little plants called trichodesmids, of which it takes forty thousand to fill up the space of a square millimeter. Maybe you'll see this phenomenon when we get to Tor."

"So this isn't the first time you've taken the *Nautilus* into the Red Sea?"

"No, Monsieur."

"Then, since a while ago you mentioned the passage of the Israelites and the catastrophe that overtook the Egyptians, I would like to know if with your submarine you have been able to discover the site of this great historic event?"

"No, Professor, and there's a good reason why I haven't."

"Why?"

"Because the place where Moses crossed with all his people is so covered with sand, that nowadays camels can scarcely even wet their legs there. As you can see, that wouldn't be quite enough water for my *Nautilus* to float in."

"And where is this place?" I asked.

"It is situated a little above Suez, within that sound which once formed a deep estuary in the days when the Red Sea stretched to the salt lakes. Now whether or not this passage was a miracle, it was precisely there that the Israelites crossed to reach the Promised Land and that Pharaoh's army perished. I therefore think that if archeologists dug in among these sands, they would find a great quantity of arms and utensils of Egyptian origin."

"Obviously," I replied, "and one can only hope for the archeologists' sake that this work will be done someday, when new towns spring up after the Suez

Canal is completed. But speaking of this canal, even when it is finished, it won't be of much use to a ship like the *Nautilus*!"

"No, but very useful for the rest of the world," said Captain Nemo. "People in ancient times understood only too well how important it was for commerce to connect the Red Sea with the Mediterranean. But they did not think of digging a direct canal, and instead did it by way of the Nile. If one can believe traditional accounts, the canal connecting the Nile and the Red Sea was probably begun under Sesostris. In any case, it is certain that in 615 B.C., Necos started work on a canal which was fed by Nile water and crossed the plains of Egypt opposite Arabia. It took four days to travel the length of this canal, and it was wide enough for two triremes to pass side by side. It was continued by Darius, the son of Hytaspe, and probably finished by Ptolemy II. Strabo saw it used for shipping, but because it sloped gently down from Bubastis to the Red Sea, it was only usable for several months a year. This canal served commerce till the period of the Antonine emperors; it was then abandoned and became sanded over, until it was finally put back into use by the Calif Omar. But then it was filled in once and for all in 761 or 762 by the Calif al-Mansur in order to prevent Mohammed ben Abdallah, who had rebelled against him, from receiving supplies. During Napoleon's Egyptian campaign, he discovered traces of these canals in the desert near Suez, and while searching for them he was overtaken by the tide and almost drowned several hours before reaching Hadjaroth, where Moses had camped three thousand years before."

"Well, Captain, what the ancients did not dare undertake—this junction of two seas which will shorten the route from Cadiz to India by 5600 miles—de Lesseps is now doing, and before long he will have changed Africa into an immense island."

"Yes, Monsieur Aronnax, and you have the right to be proud of your compatriot. Such a man honors a country even more than a great sea captain! Like so many others, he at first only encountered difficulties and refusals, but in the end he triumphed, for he has the will of a genius. And it is a sad thought that this work which should have been done by an international body and which would have been enough to make one country proud, succeeded thanks to the efforts of a single man. All honor to Monsieur de Lesseps!"

"Yes, all honor to a great man," I answered, completely taken aback by the manner in which Captain Nemo had spoken.

"Unfortunately," he went on, "I shan't be able to take you through the Suez Canal, but you will be able to see the long jetties of Port Said when we arrive in the Mediterranean the day after tomorrow."

"In the Mediterranean!" I cried.

"Yes, Professor. Does that surprise you?"

"What surprises me is the thought that we'll be there the day after tomorrow."

"Really?"

"Yes, Captain, even though scarcely anything surprises me anymore aboard your ship!"

"But just what is it that surprises you?"

"The fantastic speed at which the *Nautilus* will have to travel if it is to be in the Mediterranean the day after tomorrow, after going all the way around Africa by way of the Cape of Good Hope!"

"But who said we were going around Africa, Professor? Why bring up the Cape of Good Hope?"

"But unless the *Nautilus* can sail over dry land and cross the isthmus . . ."

"Or under it, Monsieur Aronnax."

"Under it?"

"Yes," replied Captain Nemo calmly. "A long time ago, beneath this strip of land, nature did the same thing man is now doing on the surface."

"What! There's a passage!"

"Yes, an underground passage which I've called the Arabian Tunnel. It starts beneath Suez and ends in the Gulf of Pelusium."

"But the Isthmus of Suez is made of shifting sand."

"Only to a certain depth. A hundred and fifty feet down one meets a layer of solid rock."

"Did you discover this passage by chance?" I asked, more and more surprised.

"By both chance and logic, Professor, and more by logic than by chance."

"I'm listening, Captain, but my ears can scarcely believe what they hear."

"Ah, Monsieur, 'They have ears, but they hear not' is an eternal truth. Not only does this passage exist, but I have used it several times. If not, I never would have wandered into such a dead end as the Red Sea."

"Would it be asking too much to know how you discovered this tunnel?"

"Monsieur," answered the captain, "there can be no secrets between people who will never part."

I paid no attention to this insinuation and awaited Captain Nemo's account.

"Professor, it was simple naturalist's logic that led me to discover this hitherto unknown passage. I had noticed that the Red Sea and the Mediterranean contained certain identical species of fish, ophidions, fiatolae, girelles, persegae, joels and exocoeti. Knowing this, I began to wonder if there didn't exist some passage between the two seas. If it did exist, the underground current must necessarily flow from the Red Sea to the Mediterranean because of their different levels. I therefore hauled up a large number of fish around Suez, slipped a brass ring around their tails and threw them back in the water. Several months later, off the coast of Syria, I caught several specimens of my fish with their rings. I had therefore proved that there existed some passage between the two seas. I looked for it with my *Nautilus*, found it and explored it. And very soon now, Professor, you too will have traveled through my Arabian Tunnel!"

CHAPTER XXIX
The Arabian Tunnel

On that same day, I recounted to Conseil and Ned Land that portion of the conversation which would most interest them. When I said that in two days we would be in the Mediterranean, Conseil clapped his hands, but the Canadian only shrugged his shoulders.

"An underwater tunnel!" he cried, "connecting the two seas! Who ever heard of such a thing?"

"Ned, my friend," replied Conseil, "who had ever heard of the *Nautilus?* Nobody, but it existed all the same. So don't shrug your shoulders and try to brush off ideas just by claiming nobody's ever heard of them."

"We'll see!" retorted Ned Land, shaking his head. "But just remember, I'd give anything to be able to believe in this tunnel, and in fact, I pray to God that it does take us into the Mediterranean."

That same afternoon at 21° 30' N. Lat., the *Nautilus* surfaced and drew near the coast of Arabia. We sighted Jiddah, an important trading center for Egypt, Syria, Turkey and India. I could clearly make out its houses, the ships moored to its docks and the larger vessels which had to anchor further out. The sun was now quite low on the horizon and struck full on the houses of the town, bringing out their whiteness. Outside, several wood or reed cabins indicated where the Bedouins lived.

Soon Jiddah disappeared in the evening shadows, and the *Nautilus* once again dove beneath the surface of the somewhat phosphorescent water.

On the next day, February 10, the *Nautilus* sighted several ships heading in the opposite direction and was once more obliged to cruise under water. But at noon the sea was found to be deserted and we came back up to take our position.

Accompanied by Ned and Conseil, I went up and sat on the platform. The shoreline off to the east could only be seen as a vague blur through the mist.

We were leaning on the side of the dinghy and chatting about one thing and another, when Ned Land pointed out to sea and said: "Do you see something over there, Professor?"

"No, Ned, but as you well know, my eyes aren't as good as yours."

"Take a good look," Ned went on, "there off the starboard bow. Can't you see something moving?"

"Yes," I said after looking carefully, "I can make out something long and black on the surface."

"Another *Nautilus?*" said Conseil.

"No," answered the Canadian, "and unless I'm very mistaken, it's some sea animal."

"Are there whales in the Red Sea?" asked Conseil.

"Yes, every now and then they're seen here."

"But it isn't a whale," Ned Land continued, not losing sight of the object. "Whales and I are old friends, and I can tell them by the way they move."

"The *Nautilus* is heading that way," said Conseil, "and in a little while we'll be able to know for sure what it is."

And in fact, this blackish object was soon only a mile away. It looked like a large reef stuck in mid-ocean. What was it? I had no idea.

"Look, it's moving! It's diving!" cried Ned Land. "What in God's name is it? It hasn't got the forked tail of a whale, and its fins look like sawed-off legs."

"That means . . ." I said.

"Now it's rolled over on its back," continued the Canadian, "with its mammaries in the air!"

"It's a mermaid," cried Conseil, "a real mermaid, begging Monsieur's pardon."

This word "mermaid" put me on the right track, and I realized that this animal belonged to that species from which had sprung the legends about mermaids, creatures which were half woman and half fish.

"No," I said to Conseil, "it isn't a mermaid, but a strange animal of which only a few specimens remain in the Red Sea. It's a dugong."

"Order of Sirenia, division of Pisciformae, subclass of monodelphians, class of mammals, subkingdom of vertebrates," replied Conseil.

Once he had stated this, Conseil had nothing more to say.

Meanwhile Ned Land was still watching. His eyes burned with desire at the sight of the animal. He seemed all set to harpoon it, or even throw himself in the water and attack it in its own element.

"Oh, Monsieur," he said in a trembling voice, "I've never killed 'that kind of critter.'"

All his harpooner's soul was contained in this one phrase.

Just then Captain Nemo appeared on the platform. He noticed the dugong, and realizing how the Canadian felt, said: "If you were holding a harpoon right now, Master Land, I'll bet it would be burning right through your hand."

"It certainly would, Captain."

"Would you like to take up your old profession again for one day, and add this creature to the list of fish you've already caught?"

"There's nothing I'd like more."

"Well then, go ahead and try."

"Thank you, Captain," replied Ned Land, his eyes aflame.

"Only you must promise not to miss it," the captain went on, "and I say that in your own interest."

"Is a dugong dangerous when attacked?" I asked, in spite of the Canadian's shrug.

"Yes," the captain replied, "sometimes it turns on its attackers and capsizes their boat. But with Ned Land, there's nothing to fear. His eye is sharp and his arm sure. I only advise him not to lose this dugong, because it is rightly regarded as a fine food fish, and I know that Master Land does not dislike a good meal."

"You mean to say," exclaimed the Canadian, "that in addition to everything else, this animal's good to eat?"

"Yes, Master Land. Its flesh is like real meat and is held in high esteem. Throughout the East Indies it is reserved for princes. As a result, it's been so relentlessly hunted that, just like its close cousin the manatee, it's becoming rarer and rarer."

"Well then, Captain," said Conseil gravely, "if by chance this one here is the last of his race, wouldn't it be better to spare him—in the interests of science?"

"Maybe," retorted the Canadian; "but in the interests of cooking, it would be best to hunt him."

"Go ahead then, Master Land," said Captain Nemo.

Just then, seven members of the crew, as mute and impassive as ever, came up on deck. One carried a harpoon and line of the type used by whalers. The dinghy was uncovered, taken from its niche and put to sea. Six oarsmen took their places at the oars and the coxswain took the tiller. Ned, Conseil and I got in and sat down in the stern.

"Aren't you coming, Captain?" I asked.

"No, Monsieur, but I wish you good luck."

The dinghy was shoved off and, propelled by its six oars, made rapid headway toward the dugong, which was then floating about two miles from the *Nautilus*.

When we got about five hundred yards away, the dinghy slowed down and its oars dipped noiselessly into the silent waters. Ned Land took up his harpoon and went up to stand in the bow of the boat. A whaler's harpoon is usually attached to a very long line which unwinds rapidly as the wounded animal dives. This line, however, was no longer than fifty or sixty feet, and was attached at the other end to a little barrel which was intended to float and indicate the dugong's position.

I stood up and took a close look at the Canadian's adversary. The dugong, which is also called a halicore, is somewhat similar to the manatee. It has an oblong body ending in a long tail, and its side fins are tipped with veritable fingers. It differs from the manatee in that its upper jaw is armed with two long and pointed teeth which stick out on each side.

The dugong Ned Land was preparing to attack was enormous; it must have been around twenty-five feet long. It wasn't moving and seemed asleep on the surface; this would make it easier to capture.

The dinghy cautiously approached to within twenty feet of the animal. The oars hung in mid-air. I rose to a crouching position. Ned Land was leaning back brandishing the harpoon in his experienced hand.

Suddenly I heard a whistling noise, and the dugong disappeared. The harpoon had been thrown with great force, but it seemed only to have struck water.

"Curses!" cried the Canadian in a rage. "I missed it!"

"No," I said, "you wounded it. See the blood over there. But your harpoon didn't stay in its body."

"My harpoon! My harpoon!" cried Ned Land.

The sailors started rowing again and the coxswain steered the boat toward the floating barrel. Once the harpoon had been recovered, the dinghy once again set out after the dugong.

From time to time it would come to the surface to breathe. Its wound had not weakened it, for it swam at great speed. The six oarsmen pulled with all their strength and the dinghy flew across the sea in pursuit of the animal. Several times it got to within twenty or twenty-five feet, but then the dugong would suddenly dive and disappear again.

One can imagine Ned Land's anger. He was shouting at the poor creature with all the worst swear words in the English language. As for me, I was merely disappointed that the animal was able to thwart us at every turn.

We chased it without stopping for an hour, and I had begun to think it would be almost impossible to capture it, when this animal got the unfortunate idea of getting his revenge. This was to be his downfall. He turned on the dinghy and got ready to attack.

This maneuver did not escape the Canadian's attention. "Watch out!" he cried.

The coxswain said several words in their strange language, undoubtedly warning the men to be on their guard.

The dugong came within twenty feet of the dinghy, stopped and sniffed the air with its huge nostrils. Then it started moving again, and rushed headlong in our direction.

The dinghy could not avoid the blow. We were almost capsized and the dinghy shipped a ton or two of water which had to be bailed out; we had been saved from actually going over by the coxswain's skill in maneuvering so that we were struck at an angle and not full on the side. Ned Land was clinging to the bow and harpooning the giant animal again and again, as it sunk its teeth into the gunwale and lifted the boat out of water like a lion attacking a deer. We were thrown on top of one another and things might have ended badly if the Canadian, carrying on the struggle relentlessly, had not finally struck the animal in the heart.

I could hear a grinding of teeth on the iron hull, and then the dugong disappeared, taking the harpoon with it. But soon the barrel came back to the surface, and a little later the animal's body also appeared floating on its back. The dinghy went over, took it in tow and headed for the *Nautilus*.

Very powerful pulleys had to be used to haul it up on the platform. It weighed eleven thousand pounds. When it was cut up, the Canadian watched every detail of the operation. That same day at supper, the steward served me several slices of this meat very well prepared by the cook on board. I found it excellent, and even better than veal, to say nothing of beef.

On the next day, February 11, the ship's galley was enriched by yet another delicate piece of game. A flock of terns had descended on the *Nautilus* and been caught. They were of a species called *Sterna nilotica* found only in

Egypt and had a black beak, a gray, pointed head, white dots around their eyes, grayish black wings and tail, white stomach and throat and red feet. We also captured a few dozen Nile ducks, which make an excellent dish; these birds have white heads and necks, and the rest of their body is covered with black spots.

The *Nautilus* had reduced its speed. It moved as if it were just out for a stroll, so to speak. I observed that the water of the Red Sea became less and less salty as we drew near Suez.

Toward five in the afternoon, we sighted Cape Ras Mohammed, which forms the tip of Arabia Petraea, that portion of land between the Gulf of Suez and the Gulf of Akaba.

The *Nautilus* then entered Jubal Straits leading to the Gulf of Suez. I could see clearly a high mountain dominating the land between the two gulfs. It was Mount Horeb (or Sinai), on which Moses saw God face to face, and which one always imagines sheathed in lightning.

The *Nautilus* continued cruising alternately on the surface and under water, and at six o'clock we passed Tor, situated inside a bay whose waters seemed tinted with red—a phenomenon Captain Nemo had mentioned earlier. Then night came on in the midst of a heavy silence occasionally broken by the cry of a pelican, by the crash of surf on rocks or by the faraway panting of a steamer as its paddle wheels struck the water with a resounding splash.

From eight to nine o'clock the *Nautilus* cruised only a short distance below the surface. According to my calculations, we were probably very near Suez. Through the panels in the lounge, I could see the rock walls brightly illuminated by our electric light. It seemed as if the gulf were getting narrower and narrower.

At nine-fifteen the boat returned to the surface and I went up on deck. I was very impatient to go through Captain Nemo's tunnel; I could not sit still and had come up to take a breath of the fresh night air.

Soon I could make out through the darkness a pale light, half discolored by the mist, shining about a mile away.

"A floating beacon," someone near me said.

I turned around and recognized the captain.

"It's the floating beacon of Suez," he went on. "It won't be long now before we're at the mouth of the tunnel."

"It must be rather difficult to enter."

"Yes, it is. That is why I stay in the helmsman's compartment during the entire operation. And now, if you would kindly go below, Monsieur Aronnax, the *Nautilus* is going to dive and will not surface again until we have gone through the Arabian Tunnel."

I followed Captain Nemo. The hatch closed, the reservoirs filled with water and the submarine dove to a depth of thirty or thirty-five feet.

"Professor," he said, "would you like to keep me company in the helmsman's compartment?"

"I would be very flattered," I answered.

"Come, then. You will be able to see everything of this trip that will take us both under water and under land."

Captain Nemo led me toward the central companionway. Halfway up he opened a door, went down the upper gangways and finally entered the helmsman's compartment, which, as the reader already knows, was situated on the forward part of the platform.

It was a cabin about six feet square and more or less resembling the bridges on Mississippi and Hudson steamboats.

In the middle was a vertical wheel connected to the rudder chains running to the stern of the ship. Four portholes made of lenslike glass, one in each wall, permitted the helmsman to see in all directions.

Once my eyes became accustomed to the darkness in the compartment, I could make out the helmsman, a powerfully built man, gripping the rim of the wheel. Outside, the sea was brilliantly lit by the searchlight behind us, at the other end of the platform.

"Now," said Captain Nemo, "let's find the tunnel."

Electric wires ran between this compartment and the engine room, thus permitting the captain to communicate directly. He pressed a metal button, and immediately the engines slowed down considerably.

I looked out in silence at the high, sheer wall—the solid rock base of the sandy mountains on the coast—near which we were traveling. We followed it for an hour, only a few feet away. Captain Nemo did not take his eyes off the compass installed inside the cabin. At a mere gesture from him, the helmsman would instantly alter his course.

I had taken my place at the port window, and I could make out magnificent coral foundations, zoophytes and seaweed, and from cracks in the rock I could see crustaceans waving their enormous claws.

At 10:15 Captain Nemo took the wheel. A large gallery, black and deep, opened up before us. The *Nautilus* boldly entered it. A strange rumbling could be heard on either side. It was the sound of the water rushing down the sloping tunnel from the Red Sea to the Mediterranean. In spite of the fact that the engines had been reversed to counteract the force of this current, the *Nautilus* shot forward like an arrow.

Along the narrow walls of the tunnel I could make out nothing but brilliant streaks, straight furrows of fire created by our speed and the strong electric light. My heart was beating fast, and I brought my hand to my chest in order to calm it.

At 10:35, Captain Nemo left the wheel, turned toward me and said: "The Mediterranean."

The *Nautilus* had been carried along by the current at such speed that it had crossed the Isthmus of Suez in less than twenty minutes.

CHAPTER XXX
The Greek Islands

At dawn of the next day, February 12, the *Nautilus* once again came to the surface. I rushed up to the platform. Three miles to the south I could make out the vague outline of Pelusium. Our passage through the tunnel had been easy, but the current carrying us along had been so strong as to make it impossible to go back through this tunnel in the other direction.

At about seven o'clock, I was joined by Ned and Conseil. These two inseparable companions had slept soundly without giving a thought to the extraordinary thing the *Nautilus* had done.

"Well, Professor," asked the Canadian in a slightly mocking tone, "what about the Mediterranean?"

"We're in it, Ned, my friend."

"What!" said Conseil. "You mean to say that during the night . . . ?"

"Yes, during the night, we crossed this uncrossable isthmus in a matter of minutes."

"I don't believe it," replied the Canadian.

"Well you'd better, Ned," I said. "That land you see to the south is the coast of Egypt."

"Go tell that to the marines," retorted the stubborn Canadian.

"But if Monsieur says so," replied Conseil, "it must be true."

"Moreover, Ned, the captain did me the honor of letting me stay in the helmsman's compartment while he himself steered the *Nautilus* through his narrow tunnel."

"Do you hear that, Ned?" said Conseil.

"And with eyes like yours, Ned," I added, "you ought to be able to make out the jetties of Port Said stretching out into the sea."

The Canadian looked carefully. "Yes, you're right, Professor," he said. "Your captain's an extraordinary man. There's no doubt about it, we're in the Mediterranean. All right then, let's have a little chat, and make sure that no one can overhear us."

I knew what it was the Canadian wanted to discuss, and I thought it best to let him get it off his chest. So the three of us went to sit by the searchlight where we would be less exposed to the wet spray of the waves.

"All right, Ned, we're listening," I said. "What is it?"

"It's very simple," replied the Canadian. "We're in Europe, and I want to leave the *Nautilus* before Captain Nemo's whims take us to faraway Arctic seas or back to the south Pacific."

As always, this kind of discussion with the Canadian put me in an embarrassing spot. I did not want to deprive my companions of their freedom, and yet I had no desire to leave Captain Nemo. Thanks to him and his submarine, day by day I drew nearer to completing my studies of underwater life, and I was rewriting my book on the ocean depths in the midst of the very place I was describing. Where would I ever find another opportunity like this to observe the wonders of the ocean? Nowhere. I therefore had no desire to leave the *Nautilus* before our investigations had been completed.

"Tell me frankly, Ned," I said, "are you bored on board? Do you regret the stroke of fate that threw you into Captain Nemo's hands?"

The Canadian did not answer for a few moments. He then crossed his arms and said: "Frankly, I don't regret having made this trip beneath the seas. I'll be happy to have done it, but in order to have done it, it has to end. That's the way I feel about it."

"It'll come to an end, Ned."

"Where and when?"

"I don't know where. As to when, I couldn't say; I can only suppose that it will come to an end when the seas have nothing more to teach us. Everything that begins has to come to an end."

"I agree with Monsieur," said Conseil, "and it seems very possible that after we've covered all the earth's seas, Captain Nemo will let us loose."

"Loose! He's more likely to put us in a noose!" cried the Canadian.

"Let's not exaggerate, Ned," I said. "We have nothing to fear from the captain, but I still don't agree with Conseil. We know the secrets of the *Nautilus*, and I can't imagine its commander is going to let us go and thereby risk having them spread all over the world."

"So what do you think will happen?" asked the Canadian.

"We'll get an opportunity some time, if not now, then maybe in six months."

"Hah!" exclaimed Ned Land. "And could you please tell us just where we'll be in six months, Professor?"

"Perhaps here, perhaps in China. You know how fast the *Nautilus* can travel. It crosses oceans like a swallow flying through the air or like an express train traveling over continents. It doesn't even avoid regions full of shipping. Who is to say it won't go near France, England or America where we would have as good a chance of escaping as here?"

"Monsieur Aronnax," answered the Canadian, "there's one thing wrong with all your reasoning. You're talking in the future: 'We'll be here, we'll be there!' I'm talking about right now: 'We're here and we should take advantage of it.'"

I felt hard pressed by Ned Land's logic and close to defeat. I no longer knew what arguments to use.

"Monsieur," Ned continued, "even though it's impossible, let's say that Captain Nemo offered you your freedom today. Would you accept it?"

"I don't know," I replied.

"And if he added that the offer would never be renewed, would you accept then?"

I did not answer.

"What does my friend Conseil think?" asked Ned Land.

"Your friend Conseil has nothing to say," he answered calmly. "He has no interest whatsoever in the whole matter. He's a bachelor, just like his master and his comrade, Ned. He has no wife, relations or children waiting for him at home. He's in the service of Monsieur, he thinks like Monsieur, he talks like Monsieur, and to his great regret, he can't be counted on to make a majority. Only two people are confronting each other here: Monsieur and Ned. Conseil is here to listen and keep score."

I could not help smiling at the way Conseil effaced his own personality. Ned must have been delighted at heart not to have him as an adversary.

"Well then, Monsieur," said Ned Land, "since Conseil doesn't exist, let's discuss this matter between the two of us. I spoke my piece and you heard me. What's your answer?"

I obviously had to say something, and I did not like the idea of trying to dodge the issue.

"Well, Ned," I said, "here's my answer. You're right, and my arguments can't stand up to yours. We can't rely on Captain Nemo's good will. The most elementary caution would prevent him from letting us go. So we must be on the lookout and take advantage of the first opportunity we get to leave the *Nautilus*."

"Good, Monsieur Aronnax."

"But let me say one thing," I added. "The opportunity must be a good one. Our first attempt has to succeed; if it doesn't, we won't get another chance, and Captain Nemo won't forgive us."

"That's right," replied the Canadian. "But what you say applies to any attempt we make, whether it's in two years or two days. And that means there's only one thing to keep in mind: if the right opportunity comes along, we have to take it."

"Agreed. But just tell me, Ned, what you mean by the right opportunity."

"It'll come when the *Nautilus* gets near the coast of Europe on some dark night."

"Would you try swimming?"

"Yes, if we were near enough to the shore and if the submarine were on the surface. But not if we were far from shore or the submarine under water."

"What would you do in that case?"

"I'd try to get ahold of the dinghy. I know how to sail it. We'd get inside it, unfasten it and rise to the surface. And since it's behind the helmsman's compartment, he wouldn't even see us."

"All right, Ned. Keep an eye open for such a chance. And don't forget that we're lost if we don't succeed."

"I won't forget it, Monsieur."

"And now, Ned, do you want to know what I think about your plans?"

"What, Monsieur Aronnax?"

"Well, I think—I don't say that I hope—that this opportunity will never come up."

"Why not?"

"Because Captain Nemo can't possibly believe that we've given up all hope of regaining our freedom, and he'll be on his guard, especially when we're near the coast of Europe."

"I agree with Monsieur," said Conseil.

"We'll see," replied Ned Land, shaking his head with an air of determination.

"Now, Ned," I added, "let's leave it there. Not another word about all this. The day you're ready to go, tell us and we'll follow you. I leave it completely up to you."

Thus ended this conversation which was to have such serious consequences later on. But I must add that, at the moment, events seemed to confirm my predictions, to the Canadian's great disappointment. Was Captain Nemo afraid of what we might do in these waters, or did he merely want to stay out of sight of the many ships sailing in the Mediterranean? I have no idea, but most of the time we cruised under water and far from any shore. The *Nautilus* would either come up only far enough for the helmsman's compartment to appear above the surface, or else it would dive to great depths.

I only knew, for instance, that we were passing Karpathos Island, one of the Sporades, because of the line of Virgil that Captain Nemo quoted as he put his finger on the map:

In the Karpathian sea
Lives Proteus, dark prophet of Neptune.

It had in fact been the dwelling place of Proteus, the shepherd of Neptune's flocks, and it was situated between Rhodes and Crete. I saw only its granite foundations through the glass panels of the lounge.

On the next day, February 14, I had resolved to spend several hours studying the fish of the Greek Islands, but for some reason the panels remained completely closed. On checking the *Nautilus'* direction, I realized that it was heading for Candia, the ancient isle of Crete. When I had boarded the *Abraham Lincoln* this island had just risen up against its Turkish tyrants. But of what had since happened to this insurrection I had absolutely no idea, and Captain Nemo, cut off as he was from all communication with dry land, was not the man who could inform me.

I therefore did not even mention this when I found myself alone with him that night in the lounge. Moreover, he was silent and seemed preoccupied.

Then, contrary to his usual custom, he ordered the panels to be opened and started pacing back and forth between them, carefully observing the surrounding sea. Why? I could not imagine, and contented myself with studying the fish that passed before my eyes.

Among others I noticed a certain species of goby mentioned by Aristotle. It is called a "rockling" and is particularly frequent in the salt water near the Nile delta. Near them were swimming some semiphosphorescent schnappers, a sparoid fish which the Egyptians classed among their sacred animals, and whose arrival in the Nile announced the arrival of the flood season and was greeted with religious ceremonies. I also noticed some foot-long cheilinae, bony fish with transparent scales and pale coloration accentuated by red spots. They eat large quantities of marine plants which gives them an excellent taste. As a result they were much sought after by the gourmets of ancient Rome, and their entrails, cooked with soft roe of moray, peacock brains and flamingo tongues, made a dish which delighted the emperor Vitellius.

I then noticed another inhabitant of these seas which brought back yet more memories of what I had learned about classical times. It was the remora, which often attaches itself to the bellies of sharks. According to ancient writers it could stop a ship by sticking to its hull, and it was said that one of these remora had held back Anthony's ship in the battle of Actium and thereby helped Augustus gain his victory. On how little hangs the destiny of nations! I also observed marvelous anthias belonging to the order of Lutianidae; the Greeks considered them sacred and claimed they had the power to chase off sea monsters. Their name comes from the word for "flower," and it is well justified by their shimmering shades of red going from light pink to a deep ruby color as well as by the slightly mottled effect on their dorsal fin. I could not take my eyes off these wonders of the sea. But then suddenly I was thunderstruck by an unexpected apparition.

A man had appeared in the midst of the water, a diver carrying a small leather bag attached to his belt. It was not a body floating in the water. It was a live man swimming vigorously, disappearing from time to time to catch his breath at the surface.

I turned to Captain Nemo and said excitedly: "A man drowning! We must save him!"

The captain came over to the window without saying a word.

The man drew nearer, and he was now looking at us with his face pressed against the glass.

To my complete amazement, Captain Nemo motioned to him. The diver answered with a wave of his hand and then immediately went back to the surface. He did not reappear.

"Don't worry," said the captain. "That's Nicholas from Cape Matapan. They call him 'the Fish.' He's well known throughout the Cyclades. A marvelous diver! Water is his element, and he lives in it more than he does on land, constantly going back and forth from one island to another, and even to Crete."

"Do you know him, Captain?"

"Why shouldn't I, Monsieur Aronnax?"

With this, Captain Nemo went over to a bureau beside the left-hand window of the lounge. Near it I noticed a steel banded chest with a brass plaque on the lid bearing the monogram of the *Nautilus* with the motto, *Mobilis in mobile*.

Then, without taking any notice of my presence, the captain opened the bureau, which turned out to be a kind of strongbox containing ingots.

They were ingots of gold. Where did it come from, this precious metal worth such a vast amount? Where had the captain gotten this gold, and what was he going to do with it?

I didn't say a word. I just looked. The captain took out the ingots one by one and placed them neatly in the chest, which was soon filled to the top. I estimated that it contained more than twenty hundred pounds of gold, or in other words an amount worth about a million dollars.

The chest was securely fastened, and on its lid the captain wrote an address in letters which must have been Greek.

He then pressed a button communicating with the crew's quarters. Four men appeared and, not without some difficulty, pushed the chest out of the room. I soon could hear them lifting it up the companionway by means of pulleys.

Then Captain Nemo turned toward me and asked: "You were saying, Professor?"

"I wasn't saying anything, Captain."

"Then with your permission, Monsieur, I shall wish you good night."

And with that, Captain Nemo left the room.

I went to my room very puzzled, as one might well imagine. I tried in vain to sleep. I attempted to find some relationship between the appearance of the diver and the chest filled with gold. Soon I felt the ship rolling and pitching, and realized that the *Nautilus* had surfaced.

Then I heard the sound of steps on the platform. I realized the dinghy was being unfastened and put to sea. It knocked against the *Nautilus* for a moment, and then all noise ceased.

Two hours later I heard the same noises, the same goings and comings. The dinghy was hauled on board, refastened in its place and the *Nautilus* once again dove under water.

So all this gold had been taken some place. Where? With whom was Captain Nemo in communication?

The next day I told Conseil and Ned what had happened. My companions were no less surprised than I.

"But where did he get all this gold?" asked Ned Land.

I had no answer to that question. After lunch I went to the lounge and started working. Till five in the afternoon I was busy drawing up my notes. Then suddenly—I thought at the time it might have been due to some personal indisposition—I felt very hot and had to take off my byssus coat. This was very strange as we were not in the tropics, and besides with the *Nautilus* submerged we should have been insulated against the outside climate. I looked at the pressure gauge. It indicated a depth of sixty feet, or in other words beyond reach of atmospheric heat.

I continued working, but soon the temperature had risen to the point of being almost unbearable. "Could it be that there's a fire on board?" I thought.

I was about to leave the lounge when Captain Nemo entered. He went over to the thermometer and said: "A hundred and eight."

"I don't doubt it, Captain," I replied; "and if it gets any hotter, we won't be able to stand it."

"Professor, it won't get any hotter unless we want it to."

"Can you change it at will?"

"No, but I can go farther from the area producing it."

"You mean to say it's coming from outside?"

"Yes, we're cruising through a current of boiling water."

"How is that possible?" I cried.

"Look."

The panels opened, and I could see that the ocean around us was completely white. Steaming sulfurous fumes were bubbling up through the sea, which was boiling like water in a pot. I touched one of the panes of glass, but it was so hot I immediately had to remove my hand.

"Where are we?" I asked.

"Near Santorin Island, Professor," replied the captain, "and to be more precise, in the channel separating Nea Kaumenc from Palea Kaumene. I wanted to show you the strange spectacle of an underwater volcanic eruption."

"I thought that the formation of these new islands was finished."

"Nothing is ever finished in volcanic areas," answered Captain Nemo, "and the earth is continually being altered by underground fire. Already in the year nineteen of our era, according to Cassiodorus and Pliny, a new island called Theia appeared in the same place as these more recently formed little islands. Later it sank beneath the surface, only to reappear in the year sixty-nine and then sink once more. From that period till now, the area was calm. But on February 3, 1866, a new island called George Island emerged in the midst of sulfurous vapors near Nea Kaumene and then became joined to it on the sixth of that same month. Seven days later, on February 13, the island of Aphroessa appeared, leaving a thirty-foot channel between it and Nea Kaumene. I was in these waters when it happened, and I was able to observe all the various phases. Aphroessa was a round island about three hundred feet in diameter and thirty feet in height. It was composed of black, vitreous lava mixed with feldspar. Finally, on March 10, a yet smaller island called Reka appeared next to Nea

Kaumene, and then the three became fused together, forming one entire island."

"Are we in one of these channels now?" I asked.

"This one," replied Captain Nemo, pointing to a chart of the area. "As you can see, I've drawn in the new islands."

"But will this channel also be filled in one day?"

"Probably, Monsieur Aronnax, for since 1866 eight little lava islands have arisen in front of the port of Saint Nicholas on Palea Kaumene. It is therefore obvious that Nea and Palea Kaumene will soon be joined. Whereas it's microscopic animals that form islands in the Pacific, here it's volcanic action. Look, Monsieur; you can see it going on right now beneath the surface."

I went back to the glass panel. The *Nautilus* was no longer moving. The heat was becoming unbearable. There was some iron salt in the water turning it from white to red. In spite of the lounge being hermetically sealed, it was becoming filled with an unbearable smell of sulfur, and outside scarlet flames shone brighter than the electric light.

I was covered with perspiration; I was stifling; I was being cooked alive. Yes, I really felt as if I were being cooked alive!

"We can't stay much longer in the midst of this boiling water," I said to the captain.

"No, it wouldn't be wise," Captain Nemo answered calmly.

An order was given; the *Nautilus* veered off and drew away from this dangerous furnace. A quarter of an hour later, we were breathing freely on the surface.

The thought came to me that if Ned Land had chosen to escape in these waters, we would not have come out of this sea of fire alive.

On the next day, February 16, we quit that basin which, between Rhodes and Alexandria, goes down to depths of ten thousand feet, and the *Nautilus,* cruising past Cerigo Island and Cape Matapan, left the Greek Islands.

CHAPTER XXXI
Through the Mediterranean in Forty-eight Hours

The Mediterranean, the bluest of all seas, the "Great Sea" of the Hebrews, the "Sea" of the Greeks and the "Mare Nostrum" of the Romans, bordered with orange trees, aloes, cactus, sea pines, scented with the perfume of the myrtle, framed by rugged mountains, saturated with a pure, clear air and yet incessantly troubled by volcanic action, is a true battlefield in which Neptune and Pluto still struggle for domination of the world. There on its banks and waters, as Michelet said, man gains new strength in one of the most invigorating climates of the globe.

But however beautiful it may be, I was only able to get a rapid glimpse of its basin, which covers an area of 850,000 square miles. Even Captain Nemo's knowledge was of no help to me, for this enigmatic person didn't appear once during our rapid crossing. I estimated that it took the *Nautilus* forty-eight hours to travel about thirteen hundred miles beneath the surface. We left Greek waters on the morning of February 16, and by sunrise on the eighteenth we had crossed the Straits of Gibraltar.

It was obvious to me that Captain Nemo did not like the Mediterranean, surrounded, as it was, by those countries he was fleeing. Its waves and breezes brought him too many memories, or perhaps regrets. He no longer had the same freedom of movement as in larger oceans, and his *Nautilus* felt hemmed in by the shores of Africa and Europe.

We traveled at a speed of twenty-five knots, and it therefore goes without saying that Ned Land, to his great annoyance, had to give up his plans of escape.

He couldn't use the dinghy while we were cruising at over forty feet per second. Leaving the *Nautilus* under such conditions would have been like jumping from a train traveling at the same speed, a rash move if there ever was one. Moreover, the submarine only surfaced at night to renew its air supply; it was guided merely by its compass and log.

I therefore only saw the Mediterranean as the traveler in an express train sees the landscape rushing past, or in other words, only the objects farther away and not the foreground, which passes by with the speed of lightning. Nevertheless, Conseil and I were able to observe several types of fish whose powerful fins permitted them to keep up with the *Nautilus* for short periods of time. We stayed on watch at the windows of the lounge, and our notes permit me to describe the animal life of the Mediterranean.

Of the various fish living there, some I saw clearly, others I merely glimpsed and there were yet others completely hidden from our view by the *Nautilus'* speed. I therefore hope I will be allowed to classify them according to these three rather odd categories. This will give a better idea of what I saw.

In the midst of the waters brilliantly illuminated by our electric light, I saw three-foot-long lampreys of a kind found in all seas. There were also oxyrhinchae, a kind of ray five feet across with a white belly and spotted ash-gray back, looking like vast shawls carried off by the ocean currents. Other rays passed by so fast that I could not tell whether they merited the name of eagles given them by the Greeks, or that of rats, toads or bats which modern fishermen have bestowed on them. Twelve-foot-long milander sharks—a species particularly feared by divers—vied with each other in speed. Thresher sharks, eight feet long and gifted with a very sensitive sense of smell, passed by looking like blue shadows. Sparoid dorados, some of which measured over four feet in length, passed dressed in silver and azure surrounded with stripes all contrasting sharply with the somber hue of their fins; these fish, once upon a time sacred to Venus, had golden eyebrows above their eyes; they are a valuable species, equally at home in salt or fresh water—living in rivers, lakes and oceans, and able to withstand any climate or temperature; they are also a rarity in that they have conserved all the beauty of their forebears in geological times. Magnificent sturgeons, nine or ten feet long and able to travel at great speeds, hurtled against the windows of the lounge, letting us get a glimpse of their bluish backs covered with little brown spots; these fish, which are like a weaker variety of shark, are found in all the world's oceans; in the spring they like to go up large rivers, struggling against the currents of the Volga, Danube, Po, Rhine, Loire and Oder, and they live on herring, mackerel, salmon and rockling; although they belong to the class of cartilaginous fish, their flesh is delicate; they are eaten fresh, dried or salted, and once upon a time they were brought triumphantly to Lucullus' table. But as the *Nautilus* cruised near the surface, those inhabitants of the Mediterranean which I could best observe belonged to the sixty-third genus of bony fish. They were tunas with their blue-black backs, silver bellies and dorsal stripes giving off a golden gleam. They are said to follow vessels in search of shade from the hot tropical sun, and they did just this with the *Nautilus,* as they had once done with La Pérouse's ships. For hours they would race against us. I never tired of admiring these creatures so beautifully built for speed, with their small heads, streamlined bodies up to ten feet long, extraordinarily powerful pectoral fins and forked tails. Like certain birds, they swam in triangle formation, which caused the Greeks and Romans to say that these fish knew about geometry and strategy. Nevertheless they do not escape Provençal fishermen, who esteem them as much as did the inhabitants of Propontis and Italy, and thousands upon thousands of these precious animals hurl themselves blindly and heedlessly into the nets awaiting them.

I will mention—only as a reminder—those Mediterranean fish of which Conseil and I merely got a fleeting glimpse. There were whitish gymnotes which swept past like clouds of mist; congers ten to thirteen feet long and brightly colored with green, blue and yellow; three-foot-long hakes, whose liver is so tasty; coepolae-teniae floating like thin seaweed; gurnards, which poets call lyrefish and fishermen call pipers, whose snouts are adorned with two triangular plates which resemble Homer's instrument; flying gurnards, which can swim as fast as birds can fly; a species of perch with a red head, whose dorsal fin is decorated with a kind of filament; shad covered with black, gray, brown, blue, yellow and green spots—a fish that is easily affected by the silvery sound of little bells; magnificent turbots, those pheasants of the sea whose diamond-shaped bodies are marbled with brown and yellow on top and whose yellow fins are flecked with brown; and finally schools of marvelous red mullets, the ocean's equivalent of birds of paradise, for which Romans would pay as much as ten thousand sesterces apiece so they could cruelly watch them change from deep vermilion to pale white as they died on their table.

But I was able to see no miralets, triggerfish, tetraodons, sea horses, juans, bellows fish, blennies, surmullets, wrasse, smelt, flying fish, anchovies, sea breams, boöps, orphes, or any representatives of the order Pleuronectidae common to the Atlantic and Mediterranean, such as dabs, flounders, plaice or sole. This was because of the dizzy speed with which the *Nautilus* traveled through these rich waters.

As for sea mammals, I thought I saw, near the mouth of the Adriatic, two or three cachalots belonging to the genus of the sperm whale with one dorsal fin; several dolphins of the genus Globicephala, found only in the Mediterranean, which have the front part of their heads striped with little bright lines; and also a dozen or so seals with white bellies and black fur, known as monk seals and looking just like ten-foot-long Dominicans.

Conseil thought he could make out a turtle with a shell six feet across and with three ridges down its back. I was sorry not to have seen this reptile, for from Conseil's description I thought it must have been a rather rare species called a leatherback. The only reptiles I saw were several cacuans with elongated shells.

As for zoophytes, I was able to gaze admiringly for several seconds at a marvelous orange-colored galeolaria which stuck to the port window; it consisted of a long slender filament spreading out into an infinite number of branches and ending in the finest lace ever spun by Arachne's rivals. I was unfortunately not able to capture this splendid specimen, and I undoubtedly would have seen no other Mediterranean zoophytes if, during the night of the sixteenth, the *Nautilus* had not reduced its speed considerably.

It did so because we were then passing between Sicily and the coast of Tunis, and in this narrow space between Cape Bon and the Straits of Messina, the ocean floor rises abruptly. At this point it comes up to within 60 feet of the surface, whereas on each side it goes down to depths of 250 feet. The *Nautilus* therefore had to maneuver carefully in order to avoid this underwater barrier.

I showed Conseil the position of this long reef on a chart of the Mediterranean.

"If Monsieur doesn't mind my saying so," observed Conseil, "it's like an isthmus connecting Europe to Africa."

"Yes, my boy," I answered, "it cuts across the entire Straits of Libya, and Smith's soundings have proved that between Cape Boeo and Cape Farina the continents were once upon a time connected."

"I can easily believe it," said Conseil.

"And what's more," I went on, "a similar barrier existed once between Gibraltar and Ceuta, completely closing off the Mediterranean."

"What would happen," asked Conseil, "if someday volcanic action again raised these barriers above the surface of the water?"

"I doubt that would ever happen, Conseil."

"But—with Monsieur's permission—if it ever did happen, it would come as quite a shock to Monsieur de Lesseps who's going to so much trouble to build the Suez Canal."

"Yes, but as I said before, it won't happen. The violence of the forces beneath the earth's surface is constantly diminishing. Volcanoes, which were so numerous when the world was young, are slowly dying down. The temperature of the earth's inner surfaces lowers appreciably each century, which will eventually have unfortunate results, for this heat is life."

"But there's the sun . . ."

"The sun isn't enough, Conseil. Can the sun give heat to a corpse?"

"No, not that I know of."

"Well, my friend, one day the earth will be a cold corpse. It will become uninhabitable, and it will be as deserted as the moon which lost its vital heat long ago."

"How many centuries will that take?" asked Conseil.

"Several hundred thousand years, my boy."

"Well then," said Conseil, "we'll at least have enough time to finish our trip, unless Ned Land botches things up!"

Conseil felt reassured and went back to studying the shallow bottom above which the *Nautilus* was slowly cruising.

There on a rocky volcanic bottom lay a whole world of living flowers: sponges; sea slugs; transparent cydippiae with reddish cirri, emitting a light phosphorescence; beroës, commonly known as sea cucumbers, bathed in a gleaming rainbow of light; feather stars a yard across turning the water red; treelike euryales of great beauty; pavonaceae with long stems; a great number of edible sea urchins of various species; and green sea anemones with grayish trunks and brown disks almost lost beneath their mass of olive-colored tentacles.

Conseil spent his time more especially observing mollusks and articulata, and even though a list of what he saw might make somewhat dry reading, I feel it would be wrong to leave out his personal observations.

In the subkingdom of mollusks he cites numerous scallops, spondyli, triangular wedge shells, trident-shaped hyalaea with yellow fins and transparent shells, orange-colored pleurobranchia looking like eggs flecked with green spots, aplysia, also known as sea hares, dolabellae, chubby acerae, umbrella shells, found only in the Mediterranean, ear shells, which produce a much sought after mother-of-pearl, red scallops, beaked cockles, which the people from the south of France prefer to oysters, another kind of cockle very popular in Marseilles, some of those clams so common off the coast of North America and which are eaten in such quantities in New York, comb shells of various colors, lithodes hiding inside their holes, whose flesh has a peppery taste I like very much, furrowed venericardiae, whose bulging shells are covered with ridges, cynthiae covered with scarlet bumps, carniaria bent up at each end and looking like small gondolas, atlantes with spiral shells, gray thetys with white spots and covered with their fragile mantilla, aeolides looking like little slugs, cavoliniae crawling along on their backs, auriculae—and among others the auricula myosotis with its oval shell—fawn-colored scalariae, periwinkles, ianthinae, cinerariae, petricolae, lamellariae, cabochons, pandoras, etc.

As for articulata, in Conseil's notes they are rightly divided into six classes, three of which belong to the marine world. These are crustaceans, cirrhopoda and annelids.

Crustaceans are divided into nine orders, and the first of these comprises the decapods, that is to say animals whose head and thorax is usually united, whose mouth consists of several pairs of jaws and who possess four, five or six pairs of legs on their thorax. Conseil followed the method of our master Milne-Edwards and divided them into three sections: brachyura, macrura and anomura. Even though these names are somewhat uncouth, they are correct and precise. Among the brachyura, Conseil cites amathiae, whose head is armed with two horns going off to each side, inachidae, which—and I have no idea why—the Greeks used as a symbol of wisdom, several kinds of spider crabs, one species of which had probably wandered into this shallow water, for it usually lives at great depths, xanthi, pilumnae, rhomboides, granular calappae—very easy to digest, as Conseil notes—toothless corystes, ebaliae, cymobolidae, wooly dorripi, etc. Among the macrura, which are divided into five families, ceriaceae, burrowers, astaci, palaemonidae and ochyzopodes, he cites rock lobsters, the female of which is so good to eat, scyllari or squills, and all sorts of edible species, but he says nothing of the subdivision of astaci which includes the lobsters proper. Finally, among the anomura, he saw drocinae sheltered inside the abandoned shells they had picked up, homolae with their spiny head, hermit crabs, porcelain crabs, etc.

There Conseil stopped. He did not have enough time to complete the class of crustaceans by an examination of stomatopods, amphipods, homopods, isopods, trilobites, branchiopods, ostracods and entomostracae. And in order to complete his study of marine articulata, he should have mentioned the class of cirrhopoda, which comprises cyclopes, arguli, and the class of annelids, which he would not have forgotten to divide into tubicoles and dorsibranches. But once the *Nautilus* had passed the shallow water of the Straits of Libya, it again started cruising at its usual speed in the deeper water. From then on, observing mollusks, articulata or zoophytes was out of the question. We saw only large fish which passed by like shadows.

During the night of February 16–17, we entered the second basin of the Mediterranean, which in places goes down to depths of ten thousand feet. By using its inclined planes and the force of its propeller, the *Nautilus* dove down to the deepest parts of the sea.

There, although there were no natural wonders to admire, the ocean offered many moving and horrifying scenes. We were crossing that part of the Mediterranean in which so many ships had gone down. How many ships had disappeared forever between the coast of Algeria and the shores of Provence! The Mediterranean is only a lake compared to the vast expanses of the Pacific, but it is a capricious lake with changing moods. Today it is gentle and caressing for the frail tartan which seems to float between the ultramarine blue of its water and sky; and tomorrow it is raging and tormented, lashed by winds, smashing the strongest ships with its narrow waves which strike without warning.

So in this trip through the depths, I saw innumerable wrecks lying on the ocean floor, some already encrusted with coral and others only covered with a layer of rust. I also saw anchors, cannons, shot, iron fittings, parts of engines, broken cylinders, staved-in boilers and hulls occasionally floating upright and other times upside-down.

Of these wrecked ships, some had perished in collisions, and others had struck granite reefs. I saw ships which had foundered with their masts still in place and their rigging stiffened by the water. They looked as if they were anchored in some open roadstead and waiting for the moment to depart. When the *Nautilus* passed among them and bathed them in its electric light, I felt as if these ships were going to dip their flags and salute. But no, there was nothing but silence and death in this field of sorrow.

I noticed that the number of wrecks increased as we approached the Straits of Gibraltar. The shores of Africa and Europe are closer together there, and collisions are common in this narrow space. I saw many iron hulls, eerie wrecks of steamers, some lying flat on the bottom and others standing on end like huge animals. One of these boats presented a terrifying spectacle with holes in its side, its funnel bent, its paddle wheels destroyed except for their mountings, its rudder separated from its stern-post but still held on by a chain, and its rear name plate eaten away by the sea! How many lives must have been lost in this shipwreck! How many victims must have gone down with it! Had some sailor survived to tell of this terrible disaster, or did the ocean still keep the secret of what had happened? I don't know why, but it struck me that this boat buried in the ocean could be the *Atlas* which had disappeared with all hands about twenty years before, without another word ever being heard of it! What a grim task it would be to write a history of the Mediterranean depths, this vast cemetery where so much wealth has been lost and where so many victims have met their death!

Nevertheless, the *Nautilus* cruised at full speed past all these wrecks with total indifference. On February 18, toward three in the morning, it reached the entrance to the Straits of Gibraltar.

There are two currents in these straits: one on the surface, which men have known about for a long time and which brings water from the Atlantic into the Mediterranean; then a lower counter-current, whose existence has been proved in recent times by means of simple logic. For the amount of water in the Mediterranean, if it were constantly increased by that entering from the Atlantic and from rivers, would increase year by year, since mere evaporation would not be enough to re-establish the balance. Now since the water level in fact stays the same, people were forced to admit to the existence of a lower current which empties water from the Mediterranean into the Atlantic.

And this fact is undisputable. It was this counter-current of which the *Nautilus* took advantage. It moved rapidly through the narrow straits. For an instant I could make out the marvelous ruins of a temple of Hercules, which according to Pliny and Avianus had been buried along with the low island on which it stood. Then several minutes later, we were floating on the surface of the Atlantic.

CHAPTER XXXII
Vigo Bay

The Atlantic, that vast body of water with an area of 25,000,000 square miles, a length of 9000 miles and an average width of 2700 miles! This great ocean was almost completely unknown to the ancients, except perhaps to the Carthaginians, those Dutchmen of antiquity who in their commercial wanderings explored the western coasts of both Europe and Africa! This ocean with its immense parallel coasts is watered by the world's largest rivers, the St. Lawrence, the Mississippi, the Amazon, the Plata, the Orinoco, the Niger, the Senegal, the Elbe, the Loire and the Rhine, which bring it water from both the most civilized and the most barbaric countries on earth! It is a magnificent plain, constantly furrowed by ships of all nations and ending in those two terrible capes so feared by mariners, Cape Horn and the Cape of Good Hope!

The *Nautilus'* prow was now cutting through the waters of this ocean, after having covered almost ten thousand leagues in three and a half months, a distance greater than a great circle of the earth. Where were we going now, and what did the future have in store for us?

After leaving the Straits of Gibraltar, the *Nautilus* had headed for the open sea. It could now surface without fear, and we could resume our daily walks on the platform.

I immediately went up with Ned Land and Conseil. Twelve miles away we could vaguely make out Cape St. Vincent, the southwestern tip of the Spanish peninsula. A fairly strong wind was blowing from the south, and the sea was running high, making the *Nautilus* roll considerably. It was almost impossible to stand up on the platform because of the waves constantly buffeting the ship. We therefore went back down after taking several breaths of air. I returned to my cabin and Conseil to his; but the Canadian, looking rather preoccupied, followed me. Our quick trip through the Mediterranean had not allowed him to carry out his plans, and his disappointment could be clearly read in his face.

After closing the door of my room, he sat down and looked at me silently.

"Ned," I said, "I know how you feel, but you're not to blame. At the speed the *Nautilus* was traveling, it would have been madness to try and escape!"

Ned Land didn't answer. I could tell by his frown and pursed lips that he was obsessed by a single thought.

"Look," I continued, "all hope isn't lost. We're heading for Portugal, and from there it isn't far to France or England where we'll easily be able to find refuge. Now if the *Nautilus* had headed south after leaving the Straits of Gibraltar and made for the open sea, then I would be worried too. But now we know Captain Nemo doesn't avoid civilized regions, and in several days I think we'll be able to act with some security."

Ned Land looked at me yet more fixedly and then, finally parting his pursed lips, he said: "We'll do it tonight."

I got up suddenly. I must admit I was not prepared for this. I wanted to answer him, but words failed me.

"We agreed to wait for an opportunity," Ned Land continued, "and now it's come. Tonight we'll be only several miles from the Spanish coast. It'll be dark and the wind's coming from the sea. You gave me your word, Monsieur Aronnax, and I'm counting on you."

Since I still said nothing, the Canadian got up and came over to me.

"Tonight at nine," he said. "I've told Conseil. At that time Captain Nemo will be in his room and probably in bed. Neither the mechanics nor any members of the crew can see us. Conseil and I will go to the central companionway while you wait in the library right next door, waiting for my signal. The oars, mast and sail are in the dinghy. I've even been able to store some provisions in it. I've also gotten ahold of a monkey wrench to undo the bolts which fasten the dinghy to the hull of the *Nautilus*. So everything's ready. I'll see you tonight."

"But the sea's quite rough," I said.

"I know it is," replied the Canadian, "but that's a risk we have to take.

Freedom's worth paying for. Besides the boat's well built, and several miles with a following wind is nothing much to worry about. We have to try it tonight, because for all we know by tomorrow the *Nautilus* might be two hundred miles out to sea. If things run according to plan, between ten and eleven o'clock either we'll have reached some spot on dry land or we'll be dead. May God be with us! Till tonight."

With that the Canadian departed, leaving me dumfounded. I had assumed that in such a situation I would have time to think it over and discuss it. My stubborn companion had not allowed this to happen. But then what could I have said? Ned Land was right a hundred times over. A reasonably good chance was being offered us, and we had to take advantage of it. How could I go back on my word and jeopardize the future of my companions for purely personal reasons? Besides, it was true that by tomorrow Captain Nemo might have taken us far from any land.

Just then a rather loud whistling noise told me that the reservoirs were being filled, and the *Nautilus* dove beneath the surface.

I stayed in my room. I wanted to avoid the captain so that my emotions would not betray me. It was a sad day for me, torn as I was between the desire to regain my freedom and regret at abandoning this marvelous *Nautilus* and leaving my underwater studies incomplete! How I hated leaving "my Atlantic," as I called it, without having seen its deepest waters and uncovered its secrets, as I had with the Indian Ocean and the Pacific! It was like putting down a novel after the first volume, or interrupting a dream at its most exciting moment! The hours passed by painfully as I either imagined myself safely on land with my companions, or wished, in spite of what reason told me, that some unforeseen circumstance would prevent Ned Land from carrying out his plan.

Twice I went to the lounge. I wanted to check the compass. I wanted to see if the *Nautilus* was taking us nearer or farther from the coast. But the ship stayed in Portuguese waters. It was heading north, fairly near the shore.

I therefore had to make up my mind and prepare to escape. My luggage wasn't heavy; there were only my notes and nothing else.

As for Captain Nemo, I wondered what he would think of our escape, whether it would worry him or actually do him harm, and I also wondered what he would do in the case either that our attempt did succeed or did not. I certainly had no cause for complaint, quite on the contrary. I had never seen such hospitality as his; but he could not consider me ungrateful for wanting to leave him. No promise bound us to him. He counted on retaining us on board merely by the force of circumstance and not by our word. But his frankly admitted intent of keeping us forever prisoners justified any attempt we might make to escape.

I had not seen the captain since our visit to Santorin Island. Would fate bring us face to face again before my departure? This was something I both desired and feared. I listened for his footsteps in the room next to mine. There was nothing but silence. His cabin was undoubtedly empty.

Then I began to wonder if this strange person was really on board. Since the night the dinghy had left the *Nautilus* on some mysterious errand, I had somewhat changed my ideas about him. In spite of what he had told me, I felt that Captain Nemo had perhaps maintained some kind of communication with dry land. Was it true that he never left the *Nautilus*? Often I had not seen him for weeks on end. What was he doing during that time? Wasn't it possible that he was carrying out some secret mission completely unknown to me?

All these ideas and a thousand others passed through my mind. In our peculiar situation, I could go on guessing like this forever. I felt very uneasy. This waiting was unbearable. The hours passed by much too slowly for my impatient mood.

As always, dinner was served in my room. I ate badly, for I was too preoccupied. I got up from the table at seven. There were a hundred and twenty minutes to go—I had begun counting them—before I was to rejoin Ned Land. I became more and more nervous. My heart was beating violently. I couldn't stay still. I paced back and forth, hoping that the physical movement would calm me down. The idea of dying in our daring venture was the least of my worries; but the thought of our plans being discovered before we could get away from the *Nautilus* and of being brought before a Captain Nemo who was angry, or worse yet, saddened by my wanting to abandon him, made my heart beat yet faster.

I wanted to see the lounge one last time. I went down the gangway and entered this museum in which I had spent so many pleasant and useful hours. I looked at all the riches and treasures as would a man about to be exiled for life, one leaving never to return. Never again would I see these wonders of nature and these masterpieces of art among which so much of my life had been spent lately. I wanted to look out the window at the Atlantic, but the panels were hermetically closed and a steel-plated wall separated me from this ocean I did not yet know.

As I wandered about the lounge, I arrived at the door giving onto the Captain's cabin. To my great astonishment it was ajar. I stepped back involuntarily. I was afraid Captain Nemo might see me if he were in his room. But hearing no noise, I drew near. The room was empty. I pushed the door further open and took several steps inside. Still the same stark, monastic look.

Just then I was struck by several etchings hanging on the wall which I had not noticed on my first visit. They were portraits of those great men of history who had devoted their lives to some human ideal: Kosciusko, the hero whose dying words were *Finis Poloniae*, Bozaris, the Leonidas of modern Greece, O'Connell, the defender of Ireland, Washington, the founder of the American union, Manin, the Italian patriot, Lincoln, felled by the bullet of a partisan of slavery, and finally that martyr for the cause of Negro emancipation, John Brown, hanging on his gallows just as Victor Hugo had drawn him.

What bond existed between these heroic souls and Captain Nemo? Could I unravel some of the mystery of his existence from this collection of portraits? Was he a champion of oppressed peoples, a liberator of enslaved races? Had he played a role in the latest political and social upheavals of our century? Had he been one of the heroes of that terrible American civil war which had been both unfortunate and forever glorious . . . ?

Suddenly the clock struck eight. The first blow of the hammer on the bell shook me from my reverie. I trembled as if an invisible eye had penetrated my most secret thoughts, and I rushed out of the room.

I looked at the compass. We were still heading north. The log indicated a moderate speed and the pressure gauge showed we were at a depth of about sixty feet. So everything was favoring the Canadian's projects.

I went back to my room. I dressed myself warmly—sea boots, otter-skin cap and byssus coat lined with seal fur. I was ready. As I waited, only the vibration of the propeller broke the deep silence on board. I listened, half expecting to hear shouts telling me that Ned Land had been caught trying to escape. I was seized by a mortal dread. I vainly tried to be calm and cool.

At a few minutes before nine, I put my ear to the captain's door. Not a sound. I left my room and went to the dimly lit, deserted lounge.

I opened the door leading to the library. The same half light, the same solitude. I went over and took up my position near the door leading to the central companionway. I waited for Ned Land's signal.

Suddenly the vibrations of the propeller diminished considerably, and then stopped completely. Why this change of speed? Would it help or hinder Ned's plans? I had no way of knowing.

The silence was only broken by the beating of my heart.

Then I heard a slight bump. I realized that the *Nautilus* had just come to rest on the ocean floor. My uneasiness increased. No signal from the Canadian. I wanted to find Ned Land and put off our attempt. We were no longer sailing under usual conditions. . . .

Just then the door leading to the lounge opened and Captain Nemo appeared. He noticed me, and without any kind of preamble, said amiably: "Ah, Professor! I was looking for you. Do you know your Spanish history?"

Even if a person knew the history of his own country backward and forward, under such conditions, with his head swimming, he could not have remembered a single date.

"Well?" repeated Captain Nemo. "Did you hear what I said? Do you know Spanish history?"

"Very little," I replied.

"Learned men often have a lot to learn," said the captain. "Well then, sit down and I'll tell you about a strange episode in Spain's history."

The captain sat down on a divan and I mechanically sat down next to him in the dimly lit room.

"Professor," he said, "listen carefully. This story will be especially interesting to you, for it will answer at least one question you have not been able to solve."

"I'm listening, Captain," I said, not knowing what he was driving at, and wondering if this story would lead him around to our attempted escape.

"With your permission, Professor," said Captain Nemo, "we'll go back to seventeen-two. As you undoubtedly know, your king, Louis XIV, thinking he could make the Pyrenees disappear with a mere wave of his hand, had imposed his grandson, the Duke of Anjou, on the Spaniards. This prince, who took the name of Philip V, was not an especially good king and had a particularly difficult time with foreign affairs.

"In fact, the previous year the royal houses of Holland, Austria and England had signed a treaty of alliance at the Hague with the intent of taking the crown of Spain from Philip V and placing it on the head of an archduke to whom they prematurely gave the name of Charles III.

"Spain had to face this coalition with scarcely any army or navy. But she was not without money, provided her galleons loaded with gold and silver from America could reach her ports. Now toward the end of seventeen-two she was awaiting a rich convoy which was being escorted by twenty-three French ships commanded by Admiral Château-Renaud in order to protect it from the coalition's ships cruising the Atlantic.

"This convoy was due to put into Cadiz, but when the admiral found out that an English fleet was cruising in those waters, he decided to make for a French port.

"However, the Spanish commanders in the convoy protested against such a decision. They insisted on being taken to a Spanish port, and since Cadiz was out of the question, they resolved to go to Vigo Bay on the northwest coast of Spain.

"Admiral Château-Renaud feebly gave in to their demands, and the galleons put into Vigo Bay.

"Unfortunately this bay forms an open roadstead impossible to defend. The galleons therefore had to be unloaded quickly before the coalition's ships could arrive, and there would have been plenty of time for this unloading if a miserable question of rivalry had not intervened.

"Are you following all this?" asked Captain Nemo.

"Yes," I replied, still not knowing why he was giving me this history lesson.

"I'll continue. This is what happened. By law, the merchants of Cadiz had the sole privilege of receiving all goods coming from the West Indies, and hence it would be going against their rights to unload the ingots at Vigo. They therefore complained to Madrid and persuaded the weak Philip V to order that the convoy should remain at Vigo without unloading until the enemy fleet had disappeared.

"Now while this decision was being taken, on October 22, 1702, the English vessels arrived at Vigo Bay. Admiral Château-Renaud fought courageously in spite of his inferior forces. But when he saw that all the wealth of the convoy was about to fall into enemy hands, he set fire to the ships and scuttled them, and they all sank with their huge treasure."

Captain Nemo stopped. I must admit that I had no idea why this story should be of any special interest to me.

"Well then?" I asked.

"Well then, Monsieur Aronnax," replied Captain Nemo, "we're now in Vigo Bay, and I leave it to you to unravel the rest of the story."

The captain got up and asked me to follow him. By then I had recovered, and I obeyed. The lounge was dark, but through the transparent windows lay the sparkling sea. I looked out.

Within a half-mile radius around the *Nautilus* the waters were bathed in electric light. The sandy bottom was neat and clear. Some members of the crew had put on their diving suits and were clearing off half-rotted casks in the midst of the black wrecks of ships. The ground was strewn with bars of gold and silver, coins and jewels spilling out of these casks. The men would pick up this precious booty, take it to the *Nautilus*, put down their loads and then go back to this inexhaustible fishery of gold and silver.

I understood. This was the scene of the battle of October 22, 1702. This was the spot where the Spanish galleons had sunk. This was where Captain Nemo came to take the millions with which he would ballast his *Nautilus*. It was to him and him alone that South and Central America had delivered their precious metals. He was the direct and sole heir of this treasure snatched from the Incas and the Indians conquered by Hernán Cortés!

"Did you know, Professor," he asked with a smile, "that the sea contained such wealth?"

"I know that the amount of silver suspended in sea water," I answered, "has been evaluated at two million tons."

"Undoubtedly, but in order to extract this silver, your expenses would be greater than your profits. But here I have only to pick up what other men have lost, and not only in Vigo Bay, but also at a thousand other scenes of shipwrecks marked on my underwater charts. Now do you understand why I am a billionaire?"

"Yes I do, Captain. But let me say that by doing what you are here in Vigo Bay, you are merely anticipating the work of a rival company."

"What company?"

"A company to which the Spanish Government has given the right to search for these sunken galleons. The stockholders have had their appetites whetted by the thought of enormous profits, for the amount of gold and silver at the bottom of the bay has been evaluated at a hundred million dollars."

"A hundred million dollars!" replied Captain Nemo. "There used to be that much, but it's no longer there."

"The charitable thing to do, therefore," I said, "would be to warn the stockholders. But who knows if such a warning would be well received. Gamblers usually prefer to lose their money than abandon their mad hopes. But when all's said and done, I feel less sorry for them than for those thousands of poor people who could have benefited by such wealth if it had been well distributed, whereas now it will be forever useless to them."

I had no sooner expressed this regret when I felt that it must have offended Captain Nemo.

"Useless!" he replied excitedly. "Do you think, Monsieur, that this wealth is lost when I am the one gathering it? Do you think I do it just for myself? What makes you assume I don't make good use of it? Do you think I don't know that there's suffering and oppression on earth, poor people to be comforted, victims to be avenged? Don't you understand . . ."

Captain Nemo stopped, perhaps regretting he had talked so much. But it was enough for me to see that whatever had forced him to seek freedom beneath the sea, he was still a man! His heart still beat for the sufferings of humanity, and his immense charity extended to enslaved races as well as to individuals!

And then I understood for whom those millions had been destined when the *Nautilus* had stopped near rebel Crete!

CHAPTER XXXIII
A Lost Continent

On the next day, February 19, the Canadian entered my room. I had been expecting him to visit me. He looked very disappointed.

"Well, Monsieur?" he said.

"Yesterday our luck wasn't with us, Ned."

"That darned captain would stop just as we were about to leave."

"Yes, Ned, he had to see his banker."

"His banker!"

"Or rather his bank. I mean the ocean, where wealth is even safer than in the coffers of a state."

I told the Canadian what had happened the night before, with the secret hope of making him give up the idea of leaving; but my recital had no other effect on Ned than making him regret he himself hadn't taken a stroll over the battlefield of Vigo.

"But everything's not over!" he said. "The harpoon missed its mark that time, that's all. But we'll succeed next time, tonight if we have to . . ."

"What is the *Nautilus'* direction?" I asked.

"I don't know," answered Ned.

"Well then, at noon we'll find out our position."

The Canadian went back to Conseil. As soon as I had dressed I went to the lounge. The compass was not reassuring. The *Nautilus* was heading south by southwest. We were turning our backs on Europe.

I waited somewhat impatiently for our position to be marked on the chart. Toward eleven-thirty the reservoirs were emptied and the submarine rose to the surface. I rushed out on the platform. Ned Land was already there.

No more coastline in sight. Nothing but the vast sea. Several sails on the horizon, probably of ships going all the way to Cape San Roque to find favorable winds to carry them around the Cape of Good Hope. The sky was clouded with a wind blowing up.

Ned was furious and tried desperately to pierce the misty horizon. He still hoped that behind the fog he could see the land for which he so longed.

At noon the sun shone through for a moment. The first mate took advantage of this to take his bearings. Then, since the sea was getting rough, we went below and the hatch was closed.

When I consulted the chart an hour later, I saw that the *Nautilus* was at 16° 17' W. Long. and 33° 22' N. Lat., 325 miles from the nearest shore. It was no use even thinking about escape, and I leave the reader to imagine Ned's anger when I told him of our situation.

As for me, I was not too unhappy. I felt as if a weight had been taken off my chest, and I was able to go back to work with relative calm.

At about eleven o'clock at night I received a very unexpected visit from Captain Nemo. He asked me very politely if I was tired from having been up so late the previous night. I said I wasn't.

"Then, Monsieur Aronnax, I would like to invite you on a rather curious excursion."

"What sort of an excursion, Captain?"

"So far you have only seen the ocean depths during the day when the sun is out. How would you like to see them on a dark night?"

"Very much."

"This excursion will be tiring, I warn you. We'll have to do a lot of walking and mountain climbing. The roads aren't very well kept up."

"Your description only increases my curiosity. I'm ready to go."

"Splendid. Let's go put on our diving suits."

When I got to the dressing room, I saw that neither my companions nor any member of the crew were to go with us. Captain Nemo had made no mention of inviting Ned or Conseil.

It only took us a few minutes to put on our suits. The tanks, filled with considerable amounts of air, were put on our backs, but we weren't given our electric lamps. I mentioned this to the captain.

"We won't need them," he answered.

I thought I had not heard him correctly, but I could not repeat what I had said, for the captain's head had already disappeared inside the metal helmet. When I finished my preparations, I felt an iron-tipped stick being placed in my hand, and several minutes later, after the usual operations, we set foot on the floor of the Atlantic at a depth of a thousand feet.

It was almost midnight. The water was completely dark, but Captain Nemo showed me a reddish spot, a kind of large gleam shining about two miles away from the *Nautilus*. What this fire was, what was feeding it, why it was burning at all in the midst of the water, I had no idea. But in any case, it lit our way, dimly to be sure, but I soon became accustomed to the darkness and realized that the Ruhmkorff lamps had really not been necessary.

Captain Nemo and I, walking near each other, headed straight for the spot of light. The flat ground started to rise a bit. We took large strides, helping ourselves along with our sticks; but all the same our progress was slow, for our feet often sank in a kind of mud mixed with seaweed and strewn with flat stones.

As we walked I could hear a kind of crackling overhead, a continual pattern that would occasionally increase a bit in intensity. I soon understood what caused it. It was rain pounding on the surface of the ocean. I found myself worrying about getting soaked! Soaked by water in the midst of water! I could not help laughing at such a crazy idea. But to tell the truth, in a thick diving costume one has no sensation of being in water; it feels rather as if one were in the midst of a slightly denser atmosphere than that above the surface, and nothing more.

After we had walked for half an hour the ground became rocky. Jellyfish, microscopic shellfish and sea pens lit it up with their glimmers of phosphorescence. I could make out heaps of stones covered with masses of zoophytes and seaweed. I often slipped on this viscous bed of marine plants, and I would have fallen more than once had it not been for my stick. When I turned around I could still make out the whitish light from the *Nautilus* growing paler in the distance.

The heaps of rocks I have just mentioned were laid out on the ocean floor with a certain regularity of pattern that I could not explain. I noticed gigantic furrows which went off into the murky distance and whose length it was impossible to calculate. There were also other details which struck me as even more incredible. It seemed as if my heavy lead soles were trampling on a litter of bones, making them crack with a dry sound. What was this vast plain we were crossing? I wanted to ask the captain, but unfortunately I did not know the sign language he and his companions used under water.

Nevertheless, the reddish light guiding us was growing larger, and it now lit up the entire horizon. This source of light beneath the surface of the sea aroused my curiosity to the highest degree. Was it some electrical phenomenon? Was I about to see something unknown to scientists on land? Or was this thing—for the thought occurred to me—produced by the hands of man? Was I going to meet at these great depths companions or friends of Captain Nemo, living an existence as strange as his and whom he was now going to visit? Would I find there a whole colony of exiles who had grown weary of a miserable existence on earth and had sought and found freedom in the ocean depths? All these mad, inadmissible ideas raced through my brain, and with my mind constantly overstimulated by one wonder after another, I would not have been surprised to encounter one of those underwater cities of which Captain Nemo dreamed.

Our path grew lighter and lighter. The whitish gleam came from the top of a mountain about eight hundred feet high. But what I saw was only a reflection produced by the water itself; the source of this mysterious light was on the opposite side of the mountain.

Captain Nemo pushed on unhesitatingly through the maze of rocks covering the floor of the Atlantic. He knew this dark route. He had undoubtedly been here often, and there was no danger of his getting lost. I followed him with unshakable confidence. He seemed like a spirit of the waters, and when he walked in front of me, I admired his tall build outlined in black against the lights on the horizon.

It was one in the morning. We had arrived at the foot of the mountain. But in order to climb it we had to go up difficult paths through a vast forest.

Yes, it was a forest of dead trees, without leaves or sap, trees petrified by the sea, with an occasional gigantic pine towering high into the water. It was like a coalfield still standing, holding on to the furrowed soil with its roots, and its branches looking as if they had been delicately cut out of black paper. The reader might get some idea of it by trying to imagine the forest clinging to the sides of the Harz Mountains, but all under water. The paths were cluttered with seaweed and sea wrack, and among it crawled a whole world of shellfish. I climbed up rocks and stepped over fallen tree trunks, breaking the sea vines stretching from one tree to another and startling the fish flying from branch to branch. In my excitement I no longer felt any fatigue. I followed my guide, who never seemed to tire.

What a sight! How can I describe it? How can I depict the spectacle of these woods and rocks in the midst of the water, their undersides dark and forbidding, their upper sides tinted with the red light whose intensity was increased as it was reflected by the water? We would climb over rocks, enormous chunks of which would then fall down with the mute rumbling sound of an avalanche. On either side of the path were hollowed out dark caves in which one could see nothing, and I occasionally wondered if some inhabitant of these underwater regions was not suddenly going to spring up before me.

But Captain Nemo kept on climbing. I did not want to lag behind, and I followed boldly. My stick helped me greatly. One false step would have been dangerous on these narrow paths beside huge chasms; but I walked resolutely, without the slightest feeling of giddiness. Sometimes I would jump over a crevasse whose depth would have made me hesitate had it been in a glacier on dry land; other times I would venture out on the wobbling trunk of a tree fallen over the top of an abyss without looking down, only interested in admiring the wild scenery of the region. There were huge rocks resting on strangely shaped bases, leaning as if to defy the laws of gravity. Between their stony joints trees sprouted up like jets of water under great pressure, and supported other trees which in turn helped support them. Then there were natural towers with sheer walls between them, all leaning at an angle that would have been impossible on land.

And I could also feel a difference brought about by the density of the water, for in spite of my heavy costume, my copper helmet and metal soles, I could climb up almost impossibly steep slopes with the agility of an izard or a chamois!

I realize that my description of this underwater excursion must be scarcely credible. But I am fated to recount things which, although apparently impossible, are in fact real and undeniable. It wasn't a dream, but something I saw and felt!

Two hours after leaving the *Nautilus* we had passed the tree line, and a hundred feet above rose the mountain peak which stood between us and the brilliant light coming from the other side. Several petrified shrubs ran in twisting, zigzag lines. Schools of fish rose from beneath our feet like birds flushed in high grass. The massive rocks were rent with impenetrable crevasses, deep caves and unfathomable holes at the bottom of which one could hear formidable creatures moving. My blood would curdle when I would see a huge feeler blocking my path, or hear frightful pincers snapping shut in the shadows of some hollow! Thousands of luminous spots shone in the midst of the darkness. They were the eyes of giant shellfish hidden in their lairs, huge lobsters drawing themselves up like soldiers and moving their claws with a metallic clanking noise, titanic crabs set like guns on their carriages, and frightful octopuses intertwining their tentacles like an underbrush of live snakes.

What was this luxuriant world I did not yet know? What kind of creatures were these for whom the rock formed a second shell? Where had nature found the secret of their plantlike existence, and for how many centuries had they been living like this in the deepest layers of the ocean?

But I could not stop. Captain Nemo was already familiar with these terrible animals and no longer paid any attention to them. We arrived on a plateau where yet other surprises were awaiting me. I made out picturesque ruins which betrayed the hand of man and no longer that of the Creator. There were vast heaps of stones among which one could make out vague shapes of castles and temples decked in a whole world of zoophytes and flowers, which were covered, not with ivy, but with a mantle of seaweed.

But what was this part of the globe swallowed by some cataclysm? Who had laid out these rocks and stones like the dolmens of prehistoric times? Where was I? What was this place to which Captain Nemo had led me?

I wanted to ask him. But since I could not, I stopped and seized his arm. He merely shook his head and pointed to the highest point on the mountain, as if to say: "Come on! Follow me! Further on!"

I followed him in a last burst of effort, and in several minutes I had climbed the peak rising fifty or so feet above the surrounding mass of rocks.

I looked back to the slopes we had just climbed. There the mountain only rose seven or eight hundred feet above the plain; but on the other side it rose twice that height over a deeper portion of the ocean floor. My eyes wandered into the distance and I saw a vast space lit by violent flashes. This mountain was in fact a volcano. Fifty feet below the peak, in the midst of a rain of stones and cinders, a large crater vomited forth torrents of lava which spread out in a fiery cascade in the midst of the waters. Placed as it was, this volcano acted like an immense torch lighting up the lower plain out to the farthest reaches of the horizon.

This underwater crater threw up lava, but no flames. Flames need oxygen from the air, and they cannot exist under water; but streams of incandescent lava can achieve a reddish-white color, struggle victoriously against the surrounding water and become vaporized upon contact. Fast currents carried off all these diffused gases, and the torrents of lava slid to the base of the mountain, like those of Vesuvius threatening another Torre del Greco.

And in fact, there beneath my eyes, ruined, crumbled and destroyed, lay a town with its roofs caved in, its temples falling down, its arches out of place and its columns lying on the ground. In all these fragments one could see the solid proportions of a kind of Tuscan architecture. Farther on there were the remains of a giant aqueduct; here lay an encrusted mound of some Acropolis, with the floating forms of a Parthenon; there the remains of a dock, as if from some antique port that had once sheltered merchant ships and triremes of war at the shore of an extinct sea; yet further on, long lines of crumbling walls and deserted streets. Captain Nemo was showing me an entire Pompeii buried beneath the ocean!

Where was I? I had to know. I wanted to speak—I wanted to tear off the copper helmet enclosing my head.

But Captain Nemo came over and took me by the arm. He then picked up a piece of chalky stone and went over to a rock of black basalt, where he wrote only a single word:

ATLANTIS

Suddenly everything became clear! This was the ancient Meropis of Theopompus, the Atlantis of Plato. This was the continent which Origen, Porphyry, Iamblichus, D'Anville, Malte-Brun and Humboldt had said was pure legend, as opposed to Posidonius, Pliny, Marcellinus Ammianus, Tertullian, Engel, Scherer, Tournefort, Buffon and d'Avezac, who believed it had really existed. There it was before my eyes, with undeniable evidence of its catastrophic end! This was that submerged region which had once existed beyond Europe, Asia or Libya, beyond the Pillars of Hercules and inhabited by the powerful Atlantides against whom the early Greeks had fought!

It is Plato himself who has written the history of these mighty deeds of far-off heroic times. His dialogues with Timaeus and Critias were written, so to speak, under the inspiration of Solon, the poet and lawmaker.

One day Solon was chatting with several wise old men of Sais, a city already eight hundred years old, as witnessed by the annals engraved on the sacred wall of its temple. One of these old men recounted the history of another city yet a thousand years older. This first Athenian city, nine hundred centuries old, had been invaded and partly destroyed by the Atlantides. These people, he said, occupied an immense continent larger than Africa and Asia put together, and stretching from 12° to 40° N. Lat. Their sway extended even to Egypt. They also tried to conquer Greece, but they had been forced to retreat before the indomitable resistance of the Hellenes. Centuries went by and then suddenly they were overtaken by a cataclysm, with floods and earthquakes. One night and one day were enough to annihilate Atlantis, whose highest summits, the Madeira Islands, the Azores, the Canaries and the Cape Verde Islands, still emerge above the surface of the sea.

Such were the historical memories evoked by Captain Nemo's inscription. Thus, through the strangest of destinies, I was now standing on a mountain of this lost continent! My hand was touching ruins thousands of centuries old, contemporary with geological epochs! I was walking over the very ground tread by the contemporaries of earliest mankind! My heavy soles were crushing the skeletons of ancient animals which these now petrified trees had once covered with their shade!

Ah, why was there so little time! How I would have liked to go down the steep slopes of the mountain and cross the entire huge continent stretching from Africa to America, visiting its great prehistoric cities. I was perhaps now looking at Makhimos, the warrior city, or Eusebos, the pious city whose gigantic inhabitants lived for entire centuries and who had strength enough to build with blocks of stone which still stood up against the action of the water. Maybe one day volcanic action would bring these sunken ruins back to the surface! Many underground volcanoes have been observed in this part of the ocean, and ships have often been violently tossed about while passing over these tortured regions. Some have heard muted sounds indicating a struggle of the elements deep down; others have picked up volcanic ash thrown up into the air. As far as the equator, this area is still prey to the earth's eruptive forces. And who knows but that in the distant future the summits of these underwater mountains may be raised up by volcanic ash and successive layers of lava, and once again appear above the surface of the Atlantic.

While I was dreaming about all this and trying to fix in my memory all the details of this grandiose landscape, Captain Nemo was leaning on a mossy slab of stone without moving, and as if petrified in mute ecstasy. Was he thinking of those generations long since dead and asking them the secret of human destiny? Was it here that this strange man came to steep himself in history and relive the life of ancient times, he who would have nothing to do with the world around him? How much I would have given to know his thoughts, to share and under-stand them!

We stayed there for a whole hour, contemplating the vast plain lit by the hot lava, which occasionally took on surprising brilliance. Sometimes an under-ground bubbling would make the mountain tremble. Noises from the deep, clearly transmitted by the water, resounded with majestic grandeur.

For an instant the moon appeared and threw its pale rays on the sunken con-tinent. It was only a glimmer, but the effect was indescribable. The captain straightened up, took one last look at the vast plain, and then motioned for me to follow him.

It took us little time to climb back down the mountain. Once we had gotten past the petrified forest, I made out the *Nautilus'* light shining like a star. The captain made straight for it, and we were back on board just as the first rays of dawn were whitening the surface of the ocean.

CHAPTER XXXIV
Underwater Coal Mines

The next day, February 20th, I got up very late. I had been so tired from the night before that I slept till eleven o'clock. I got dressed quickly. I was anxious to find out the *Nautilus'* direction. The instruments told me that it was still head-ing south at a speed of twenty knots and at a depth of three hundred feet.

Conseil entered. I told him about our excursion of the previous night, and since the panels were open, he could still make out part of this submerged continent.

For the *Nautilus* was cruising only thirty feet above the plain of Atlantis. It scurried along like a balloon carried by the wind over earthly prairies; but it would be nearer the truth to say that we sat in this lounge as if in the carriage of an express train. In the foreground we could see rocks hewn into fantastic shapes, and forests of trees which had passed to the mineral from the vegetable kingdom and whose immobile silhouettes stood out grimly beneath the ocean. There were also masses of rock buried under layers of axidiae and anemones, and bristling with long, vertical marine plants; among these I could make out strangely shaped blocks of lava bearing witness to the fury of volcanic action.

While this peculiar scenery was gleaming beneath our electric light, I told Conseil the history of Atlantis, which, from the purely fictional point of view, had inspired Bailly to write so many charming pages. I told him about the wars of these heroic people, and discussed the question of Atlantis from the point of view of a man who no longer entertained the slightest doubt. But Conseil seemed distracted and not really listening, and I soon realized what caused this indifference to matters of history.

Numerous fish were attracting his attention, and when fish passed by, Conseil would become lost in the abyss of classification and leave the world of reality. In a situation like that, I could do nothing but follow his lead and once again take up our study of marine life.

These fish in the Atlantic, however, differed little from those we had already seen. There were gigantic rays fifteen feet long and powerful enough to leap out of water; various kinds of sharks, and among others, one blue-green in color and fifteen feet long, with sharp, triangular teeth and so transparent as to be almost invisible in the water; brown sargos; humantins shaped like prisms and armored with a tubercular skin; sturgeons similar to their cousins in the Mediterranean; and pipefishes eighteen inches long, yellowish brown in color with little gray fins, lacking teeth or tongue, which passed by like delicate, supple snakes.

Among the class of bony fish, Conseil noted some blackish makairas ten feet long and armed with a sharp sword on their upper jaw; brightly colored sting-fish, known in Aristotle's time as sea dragons and very dangerous to pick up because of the spines on their dorsal fin; spiny dolphins, their brown backs striped with blue and edged with gold; lovely dorados; moonfish resembling disks with a bluish glint, which, when lit from above by the sun's rays, looked like spots of silver; and finally swordfish twenty-five feet long swimming in schools, waving their sickle-shaped fins and brandishing their six-foot swords—these fearless animals eat plants rather than other fish and obey the least signal from their females, like all well-trained husbands.

But while observing these various specimens of marine life, I never grew tired of examining the long plains of Atlantis. Sometimes capricious altera-tions in the terrain would force the *Nautilus* to slow down and slip like a whale through the narrow passes between hills. And if the maze became impossible, it would merely rise like an airship, go over the obstacle and then once again take up its rapid course a few feet above the ocean floor. It was an admirable and charming way to travel, somewhat like being in a balloon, but with the important difference that the *Nautilus* responded instantly to the helmsman's command.

Toward four in the afternoon, the terrain, which till then had been composed mainly of thick mud intermingled with petrified branches, began to change little by little; it became more stony and seemed littered with conglomerate and basalt mixed with bits of lava and sulfurous obsidian. I felt sure that the long plains would soon end in mountains, and indeed I could soon see that the south-ern horizon was blocked by a high wall which seemed to bar all roads. Its sum-mit obviously rose above the surface. It must have been a continent, or at least an island—either one of the Canaries or one of the Cape Verde Islands. Since our position had not been marked on the chart—perhaps on purpose—I did not know where we were. In any case, such a wall seemed to mark the end of Atlantis of which we had covered only such a small portion.

Night interrupted my observations. I remained alone when Conseil went back to his cabin. The *Nautilus* reduced its speed and hovered over the ocean floor, sometimes almost touching it as if it wanted to settle on the bottom, and sometimes capriciously going back up to the surface. Through the crystalline waters I could make out several bright constellations, and specifically five or six of those zodiacal stars behind Orion.

I would gladly have remained at the window much longer, admiring the beauties of sea and sky, but the panels closed. Just then the *Nautilus* had arrived before the sheer face of the wall. I had no idea what sort of maneuvers it was trying to make. I went back to my room. The *Nautilus* was no longer moving. I went to sleep with the firm resolve of getting up after several hours.

But on the next day, it was past eight when I returned to the lounge. I looked at the pressure gauge; the *Nautilus* was floating on the surface. Moreover, I could hear the sound of footsteps on the platform. But there was no rolling or pitching.

I went up the companionway. The hatch was open. But instead of the bright daylight I had expected, I found myself surrounded by total darkness. Where were we? Had I made a mistake? Was it still night? No, not a single star was shining, and besides night is never as totally dark as that.

I didn't know what to think, when suddenly a voice said: "Is that you, Professor?"

"Oh! Captain Nemo," I answered. "Where are we?"

"Underground, Professor."

"Underground!" I cried. "But the *Nautilus* is still floating!"

"It always floats."

"I don't understand."

"Wait a minute till our light is turned on and everything will be cleared up."

I got out on the platform and waited. It was so dark that I couldn't even see Captain Nemo. But directly overhead, I thought I could make out a vague glimmer, a kind of half-light filtering through a round hole. Just then the searchlight suddenly was turned on, and its strong gleam made this dim light vanish.

For a moment my eyes were completely dazzled, but soon I could open them and look around. The *Nautilus* was moored to a bank shaped like a dock. It was floating in a lake enclosed within circular walls two miles in diameter, or in other words six miles in circumference. The level of the lake—this fact was confirmed by the pressure gauge—was necessarily the same as that outside, for there had to be a passage between this lake and the ocean. The high walls curved in to form a vault like a huge, upside-down funnel 1500 to 2000 feet high. At the top there was a round hole through which daylight could enter—this explained the vague glimmer I had seen.

Before examining the inside of this enormous cavern more carefully and asking myself if it had been made by nature or by man, I went over and asked Captain Nemo: "Where are we?"

"At the center of an extinct volcano," replied the captain, "that was invaded by the sea after some convulsion of the earth. While you were sleeping, Professor, the *Nautilus* entered this lagoon through a channel thirty feet below the surface of the ocean. This is my harbor—safe, convenient, secret and sheltered from any wind! Find me a single harbor on the coasts of your continents that is so protected as this one from the fury of gales."

"Yes," I replied, "you are certainly safe here, Captain Nemo. Who could ever disturb you in the middle of a volcano? But didn't I see an opening at the top?"

"Yes, that is the crater, which was once filled with lava, steam and flames; but now it merely brings us the air we breathe."

"But what mountain is this?" I asked.

"It's one of those innumerable little islands which dot the surface of the ocean. For ships it's just a reef to be avoided; for us it's an immense cavern. I discovered it quite by chance, and this was a great stroke of luck for me."

"But couldn't someone enter through that hole at the top?"

"No more than I could get out through it. The inside base of this mountain can be climbed for about a hundred feet up, but above that the walls lean in and nobody could scale them."

"I can see that nature helps you wherever you go, Captain. You're safe in this lake, and no one could visit these waters. But what good is this refuge? The *Nautilus* doesn't need a harbor."

"No, Professor, but it needs electricity for its power, batteries to produce the electricity, sodium for the batteries, coal to make the sodium, and therefore coal mines to get the coal. In this very spot there are whole forests which were buried millions of years ago; now they have turned to coal, and for me they are an inexhaustible mine."

"So here, Captain, your men act as miners?"

"That's right. These mines reach out beneath the ocean like those of Newcastle. My men, dressed in their diving suits and equipped with pick and shovel, go down to extract the coal, thereby making me independent of dry land even for that substance. When I burn it to make sodium, the smoke which escapes through the crater merely makes the mountain look like a volcano that's still active."

"Will I see your companions doing this?"

"No, not this time, for I'm in a hurry to continue our underwater tour of the earth. Now I shall merely take sodium from my reserve stock. We'll stay here long enough to put it on board—which won't take more than one day—and then we'll be on our way again. So if you want to see this cavern and take a walk around the lake, take advantage of what time you have today, Monsieur Aronnax."

I thanked the captain and went to get my two companions, who had not yet left their cabin. I invited them to come along, without telling them where they were.

They climbed up onto the platform. Conseil, who was never surprised by anything, acted as if it were perfectly natural to wake up under a mountain after going to sleep under the sea. But Ned Land had only one idea—to see if there was some way out of the cavern.

After breakfast, at about ten o'clock, we got off onto the bank.

"Here we are on land again," said Conseil.

"This isn't exactly what I'd call 'land,'" replied the Canadian. "And besides, we're not on it but under it."

Between the base of the mountain walls and the lake itself there was a sandy shoreline five hundred feet across at its widest point. On this beach one could easily walk around the lake. The base of the high walls was a picturesque pile of volcanic rocks and enormous pumice stones. All these broken fragments had been polished by subterranean fires and glistened beneath the ship's electric light. Along the shore, mica dust kicked up by our feet rose up like clouds of sparks.

As we got away from the water's edge, the ground rose considerably, and we soon arrived at some long, narrow ramps—abrupt paths on which we could climb slowly. But we had to walk carefully over the loose stones and the slippery glasslike trachyte made of feldspar and quartz crystals.

Every detail of this enormous cavern, as I pointed out to my companions, confirmed its volcanic origin.

"Can you imagine what this funnel must have been like," I said, "when it was full of boiling lava rising to the crater on top like molten metal in a furnace?"

"I can well imagine what it was like," replied Conseil. "But could Monsieur tell me why this particular furnace went out of operation and was replaced by calm lake water?"

"Very probably, Conseil, because the earth, as it shook and trembled, opened up an underwater channel (the one through which the *Nautilus* passed), allowing sea water to rush in. This must have been followed by a terrible struggle between these two elements, with the ocean finally winning. But many centuries have passed by since then, and now the submerged volcano is nothing but a peaceful cavern."

"That's all very fine," retorted Ned Land, "but it's too bad for us that this channel formed under water."

"But Ned," replied Conseil, "if it hadn't been under water, the *Nautilus* couldn't have gotten in!"

"And what's more, Ned, the ocean wouldn't have entered and this mountain would still be a volcano. So your regrets don't make much sense."

We continued to climb. The path became steeper and narrower. Sometimes there were deep gaps we had to jump across; sometimes great rocks we had to go around. Occasionally we had to crawl on our hands and knees, and even on our bellies. But between Conseil's skill and the Canadian's strength, we overcame all these obstacles.

When we were about a hundred feet up, the terrain changed, but without becoming any easier for us. We were now in an area of black basalt, in some places all eaten away and honeycombed, in others forming regularly shaped prisms which supported the vaulting in a splendid display of natural architecture. Among these basalt rocks ran long trickles of hardened lava streaked with coal and occasionally covered with broad layers of sulfur. The light entering from the overhead crater was now stronger, dimly illuminating our path among these volcanic formations forever buried in the heart of this mountain.

At a height of about 250 feet, a series of impassable obstacles prevented us from climbing further. The interior vaulting began to lean in sharply, and we therefore had to start walking horizontally around the inside of the mountain. At this level the vegetable kingdom began its struggle for existence. There were several shrubs and even a few trees growing out of cracks in the wall. I saw spurge with its bitter sap seeping from its bark. There were heliotropes unable to justify their name since the sun's rays never reached them, with their bunches of flowers hanging down half wilted. Here and there, several chrysanthemums grew timidly at the foot of sad and sickly-looking long-leafed aloes. But between the streams of dried lava I noticed little violets, and I must confess to having sniffed them with delight. Scent is the soul of flowers, and sea flowers, as splendid as they may be, have no soul!

We had reached a clump of hardy dragon trees prying the rocks apart with their powerful roots, when suddenly Ned Land cried: "Monsieur! A beehive!"

"A beehive!" I cried with a gesture of disbelief.

"Yes, a beehive," repeated the Canadian, "and with the bees buzzing around it."

I drew nearer and was forced to believe what I saw. There, around a hole in the trunk of a dragon tree, swarmed several thousand of those clever insects which are so common on the Canary Islands and whose produce is so highly esteemed.

Naturally, the Canadian wanted to stock up on honey and I could not very well say no. He mixed some dried leaves with sulfur, lit them with his flint and began to smoke out the bees. Little by little the buzzing ceased, and the hive, after being broken open, yielded several pounds of perfumed honey. Ned Land filled his haversack with it.

"I'll mix this honey with breadfruit paste," he said, "and we'll have a really delicious cake."

"Or rather gingerbread," said Conseil.

"Never mind the gingerbread," I said; "let's keep walking."

From several points in our path we could see the entire lake. The light from the submarine lit up its whole peaceful surface. The *Nautilus* was completely immobile. On its platform and on the shore, members of the crew were milling about looking like black shadows clearly outlined in the luminous atmosphere.

We now reached the highest crest of that wall of rocks supporting the vault. I saw then that bees were not the only animals inside this volcano. Birds of prey soared and whirled here and there in the shadows, or fled from their nests on the tips of rocks. There were sparrow hawks with white bellies, and screeching kestrels. There were also fine, fat bustards scampering over the slopes as fast as their legs would carry them. I shall let the reader imagine how the Canadian's appetite was whetted at the sight of such a tasty game bird and how he regretted not having a gun with him. He tried using stones instead of bullets, and after several fruitless attempts, he succeeded in wounding one of these splendid bustards. It is no exaggeration to say that he risked his life twenty times in order to get the bird, but finally it was placed in his haversack alongside the honeycombs.

We then had to go back down, for we could climb no farther. The yawning crater above us looked like the mouth of a large well. We could now see the sky quite clearly, with scattered clouds scudding along and occasionally grazing the top of the mountain. This was certain proof that the clouds were not very high, for the volcano did not rise more than eight hundred feet above the surface of the ocean.

A half an hour after the Canadian's last exploit, we reached the shore of the lake. There the vegetable kingdom was represented by blankets of sea fennel, that umbrella-shaped plant which makes such a good preserve. Conseil picked several bunches of it. As for the animal life, it consisted of thousands of shellfish of all sorts, lobsters, crabs, prawns, musis, spider crabs and a prodigious number of shells, cowries, murices and limpets.

While we were standing there, we spotted the mouth of a magnificent cave. My companions and I delightedly stretched out on its fine sand. Fire had polished its sparkling, enameled walls sprinkled with mica dust. Ned Land felt the walls and tried to see how thick they were. I could not help smiling. The conversation then turned to his eternal plans for escaping, and I felt I could give him the following hope, without too great a risk of being wrong. Namely, that Captain Nemo had headed south only to renew his supply of sodium. I felt he would now return to the coasts of Europe or America, thus permitting the Canadian to have another and more successful try at escaping.

The conversation had been very lively at first, but after we had been stretched out in this cave for about an hour, it began to lag. A certain drowsiness came over us, and since there was no reason not to give in, I let myself fall into a deep sleep. I dreamed—one doesn't choose one's dreams—that my life had been reduced to the simple vegetablelike existence of a mollusk. It seemed as if the cave formed the double valve of my shell . . .

Suddenly I was awakened by Conseil shouting, "Wake up, wake up!"

"What is it?" I asked, sitting up.

"We're being swamped!"

I got up. The sea was rushing into our cave, and since we weren't mollusks, we had to get out.

In a few moments we had climbed to safety above the cave. "What's going on?" asked Conseil. "Is this some new phenomenon?"

"No, my friends," I answered, "it's just the tide, and it came close to catching us the way it did Sir Walter Scott's hero! The ocean outside is rising, and by a natural law of equilibrium, the level of the lake is also rising. We're lucky nothing worse happened than our getting half wet. Let's go back to the *Nautilus* and change."

Three-quarters of an hour later we had completed our circular walk and were back on board. The sailors had just finished loading the sodium, and the *Nautilus* could have left then and there.

But Captain Nemo gave no orders for departure. Did he want to wait for the night and leave secretly by his underwater channel? Perhaps.

Whatever the reason, by the next day the *Nautilus* had left its port and was cruising several yards below the surface of the Atlantic far from any land.

CHAPTER XXXV
The Sargasso Sea

The *Nautilus* had not altered its course. For the moment, therefore, we had to give up any hope of returning to European waters. Captain Nemo kept heading south. Where was he taking us? I did not dare think.

That day the *Nautilus* crossed a strange part of the Atlantic Ocean. Everyone knows about that great current of warm water known as the Gulf Stream. After leaving the channels around Florida, it heads for Spitsbergen. But before it reaches its destination, it splits in two near the forty-fourth parallel. One current continues toward the coasts of Ireland and Norway, while the other bends southward near the Azores, touches the coast of Africa and then swings back toward the West Indies.

Now this second branch forms a kind of ring of warm water around an area of colder water called the Sargasso Sea, which is always calm and immobile. It is like a lake in the middle of the Atlantic, and the waters of the Gulf Stream take three years to travel around it.

The Sargasso Sea properly speaking covers all the submerged region of Atlantis. Certain authors have even stated that the numerous plants it contains have been uprooted from the plains of this ancient continent. Nevertheless, it is more probable that this algae and sea wrack have been taken from the shores of Europe and America and brought there by the Gulf Stream. This was one of the

Where was I? I had to know.

factors which led Columbus to believe in the existence of a New World. When this hardy sailor's ships arrived in the Sargasso Sea, they had considerable difficulty navigating in the midst of all the plant life impeding their progress. The crews were terrified, and it took them three long weeks to cross it.

Such was the region the *Nautilus* was now visiting—a real prairie, a thick carpet of seaweed, sea wrack and bladder wrack, so dense and compact that the keel of a ship would have had difficulty cutting through it. Captain Nemo did not want to get his propeller entangled in this mass of plants, and he therefore kept his ship a short distance below the surface.

This word "Sargasso" comes from the Spanish "sargazo," which means gulfweed—the principal constituent of this immense bed. The scientist Maury, in his *Physical Geography of the Earth,* gives the following explanation for the presence of marine plants in such a peaceful portion of the Atlantic: "It seems to be caused," he said, "by a phenomenon familiar to everybody. If one places pieces of cork or any other small floating objects in a glass of water and then makes the water in the glass go round and round, one will soon see the scattered fragments come together in the center of the liquid surface, or in other words, at the place with the least motion. In the phenomenon under discussion, the glass is the Atlantic, the circular current of water is the Gulf Stream, and the central point where all the floating bodies come together is the Sargasso Sea."

I share Maury's opinion, and I was able to study the phenomenon in its very midst, where vessels rarely penetrate. Above us there were all sorts of strange objects floating among the brownish seaweed: tree trunks uprooted from the Andes or the Rocky Mountains and brought down the Amazon or the Mississippi, many wrecks, and parts of keels and hulls so weighted down with shells and barnacles that they could no longer rise to the surface. And someday Maury's other idea will find proof, namely that these objects will eventually turn to coal and form an inexhaustible mine—a precious reserve prepared by farsighted nature for the time when men will have exhausted the mines on land.

In the midst of this inextricable fabric of plants and seaweed, I noticed some charming pink star-shaped alcyonia, some sea anemones dragging their long hairlike tentacles behind them, and green, red and blue jellyfish, among which I particularly remarked Cuvier's large rhyzostomae with their bluish swimming bell edged with violet.

We spent the entire day of February 22 in the Sargasso Sea. We saw great quantities of fish who, since they are great lovers of marine plants and shellfish, find abundant food there. The following day the ocean once again took on its normal aspect.

Then for nineteen days, from February 23 to March 12, the *Nautilus* remained in mid-Atlantic, traveling at a constant speed of a hundred leagues every twenty-four hours. Captain Nemo obviously was anxious to complete his underwater program, and I had no doubts that after going around Cape Horn, he would return to the south Pacific.

Ned Land was therefore right to worry. Escape was out of the question in these broad seas without islands. Nor was there any way to oppose Captain Nemo's will. There was nothing to do but give in; and what we could no longer obtain by force or trickery, I liked to think we might obtain by persuasion. Once this voyage was over, might Captain Nemo not set us free under oath never to reveal his existence? We would have kept our word. But how could I broach this delicate subject to the captain? How could I ask him to set us free? Had he not stated plainly from the start that the secret of his life required us to be perpetual prisoners aboard the *Nautilus*? Wouldn't my four months' silence on this subject seem like a tacit acceptance of our situation? Wouldn't bringing this subject up again only result in arousing his suspicion and lessening our chances of escape if some favorable circumstance should come up later on? I thought about these various points, weighed them, turned them over in my mind and discussed them with Conseil, but he was no less perplexed than I. In short, even though I am not easily discouraged, I realized that my chances of ever seeing my fellow men again were lessening day by day, and above all just then when Captain Nemo was rashly heading for the south Atlantic!

During these nineteen days, nothing unusual occurred. I saw the captain little. He spent his time working. In the library I would often come across books he had left open, and especially books on natural history. He had apparently been leafing through my work on the ocean depths, for it lay open with his notes in the margins, sometimes contradicting my theories and systems. But this was the only way in which the captain corrected my work, for he hardly ever discussed it with me. Sometimes I could hear melancholy sounds from the organ which he played very expressively; but this he would only do in the depth of the night, when the *Nautilus* was asleep in the wastelands of the ocean.

During this part of our voyage, we cruised for entire days on the surface. The sea seemed deserted. We only saw a few sailing vessels heading for the East Indies via the Cape of Good Hope. One day we were chased by dories from a whaling ship which undoubtedly took us for some huge whale of great value. But Captain Nemo did not want these worthy people to lose their time and trouble, and he ended the chase by diving below the surface. This incident seemed to greatly interest Ned Land. I am sure he regretted that our iron whale had not been killed by the whaler's harpoons.

The fish Conseil and I saw during this period differed little from those we had already studied in other latitudes. We mainly saw some specimens of that terrible genus of cartilaginous fish which is divided into three subgenera and includes no less than twenty-three species. There were striped sharks fifteen feet long with rounded tails and seven black lines running parallel down their backs, and ash-gray perlon sharks with seven gill openings and only one dorsal fin placed almost exactly in the middle of their bodies.

We also saw some large dogfish, a voracious species of fish if there ever was one. Even though fishermen's stories are not to be believed it is said that in one of these fish was found a buffalo head and an entire calf; in another two tuna and a sailor still in his uniform; in another a soldier with his saber; and in yet another, a horse with its rider. It must be said, though, that these stories seem a bit doubtful. In any case, none of these animals ever allowed itself to be captured in the *Nautilus'* nets, and I therefore had no way of finding out how voracious they were.

A school of playful elegant porpoises accompanied us for several days. They traveled in groups of five or six, like wolves hunting in packs. Apparently these animals are no less voracious than dogfish, if one is to believe a Danish professor who claims to have removed thirteen sea hogs and fifteen seals from the stomach of a porpoise. To be sure it was a grampus, the largest known species of porpoise, sometimes exceeding twenty-four feet in length. The family of the delphinians includes ten genera, and those I saw were from the genus of Delphini, noted for their muzzle which is very narrow and four times as long as their head. Their ten-foot-long bodies were black on top and pinkish white with occasional spots underneath.

We also noted strange fish of the order of Acanthopterygii and the family of Sciaenidae. Some authors—who are better poets than naturalists—claim that these fish sing melodiously, and that together they form a choir that could scarcely be equaled by human voices. I do not deny this, but the Sciaenidae we saw did not serenade us as we passed, much to my regret.

In addition, Conseil classified a great number of flying fish. We were fascinated by the extraordinary sense of timing with which porpoises chased them. No matter how far or in what direction they flew—and they sometimes even flew over the *Nautilus*—when they landed, these poor fish always found porpoises awaiting them with open mouths. There were both pirapedes and red gurnards with luminous mouths who at night would trace fiery lines through the air and then plunge into the dark waters like shooting stars.

We continued cruising in this same fashion until March 13. But on that day, the *Nautilus* was used for experiments in sounding the ocean depths which were of great interest to me.

By then we had covered almost thirteen thousand leagues from our point of departure in the high Pacific. As marked on the chart, our position was 45° 37' S. Lat. and 37° 53' W. Long. These were the same waters in which Captain Denham of the *Herald* had taken soundings down to 45,000 feet without touching bottom. It was also there that Lieutenant Parker of the American frigate *Congress* had not been able to reach the bottom with soundings of 49,670 feet.

Captain Nemo decided to send his *Nautilus* down to check these soundings. I got ready to take notes on this experiment. The panels in the lounge were opened, and the necessary preparations were made for diving to such prodigious depths.

As one might well imagine, it was out of the question to make such a dive merely by filling the reservoirs. They might not have sufficiently increased the ship's specific gravity. Moreover, in order to come back up, this excess water would have to be expelled, and the *Nautilus'* pumps would not have been strong enough to overcome the outside pressure.

Instead, the side fins were placed at a 45° angle with the *Nautilus'* waterline. Then the propeller was made to go at full speed, and its four blades churned the water with indescribable violence.

The force of this vibration made the *Nautilus'* hull quiver like the string of a violin as we went deeper and deeper. The captain and I sat in the lounge and watched the pressure gauge with its needle moving rapidly across the dial. Soon we had left the zone in which most fish can live. Although some can only live on the surface of seas or rivers, others—though not so many—live at fairly great depths. Among this latter kind, I noted a hexanchus, a sort of shark with six gill clefts; a telescope fish with enormous eyes; an armored malarmat with gray lower fins and black upper fins and protected by a pale red layer of bone; and finally a grenadier, who, since we saw him at a depth of four thousand feet, was capable of living under a pressure of 120 atmospheres.

I asked Captain Nemo if he had ever seen fish living even deeper.

"Fish?" he replied. "Hardly ever. But in the present state of science, what can we presume to say? What do we know?"

"We know, Captain, that as you go into the deeper regions of the ocean, plant life disappears faster than animal life. We know that in places where one still encounters living creatures, one will not find a single marine plant. We know that scallops and oysters live at depths of 6500 feet, and that McClintock, the hero of the polar seas, brought up a live starfish from a depth of 8000 feet. We also know that the crew of the H.M.S. *Bulldog* brought up another kind of starfish from a depth of 15,720 feet, or more than a league down. Would you therefore still say, Captain Nemo, that we know nothing?"

"No, Professor," replied the captain. "I would not be that impolite. But all the same, I would like to know your explanations as to how creatures can live at such depths."

"There are two explanations," I replied. "First of all, there are vertical currents, caused by differences in the salinity and density of water, which produce sufficient movement to sustain the rudimentary life of encrinidae and starfish."

"Right," said the captain.

"Secondly, we know that oxygen is the basis of life and that the amount of oxygen dissolved in sea water increases with depth, or in other words the greater the pressure the more of it goes into solution."

"Oh! Did you know that?" replied Captain Nemo, somewhat surprised. "Well, Professor, what you say is true. I shall merely add that fishes' air bladders contain more nitrogen than oxygen when they are caught near the surface, and more oxygen than nitrogen when they are caught from great depths. And this proves that you are right. But let us go back to our observations."

I looked at the pressure gauge. It showed we were at a depth of 20,000 feet. We had been diving for an hour, and the *Nautilus* was still going down. The empty water around us was extraordinarily clear and transparent. An hour later we were down to 43,000 feet—about three and a quarter leagues—and we still couldn't see the bottom.

Nevertheless at 46,000 feet I could make out blackish peaks rising in the midst of the waters. But these could have been the tops of mountains as high as the Himalayas or Mont Blanc, or even higher, and we still had no way of evaluating the depth of the valleys between them.

In spite of the powerful pressure around it, the *Nautilus* went down yet farther. I could feel its iron plates quivering where they were bolted together; steel bars bent and bulkheads groaned; the glass panels in the lounge seemed to warp under the pressure of the water. And this strong ship would undoubtedly have been crushed if, as the captain had said, it had not been built to withstand pressure like a solid object.

As we brushed past these rocky slopes lost beneath the sea, I could still see shells, serpulae, spinorbis and several specimens of starfish.

But soon these last representatives of animal life disappeared, and below a depth of three leagues, the *Nautilus* passed the limits of underwater life like a balloon rising into the atmosphere where no one can breathe. We had reached a depth of 52,500 feet—four leagues—and the *Nautilus'* hull was withstanding a pressure of 1600 atmospheres, or 23,500 pounds on each square inch of its surface!

"How extraordinary," I cried, "to sail through regions where man has never been! Look, Captain, look at these magnificent rocks and these uninhabited caves in a place where life is no longer possible! What a shame that we can bring back nothing but the memory of these unknown sites!"

"Would you like to bring back more than the memory?" asked Captain Nemo.

"What do you mean?"

"I mean that nothing would be easier than to take a photograph of this area!"

I was about to express my astonishment at this new proposition when, at an order from the captain, a camera was brought into the lounge. The water outside the panels was absolutely clear. Our artificial light caused no fuzziness or shadowiness. Even the sun could not have served our purposes better. By controlling the speed of its propeller and the angle of its side fins, the *Nautilus* remained immobile. The camera was pointed at the ocean floor, and in several seconds we had obtained a negative of great clarity.

And here I give the proof. One can see the primeval rocks which have never seen the light of day, granite formations which form the globe's solid base, deep caves hollowed out in the mass of rock, and everything outlined with the incomparable clarity and shading of certain Flemish masters. Then in the background there is a horizon of mountains. I cannot describe this ensemble of smooth, black, polished rocks with no moss or other growth to spot their surface, cut into strange shapes and resting firmly on a carpet of sand sparkling beneath the electric light.

After taking this picture, Captain Nemo said: "Now let us go back up, Professor. We must not expose the *Nautilus* to such pressure for too long a time."

"All right," I said.

"Hold on tight."

Before I had time to understand why the captain had given me this piece of advice, I was thrown to the floor.

At a signal from the captain, the propeller had been disengaged and the fins placed vertically; then the *Nautilus* had shot up at a terrifying speed, like a balloon being carried into the atmosphere. It cut through the water with a loud quivering noise. We could see nothing. In four minutes we had covered the four leagues between us and the surface, and after leaping into the air like a flying fish, we came hurtling back down onto the water, making it splash up to a prodigious height.

CHAPTER XXXVI
Whales

During the night of March 13–14, the *Nautilus* once again started heading south. I thought that once it got on a parallel with Cape Horn, it would turn west in order to return to the Pacific and finish our tour of the world. But it did nothing of the sort, and merely continued in the direction of the Antarctic. I began to think that the captain's rashness justified Ned Land's worst fears.

For some time now, the Canadian had said nothing about escaping. He had become less talkative, and now remained silent much of the time. I could see how this prolonged imprisonment weighed on him. Whenever he met the captain, his eyes would gleam with a sullen fire, and I was constantly afraid that his violent instincts would cause him to do something rash.

On that day, March 14, Conseil and he came to find me in my room. I asked them why they had come.

"We just want to ask you one question, Monsieur," said the Canadian.

"What is it, Ned?"

"How many men do you think there are aboard the *Nautilus?*"

"I couldn't say."

"I can't imagine," Ned Land went on, "that it would take a very large crew to operate a ship like this."

"The way it's built," I said, "ten men should be enough."

"Well then," said the Canadian, "why should there be more?"

"Why?" I retorted, looking fixedly at Ned Land, whose intentions were easy to guess. "Because if my guess is correct, and if I've understood what kind of a man the captain is, the *Nautilus* is not only a ship, but also a place of refuge for all those who, like the captain, have broken off relations with life on land."

"Maybe," said Conseil, "but the *Nautilus* can only hold a certain amount of men, and possibly Monsieur could calculate this maximum."

"How, Conseil?"

"By working it out mathematically. Given the ship's capacity, which Monsieur knows, and therefore the amount of air it contains; given the quantity of air one man needs for breathing, and comparing these results with the fact that the *Nautilus* has to surface every twenty-four hours . . ."

Conseil did not finish his sentence, but I saw what he was driving at.

"I understand," I said; "but even though this wouldn't be difficult to calculate, the results might only be very approximate."

"That's all right," said Ned Land insistently.

"Then here it is," I answered. "The amount of oxygen a man uses per hour is equivalent to that contained in a hundred liters of air, and therefore in twenty-four hours he would need 2400 liters of air. So we have to find out how many times 2400 liters the *Nautilus* can contain."

"Precisely," said Conseil.

"Now the capacity of the *Nautilus* is 1500 tons, and since there are a thousand liters in a ton, the *Nautilus* contains 1,500,000 liters of air, which divided by 2400 . . ."

I made a rapid calculation with a pencil.

". . . gives 625. This means that strictly speaking the air in the *Nautilus* would be enough to support 625 men for twenty-four hours."

"Six hundred and twenty-five!" repeated Ned.

"But you can be certain," I added, "that between passengers, sailors and officers, there isn't one-tenth of that number on board."

"That's still too much for three men!" murmured Conseil.

"So, Ned, I can only advise you to be patient."

"Not only patient," replied Conseil, "but resigned."

Conseil had indeed found the right word.

"After all," he went on, "Captain Nemo can't head south forever! He has to stop sometime and come back to more inhabited regions! Then we'll be able to think about escaping again."

The Canadian shook his head, rubbed his forehead and left without saying a word.

"With Monsieur's permission, I would like to point out something," Conseil said. "Poor Ned keeps thinking about all the things he can't have. He keeps going over his past life. He frets about everything that's now beyond his reach. His memories weigh on him and his heart is heavy. We must try to understand how he feels. What is there for him to do here? Nothing. He is not a scientist like Monsieur and he can't share our delight in all the wonders of the sea. He would risk everything just to be in some tavern in his own country!"

The monotony of life on board must have been unbearable to the Canadian, accustomed as he was to freedom and activity. Very seldom did anything happen that could really interest him. But nevertheless, that day something occurred which reminded him of his old harpooning days.

Toward eleven in the morning, with the *Nautilus* cruising on the surface, we found ourselves in the midst of a herd of whales. This encounter did not surprise me, for I knew that these creatures had been so mercilessly hunted that they had gone to seek refuge in colder waters.

The role played by whales in the sailing world and their influence on geographic discoveries has been considerable. It was while following whales that first the Basques, then the Asturians, English and Dutch learned to brave the dangers of the ocean from one pole to the other. Whales like to frequent Arctic and Antarctic waters. Ancient legends even claim that these creatures had led

whalers to within only fifteen miles of the North Pole. Even though this statement is false, it is prophetic, for it will probably be through chasing whales into
Arctic or Antarctic regions that man will reach one of these unexplored points
on the globe.

We were sitting on the platform in the midst of a calm sea. The October of
these latitudes had been bringing us lovely weather. It was the Canadian—and
he never made mistakes about that sort of thing—who first sighted a whale on
the eastern horizon. By looking carefully I could see its blackish back rise and
fall above the surface five miles from the *Nautilus*.

"Ah!" cried Ned Land, "if I were only on board a whaler, what fun this
would be! It's a big one! Look what a powerful jet of water it's sending up!
Confound it! Why do I have to be chained to this hunk of steel plate!"

"What! You still haven't gotten over your old ideas about fishing, Ned?"

"Can a whaler ever forget his old profession? Can a man ever get bored with
a job that's so exciting?"

"Have you ever hunted whales in these waters, Ned?"

"Never, Monsieur. Only in northern waters, in the Bering Straits and the
Davis Straits."

"So then you don't know about southern whales. Until now you've only
hunted the right whale, a species that would never venture to cross the warm
waters near the equator."

"What are you trying to tell me, Professor?" said the Canadian in a somewhat incredulous tone of voice.

"Just what I said."

"Rubbish! In sixty-five—that's two and a half years ago—I myself harpooned a whale off Greenland, and embedded in its body we found another harpoon with the mark of a whaler from the Bering Sea. Now I ask you, how could
this animal, after being wounded west of America, come to be killed east of
America without crossing the equator and making his way either around Cape
Horn or the Cape of Good Hope?"

"I agree with Ned," said Conseil, "and I'm waiting to see what Monsieur
will say."

"Monsieur will say, my friends, that every species of whale lives within a certain area which it never leaves. And if one of these animals came from the Bering Straits to the Davis Straits, it's quite simply because there exists a passage from one sea to the other along either the coast of America or of Asia."

"You wouldn't be pulling my leg?" asked the Canadian with a wink.

"No, Monsieur is being perfectly serious," answered Conseil.

"In any case," the Canadian went on, "since I've never fished in these waters, I don't know what whales are to be found here."

"That's what I said, Ned."

"All the more reason to get to know them," retorted Conseil.

"Look! Look!" said the Canadian excitedly. "It's coming, it's coming toward us! It's thumbing its nose at me—it knows I can't do a thing!"

Ned stamped his foot. He brandished an imaginary harpoon with his trembling hand.

"Are these whales as big as those in northern waters?"

"Just about, Ned."

"Because I've seen big whales in my day, up to a hundred feet long! And I've even heard tell of a certain kind of whale around the Aleutian Islands that gets up to a hundred and fifty feet long."

"That seems a bit exaggerated," I answered. "Those that live around the Aleutians belong to the family of the Balaenopteridae, which have dorsal fins, and, like the sperm whale, are usually smaller than the right whale."

"Look!" cried the Canadian, who hadn't taken his eyes off the ocean, "it's coming nearer, right up to the *Nautilus*!"

Then he once more took up the thread of the conversation. "You talk about sperm whales as if they were small! But I've heard people tell of gigantic sperm whales. They're supposed to be very intelligent. They say that some of them cover themselves with seaweed and people take them for little islands. People get onto them, set up camp, build a fire . . ."

"And even build houses?" said Conseil.

"You joker!" retorted Ned Land. "And then one fine day the creature dives and all the people living on it drown."

"Just like Sinbad the Sailor," I said laughing. "Ah, Master Land, you seem to be awfully fond of tall stories! Those are pretty stupendous sperm whales of yours! I hope you don't believe in them!"

"Professor," the Canadian answered seriously, "when it comes to whales, you have to believe just about anything!—Look how this one travels! Look how it dives under!—They say these animals can go around the world in two weeks."

"I don't doubt it."

"But what you undoubtedly don't know, Monsieur Aronnax, is that at the beginning of time, these whales could swim even faster than they can now."

"Oh really, Ned! Why?"

"Because in the old days they had vertical tails like fish, and they moved them from side to side in the water. But the Creator saw that they swam too fast and He twisted their tails, and from then on they have had to move their tails up and down in the water and they haven't been able to swim as fast."

"You wouldn't be pulling my leg, would you, Ned?" I said, using his same expression.

"Not too much," answered Ned Land, "no more than if I told you about whales three hundred feet long and weighing a hundred thousand pounds."

"That would be quite a lot, wouldn't it," I said. "Nevertheless, it must be said that certain whales reach enormous sizes, since some have been said to have furnished up to a hundred and twenty tons of oil."

"I've seen them that big," said the Canadian.

"I believe you, Ned, just as I believe that certain whales are equal in size to a hundred elephants. Can you imagine the effect of such a weight traveling at full speed!"

"Is it true," asked Conseil, "that they can sink ships?"

"No, or at least I don't think so," I answered. "But they say that in eighteen-twenty, in just these southern waters, a whale rushed at the *Essex* and pushed it backward at a speed of thirteen feet per second. Water entered astern, and the *Essex* sank almost immediately."

Ned looked at me mockingly. "As for me," he said, "I've been hit by the tail of one of these animals—it happened in a longboat, of course. My companions and I were thrown twenty feet in the air. But alongside Monsieur's whale, mine was just a baby."

"Do these animals live a long time?" asked Conseil.

"A thousand years," answered the Canadian without hesitation.

"How do you know that, Ned?"

"Because that's what people say."

"But why do they say it?"

"Because it's a known fact."

"No, Ned, it isn't a known fact, but just a supposition, and this is what it's based on. Four hundred years ago, when men first hunted whales, they grew larger than they do now. It's therefore supposed, and rather logically, that the smaller size of present-day whales is due to the fact that they haven't had time to reach their full development. This is what made Buffon say that whales could—and undoubtedly did—live a thousand years. Do you understand?"

Ned Land didn't understand; he wasn't even listening. The whale was getting closer. He couldn't take his eyes off it.

"Look!" he cried. "It isn't just one whale, it's ten, twenty, a whole herd! And to think I have to sit here doing nothing, tied hand and foot!"

"But Ned," said Conseil, "why don't you ask Captain Nemo's permission to hunt them . . . ?"

Conseil hadn't finished his sentence when Ned Land dropped down through the hatch and rushed off in search of the captain. Several moments later, both of them appeared on the platform.

Captain Nemo looked at the herd of whales playing in the water a mile or so from the *Nautilus.*

"They're black whales," he said, "and there are enough of them out there to make a whole fleet of whalers rich."

"Well, Captain," asked the Canadian, "couldn't I go out and hunt them, if only so I don't forget how to use a harpoon?"

"What good would it do," answered Captain Nemo, "hunting just to destroy? We have no use for whale oil on board."

"But Monsieur," said the Canadian, "in the Red Sea you let us hunt a dugong!"

"Then it was a question of getting fresh meat for my crew. Here it would be killing just for the sake of killing. I know very well that this is one of man's privileges, but I won't permit such murderous pastimes. People like you, Master Land, are very wrong to destroy kind, inoffensive creatures like black whales and right whales. You've already cleared out Baffin Bay and you're on the way to exterminating a useful class of animals. So leave these poor whales alone. They have enough trouble with their natural enemies, such as sperm whales, swordfish and sawfish, without you getting into the act."

I leave the reader to imagine the expression on Ned's face during this little lecture. It was a waste of words to use such arguments with a born hunter. Ned Land looked at Captain Nemo and obviously didn't understand what he meant. Nevertheless, the captain was right. The barbarous, unthinking way these animals are hunted will one day wipe the last whale from the ocean.

Ned Land whistled "Yankee Doodle" between his teeth, stuck his hands in his pockets and turned his back to us.

After watching the whales for a while, Captain Nemo came over to me and said: "I was right to say that whales have enough natural enemies without men trying to kill them off. These whales are soon going to be in trouble. Do you see those black dots moving about eight miles to leeward, Monsieur Aronnax?"

"Yes, Captain," I answered.

"Those are sperm whales—terrible animals. I've sometimes seen them in herds of two or three hundred! They're cruel and destructive, and people are right to kill them."

The Canadian turned around brusquely at these last words.

"Well, Captain," I said, "there's still time to help out the black whales . . ."

"There's no use running any risk, Professor. We can disperse these sperm whales well enough with the *Nautilus* itself. It has a steel spur on its prow that I imagine is just as effective as Master Land's harpoon."

The Canadian didn't even bother shrugging his shoulders. The idea of attacking whales with a ship's prow! Who had ever heard of such a thing?

"In a few minutes, Monsieur Aronnax," said Captain Nemo, "you'll see such hunting as you've never seen before. We'll give them no quarter. These ferocious whales are nothing but mouth and teeth!"

Mouth and teeth! There was no better way to describe the sperm whale, which sometimes exceeds eighty feet in length. Its huge head takes up roughly a third of its body. It is better armed than the ordinary whale, whose upper jaw is only furnished with whalebone, for it has twenty-five large teeth eight inches high, round and cone-shaped on top, which weigh about two pounds apiece. Inside the upper part of the creature's head there are big cavities separated by cartilage which contain up to eight or nine hundred pounds of that precious whale oil called "spermaceti." The sperm whale is a very ungraceful animal, shaped more like a tadpole than a fish, as Frédol put it. It is badly built, being more or less defective on its left side with the result that its sight is almost totally confined to its right eye.

Meanwhile the huge herd was drawing nearer. They had noticed the black whales and were preparing to attack. I knew that the sperm whales would win, not only because they were better adapted for fighting than their harmless adversaries, but also because they could stay longer under water without coming to the surface to breathe.

There was no time to be lost in going to the rescue of the black whales. The *Nautilus* dove. Conseil, Ned and I took our places by the glass panels in the lounge. Captain Nemo went up to the helmsman's compartment to wield his ship like a weapon. Soon I could feel our speed increasing.

The struggle between the sperm whales and the black whales had already begun when the *Nautilus* arrived on the scene. It maneuvered in such a way as to cut off the sperm whales. At first they seemed to pay no attention to the new monster which had joined the fray, but soon they found they had met their match.

What a fight! Even Ned Land became enthusiastic and began clapping his hands. The *Nautilus* had become a formidable harpoon brandished by the hand of its captain. It would hurl itself against one of these massive creatures and run clean through it, leaving behind two twisting halves of a whale. The submarine was impervious to the blows of their powerful tails, nor did we even notice the impact when it struck a whale. Once it had killed one, it would rush on to the next, turning so as not to miss its prey, going forward and backward, obedient to its helm, diving when a whale went for deep water and then coming back up with it when it surfaced, striking it full on or obliquely, cutting it in two or merely tearing it open, and piercing with its terrible spur in any direction or at any speed.

What carnage! What a noise on the surface! What sharp hissings and strange roars these terrified animals let out! Lower down, where the water is usually so calm, their tails churned up the sea as if a storm were raging.

This Homeric massacre went on for an hour, and there was no way the sperm whales could escape. Several times ten or twelve of them got together and tried to crush the *Nautilus* with their weight. Through the glass panels we could see their huge mouths full of teeth and their formidable eyes. Ned Land was beside himself, menacing and cursing them. We could feel them clinging to the submarine like dogs seizing a wild boar. But the *Nautilus* would merely put on speed and either drag them along or force them back up to the surface, indifferent both to their enormous weight and the power of their huge jaws.

Finally the herd of sperm whales began to thin out. The waters once again became calm. I could feel the ship surfacing. The hatch was opened and we rushed out on the platform.

The sea was covered with mutilated carcasses. A powerful explosion could not have torn open these huge creatures more violently. We were floating amid gigantic humped bodies with bluish backs and white bellies. Several terrified sperm whales were fleeing out toward the horizon. The water had turned red for several miles in either direction and the *Nautilus* was floating in a sea of blood.

Captain Nemo rejoined us. "Well, Master Land?" he said.

"Well, Monsieur," answered the Canadian, whose enthusiasm had by now died down, "there's no doubt about it, it was a terrible sight. But I'm a hunter, not a butcher, and this was nothing but a massacre."

"It was a massacre of harmful animals," answered the captain; "the *Nautilus* is not a butcher knife."

"I prefer my harpoon," retorted the Canadian.

"Each man to his own weapon," answered the captain, looking fixedly at Ned Land.

I feared Ned might get carried away and do something violent, which would have had serious consequences for us. But his anger was distracted by the sight of a whale floating near the *Nautilus*.

It was one which had not been able to escape from the sperm whales. I recognized the black or southern whale with its compressed head. Anatomically it is distinguished from the right whale and the North Cape whale by the fact that its seven cervical vertebrae are joined together and that it has two more ribs. This poor creature was dead, lying on its side with its belly bitten open. A baby whale, which the mother had not been able to save from the massacre, still hung on to her mutilated fin. The water ran in her mouth and over her whalebone like a murmuring undertow.

Captain Nemo brought the *Nautilus* alongside the cadaver. Two of his men got off onto the whale and, to my great surprise, started milking her. By the time they were through, they had enough to fill two or three casks.

The captain offered me a glass of this still warm milk. I could not refrain from showing my distaste for this sort of drink. But he assured me that it was not only excellent, but indistinguishable from cow's milk.

I tasted it and was forced to agree with him. It therefore provided us with a useful reserve stock, for this milk—in the form of salted butter or cheese—brought a pleasant change in our usual diet.

From that day on, I began to worry about Ned Land, for I noticed that his ill will toward Captain Nemo was increasing. I resolved to keep a close watch on the Canadian.

CHAPTER XXXVII
The Great Ice Barrier

The *Nautilus* once again took up its steady southern course. It followed the fiftieth meridian, traveling at a considerable speed. Did the captain want to try to reach the South Pole? I did not think so, for till then every attempt to reach it had failed. Moreover, it was already nearly too late in the season, for the thirteenth of March in the Antarctic corresponds to the thirteenth of September in northern regions.

On the fourteenth of March I saw floating ice near 55° S. Lat., but it was no more than bits or pieces twenty to twenty-five feet long, forming reefs against which the sea broke into foam. The *Nautilus* stayed on the surface. To Ned Land, who had already fished in Arctic waters, icebergs were a familiar sight; but Conseil and I were admiring them for the first time.

Toward the southern horizon there was a shining white streak in the sky. English whalers have named it "ice blink." No matter how many clouds there are, it is never hidden from view. It announces the presence of a pack or bank of ice.

And in fact, we soon began to see real icebergs shining with a brilliance which varied according to the changing mist. Some of them contained green veins, as if streaked with wavy lines of copper sulfate. Others seemed like enormous transparent amethysts, reflecting the sunlight in the thousand facets of their crystals. Others, tinted by the limestone they contained, would have supplied enough marble to construct a city.

The farther south we went, the more numerous and large these icebergs became. Polar birds were nesting on them by the thousands. There were petrels and puffins deafening us with their cries. Some of them, mistaking the *Nautilus* for the body of a dead whale, would alight on its deck and try pecking at its steel plates.

While we were navigating among these icebergs, Captain Nemo remained on deck a good deal of the time. He was carefully observing these deserted waters. Every now and then I would see his calm eyes light up. Was he saying to himself that since the Antarctic Sea was closed off to other men, he was at home and master of these impassable spaces? Perhaps, but he said nothing. He remained immobile, only coming out of his reverie when his helmsman's instincts finally got the upper hand. He then took the wheel and guided the ship with consummate skill, cleverly avoiding collisions with these masses of ice, some of which were several miles long and 200 to 250 feet high. Often the horizon seemed completely blocked. Then finally when we had reached 60° S. Lat., every passageway had disappeared. But after a careful search, Captain Nemo soon bravely maneuvered the ship into a narrow opening, knowing only too well that it would close in behind him.

Thus the *Nautilus*, guided by his skillful hand, passed through all that ice which, to Conseil's delight, has been classified with great precision according to its shape and size. There are icebergs, which are shaped like mountains; ice fields, stretching out in vast, unbroken plains; drift ice or floating ice; and ice packs, called "palchs" when they are round and "streams" when they are arranged in elongated strips.

The temperature was quite low. The outside thermometer registered between 27° and 28°. But we were warmly dressed in clothes made of seal or polar-bear fur. The inside of the *Nautilus* was heated by its electrical apparatus and could maintain an even temperature against the severest cold. Moreover, we merely had to dive several fathoms down to find a more comfortable temperature.

Two months earlier in these latitudes we would have had a period of perpetual daylight; but now there were already three or four hours of night, and later on six months of darkness would descend on these regions around the Pole.

But March 15 we had passed the latitude of the South Shetland and South Orkney Islands. The captain told me that large herds of seals used to inhabit these islands, but that English and American whalers, in their rage for destruction, had massacred the adult males and pregnant females, and left behind them the silence of death.

Toward eight in the morning of March 16, the *Nautilus,* cruising along the fifty-fifth meridian, crossed the Antarctic Circle. We were so surrounded by ice that the horizon was hidden from view. Nevertheless, Captain Nemo went from one passageway to the next, always heading south.

"Where do you suppose he's going?" I asked.

"Straight ahead," replied Conseil. "After all, when he can't go any farther, he'll stop."

"I wouldn't swear to that!" I answered.

And to be frank, I did not dislike the idea of this new adventure on which we had embarked. I cannot describe the beauties of this new region. The ice took on extraordinary shapes. Here it would look like an oriental town with its innumerable minarets and mosques; there like a ruined city, destroyed by some earthquake. The scenery was constantly varied by the sun's oblique rays or lost in gray mists or blizzards. From all sides came the sound of icebergs cracking apart, crumbling or falling over.

If the *Nautilus* happened to be cruising under water when these things took place, the sound would travel through the ocean with incredible intensity, and these masses of falling ice would create a backwash which could be felt to the deepest parts of the ocean. The *Nautilus* would then roll and pitch like a ship at the mercy of the elements.

Often I could see no way out and thought we would be imprisoned forever. But, guided by his instinct, Captain Nemo would find tiny openings and lead us into new passageways. He never erred in picking out the tiny threads of bluish water running through the ice fields. I therefore felt sure he had already sailed the *Nautilus* through Antarctic waters.

Nevertheless, on March 16, our path was finally completely blocked by ice. We had not yet reached the Great Ice Barrier, but we were among vast ice fields cemented together by the cold. This obstacle, however, did not stop Captain Nemo, and he sent the *Nautilus* hurtling against the ice with incredible violence. The submarine entered this brittle mass like a wedge and split it open with terrible cracking sounds. It was like a battering-ram with infinite power behind it. Pieces of ice were thrown high in the air and then fell around us like hail. Our ship carved out a path for itself by brute force. Occasionally its momentum would be such that it would rise up on top of the ice field and then crush it beneath its weight, or sometimes, when it became imbedded within the ice field, it would split it open by pitching back and forth.

During this time we were assaulted by violent squalls. Then there would be fogs so thick we could not see from one end of the platform to the other. Sudden winds would spring up from any point of the compass. Snow would pile up so deep and compact on the ship that it would have to be chipped off with pick-axes. The temperature would only have to go down to 23° for the whole outside of the *Nautilus* to become covered with ice. Rigging would have been unusable, for all the tackle would have become frozen; only a ship without sails and propelled by electricity could venture into these latitudes.

During this whole period the barometer remained very low. Moreover, the compass no longer gave reliable readings. Its needle would madly point in all directions as we got nearer the south magnetic pole, which must not be confused with the South Pole itself. In fact, according to Hansten, the magnetic pole is situated at about 70° S. Lat. and 130° Long., and according to Duperrey's observations at 135° Long. and 70° 30' S. Lat. We therefore had to take numerous readings on compasses placed in different parts of the ship and then take a mean. But often we could only chart our route by guesswork, a highly unsatisfactory method in the midst of these winding passageways among continually shifting landmarks.

Finally, on March 18, after twenty useless assaults, the *Nautilus* found itself completely blocked. This was no longer an ice stream, "palch" or ice field, but an interminable, immobile chain of mountains welded together.

"The Great Ice Barrier!" said the Canadian.

I realized that for Ned Land, as well as for all the other sailors who had preceded us, this was the impassable obstacle. Toward noon the sun appeared for a moment and permitted Captain Nemo to obtain a fairly exact reading for our position: 51° 30' W. Long. and 67° 39' S. Lat. We were already far into Antarctic regions.

Before us we could no longer see any water. Beyond the *Nautilus'* prow stretched a vast plain, twisted and tangled in a confused mass of ice. It had the capricious, helter-skelter look of the surface of a river just before the ice breaks up, but on a gigantic scale. Here and there were sharp peaks rising like thin needles two hundred feet into the air; farther on a row of sheer, grayish cliffs reflected the sun's rays like huge mirrors lost in the mist. And over this desolate expanse reigned a grim silence, only occasionally broken by the wingbeat of petrels or puffins. Everything, even sound, was frozen.

Here the *Nautilus* was forced to halt in its daring journey through the ice fields.

"Monsieur," said Ned Land, "if that captain of yours goes any farther . . ."

"What then, Ned?"

"Why then he's a superman."

"Why, Ned?"

"Because no one can cross the Great Ice Barrier. Captain Nemo may be quite a man, but he can't overcome nature, and where nature tells you to stop you have to stop whether you like it or not."

"You're right, Ned, but all the same I'd like to know what's behind this barrier! Nothing infuriates me more than a wall!"

"Monsieur's right," said Conseil. "Walls were invented to frustrate scientists. There shouldn't be walls anywhere."

"That's all very fine," said the Canadian, "but anyone can tell you what you'll find behind this barrier."

"What?" I asked.

"Ice, and more ice!"

"I'm not so sure about that, Ned. That's why I would like to go farther."

"Give up that idea, Professor," replied the Canadian. "You've gotten as far as the Great Ice Barrier; that should be enough. Even with Captain Nemo and his *Nautilus* you won't get any farther. And whether he wants to or not, he'll have to head back north where normal people live."

I must admit that Ned Land was right, and until they make ships that can sail over ice fields, they will have to stop before the Great Ice Barrier.

And true enough, in spite of its efforts and its powerful means of splitting ice, the *Nautilus* became completely hemmed in. Ordinarily, if one does not want to go any farther, one can merely turn back. But here, turning back was as impossible as going forward, for all passages had closed in behind us. Although we were now merely hemmed in, the submarine would soon become imbedded in the ice. And this is what began happening toward two in the afternoon, when new ice formed along the sides of the ship with astonishing speed. I had to admit that Captain Nemo's conduct had been exceedingly rash.

I was then on the platform. The captain, who had been watching the situation for several moments, said to me: "Well, Professor, what do you think of our situation?"

"I think we're trapped, Captain."

"Trapped! What do you mean?"

"I mean that we can't go forward, backward or sideways. I think that's what's meant by 'trapped' in the inhabited parts of the earth."

"So, Monsieur Aronnax, you think the *Nautilus* won't be able to get free?"

"It will be very difficult, Captain, for it's already too late in the year to be able to count on the ice breaking up."

"Oh, Professor," replied Captain Nemo in an ironic tone of voice, "you'll always be the same! You never see anything but difficulties and obstacles! But let me say that not only will the *Nautilus* free herself, but she will take us even farther!"

"Farther south?" I asked, looking at the captain.

"Yes, Monsieur, to the South Pole."

"To the South Pole!" I cried, unable to repress a gesture of disbelief.

"Yes," the captain answered coldly, "to the South Pole, that unknown point where all the meridians of the globe meet. As you know, I can make the *Nautilus* do what I want."

Yes, that much I knew! I also knew that this man was brave to the point of being foolhardy! But the South Pole! It was surrounded by many more obstacles than the North Pole, which even the bravest navigators had not yet reached. To go there would be absolutely mad; it was an idea that could only arise in the mind of a crazy man!

I then got the idea of asking the captain if he had already discovered the South Pole.

"No, Monsieur," he answered, "but we will discover it together. Where others have failed, I shall succeed. I have never taken my *Nautilus* this far south; but I repeat, she will go yet farther."

"I would like to believe you, Captain," I said in a somewhat ironic tone of voice. "In fact it ought to be easy! No obstacle's too great for us! We'll just smash the barrier! We'll blow it up, and if it can't be blown up, we'll put wings on the *Nautilus* and fly over it!"

"Over it, Professor?" Captain Nemo replied calmly. "No, not over it, but under it."

"Under it!" I cried.

Suddenly I realized what the captain had in mind; I understood what he was going to do. The *Nautilus'* marvelous powers were once again going to be employed in a superhuman undertaking!

"I think we're beginning to understand one another, Professor," said the captain, half smiling. "You're beginning to see the possibility—or the success, as I prefer to think of it—of this attempt. Things you cannot do with an ordinary ship become easy with the *Nautilus*. If there is a continent at the pole, we will be forced to stop before this continent. But if on the contrary there's open ocean there, we will sail to the very pole!"

"That's right," I said, carried away by the captain's reasoning, "for although the surface of the sea is frozen, the water deeper down must be free, for the heaven-sent reason that the maximum density of water occurs at 2 degrees above freezing point. And unless I'm mistaken, the submerged portion of this barrier is in a ratio of four to one to the part above water."

"Very nearly, Professor. For every foot of an iceberg that is above water, there are three feet below. Now since none of these mountains of ice are higher than three hundred feet, they won't go deeper than nine hundred feet into the water. And what is nine hundred feet for the *Nautilus*?"

"Nothing, Captain."

"It could even go deeper to find that area of temperature common to all oceans, and there we could be completely impervious to the thirty or forty degrees below zero on the surface."

"Absolutely, Captain," I said, becoming more animated.

"The only difficulty," Captain Nemo continued, "will be to remain submerged for several days without renewing our air supply."

"Is that the only difficulty?" I retorted. "The *Nautilus* has vast reservoirs which can be filled and thereby furnish us with all the oxygen we'll need."

"Well thought out, Monsieur Aronnax," replied the captain with a smile. "But since I don't want you to accuse me of being rash, I am reminding you in advance of all my objections."

"Are there any others?"

"Only one. If there is water at the South Pole, it's possible that it will be entirely frozen over and that we would therefore be unable to surface!"

"But, Captain, you're forgetting that the *Nautilus* is armed with a powerful spur! Why couldn't we come up under these ice fields from below and break them open?"

"Ah-hah, Professor! You're full of ideas today!"

"Moreover, Captain," I added, working up to a pitch of enthusiasm, "why shouldn't there be open water at the South Pole just as there is at the North Pole? The poles of cold and those of the earth are not the same either in the Arctic or the Antarctic, and until we have proof to the contrary, we must suppose that at these two points there is either land or open ocean."

"I think so too, Monsieur Aronnax," replied Captain Nemo. "Let me merely remark that after raising so many objections to my plan, you're now flooding me with arguments in its favor."

This was true. I was getting bolder than he! I was the one persuading him to go to the Pole! I was the leader, the man willing to . . . No, stop your daydreaming, you poor fool! Captain Nemo knew better than you the pros and cons of the question; he was just playing a game with you, watching you being carried away with visions of the impossible.

Meanwhile, he did not lose a moment. He signaled and the first mate appeared. The two of them spoke rapidly in their incomprehensible language, and either because the first mate had been warned beforehand or because he considered the project reasonable, he showed no surprise.

But as impassive as he may have been, he could not compare with Conseil when I told him of our intent to push on to the South Pole. As an answer I received a mere "As Monsieur wishes" and had to be content with that. As for Ned Land, he gave the largest shrug I've ever seen.

"Believe me, Monsieur," he said, "I feel sorry for you and your Captain Nemo!"

"But we'll reach the South Pole, Ned."

"Maybe, but you won't come back!"

And then Ned Land went back to his cabin so he wouldn't "do something desperate," as he said upon leaving.

Meanwhile, the ship was made ready for this bold attempt. The *Nautilus'* powerful pumps brought air into the reservoirs and stored it there under high pressure. Toward four o'clock Captain Nemo announced that the hatches leading to the platform would be closed. I took one last look at the thick barrier we were about to cross. The sky was clear, and the air pure and cold (it was 10° above zero), but now that the wind had died down, this temperature did not seem too unbearable.

Ten or so men got onto the sides of the *Nautilus* and broke the ice around the hull with pickaxes. Soon we were free. It took little time, for the new ice was still thin. We all went back inside. The reservoirs were filled with the water that had not frozen around the hull, and the *Nautilus* started down.

I and Conseil had taken up our posts in the lounge. Through the open panels we looked out into the waters of this southern sea. The thermometer rose. The needle on the pressure gauge started moving down.

As Captain Nemo had predicted, at about 900 feet we found ourselves floating beneath the undulating surface of the barrier. But the *Nautilus* went yet farther down. We finally stopped at a depth of 2600 feet. The temperature of the water had risen two degrees, from 10° at the surface to 12° at this depth. It goes without saying that the temperature inside the *Nautilus,* maintained by its heating devices, was much higher than this. Every operation was carried out with extraordinary precision.

"If Monsieur will permit me to say so, I think we will pass the ice barrier," said Conseil.

"I'm sure we will!" I answered with deep conviction.

Now that it was in open water, the *Nautilus* headed straight for the South Pole, cruising along the fifty-second meridian. We had to go from 67° 30' to 90°, twenty-two and a half degrees of latitude, or more than a thousand miles. The *Nautilus* was traveling at an average of twenty-six knots, the speed of an express train. If it kept going at this rate, we would be there in forty hours.

The novelty of our situation kept Conseil and me at the glass panels of the lounge for a good part of the night. The sea was lit up by the electric light, but it was empty. No fish lived in these imprisoned waters. For them it was only a way of getting from the Antarctic Ocean to the open water around the Pole. We were traveling fast, and the long steel hull trembled as it sped through the water.

Toward two in the morning I went to get several hours of sleep. Conseil did the same. As I went down the gangway, I did not meet Captain Nemo. I supposed he was at the helm.

At five on the following morning, I went back to my post in the lounge. The electric log showed that we had reduced our speed. The *Nautilus* was cautiously returning toward the surface, emptying its reservoirs slowly.

My heart was beating fast. Were we going to come up and find ourselves in open water near the South Pole?

No. A sudden thud told me that the *Nautilus* had struck the underside of the ice barrier, which was still very thick judging by the dead sound of the blow. We had in fact "touched ground," to use the nautical term, but upside down and at a depth of a thousand feet. This meant that there were 1,333 feet of ice above us, 333 feet of which were above the surface. The barrier was slightly higher here than it was at the edge. Not a very comforting thought.

The *Nautilus* tried the same experiment several times that day, and every time it was stopped short by the wall overhead. In certain places it met ice at a depth of three thousand feet, which meant that the ice was four thousand feet thick with a thousand feet protruding above the surface. This was three times the height of the barrier at the point where the *Nautilus* had first gone under.

I carefully noted these various depths, and I was thus able to obtain an underwater outline of this icy mountain chain.

That evening our situation remained unchanged. We continued to find ice at depths varying from 1300 to 1600 feet. This was an improvement, but there was still quite a distance between us and the surface of the ocean!

It was then eight o'clock. At four o'clock the air should have been renewed in the *Nautilus* according to the usual custom on board. But I was not feeling the lack of it too much, even though Captain Nemo had not started using his reserve supply.

I slept fitfully that night. I was assailed by hopes and fears. I got up several times. The *Nautilus* continued trying to break through. Toward three in the morning I noticed that we met the underside of the barrier at a depth of only 150 feet. The barrier was little by little turning back into an ice field. The mountains were changing into plains.

My eyes remained fixed on the pressure gauge. We kept climbing, following the underside of the ice, which sparkled beneath the rays of the electric light. Slowly but surely the barrier was getting thinner.

Finally at six in the morning, on that memorable day of March 19, the door of the lounge opened. Captain Nemo entered and said: "Open water!"

CHAPTER XXXVIII
The South Pole

I rushed out on the platform. Yes, we were in open water! There were only a few icebergs scattered here and there. A broad sea stretched out into the distance. The sky was full of birds and myriads of fish swam in water ranging in color from a deep blue to olive green. The thermometer read 37°. Relatively speaking, it was like spring here behind the Great Ice Barrier, whose far-off masses were outlined against the northern horizon.

"Are we at the South Pole?" I asked the captain, with my heart throbbing.

"I don't know," he said. "At noon we'll take our position."

"But will we be able to see the sun through these clouds?" I asked, looking up at the gray sky.

"We will only need to get a faint glimpse of it to be able to take our position," the captain replied.

Ten miles to the south a solitary island rose about seven hundred feet above the surface. We headed for it cautiously, for these waters could have been strewn with reefs.

An hour later we had reached it, and in two more hours we had gone all the way around it. It was four or five miles in circumference. A narrow channel separated it from a considerable body of land, perhaps an entire continent, whose limits we could not see. The existence of this land seemed to prove Maury right. This clever American scientist has stated, in fact, that between the South Pole and the sixtieth parallel the sea is covered with enormous icebergs, much bigger than those found in the north Atlantic. From this he has deduced that within the Antarctic Circle there lies a considerable body of land, since icebergs cannot form over water, but only at coastlines. According to his calculations, the mass of ice surrounding the South Pole forms a cap about twenty-five hundred miles wide.

The *Nautilus* had stopped, out of fear of running aground, about six hundred yards from a beach above which rose a superb mass of rocks. The dinghy was put to sea, and the captain, two of his men carrying instruments, Conseil and myself got in. It was ten in the morning. I had not seen Ned Land. He undoubtedly did not relish the idea of having to swallow his words in the presence of the South Pole.

Several strokes of the oars brought the dinghy to the sandy shore, where it was beached. Conseil was about to jump out, but I held him back.

"Monsieur," I said to Captain Nemo, "it is your privilege to be the first to set foot on this land."

"Yes, Monsieur," answered the captain, "and if I don't hesitate to go ashore on the South Pole, it is because till now no human being has even been here."

With this he jumped out lightly onto the sand. His heart beat with emotion. He climbed up to an overhanging rock on a little promontory, and there, with his arms crossed, eyes burning, immobile and silent, he seemed to take possession of these Antarctic regions. After spending five minutes in this state of ecstasy, he turned toward us and said: "Whenever you wish, Monsieur."

Conseil and I got out, leaving the two men in the dinghy.

Over a considerable area, the terrain consisted of reddish volcanic rock, looking as if it had been made of ground bricks. It was covered with bits of slag, hardened lava and pumice stone. There was no doubt about its volcanic origin. In certain places little smoke holes gave out a sulfurous odor and bore witness to the fact that the fires inside the earth still retained their force. However, upon climbing a steep slope, I saw no volcanoes within a radius of several miles. It is well known, however, that in the Antarctic James Ross discovered the two craters called Erebus and Terror in full activity at 167° W. Long. and 77° 32' S. Lat.

The vegetation of this desolate continent seemed very limited. Some lichens of the species *Usnea melanoxantha* were spread out on the black rocks. These, along with certain microscopic plants such as diatoms with their single cells placed between two quartz shells, and long purple and crimson sea wrack thrown up on the shore by the surf, were the only signs of plant life in this region.

The coast was sprinkled with shellfish: little mussels, limpets, smooth heart-shaped cockles and especially cliones with their oblong membranous bodies and their head made of two round lobes. We also saw many of those inch-long Arctic cliones which a whale swallows by the thousands in one mouthful. The water near the shore was alive with these charming pteropods, veritable butterflies of the sea.

Among other zoophytes, in the shallows I noticed some tree-shaped corals of a type which according to James Ross live in Antarctic waters down to depths of three thousand feet. I also saw little alcyonacea belonging to the species *Procellaria pelagica*, as well as a great number of starfish peculiar to this region.

But it was in the air that life really abounded. Thousands of birds of all kinds soared and fluttered overhead, deafening us with their cries. Others were crowded together on rocks, watching us pass by so fearlessly that sometimes we even had to step over them. There were auks, so agile and supple in the water that they could be mistaken for bonitos, and yet so clumsy and heavy on land. They let out strange cries and assembled in large groups, moving little but making a great deal of noise.

Among other birds, I noticed some chionis, belonging to the wader family: they are about the size of pigeons, white in color, with a short conical beak and a red circle around their eyes. Conseil captured a few, for if well cooked these birds can make a very good dish. Overhead passed sooty albatrosses with a wing span of about thirteen feet, justly called the vultures of the ocean; giant petrels, and among others a species called the "sea eagle," which is a great killer of seals; a kind of small checkered duck; and many kinds of ordinary petrels, some whitish with brown borders on their wings and another bluish species, peculiar to Antarctic waters, which is "so full of oil," as I told Conseil, "that the inhabitants of the Faroe Islands merely stick a wick in them before lighting them."

"What a pity," said Conseil, "that nature didn't build them with the wicks already in. That way they would have made perfect lamps!"

A half a mile farther on, the ground was riddled with penguin nests. They were like burrows arranged for laying eggs, and out of them would scramble innumerable birds braying like donkeys. Later on, Captain Nemo had several hundred penguins hunted and killed, for their black flesh is very good to eat. These creatures, with their slate-colored bodies, white bellies and lemon-yellow bands around their necks, would allow themselves to be killed with stones without even trying to run away. Meanwhile, the sky was still gray, and at eleven o'clock the sun had not yet appeared. I was afraid it would not come out, and without the sun it was impossible to take our position. How then would we know if we had reached the South Pole!

When I rejoined Captain Nemo, I found him silently leaning on a rock and looking up at the sky. He seemed impatient and annoyed. But what could he do? This brave, powerful man had no sway over the sun as he did over the sea.

Icebergs shaped like mountains

Noon came without the sun having appeared for a single moment. One could not even make out where it was behind the curtain of clouds. Then it began to snow.

"We will try again tomorrow," said the captain, and we went back to the *Nautilus* amid flurries of snow.

During our absence the nets had been put out, and I was interested to see what fish had been hauled on board. Antarctic waters serve as a place of refuge for a great number of migratory fish, who flee the storms of other regions only to be eaten, it must be said, by porpoises and seals. I noticed several miller's thumbs about four inches long, whitish with pale stripes and armed with spines, and also some chimera about three feet long with slim bodies, silvery smooth skin, round heads, three fins on their back and a snout shaped like a trunk curving in toward their mouth. I tasted them, but found them flavorless; whereas Conseil found they were much to his liking.

The snowstorm lasted until the next day. It was impossible to stay on the platform. I stayed in the lounge noting down the incidents of this polar excursion, and from there I could hear the cries of the petrels and albatrosses playing about in the midst of the storm. The *Nautilus* did not remain immobile; it traveled ten or so miles farther south along the coast, cruising in a kind of half-light left by the sun as it touched the horizon.

On the next day, March 20, the snow had stopped. But it was a bit colder; the thermometer marked 28°. The clouds were lifting, and I hoped that we would be able to take our position that day.

Since Captain Nemo had not yet appeared, the dinghy took Conseil and me to shore. Here too the ground was volcanic. Everywhere there were traces of lava, slag and basalt, but I was unable to find the crater which had emitted them. Here, as before, myriads of birds flew overhead. But now they had to share their dominion with vast herds of marine mammals looking at us with their soft eyes. There were various kinds of seals, some stretched out on the ground, others lying on drift ice, and many going in or coming out of the sea. They had never seen men before and therefore did not run away as we drew near. I reckoned there were enough of them here to stock several hundred ships.

"It's lucky," said Conseil, "that Ned Land didn't come along with us!"

"Why, Conseil?"

"Because the way he feels about hunting, he would have killed them all."

"Not all of them, that's a bit too much; but I doubt that we could have prevented our Canadian friend from harpooning several of these magnificent creatures. And this wouldn't have pleased Captain Nemo, who doesn't like to shed the blood of innocent animals without reason."

"He's right."

"He certainly is, Conseil. But tell me, haven't you yet classified these superb specimens of marine fauna?"

"As Monsieur knows," answered Conseil, "I'm not very good at practical classification. If Monsieur could tell me the names of these animals . . ."

"They're seals and walruses."

"Both of these genera belong to the family of the pinnipeds," Conseil hastened to say, "order of carnivores, division of unguiculates, subclass of monodelphians, class of mammals, subkingdom of vertebrates."

"Good, Conseil," I replied, "but these two genera of seals and walruses are divided into various species which, if I'm not mistaken, we'll be able to observe. Let's go."

It was eight in the morning. We still had four hours until the sun would be usable for taking our position. I led the way to a vast bay cut into the granite cliffs along the shore.

There, as far as the eye could see, the ground and floating ice was covered with these creatures, and I involuntarily looked for old Proteus, the mythological shepherd who watched over these immense flocks belonging to Neptune. Most of them were seals. They were in groups with the males and females each carrying out their own tasks: the father watched over the family and the mother suckled her young, while those little seals already strong enough to walk wandered off a short distance. When these creatures wanted to move, they did it in a series of little jumps made by contracting their bodies and helping themselves clumsily along with their flippers. But I must say that once they are in the water, their natural element, these animals, with their flexible spinal column, narrow pelvis, close-cropped hair and webbed feet, can swim marvelously. When they rest on land, they lie in graceful positions. Thus the ancients, noting their gentle faces, their expressive eyes (which are unsurpassed by those of the most beautiful women) and their charming attitudes, poetically changed the males into tritons and the females into mermaids.

I pointed out to Conseil the highly developed cerebral lobes of these intelligent creatures. No mammal except man has a greater brain capacity. Thus seals are easily domesticated and capable of being trained to a certain extent; and I agree with certain naturalists who say that if properly taught, they could be used for fishing.

Most of them were asleep on the rocks or on the sand. Among the seals properly speaking—that is, those whose ears, unlike sea lions, do not protrude from their head—I saw several varieties of stenorhyncae ten feet long, with white hair, bulldog heads and ten teeth in each jaw—four incisors in the upper and four in the lower jaw, and two large canine teeth in each jaw shaped like lilies of the valley. Between them slithered some sea elephants, a kind of seal with a short mobile trunk; they are the giants of the species, with bodies measuring twenty-five feet around and thirty three feet in length. They did not move when we drew near.

"Aren't those animals dangerous?" Conseil asked me.

"No," I answered, "unless they're attacked. When a seal defends its young, its anger is terrible, and it isn't rare for them to break small fishing boats to pieces."

"They're only right to defend themselves."

"I can't deny that."

Two miles farther on we were stopped by a promontory which protected the bay from the south wind. It rose up vertically from the water and the surf crashed against it. From beyond it we could hear loud bellowings as if from a herd of cattle.

"What's that?" asked Conseil. "A chorus of bulls?"

"No," I said, "a chorus of walruses."

"Are they fighting?"

"Either fighting or playing."

"With Monsieur's permission, I'd love to see them."

"Let's go, Conseil."

And we started off climbing over blackish rocks, among sudden landslides and stones covered with ice and therefore very slippery. More than once I fell and hurt my back. Conseil, either because he was more careful or stronger, scarcely ever stumbled, and he would say as he picked me up: "If Monsieur would be kind enough to keep his feet apart, I think Monsieur would maintain his balance better."

When we got to the ridge running along the top of the promontory, I saw a vast white plain covered with walruses. They were playing with one another; their bellowings were of joy, not anger.

Walruses resemble seals in the shape of their bodies and the disposition of their limbs. But they have no canine teeth or incisors in their lower jaw, whereas the canine teeth in their upper jaw form two tusks thirty inches long and thirteen inches around at the base. They are made of compact, unstreaked ivory which is harder than that of elephants and does not turn yellow so quickly, and they are therefore much sought after. As a result, walruses have been hunted so indiscriminately that they will soon become extinct, for hunters kill about four thousand a year, including pregnant females and the young.

As I passed near these curious animals, I could examine them at my leisure, for they did not move. Their reddish-tan skin was thick and rough; what hair they had was short. Some of them were thirteen feet long. They seemed calmer and less fearful than their northern cousins, for they did not place sentinels around their camp.

After examining this colony of walruses, I began to think of returning. It was eleven o'clock, and if Captain Nemo found the weather favorable for taking our position, I wanted to be present while he did it. Nevertheless, I had little hope that the sun would come out that day. It was hidden from our view by clouds squashed out along the horizon. It seemed as if the sun was jealous and did not want to reveal to human beings this unapproachable part of the globe.

We started back toward the *Nautilus*, following a steep path running along the edge of the cliffs. By eleven-thirty we had reached our landing place. The dinghy had already returned with the captain. I saw him standing on a block of basalt. His instruments were next to him. His eyes were fixed on the northern horizon, near which the sun was describing its long arc.

I went over and stood beside him without saying a word. Noon came, and as on the day before, the sun did not appear.

It was bad luck for us. We still had not been able to take our position. If it was not done the next day, we would have to give up our project completely, for it was the twentieth of March. The next day, the twenty-first, would be the equinox. From then on the sun would disappear behind the horizon for six months, and with its disappearance would begin the long polar night. Since the September equinox, it had emerged from the northern horizon and risen in long spirals till December 21. On that day, the summer solstice of the Southern Hemisphere, it had started back down, and tomorrow it would send forth its last rays over the South Pole.

I told Captain Nemo my thoughts and fears on this subject.

"You are right, Monsieur Aronnax," he said. "If I cannot shoot the sun tomorrow, I will not be able to do so again for six months. But since fate has brought us here on precisely March twenty-first, our position will be easy to determine, if the sun appears."

"Why, Captain?"

"Because when the sun is traveling through the sky in such elongated spirals, it is difficult to get an exact measurement of its height above the horizon, and one is in danger of making serious errors."

"How will you do it then?"

"I will only use my chronometer," replied Captain Nemo. "If at noon tomorrow, March twenty-first, the sun's disk is cut exactly in two by the northern horizon, that will mean I'm at the South Pole."

"Right," I said, "but this won't be, mathematically speaking, absolutely correct, for the equinox doesn't fall necessarily at noon."

"No doubt, Monsieur, but the error involved will be less than a hundred yards, and that will be good enough for us. So, until tomorrow."

Captain Nemo went back on board his ship. Conseil and I stayed until five o'clock surveying the beach. I picked up nothing of interest, except for the egg of an auk, remarkable for its size, for which a collector would have paid more than two hundred dollars. It was cream colored and covered with streaks and lines which looked like hieroglyphics. I gave it to Conseil, and this worthy, sure-footed boy, carrying it as if it were a precious Chinese vase, brought it back to the *Nautilus*.

There I deposited this rare egg inside one of the showcases of the museum. That night I dined off an excellent piece of seal liver, which to me tasted rather like pork. Then I went to bed, but not before praying like a Hindu for the sun to appear.

On the next day, March 21, I was up on the platform at five in the morning. I found Captain Nemo already there.

"The weather's clearing up a bit," he said. "There's some hope. After breakfast we'll go ashore to pick out an observation post."

Once this had been decided, I went to find Ned Land. I would have wanted to take him with me. But the stubborn Canadian refused, and I could see that day by day he was becoming more taciturn and angry. In this particular circumstance, however, I did not mind his stubbornness; there were really too many seals on shore, and it was best not to expose a man with his hunting instincts to such a temptation.

After breakfast I went ashore. The *Nautilus* had moved several miles farther on during the night. It was in open water, more than two miles from the coast, above which rose a sharp peak about fifteen hundred feet high. Also in the dinghy were Captain Nemo, two members of the crew and the instruments—a chronometer, a telescope and a barometer.

During the crossing, I saw many whales belonging to the three species peculiar to southern waters: the right whale, which has no dorsal fin, the humpback whale with its wrinkled belly and huge whitish fins, and the finback whale, which is yellowish brown in color and is the liveliest of all whales. One can hear this animal a long way off when it sends up its spout of air and vapor resembling a column of swirling smoke. Herds of these various mammals were playing about in the calm water, which I realized now served them as a place of refuge from the hunters tracking them.

I also noticed long white rows of salpas, a kind of shellfish which lives in colonies, and enormous jellyfish rocking back and forth in the backwash of the waves.

At nine o'clock we reached shore. The sky was clearing and the clouds scurrying off to the south. Mist was rising from the cold surface of the water. Captain Nemo headed for the peak where undoubtedly he wanted to make his observation post. It was a difficult climb over sharp lava rock and pumice stone, through air often filled with the sulfurous gases escaping from volcanic smoke holes. Even though the captain was unaccustomed to walking on dry land, he climbed the steepest slopes with a suppleness and agility which a hunter of mountain goats would have envied, and I had difficulty keeping up with him.

It took us two hours to reach the summit of this peak composed partly of porphyry and partly of basalt. From there we could see a vast expanse of sea stretching out toward the northern horizon. At our feet there were shining white fields, and overhead a pale azure sky clear of clouds. To the north, the sun's disk looked like a ball of fire already cut off at the corner by the horizon. The whales swimming in the sea sent up hundreds of magnificent fan-shaped jets of water. In the distance, the *Nautilus* looked like yet another whale merely sleeping. Behind us, to the south and east, a vast expanse of land, chaotically heaped with rocks and ice, stretched out as far as we could see.

Upon arriving at the summit, Captain Nemo carefully calculated its altitude by means of his barometer, for this factor had to be taken into account when determining our position.

At a quarter to twelve, the sun—a golden disk we could then only see by refraction—sent its last rays over this region never before visited by men.

Captain Nemo, armed with a special telescope to correct the refraction, observed the sun as it disappeared little by little below the horizon, traveling in a long, curving path. I was holding the chronometer. My heart was pounding. If the disappearance of the sun's half-disk coincided with noon on the chronometer, we would then be at the South Pole itself.

"Noon!" I cried.

"The South Pole!" replied Captain Nemo in a solemn tone of voice, passing me the telescope through which I could see the sun cut into two equal portions by the horizon.

I watched its last rays crowning the peak and the shadows slowly climbing the slopes.

Then Captain Nemo put a hand on my shoulder and said: "In 1600, the Dutchman Gheritk, carried off his course by currents and storms, reached 64° S. Lat. and discovered the South Shetland Islands. On January 17, 1773, the famous Cook, following the thirty-eighth meridian, reached a latitude of 67° 30', and on January 30, 1774, following the hundred-and-ninth meridian, he reached a latitude of 71° 15'. In 1819, the Russian Bellinghausen got to the sixty-ninth parallel, and in 1821 to the sixty-sixth at 111° W. Long. In 1820, the Englishman Brunsfield was stopped at the sixty-fifth parallel. That same year, the American Morrel, whose accounts are doubtful, went along the forty-second meridian and discovered open sea at 70° 14' S. Lat. In 1825, the Englishman Powell could get no further than the sixty-second parallel. But that same year an Englishman named Weddel who was a mere seal fisherman got as far as 72° 14' S. Lat. along the thirty-fifth meridian, and as far as 74° 15' on the thirty-sixth. In 1829, the Englishman Forster, captain of the *Chanticleer*, took possession of the Antarctic continent at 63° 26' S. Lat. and 66° 26' W. Long. On February 1, 1831, the Englishman Biscoe discovered Enderby Land at a latitude of 68° 50', on February 5, 1832, Adelaide Land at 67° S. Lat., and on February 21 of that same year, Graham Land at 64° 45' S. Lat. In 1838, the Frenchman Dumont d'Urville was stopped by the Great Ice Barrier at 62° 57' S. Lat., but managed to discover Louis-Philippe Land; two years later in a new expedition to the south he discovered Adélie Land at 66° 30' on January 21, and a week later Clarie Coast at 64° 40' S. Lat. In 1838, the Englishman Wilkes went along the hundredth meridian as far as the sixty-ninth parallel. In 1839, the Englishman Balleny discovered Sabrina Land on the edge of the Antarctic Circle. Then on January 12, 1842, the Englishman James Ross, commanding the *Erebus* and the *Terror*, discovered Victoria Land at 76° 56' S. Lat. and 171°

7' E. Long. On the twenty-third of the same month he reached the seventy-fourth parallel, the farthest point attained till then; on the twenty-seventh he reached 76° 8', on the twenty-eighth 77° 32' and on February 2 78° 4'. Later in 1842, he returned but could get no farther than the seventy-first parallel. And then on March 21, 1868, I, Captain Nemo, reached the South Pole at a latitude of 90° and took possession of this portion of the globe equal in area to a sixth of all known continents."

"In the name of whom, Captain?"

"My own!"

With this, Captain Nemo unfurled a black banner bearing a gold letter *N*. He then turned toward the sun, whose last rays were flickering over the horizon, and said: "Farewell, sun! Leave us, O radiant orb! Go to thy rest beneath the sea and let six months of night spread its shadows over my new domain."

CHAPTER XXXIX
Accident or Incident?

At six o'clock in the morning of the next day, March 22, preparations for departure were begun. The last glimmer of twilight was melting into the night. The cold was sharp. The stars were shining with surprising intensity. Straight overhead I could make out the marvelous Southern Cross, that polar star of Antarctic regions.

The thermometer marked nine degrees above zero, and when the wind came up it was very biting. Ice was forming on the open water, and the sea started to congeal everywhere. Obviously this southern basin was frozen over for six months of the year, during which time it was absolutely inaccessible. What did the whales do then? Undoubtedly they went out under the ice barrier in search of open water. As for seals and walruses, they were accustomed to the extremely cold climate and they stayed in this frozen waste. Out of instinct, they make holes in the ice field and keep them always open; this is where they come to breathe. And when the birds migrate north to escape the cold, these marine mammals remain sole masters of the Antarctic continent.

Meanwhile the *Nautilus'* tanks had been filled and it slowly sank beneath the surface. When it reached a depth of a thousand feet it stopped. Its propeller began churning the water and it headed straight north at a speed of fifteen knots. That afternoon it was already cruising beneath the immense shell of the Great Ice Barrier.

The panels in the lounge had been closed in case the *Nautilus* should strike submerged ice. I therefore spent the day putting my notes in order. My mind was completely occupied with thoughts of the South Pole. We had reached that inaccessible point with no more fatigue or danger than if we had been traveling in a train. And now we were beginning the return journey. Would it bring new surprises? I had no doubts, for there seemed to be no end to the wonders of underwater life! Nevertheless, since fate had brought us on board this ship five and a half months ago, we had covered fourteen thousand leagues. And on this trip, which was longer than the circumference of the earth, how many fascinating or terrifying incidents had held us spellbound: the hunting expedition in the forests of Crespo Island, running aground in Torres Strait, the coral graveyard, the pearl fisheries of Ceylon, the Arabian Tunnel, the volcano of Santorin Island, the treasure in Vigo Bay, Atlantis, the South Pole! During the night, all these memories passed by one after another in my dreams and did not allow my brain to rest for an instant.

At three in the morning I was awakened by a violent blow. I sat up in bed and tried to hear what was going on, but suddenly I was hurled out into the middle of the room. Obviously the *Nautilus* had collided with something and then heeled over at a sharp angle.

Feeling my way along the walls, I dragged myself along the gangways to the lounge, where the ceiling lights were still on. The furniture had been knocked over. Luckily, the showcases were well attached to the floor and had therefore remained upright. The pictures on the starboard side of the room were flat against the wall, while those on the port side were leaning out with their lower edges a foot away from the wall. The *Nautilus* was heeled over to starboard, and moreover, completely immobile.

Inside I could hear the sound of footsteps and a confused murmur of voices. But Captain Nemo did not appear. Just as I was about to leave the lounge, Ned Land and Conseil entered.

"What happened?" I asked them at once.

"That's what we just came to ask Monsieur," replied Conseil.

"Confound it!" cried the Canadian. "I can tell you what happened! The *Nautilus* ran aground, and judging by the way it's heeled over, I don't think we're going to get away as easily as we did in Torres Strait."

"But are we at least on the surface?" I asked.

"I don't know," replied Conseil.

"It's easy to find out," I answered.

I looked at the pressure gauge. To my great astonishment it indicated a depth of 1180 feet.

"What's all this about?" I cried.

"We'll have to ask Captain Nemo," said Conseil.

"Where is he?" asked Ned Land.

"Follow me," I said to my two companions.

We left the lounge. There was no one in the library. No one either at the central companionway or in the crew's quarters. I supposed that Captain Nemo was in the helmsman's compartment. The best thing to do was to wait. All three of us returned to the lounge.

I will pass over the Canadian's recriminations. I can't say his anger was unjustified. But in any case I let him get rid of his ill humor without answering.

We remained like this for twenty minutes, listening for the slightest noise inside the *Nautilus*, when Captain Nemo entered. He seemed not to see us. His face, usually so impassive, showed signs of uneasiness. He silently checked the compass and the pressure gauge, and then went over to a map of the world and put his finger on the Antarctic seas.

I did not want to interrupt him. However, when he turned toward me several minutes later, I asked him, using a phrase he had employed in Torres Strait: "Merely an incident, Captain?"

"No, Monsieur," he replied, "this time it is an accident."

"Is it serious?"

"Perhaps."

"Is there any immediate danger?"

"No."

"Has the *Nautilus* run aground?"

"Yes."

"How did it happen?"

"By a trick of nature, not through the incompetence of men. We did not make a single mistake in our maneuvers. Nevertheless, one cannot prevent the laws of equilibrium from taking effect. One can resist the laws of men, but not those of nature."

Captain Nemo had chosen an odd moment to start philosophizing, and moreover his answer told me nothing.

"Could you please tell me, Captain, what caused this accident?"

"An enormous block of ice—as big as a mountain—has turned over," he replied. "When icebergs become eaten away underneath by warm water or by repeated blows, their center of gravity rises. Then the whole mass of ice turns upside down. This is what has happened. One of these icebergs turned and struck the *Nautilus* as it was cruising under water. The iceberg then slipped under its hull and lifted it with an irresistible force into shallower water, where it is now lying heeled over on its side."

"But can't you free the *Nautilus* merely by emptying its reservoirs and thereby returning it to an upright position?"

"That's what we're trying to do now, Monsieur. You can hear the pumps working. Look at the pressure gauge; it shows the *Nautilus* is rising. But unfortunately the block of ice is rising with it, and until some obstacle stops its upward movement, our position will not change."

And, in fact, the *Nautilus* was still lying on its side. Undoubtedly it would straighten up when the block of ice stopped turning. But who was to say that at that moment we wouldn't collide against the underside of the barrier, and thus be horribly squashed between two surfaces of ice?

I thought over all these consequences of our situation. Captain Nemo did not take his eyes off the pressure gauge. Since it was first struck by the iceberg, the *Nautilus* had risen about a hundred and fifty feet, but it was still heeling over at the same angle.

Suddenly I could feel the hull make a slight movement. Evidently the *Nautilus* was righting itself a bit. The objects hanging in the lounge began to go back to their normal positions, and the walls became more vertical. None of us said a word. With beating hearts, we watched the ship right itself. The floor became horizontal beneath our feet. Ten minutes went by.

"We're upright at last!" I cried.

"Yes," said Captain Nemo as he headed for the door of the lounge.

"Do you think we'll get free?" I asked.

"Certainly," he replied, "since the reservoirs are not yet empty."

The captain left and I soon saw that at his orders the upward course of the *Nautilus* had been stopped. We were, in fact, close to striking the underside of the ice barrier, and it was better to remain free in the water.

"Well, we got out of that one!" said Conseil.

"Yes, we could have easily been squashed between two blocks of ice, or at least imprisoned. And then, without any way of renewing our air supply . . . Yes, we're well out of that one!"

"Presuming it's all over!" murmured Ned Land.

I did not want to start a useless argument with the Canadian and I therefore did not reply. Moreover, just then the panels opened and light poured in from outside.

We were suspended in the water, but thirty feet away on each side of the *Nautilus* rose a shining wall of ice. Above and below there was the same wall. Above, because the underside of the ice barrier formed an immense ceiling; below, because the overturned iceberg had slid so as to come to rest on the two side walls. The *Nautilus* was imprisoned in a veritable tunnel of ice about sixty feet across and filled with calm water. It was therefore easy to get out by going either forward or backward, and then to set out again several hundred yards deeper on a free passage under the ice barrier.

Even though the lights in the lounge had been put out, it was brilliantly illuminated by the walls of ice acting as powerful reflectors for the light on top of the submarine. I could not possibly describe the effect of its rays on these huge blocks cut into such strange shapes; every one of their angles, ridges and facets gave off a different hue. It was a dazzling mine of precious stones, and especially of sapphires and emeralds flashing their blue and green rays in all directions. Here and there one could see soft, milky opal nuances running among fiery, diamondlike points of light shining with such brilliance that one could hardly look at them. The power of the *Nautilus* was multiplied a hundred times, like that of a lamp passing through the lenses of a beacon.

"How beautiful! How beautiful!" exclaimed Conseil.

"Yes," I said, "it's a marvelous sight. Don't you think so, Ned?"

"Yes, confound it!" he retorted. "It's magnificent, even though it makes me furious to have to admit it! I've never seen anything like it. But this sight could cost us our necks. And to be frank, I feel as if we're looking at things God didn't intend for the eyes of man!"

Ned was right. It was too beautiful. Suddenly a cry from Conseil made me turn around.

"What is it?" I asked.

"Close your eyes, Monsieur! Don't look!"

And with this, he clapped his hands over his eyes.

"What's wrong, my boy?"

"I've been blinded!"

Involuntarily I looked out the window, but my eyes could not stand the blazing light entering the room.

I then realized what had happened. The *Nautilus* had gotten under way and was now traveling at high speed. All the quiet luster from the walls of ice had changed into flashing streaks. The fire from these myriads of diamonds had blended together. The *Nautilus,* propelled by its powerful engines, was traveling through a sheath of lightning.

Then the panels in the lounge closed. We held our hands over our eyes and saw nothing but spots, as if we had been looking at the sun too long. It took our troubled eyes some time to calm down.

Finally we took away our hands.

"Goodness me, I never would have believed such a thing was possible!" said Conseil.

"And as for me, I still don't believe it!" retorted the Canadian.

"When we get back on land," said Conseil, "after seeing such wonders of nature, what will we think of those miserable continents and the tiny things produced by the hand of man? No, civilization is no longer worthy of us!"

Such words in the mouth of an impassive Belgian showed to what a point our enthusiasm had risen. But the Canadian made sure to throw cold water on our excitement.

"Civilization?" he said, shaking his head. "Don't worry, Conseil, you'll never see it again anyhow!"

It was then five o'clock in the morning. Suddenly I felt the *Nautilus* collide with something ahead; I realized its spur had just struck a block of ice. It was undoubtedly due to some error in judgment, for this underwater tunnel was full of ice and not easy to navigate. I thought that Captain Nemo would merely alter his course slightly, go around the obstacle and continue on his way. I felt sure our forward progress could not be completely blocked. Nevertheless, contrary to my expectations, the *Nautilus* started to move backward.

"Are we going backward?" asked Conseil.

"Yes," I answered. "The tunnel is probably blocked at this end."

"Then what are we going to do?"

"It's simple," I said. "We'll retrace our steps and leave by the southern end, that's all."

In saying this, I wanted to seem more sure of myself than I really was. Meanwhile the *Nautilus'* backward speed had increased and we were now traveling very fast.

"It'll take longer this way," said Ned.

"Several hours one way or the other, what difference does it make, as long as we get out."

"Yes," repeated Ned Land, "as long as we get out!"

After a while I left the lounge and went into the library. My companions remained seated, without saying a word. I stretched out on a couch, took up a book and let my eyes scan the pages mechanically.

A quarter of an hour later, Conseil came up and said: "Is that an interesting book Monsieur's reading?"

"Very interesting," I replied.

"Undoubtedly. Monsieur is reading Monsieur's book!"

"My own book?"

And to be sure, I was holding my work on the great ocean depths. I hadn't even realized it. I closed the book and started walking about. Ned and Conseil got up to go to their room.

"Stay here, my friends," I said, holding them back. "Let's stay together until we're out of this blind alley."

"As Monsieur wishes."

Several hours went by. Again and again I checked the instruments hanging on the wall of the lounge. The pressure gauge showed that the *Nautilus* was staying at a depth of one thousand feet, the compass indicated that it was still heading south, and the log showed that it was traveling at twenty knots, a speed which seemed excessive in such a narrow space. But Captain Nemo knew that he could not really go too fast, for in such a situation every minute was worth a century.

At 8:25 a second collision took place. This time it was behind. I grew pale. My companions came over. I took Conseil's hand. We looked questioningly at one another, our looks betraying our thoughts better than any words.

Just then the captain entered the lounge. I went over to him and asked: "Is our route also barred to the south?"

"Yes, Monsieur. As the iceberg turned over, it closed off every opening."

"Then we're completely hemmed in?"

"Yes."

CHAPTER XL
Lack of Air

Thus around, above and below the *Nautilus* there was an impenetrable wall of ice. We were prisoners of the Great Ice Barrier! The Canadian struck the table with his powerful fist. Conseil was silent. I looked at the captain. His face had once again taken on its usual impassivity. He had crossed his arms. He was thinking. The *Nautilus* no longer moved.

The captain then started speaking. "Gentlemen," he said in a calm voice, "there are two ways of dying under such conditions as these."

This strange person had the look of a mathematics professor explaining something to his pupils.

"The first," he went on, "is to be crushed to death. The second is to die asphyxiated. There's no question of dying of hunger, for the provisions on the *Nautilus* will last longer than we will. So let's think about our chances of being crushed or asphyxiated."

"As for asphyxiation, Captain," I answered, "we have nothing to fear, for the reservoirs are full."

"Right," said Captain Nemo, "but they only contain enough air for two days. We've now been under water for thirty-six hours and already the air inside the *Nautilus* needs to be renewed. Within forty-eight hours our reserves will be used up."

"Well then, Captain, let's get out within forty-eight hours!"

"We'll at least try, by cutting through the wall around us."

"On which side?" I asked.

"Soundings will tell us that. I am going to let the *Nautilus* down on the lower surface, and my men will put on their diving suits and start to work on the ice wherever it's thinnest."

"Could the panels in the lounge be opened?"

"I can see no objection; we're no longer moving."

With this, Captain Nemo left. Soon I could tell by a whistling noise that the reservoirs were being filled with water. The *Nautilus* slowly sank and came to rest on the ice at a depth of 1150 feet.

"My friends," I said, "our situation is serious, but I am counting on your courage and energy."

"Monsieur," replied the Canadian, "at a time like this I will forget all my complaints. I'm ready to do anything for the general safety."

"Good, Ned," I said, stretching out my hand to him.

"And what's more," he continued, "I'm as handy with a pickax as I am with a harpoon, and if I can help the captain in any way, I hope he'll let me know."

"He won't refuse your help. Come, Ned."

I led him to the room where the men from the *Nautilus* were putting on their diving suits. I told the captain about Ned's proposal, and he accepted. The Canadian put on his diving suit and soon he was ready to go with the others. Each of them carried their tanks filled with a large supply of pure air. As for the Ruhmkorff lamps, they were unnecessary in the midst of waters so brilliantly illuminated by the ship's light.

As soon as Ned Land was dressed, I went back to the lounge, where I found the panels open. I took up my post next to Conseil and examined the ice that surrounded and supported the *Nautilus*.

Several moments later, we saw a dozen men from the crew step out onto the ice, and among them Ned Land, easily recognizable by his height. Captain Nemo was also among them.

Before beginning to dig, he had to find out the best direction in which to work. Long soundings were therefore sunk into the side walls, but after fifty feet they found nothing but more and more ice. There was no use attacking the surface overhead, for this was the ice barrier itself, more than thirteen hundred feet thick. Captain Nemo then had the ice underneath sounded; he found that only thirty feet separated us from the water below. It was therefore a matter of cutting out a piece equal in area to the waterline of the *Nautilus*. About 230,000 cubic feet of ice had to be removed in order to make a hole big enough for us to pass down through.

They set to work at once, and carried on with indefatigable energy. Instead of digging around the *Nautilus,* which would have involved great difficulties, Captain Nemo had an immense trench drawn on the ice twenty-five feet off the starboard side of the submarine. Then his men started chipping away along its edges. Soon the picks were beginning to take effect, and large blocks of ice were loosened. An odd effect was produced by these blocks, which, since they were lighter than water, floated up to the ceiling of the tunnel, and this ceiling therefore got thicker by as much as was removed underneath. But this made little difference, as long as the wall beneath also got thinner by the same amount.

After two hours of hard work, Ned Land came back exhausted. His companions and he were replaced by fresh workers, including Conseil and myself. The first mate acted as our foreman.

The water seemed especially cold, but I soon got warm handling the pickax. I could move freely, even though I was undergoing a pressure of thirty atmospheres.

When I returned after two hours to get some nourishment and rest, I noticed a big difference between the air from our diving tanks and that inside the *Nautilus,* which was already full of carbon dioxide. The air in the submarine had not been renewed in forty-eight hours, and it now contained scarcely any life-giving substances.

After working for twelve hours, we had only removed a three-foot layer of ice from the trench, or in other words about twenty thousand cubic feet. Assuming that we could continue working at this rate, we would still need five nights and four days to finish.

"Five nights and four days," I said to my companions, "when we have only two days' air supply in the reservoirs!"

"Without taking into account," said Ned, "that once we're out of this darned prison, we'll still be under the ice barrier without any way of renewing our air supply!"

This was indeed true. Who could possibly calculate the minimum time required for us to get out? Might we not be asphyxiated before the *Nautilus* could surface? Was it destined to perish in this tomb of ice along with all those on board? The situation seemed terrible. But everyone faced it squarely and decided to do their duty to the end.

As I had predicted, a new slice one yard thick was removed from the pit during the night. But the next morning, when I put on my diving suit and went out into the water, whose temperature was between 18° and 20°, I noticed that the side walls of the tunnel were getting closer together. The water farther from the pit, since it was not warmed by the men working, showed a tendency to freeze. Faced with this new danger, what would now happen to our chances of escaping? How would we prevent the water from turning to ice and therefore cracking open the *Nautilus'* hull as if it were made of glass?

I did not mention this new danger to my two companions. What good would it have been to risk their becoming apathetic and giving up the rescue work? But when I came back on board, I mentioned this new danger to Captain Nemo.

"I know," he said in that same calm voice he maintained no matter how terrible the situation. "It's one more danger for us, but I don't see any way to stop it. Our only chance is to dig faster than the water freezes. We have to get there first, that's all."

Get there first! But by then I should have become accustomed to his ways of thinking!

That day I wielded the pickax for several hours with great determination. This work kept up my spirits. Moreover, this way one could leave the *Nautilus* and breathe the pure air taken from the reservoirs and stored in the tanks on our backs; it was the only way to escape the foul, thin air inside the submarine.

By that afternoon, the pit had been dug yet a yard deeper. But when I came back on board, I was nearly asphyxiated by the carbon dioxide saturating the air inside the boat. Oh, if only there had been some chemical process by which we could have gotten rid of this harmful gas! For there was no lack of oxygen; the water around us contained a considerable quantity which could have been extracted by our powerful batteries, thus giving us all we needed. I had thought of this, but it was no use since the carbon dioxide produced by our breathing had already invaded every part of the ship. In order to absorb it, we would have had to fill receptacles with potassium lye and shake them continually. But we had none of this chemical on board, and there was nothing else which would serve the same purpose.

That afternoon, Captain Nemo had to open some of the spigots on his reservoirs and let a bit of pure air into the *Nautilus*. If he had not done so, we would have never awakened from our sleep.

On the next day, March 26, I once again took up my miner's work, starting in on the fifth yard-thick layer. The ice on either side and overhead was becoming visibly thicker. It was obvious that it would come together before the *Nautilus* could get free. For a moment I fell into despair. My pickax almost dropped from my hands. What good was it to dig when I was going to die crushed by this water turning to rock, a death worse than any dreamed of by savages? It seemed as if I were between the huge jaws of some monster, and they were closing slowly and irresistibly.

Just then Captain Nemo, who was not only directing the work but also working himself, passed by near me. I tapped him on the shoulder and pointed to the walls of our prison. The starboard wall alone had advanced at least twelve feet toward the *Nautilus*' hull.

The captain understood and motioned for me to follow him. We went back on board. We took off our diving suits and went into the lounge.

"Monsieur Aronnax," he said, "we're going to have to take some heroic measures if we don't want to be sealed up inside this ice as if it were a block of cement."

"Yes," I said, "but what can we do?"

"Ah," he said, "if only my *Nautilus* were strong enough to withstand this pressure without being crushed!"

"How would that help us?" I asked, not understanding what he was driving at.

"Don't you see," he went on, "that then the fact that the water is freezing would help us? Don't you realize that this solidification would break open the ice field around us just as it does the hardest of rocks? Don't you understand how it would save us instead of destroying us?"

"Yes, perhaps, Captain. But however strong the *Nautilus* may be, it could not withstand such a pressure as that, and it would merely be flattened out into an iron leaf."

"I know, Monsieur. We must therefore not count on nature to help us, but on our own ingenuity. We have to stop this freezing. Not only are the side walls coming in closer, but there are only ten feet left fore and aft of the *Nautilus*. The ice is moving in on us from all sides."

"How much longer will the air in the reservoirs permit us to breathe on board?" I asked.

The captain looked me straight in the face. "The day after tomorrow," he said, "the reservoirs will be empty!"

A cold sweat came over me. But why should his answer have surprised me? The *Nautilus* had gone beneath the surface of the open water around the South Pole on March 22 and now it was the twenty-sixth. For five days we had been living off the air supply on board! And what was left of the good air had to be saved for the men working. As I write these lines, the impression of how I then felt is still so strong that an involuntary terror comes over my whole being and I once again feel as if there were not enough air for my lungs!

Meanwhile, Captain Nemo, silent and immobile as always, was lost in thought. Suddenly an idea seemed to cross his mind; but he apparently rejected it. Then finally some words escaped from his lips: "Boiling water!" he murmured.

"Boiling water?" I cried.

"Yes, Monsieur. We're enclosed within a relatively small space. Wouldn't jets of boiling water constantly pumped out from the *Nautilus* raise the temperature around us and retard the freezing?"

"It's our only chance," I said.

"Let's go, then, Professor."

The thermometer showed the outside water to be at 19° Fahrenheit. Captain Nemo led me to the kitchen where vast distilling machines were operating, furnishing drinking water by means of evaporation. They were filled and all the heat the batteries could produce was thrown into the coils passing through the liquid. Within several minutes the water was boiling. It was then led off toward the pumps and at the same time replaced with more water. The heat developed by the electric coil was such that the cold water from the sea had only to pass once through the mechanism in order to arrive boiling at the pumps.

It began to be injected into the surrounding water, and three hours later the outside temperature had risen to 21°. This was a gain of two degrees. Several hours after this, the thermometer registered 25°.

"It's going to work," I said to the captain after following this operation closely.

"I think so," he replied. "At least we won't be crushed to death; now we only have to worry about being asphyxiated."

During the night the temperature of the surrounding water rose to 30°. That was as high as it would go. But since seawater will only freeze at 28.4°, I at least felt reassured against this danger.

By the next day, March 27, twenty feet of ice had been removed from the trench. Only thirteen feet remained to be chipped out. But this would still take forty-eight hours of work. We could no longer renew the air inside the *Nautilus*; during the day it became worse and worse.

A terrible weariness came over me. Toward three in the afternoon this feeling had increased to the point of becoming unbearable. I yawned so much I felt my jaws would come apart. I began to pant as the fuel needed for breathing became scarcer and scarcer. I became completely lethargic. I stretched out feeling weak and almost unconscious. My good Conseil, even though he had the same symptoms as I and suffered quite as much, did not leave my side. He would take my hand, encourage me, and I could hear him murmur: "If only I could stop breathing in order to leave more air for Monsieur!"

It brought tears to my eyes to hear him talk like this.

The more intolerable life became inside the submarine, the more joyfully we would put on our diving suits to take our turns working! Our pickaxes resounded against the ice. Our arms were exhausted and our hands chafed, but what difference did it make! Lifegiving air was reaching our lungs! We were breathing! We were breathing!

Yet no one prolonged his underwater work beyond the time allotted. Once his job was over, each man would give a gasping companion the tank which would pour life into his body. Captain Nemo set the example and was the first to submit himself to this severe discipline. When the time came he would give his apparatus to another man and calmly enter the foul atmosphere on board, without flinching or murmuring.

That day the work was carried on with even more vigor. Only six feet remained to be removed. Only six feet separated us from open water. But the reservoirs were almost empty of air. The little that remained had to be saved for the men working. Not one atom for the *Nautilus*!

When I went back on board, I was half suffocated. What a night! I couldn't possibly describe it. Such suffering can't be put into words. The next day I found it difficult to breathe. Not only did I have a headache, but I felt as dizzy as if I were drunk. My companions had the same symptoms. Some members of the crew were close to death.

That day—the sixth of our imprisonment—Captain Nemo felt that our work with the pickaxes was going too slowly, and he decided to try crushing the layer of ice separating us from open water. He had retained all his coolness and energy. His moral strength dominated his physical sufferings. He could still think, plan and act.

At an order from him, the submarine was raised off the ice on which it had been resting and hauled over till it was directly above the huge trench we had dug out. Water was let into its reservoirs and it sank down into the trench.

Then all the crew came back on board, and the double door communicating with the outside was closed. At that moment the *Nautilus* was resting on a layer of ice which was less than a yard thick and had been pierced by soundings in hundreds of places.

The spigots of the reservoirs were then opened wide and 3500 cubic feet of water rushed in, increasing the *Nautilus'* weight by 220,000 pounds.

We waited and listened. Hope made us forget our sufferings. Our lives depended on this one last stroke of fortune.

In spite of the buzzing inside my head, I soon heard something trembling beneath the *Nautilus*. The ship started to go down. The ice broke with a strange noise like that of paper tearing, and the *Nautilus* continued sinking.

"We're going through!" Conseil murmured in my ear.

I couldn't answer, but merely grasped his hand.

Suddenly, carried down by its terrific excess weight, the *Nautilus* sank as if it were made of lead, or that is to say as if there were no more ice under it.

Then all the available electric power was put behind the pumps and the water began to be dispelled from the reservoirs. After several minutes we stopped sinking. Soon, in fact, the pressure gauge showed that we were rising. The propeller, turning at top speed, made the hull quiver to its very bolts and started us on our northward course.

But how long would it be before we reached the other side of the ice barrier and could surface in open water? Another day? I would be dead before then!

I was half stretched out on a sofa in the library and felt as if I were suffocating. My face was purple, my lips blue and my mind incapable of functioning. I could no longer see or hear anything. All idea of time left me. I could not even contract my muscles.

How many hours passed by like this I cannot say. But I felt I could last no longer. I was near death. . . .

Suddenly I regained consciousness. A few breaths of fresh air entered my lungs. Had we surfaced? Had we reached the other side of the ice barrier?

No! It was my worthy companions Ned and Conseil sparing themselves to save me. Several molecules of air had remained in the bottom of one of the diving apparatuses. Instead of breathing it themselves, they had preserved it for me, and while they suffocated they poured life into me drop by drop! I wanted to push the apparatus away, but they were holding my hands, and for a few moments I indulged in the pleasure of breathing.

I looked at the clock. It was eleven in the morning. It must have been March 28. The *Nautilus* was traveling at the terrifying speed of forty knots. It writhed in the water.

Where was Captain Nemo? Had he succumbed? Had his companions died with him?

At that moment the pressure gauge indicated that we were only twenty feet below the surface. A thin ice field separated us from the atmosphere. Could we break through it?

Perhaps! In any case, the *Nautilus* was going to try. I could feel it take an oblique position, lowering its stern and raising its prow. Then, impelled forward by its powerful engines, it attacked the ice field from underneath like a formidable battering-ram. It broke the ice a little bit at a time, repeatedly going back down and then striking again at full speed. Finally it made a supreme effort and rushed up at the layer of ice, crushing it beneath its weight.

The hatch was opened—one might say torn open—and pure air came flooding into the whole interior of the *Nautilus*.

CHAPTER XLI
From Cape Horn to the Amazon

How I got up onto the platform, I cannot say. Perhaps Ned Land had carried me there. But I was breathing, taking in the revivifying sea air. My two companions were next to me getting drunk on oxygen. People who have gone without food for a long time are unfortunate in that they cannot gulp down thoughtlessly the first thing given them. But we did not have to restrain ourselves; we could breathe as much as we wanted, and it was the sea breeze, nothing more than the sea breeze, which brought on our sensual intoxication.

"Ah!" said Conseil. "How good oxygen is! Monsieur need have no fear of breathing it; there's enough for everybody."

As for Ned Land, he did not say a word, but merely opened his jaws wide enough to frighten a shark. And what breaths he took! He drew in air like a furnace going full blast.

Our strength soon came back, and when I looked around I saw we were alone on the platform. None of the crew was in sight. Not even Captain Nemo. These strange sailors of the *Nautilus* seemed satisfied with the air entering the submarine. None of them had come up to taste the pleasure of the sea breeze.

The first words I uttered were of thanks and gratitude to my two companions. Ned and Conseil had prolonged my life during the final hours of our long ordeal. But no gratitude could sufficiently repay such devotion.

"Oh, Professor!" replied Ned Land. "Don't even mention it! What did we do? Nothing. It was just a matter of simple arithmetic. Your life was worth more than ours, and so it had to be preserved."

"No, Ned," I answered, "it isn't worth more. No one is superior to a man as kind and generous as you!"

"Goodness, Professor," said the Canadian in an embarrassed tone of voice.

"And you, my good Conseil, you must have suffered a lot too."

"Not too much, to tell the truth. I was lacking a few mouthfuls of air, but I felt I would scrape through. What's more, when I saw Monsieur fainting it took away my desire to inhale. It so to speak took my breath a—"

Conseil felt embarrassed at the cliché he was about to utter and did not finish his sentence.

"My friends," I replied, deeply touched, "we are bound to one another forever, and with me you have the right . . ."

"Which I'm going to take advantage of," retorted the Canadian.

"What?" exclaimed Conseil.

"Yes," continued Ned Land, "the right to take you with me when I leave this infernal *Nautilus*."

"By the way," said Conseil, "are we heading in the proper direction?"

"Yes," I replied, "since we're heading toward the sun and here the sun means north."

"That's all very well," said Ned Land, "but we still have to find out whether we're heading for the Pacific or the Atlantic, or in other words, toward inhabited or deserted regions."

There was no answer to this, and I was afraid Captain Nemo would take us to that vast ocean fringed by the coasts of Asia and America. He would thus be completing his underwater tour of the world and returning to those waters in which the *Nautilus* had its greatest freedom. But if we went back to the Pacific, far from any inhabited shores, what would happen to Ned Land's project?

We would soon find out. The *Nautilus* was traveling fast. Before long we had passed the Antarctic Circle and were heading for Cape Horn. We reached the tip of the American continent at 7:00 P.M. on March 31.

Then all of our past sufferings were forgotten. The memory of our imprisonment in the ice faded from our minds. We thought only of the future. We no longer saw Captain Nemo, either in the lounge or on the platform. But each day the first mate marked our position on the chart and this permitted me to know the *Nautilus'* exact direction. And that night, to my great satisfaction, it became evident that we were heading north by way of the Atlantic.

I told the news to Ned and Conseil.

"Good," replied the Canadian, "but where exactly is the *Nautilus* going?"

"I couldn't say, Ned."

"Do you suppose the captain would now want to go to the North Pole and return to the Pacific through the famous Northwest Passage?"

"I wouldn't present it to him in the form of a challenge," replied Conseil.

"That's all right," said the Canadian, "we would just skip out on him beforehand."

"In any case," added Conseil, "this Captain Nemo is an extraordinary man, and we won't regret having known him."

"Especially after we've left him!" retorted Ned Land.

The next day, April 1, when the *Nautilus* surfaced several minutes before noon, we sighted land off to the west. It was Tierra del Fuego, which was given this name by early navigators because of the many columns of smoke they saw rising from native huts. This Tierra del Fuego is a vast agglomeration of islands stretching out 65 miles in length and 173 miles in width, lying between 53° and 56° S. Lat., and 67° 50' and 77° 15' W. Long. The coastline seemed rather low, but in the distance rose high mountains. I even thought I could make out Mount Sarmiento, which rises 6,790 feet above sea level. It is a pyramid-shaped block of shale with a very pointed peak which, depending on whether or not it is surrounded by clouds, "announces good or bad weather," as Ned Land told me.

"So it's a well-known barometer, then, my friend."

"Yes, Monsieur, a natural weather gauge which has never deceived me in all the times I've sailed through the Straits of Magellan."

Just then we could see the peak clearly outlined against the sky. This was an omen of good weather, which turned out to be correct.

The *Nautilus* dove under water and cruised along no more than a few miles off the coast. Through the open glass panels in the lounge I saw a kind of sea vine and also some gigantic sea wrack, specimens of which I had seen in the open water around the South Pole. It had shiny, sticky filaments that measured as much as a thousand feet in length; they were like cables, bigger around than a man's thumb and very strong, so strong in fact that they were often used to moor ships. Another plant, known as "velp," with leaves four feet long, was growing among the coral and carpeting the ocean floor. It served as both a nest and food for myriads of shellfish. Seals and otters came there to gorge themselves, eating a mixture of fish and ocean vegetables rather as the English do.

The *Nautilus* passed at a high speed over this rich, luxuriant bottom. Toward evening we approached the Falkland Islands, whose high summits I saw the next day. The sea was not very deep. I therefore assumed, not without reason, that these two islands, surrounded by a great number of smaller islands, had once formed part of Patagonia. The Falkland Islands were probably discovered by the famous John Davis and first called the South Davis Islands. Later Richard Hawkins named them the Maiden Islands. Then at the beginning of the eighteenth century they were called the Malouines by Breton fishermen, and finally the Falkland Islands by the English, to whom they belong today.

In these waters our nets brought in lovely specimens of seaweed, and especially a certain kind of sea wrack whose roots were loaded with the best mussels in the world. Geese and ducks came on deck by the dozens, and they soon took their place on the ship's menu. As for fish, I particularly noted a bony species related to the goby.

I was able to admire many kinds of jellyfish, and particularly the most beautiful of all, called "chrysaor," which is found only near the Falkland Islands. Sometimes their swimming bell would be shaped like a very smooth half-globe with reddish-brown stripes and ending in twelve symmetrical tentacles; sometimes they looked like an upside-down basket from which were falling large, graceful leaves and long red twigs. They swam by moving their four leaf-shaped arms and letting their thick mass of tentacles float in the water. I would have liked to preserve several specimens of these delicate zoophytes, but they are like clouds, shadows or phantoms that melt and evaporate once they are out of their natural element.

When the last heights of the Falkland Islands had disappeared beneath the horizon, the *Nautilus* dove to a depth between sixty-five and eighty feet and followed the coast of South America. Captain Nemo still did not appear.

Until April 3, we did not leave the waters of Patagonia, sometimes cruising under water, sometimes on the surface. Then the *Nautilus* passed by the large estuary of the Rio Plata, and on April 4 we were off Uruguay, but fifty miles out to sea. We still headed north, following the winding coast of South America. By then we had covered sixteen thousand leagues since coming on board in the Japan Sea.

Toward eleven in the morning we crossed the Tropic of Capricorn at the thirty-seventh meridian and passed off Cape Frio. To Ned Land's great displeasure, Captain Nemo did not seem to like being so near the inhabited coast of Brazil, for we traveled at a dizzying speed. No fish or bird, however fast it could travel, was able to follow us, and thus whatever curiosities of nature these waters contained escaped all observation.

This speed was maintained for several days, and on the afternoon of April 9 we sighted the most easterly point of South America, Cape San Roque. But then the *Nautilus* once again headed out to sea, searching for the underwater valley which lies between this cape and Sierra Leone on the coast of Africa. This valley splits in two at the latitude of the West Indies and ends to the north in an enormous depression thirty thousand feet deep. Between there and the Lesser Antilles there rises a vertical cliff four miles high, and on a level with the Cape

Verde Islands, another wall no less imposing, and between these two barriers lies the submerged continent of Atlantis. The bottom of this immense valley is dotted with several underwater mountains which give it a very picturesque aspect. All this information is based largely on manuscript charts contained in the library of the *Nautilus*, charts evidently drawn by Captain Nemo according to his own personal observations.

For two days we visited these deep, deserted waters. The *Nautilus* would dive by means of its side fins, traveling in a long diagonal course that would take it to any depth. But on April 11, it suddenly surfaced and we saw the coastline around the mouth of the Amazon, whose estuary is so vast that one can still find fresh water several leagues out to sea.

We had crossed the equator. Twenty miles to the west lay Guiana, a French territory in which we would have found easy refuge. But the wind was blowing strong and a dinghy could not have ventured on the surface of such a raging sea. Ned Land undoubtedly realized this, for he said nothing. As for me, I made no allusion to his plans for escape, for I did not want to push him into some rash venture doomed to failure.

I took advantage of this delay by making interesting studies. During the two days of April 11 and 12, the *Nautilus* remained on the surface and its dragnet brought in a marvelous variety of zoophytes, fish and reptiles.

The chains holding the dragnet had caught several kinds of zoophytes. For the most part they were lovely phyctallinae, belonging to the family of the actinidians, and among other species there was the *Phyctalis protexta*, peculiar to this part of the ocean, whose cylindrical body was adorned with vertical lines and red dots, and which was crowned with a marvelous tuft of tentacles. As for shellfish, they consisted of species I had already observed, such as turritellae; porphyry shells with evenly crossed lines and reddish-brown spots standing out vividly against a flesh-colored background; strange pterocerae looking like petrified scorpions; translucent cavolinia; argonauts; cuttlefish, which are so good to eat; and a certain species of squid which ancient naturalists used to classify among the flying fish and which is used primarily as bait for catching cod.

Among the fish of these waters I had not yet had the opportunity to study, I noted various species. Among cartilaginous fish there was a certain kind of lamprey about fifteen inches long, with a greenish head, violet fins, bluish-gray back, silvery-brown belly with bright spots and a band of gold encircling the iris of its eye; these strange animals must have been brought out to sea by the currents of the Amazon, for they are fresh-water creatures. There was also a species of ray with a pointed muzzle, thin tail and long notched sword in front; small sharks three feet long, gray and whitish in color, whose several rows of teeth bent backward; anglers shaped like isosceles triangles about a foot and a half long, reddish in color, with long wide pectoral fins that made them look like bats, but whose hornlike appendage near their nostrils has earned them the name of sea unicorns; finally, several kinds of triggerfish, the curassavian, whose dotted sides shone with a golden tint, and the caprisca, light violet in color and with an iridescent luster like a pigeon's throat.

I will finish this somewhat dry but very accurate list with a mention of the bony fish I observed. There were some odontagnathae, whose bright silver hue and thin, pointed body made them look like foot-long sardines; a kind of mackerel with two anal fins; black centronotae, which fishermen catch by using torches—they are large fish six feet long with fatty, white, firm flesh which tastes like eel when served fresh and like smoked salmon when dried; wrasse with scales only around the base of their dorsal and anal fins; chrysopterae, whose gold and silver bodies glitter as if encrusted with rubies and topazes; giltheads, which are very tasty and whose phosphorescence makes them so easy to see in the water; sciaena with golden tails; acanthopterans; anableps from Surinam; etc.

But this "etc." will not prevent me from citing yet one more fish which Conseil will remember for a long time to come, and not without reason.

One of our nets had brought in a kind of very flat ray weighing about forty-five pounds, which, without its tail, would have formed a perfectly round disk. Its smooth skin, ending in a double-lobed fin, was white on top and reddish underneath with big dark blue spots encircled in black. Once on the platform, it writhed around trying to turn back over on its stomach, and in its struggle it got so near the edge that one last flip and it would have fallen back into the sea. But Conseil, who hated to lose a fish like this, jumped on it and grabbed

Captain Nemo hurled himself at the squid.

it with both hands before I could stop him.

He was instantly thrown back. He lay on the platform with his legs in the air and his body half paralyzed, shouting: "Help, Monsieur, help!"

Ned Land and I picked him up, massaged him and when he had finally come back to his senses, this eternal classifier murmured in halting tones: "Class of cartilaginous fish, order of chondropterygians with fixed gills, suborder of selacians, family of the rays, genus of electric ray!"

"Yes, my friend, an electric ray that almost knocked you out."

"Yes, Monsieur, believe me," retorted Conseil, "but I'll get my revenge on this animal."

"How?"

"By eating it."

And so he did that very night, but purely out of a feeling of retaliation, for it was apparently quite leathery.

Poor Conseil had attacked an electric ray of the most dangerous kind, the cumana. This strange animal, living in a medium like water which conducts electricity, can kill fish several yards away, so great is the power of his electrical organ whose two principal surfaces measure no less than twenty-seven square feet.

On the next day, April 12, the *Nautilus* approached the mouth of the Maroni River on the coast of Dutch Guiana. There we saw sea cows living in family groups. These manatees, like the dugong and Steller's sea cow, belong to the order of Sirenia. They are peaceful and inoffensive animals which grow as long as twenty or twenty-five feet and weigh up to nine thousand pounds. I told Ned Land and Conseil that farsighted nature had assigned these animals an important role. It is they and seals who have been destined to graze on underwater prairies and thus destroy those agglomerations of plants which obstruct the mouths of tropical rivers.

"And do you know," I added, "what has happened since man has almost completely destroyed these useful creatures? Rotting plants have fouled the air, and it is this foul air which has produced the yellow fever laying waste to these remarkable lands. Poisonous vegetation has increased beneath these warm seas, and this disease has spread unchecked from the mouth of the Rio Plata to Florida!"

And if one is to believe Toussenel, this scourge is nothing to that which will strike our descendants, when the seas become empty of whales and seals. Then, filled with octopus, jellyfish and squid, they will become vast centers of infection, since their waters will no longer possess "those vast stomachs which God has delegated to scour the surface of the seas."

Nevertheless, the crew of the *Nautilus* caught a half a dozen of these sea cows. It was a question of laying in a stock of excellent meat, superior to beef or veal. But the hunting was not interesting. The sea cows let themselves be caught without putting up any defense. Several thousand pounds of meat were stored on board to be dried and preserved.

That day the *Nautilus'* stock was further increased through a very strange manner of fishing. The dragnet had brought up a certain amount of fish whose heads end in an oval plaque with fleshy edges. They were echeneis, of the third family of subbrachian malacopterygians. This flat disk on their head is composed of mobile, transversal cartilaginous layers between which the animal can create a vacuum, thus permitting him to fasten on to things like a leech.

The remora, which I had observed in the Mediterranean, belongs to this species. But the one we saw here was the *Echeneis osterchara,* found only in these waters. Our sailors took them out of the nets and deposited them in tubs full of water.

Once this was done, the *Nautilus* went in nearer the coast. There, a certain number of sea turtles were sleeping on the surface. It would have been difficult to catch these precious reptiles, for the least sound awakens them, and their solid shell protects them from harpoons. But the echeneis was to help capture them with extraordinary ease and assurance. This animal, in fact, is a living fishhook, and could be of great use to the ordinary fisherman.

To the tail of these fish the sailors attached a ring large enough not to cramp their movements, and to this ring a long line which was tied on board at its other end.

The echeneis were then thrown into the sea, and immediately they started to work attaching themselves to the turtles' shells. They held on with such determination that they would have been torn apart rather than let go. They were then hauled on board, along with the turtles to whom they were attached.

In this way we caught several cacuans about three feet long and weighing about 450 pounds apiece. Their shells were covered with very valuable horny plaques, which were a transparent brown color with white and yellow spots. Moreover, their flesh was excellent to eat.

This fishing ended our sojourn in the waters off the Amazon basin, and as night came on the *Nautilus* once more headed for the open sea.

CHAPTER XLII
Squid

For several days, the *Nautilus* remained far from any shore. It obviously did not want to enter the Gulf of Mexico or the Caribbean, even though it would not have found itself in uncomfortably shallow water, since the average depth of these seas is six thousand feet. But probably a region so full of islands and so constantly crossed by steamers was not to Captain Nemo's liking.

On April 16, we sighted Martinique and Guadeloupe from about thirty miles off shore. For a moment I could make out their highest peaks.

The Canadian, who had counted on being able to escape in the Caribbean, either by reaching land or by hailing one of the many ships that ply between the various islands, was very disappointed. It would have been quite easy to get away there, if Ned Land had been able to get the dinghy without the captain's knowledge. But on the open ocean, there was no longer any question of trying.

Ned, Conseil and I had a long conversation on this subject. We had now been prisoners aboard the *Nautilus* for six months. We had covered seventeen thousand leagues and, as Ned Land put it, there was no reason to think it would ever end. He therefore made an unexpected proposal. It was to ask the captain in no uncertain terms whether or not he intended to keep us on board indefinitely.

This did not strike me as a good idea, but rather one doomed to failure. I felt that we should expect nothing from the commander of the *Nautilus* and rely only on ourselves. Moreover, for some time now, this man had become somber, more withdrawn and less sociable. He seemed to avoid me. I only saw him once in a great while. He had formerly enjoyed explaining to me the wonders of undersea life; but now he left me alone in my studies and no longer came to the lounge.

What sort of a change had come over him? What had brought it on? I had done nothing for which he could blame me. Had our presence on board perhaps begun to disturb him? Yet I had no reason to hope he would set us free.

I therefore asked Ned Land to let me think it over before doing anything. If this plan did not succeed, it could revive his suspicions, make our situation difficult and harm the Canadian's projects. I must add that I could not give our physical condition as a reason, for except for the trying experience under the Great Ice Barrier, we had never been in better health, neither Ned, Conseil nor I. The healthy food, invigorating air, regular hours and uniform temperature kept illness at bay. Moreover, for a man like Captain Nemo who did not miss life on land, for whom this was his home and who was free to go where he wanted, I could understand such an existence. But we had not broken with humanity. And as for me, I had done much interesting new research, and I did not want to have it buried with me. I now would be able to write a definitive book on the sea, and I wanted this work to see the light of day sooner or later.

And even here in West Indian waters, at a depth of thirty-five feet with the panels open, how many interesting things I was able to observe and set down in my daily notes! Among other zoophytes, there were Portuguese men-of-war, known as pelagic physalia, fat and oblong in shape with a mother-of-pearl tint, holding up their membrane to the wind and letting their blue threadlike tentacles float on the surface. To the eye they seemed like lovely jellyfish, but to the touch they were like poisonous nettles. Among the articulata, I saw some sea worms about five feet long, armed with a pink horn and equipped with seventeen hundred organs of locomotion, winding and twisting through the water, and gleaming with all the colors of the rainbow. Among various fish, I saw enormous devilfish, a kind of ray six feet long and weighing six hundred pounds, with triangular pectoral fins, a slight hump in the middle of its back and eyes placed on the extreme front sides of its head; they were floating in the water like wrecked ships and sometimes they covered our window like a thick shutter. There were also triggerfish, which nature has colored only black and white; a kind of goby with a long plump body, yellow fins and protruding lower jaw; some mackerel five feet long with short sharp teeth, their bodies covered with small scales. In addition we saw clouds of red mullets with shining fins and golden stripes running from their head to their tail. These masterpieces of jewelry were once upon a time considered sacred to Diana and they were particularly sought after by rich Romans. There was a proverb about them which said: "He who catches them can never eat them!" Lastly we saw golden pomacanthae dressed in velvet and silk and decorated with emerald-green bands, passing before our eyes like lords and ladies from a Veronese painting; spurred giltheads, which dashed off with one stroke of their powerful under fin; clupanadons fifteen inches long wrapped in a phosphorescent gleam; common mullets churning the water with their big, plump tails; red coregoni, which seemed to be mowing the ocean with their sharp pectoral fin; and silver moonfish, worthy of their name, rising on the horizon of the sea like so many pale moons.

How many other marvelous new specimens of fish I could still have observed if the *Nautilus* had not little by little dived down to deep water! Its side fins brought it to depths ranging from 6500 to 11,000 feet. There the animal kingdom was represented only by sea lilies, starfish, charming pentacrini with a straight stalk bearing a little chalice, top shells, and a type of coastal mollusk called keyhole limpets.

On April 20 we came back up to a depth of five thousand feet. The nearest land was the Bahamas, spread out like so many paving stones on the surface of the water. There we saw high underwater cliffs formed by worn blocks of stone arranged like bricks, between which there were dark holes whose depths the rays from our searchlight could not reach.

These rocks were carpeted with huge plants, giant sea tangles and sea wracks forming a bower of hydrophytes worthy of a world of Titans.

As we talked about these colossal plants, Conseil, Ned and I were naturally led into a discussion about the gigantic animals of the ocean. For one was obviously intended as nourishment for the other. Nevertheless, as I looked through the window of the now almost immobile *Nautilus,* I could make out nothing among these long filaments but the principal articulata of the division of branchipodae: sea spiders with their long legs, purplish-blue crabs and clios peculiar to West Indian waters.

It was about eleven o'clock when Ned Land drew my attention to a formidable wriggling movement among the long seaweed.

"Those are the kind of caves squid live in," I said, "and I wouldn't be surprised to see several of these monsters."

"What!" exclaimed Conseil. "Squid—mere squid from the class of cephalopods!"

"No," I said, "giant squid. But Ned must have made some mistake, for I don't see anything."

"That's too bad," said Conseil. "I'd like to come face to face with one of these giant squid I've heard so much about, and which can drag ships down to the bottom. They're called kraken, I think."

"You'll never get me to believe such animals exist," said Ned Land.

"Why not?" replied Conseil. "We believed in Monsieur's narwhal."

"And we were wrong, Conseil."

"Yes, but others still believe in it."

"Maybe they do, Conseil, but as for me, I've decided not to admit these monsters really exist until I've dissected one with my own hands."

"Doesn't Monsieur believe in giant squid either?" Conseil asked me.

"Who in the name of heaven ever has believed in them?" cried the Canadian.

"Lots of people, Ned my friend."

"Maybe scientists, but not fishermen."

"No, Ned. Both fishermen and scientists!"

"I myself can remember," said Conseil with the most serious tone of voice in the world, "having seen a large boat dragged down by the arms of a squid."

"You've seen that?" asked the Canadian.

"Yes, Ned."

"With your own eyes?"

"With my own eyes."

"Where, if you don't mind telling me?"

"At Saint-Malo," replied Conseil imperturbably.

"In the harbor?" asked Ned Land sarcastically.

"No, in a church," answered Conseil.

"In a church!" cried the Canadian.

"Yes, Ned. It was a painting of a squid."

"That's a good one!" exclaimed Ned Land as he burst out laughing. "Monsieur, Conseil's trying to pull a fast one on me!"

"He's right," I said. "I've heard about that painting; but the subject it represents is taken from a legend, and you know how trustworthy legends are when it comes to natural history! Moreover, when it's a question of monsters, people's imaginations ask nothing better than to be given free rein. Not only has it been claimed that squid and octopus could drag down ships, but a certain Olaus Magnus talks of a mile-long cephalopod which looked more like an island than an animal. They also tell of the Bishop of Midros who one day set up his altar on a huge rock to say mass. Once mass was over, the rock moved off and went back out to sea. The rock was an octopus."

"Oh! Is that all?" asked the Canadian.

"No," I replied. "Another bishop, Pontoppidan of Berghem, talks of an octopus on which a regiment of cavalry could maneuver!"

"In the old days bishops must have been good storytellers!" said Ned Land.

"And lastly, naturalists of ancient times mention monsters whose mouths were the size of gulfs and who were too big to pass through the Straits of Gibraltar."

"That's a good one, all right!" exclaimed the Canadian.

"But how much truth is there in all these stories?" asked Conseil.

"None, my friends, or at least none which does not pass the bounds of probability and enter the realm of fable or legend. Nevertheless, there must have been something which stimulated the imagination of these storytellers. It can't be denied that there exist species of octopus and squid which grow to great size, although still smaller than whales. Aristotle saw a squid five cubits long, or in other words ten feet two inches. The museums of Trieste and Montpellier have skeletons of octopuses six and a half feet long. Moreover, naturalists have calculated that one of these creatures with a body six feet long would have tentacles twenty-seven feet long, which would make a pretty formidable monster."

"Do people fish for them nowadays?" asked the Canadian.

"No, but sailors see them all the same. One of my friends, Captain Paul Bos from Le Havre, has often told me about how he met one of these enormous monsters in the Indian Ocean. But the most astonishing event, and one which dispels all doubts concerning the existence of such gigantic animals, took place several years ago, in eighteen sixty-one."

"What happened?" asked Ned Land.

"Well, in that year, to the northwest of Teneriffe, at very nearly the same latitude we're in now, the crew of the dispatch vessel *Alecton* noticed a huge squid swimming near the ship. Commander Bouguer brought the ship alongside, had the creature harpooned and shot, but without much success, for the bullets and harpoons went through its soft flesh as if it were loose jelly. After several unsuccessful attempts, the crew managed to pass a slipknot around the creature's body. The loop slid back to the caudal fins and there it stopped. They then tried hauling the monster on board, but it weighed so much that its tail merely broke off and the squid itself, separated from this part of its body, disappeared beneath the surface."

"Finally we have some facts," said Ned Land.

"Indisputable facts, my good Ned. As a result of what had happened, people suggested naming this creature 'Bouguer's squid.'"

"How long was it?" asked the Canadian.

"Wasn't it about twenty feet long?" said Conseil, standing at the window and once more examining the rugged cliffs.

"Precisely," I answered.

"And wasn't its head," Conseil went on, "crowned with eight tentacles which thrashed about on the water like a nest of snakes?"

"Absolutely."

"And didn't it have huge, popping eyes?"

"Yes, Conseil."

"And wasn't its mouth like a parakeet's beak, but enormous?"

"That's right."

"Well then, if Monsieur doesn't mind my saying so," Conseil replied calmly, "this is either Bouguer's squid or one of his first cousins."

I looked at Conseil. Ned Land rushed to the window.

"What a horrible creature!" he cried.

I then looked around, and I could not repress a gesture of repulsion. Before my eyes wriggled a terrible monster worthy of all the legends about such creatures.

It was a giant squid twenty-five feet long. It was heading toward the *Nautilus*, swimming backward very fast. Its huge immobile eyes were of a blue-green color. The eight arms, or rather legs, coming out of its head—it is this which has earned it the name of "cephalopod"—were twice as long as its body and were twisting about like the hair of a Greek fury. We could clearly make out the 250 suckers lining the inside of its tentacles, some of which fastened onto the glass panel of the lounge. This monster's mouth—a horny beak like that of a parakeet—opened and closed vertically. Its tongue, also made of a hornlike substance and armed with several rows of sharp teeth, would come out and shake what seemed like veritable cutlery. What a whim of nature! A bird's beak in a mollusk! Its elongated body, with a slight swelling in the middle, formed a fleshy mass which must have weighed between forty and fifty thousand pounds. Its color, which could change very fast according to the animal's mood, would vary from a ghastly gray to reddish brown.

What was irritating this creature? Undoubtedly it was the presence of the *Nautilus*, which was more formidable than it and on which its arms and suckers could get no hold. Yet what monsters are such squid! What vitality the Creator has given them, and what vigor of movement! And to think they possess three hearts!

We had encountered this mollusk quite by chance, and I did not want to lose the opportunity of studying it carefully. I overcame my horror at the sight of it, and taking up a pencil, started to draw it.

"This is perhaps the same one they almost caught on the *Alecton*," said Conseil.

"No," replied the Canadian, "because this one's whole, and the other one had lost his tail!"

"That doesn't make any difference," I said. "The arms and tails of these creatures can re-form by a special process, and I'm sure that in seven years Bouguer's squid has had time to grow another tail."

"Besides," said Ned, "if it isn't this one, it's maybe one of those!"

And in fact, other squid had appeared outside the starboard window. I counted seven. They were swimming in a procession around the *Nautilus* and I could hear the noise of their beaks grinding on the steel hull. Our wishes were more than satisfied.

I continued my work. These monsters kept up with us so easily that they seemed immobile, and I could easily have traced a reduced outline of one on the window. Besides, we were not traveling very fast.

Suddenly the *Nautilus* stopped. There was a blow which made it quiver throughout its length.

"Have we struck ground?" I asked.

"If we did, we're already free," replied the Canadian, "for we're floating."

But even though the *Nautilus* was floating, it wasn't moving. The blades of its propeller were not revolving in the water. After a minute or so, Captain Nemo entered the lounge followed by the first mate.

I had not seen him for some time. He seemed gloomy. Without saying a word to us—perhaps without even seeing us—he went over to the glass panel, looked at the squid and said several words to his first mate, who then left the room. Soon the panels closed and the ceiling lights came on.

I went over to the captain. "A curious collection of squid," I said in the offhand tone of voice of someone standing before the window of an aquarium.

"Indeed it is, Monsieur," he replied, "and we're going to fight them hand to hand."

I looked at the captain. I thought I had not heard him right. "Hand to hand?" I repeated.

"Yes, Monsieur. The propeller has been stopped. I think one of these squid got his horned beak caught up in the propeller, and now we can't move."

"What do you intend to do?"

"Surface the ship and wipe out all this vermin."

"That will be difficult."

"Yes, it will. Our electric bullets have no effect against these animals, for their soft flesh doesn't offer enough resistance to make them explode. But we'll attack them with axes."

"And with a harpoon, Monsieur," said the Canadian, "if you'll permit me to help you."

"I accept, Master Land."

"We'll go with you," I said, and we followed Captain Nemo to the central companionway.

There, ten or twelve men armed with boarding axes were ready for the attack. Conseil and I each took an ax, and Ned Land a harpoon.

By then the *Nautilus* had surfaced. One of the sailors at the top of the companionway unscrewed the bolts holding down the hatch. But hardly had they been unscrewed when the hatch flew up with great violence, obviously pulled up by the suckers on a squid's arm.

One of these long arms immediately slid like a snake into the opening and twenty others were waving about above. With one blow of his ax, Captain Nemo cut this formidable tentacle and it slid writhing down the companionway.

Just as we were pressing one another to get out on the platform, two other arms came slashing down through the air, grabbed the sailor in front of Captain Nemo and pulled him out with irresistible force.

Captain Nemo let out a cry and rushed up to the platform. We clambered out after him.

What a scene! The poor man was being clutched by the tentacles with their suckers and waved about in the air. He was half dead and choking, but he managed to shout, "Help! Help!" I was astounded to hear these words uttered *in French*! So I had a compatriot on board, perhaps several! All my life I shall hear this heart-rending cry.

The poor man was done for. Who could save him from such a powerful grip? Nevertheless, Captain Nemo hurled himself at the squid, and with one blow of his ax cut off yet another arm. The first mate struggled furiously with other monsters which were climbing up the sides of the *Nautilus*. The crew were flailing away with their axes. Ned, Conseil and I also dug our weapons into their soft bodies. A violent odor of musk filled the air. It was horrible.

For a moment I thought the poor man entangled in the squid would be saved from its powerful suckers. Seven of its eight arms had been cut. Only one— brandishing the victim like a feather—still writhed about in the air. But just as Captain Nemo and the first mate rushed at it, the animal let out a jet of black ink. We were blinded by it. When the cloud of spray had cleared away, the squid had disappeared, and with it my unfortunate compatriot!

With what a fury we then attacked these monsters! We were beyond ourselves. Ten or twelve squid had invaded the platform and sides of the *Nautilus*. We were struggling pell-mell in the midst of snakelike pieces of tentacles jumping about on the platform among torrents of blood and black ink. It seemed as if these slimy arms grew back instantly like a hydra's heads. Each time Ned Land wielded his harpoon it would plunge into a squid's sea-green eyes. But suddenly my brave companion was knocked over by the tentacles of a monster he could not avoid.

Oh, how close my heart came to breaking from emotion and horror! The squid's huge mouth had opened over Ned Land. The poor man was about to be cut in two. I rushed over to help him, but Captain Nemo had gotten there first. He buried his ax between the two enormous jaws, and Ned Land, miraculously saved, got up and plunged his harpoon deep into the creature's triple heart.

"I owed you this!" said Captain Nemo.

Ned bowed his head without answering.

The struggle had lasted fifteen minutes. The monsters, defeated, mutilated or killed, finally left us and disappeared beneath the surface.

Captain Nemo, covered with blood and standing immobile next to the searchlight, looked at the sea which had swallowed up one of his companions and tears ran down his cheeks.

CHAPTER XLIII
The Gulf Stream

None of us will ever be able to forget that terrible scene of April 20. When I wrote it, I still felt under the sway of violent emotions. Since then I have gone over my account. I have read it to Conseil and the Canadian. They found it factually correct, but lacking in emotional impact. But to paint such scenes, one would have to write like the greatest of our poets, Victor Hugo.

I said that Captain Nemo was crying as he looked at the sea. His sorrow was great. It was the second companion he had lost since our arrival on board. And what a way to die! This man had been crushed, stifled and torn apart by the powerful arms of a squid, ground up in its steel jaws; and unlike his companions, he would find no peaceful rest in a coral graveyard!

As for me, what had been heartrending was the cry of despair he had uttered in the midst of the struggle. This poor Frenchman, forgetting the strange speech they used on board, had uttered his last call for help in the language of his country and of his mother! This therefore meant that among the crew of the *Nautilus,* who had bound themselves to Captain Nemo body and soul, and who like him were fleeing from all contact with other men, I had a compatriot! Was he the only Frenchman in this mysterious group, obviously made up of different nationalities? This was yet another insoluble problem to torment my mind!

Captain Nemo retired to his cabin and I did not see him again for some time. But how sad, despairing and irresolute he must have felt, I could judge from the submarine whose soul he was and which received his every impression! The *Nautilus* no longer stayed on a fixed course. It would come and go, sometimes even being allowed to float like a corpse at the mercy of the waves. Its propeller had been freed, yet it was scarcely used. The captain cruised about at random. He could not tear himself away from the scene of his last struggle, from that sea which had swallowed up one of his men.

Ten days passed like this. It was only on the first of May, after sighting the Bahamas at the mouth of the Old Bahama Channel, that the *Nautilus* once again started on a definite northern course. We then followed the greatest of all ocean currents, one which has its own banks, fish and temperature. We were in the Gulf Stream.

It is, in fact, a river which flows freely through the middle of the Atlantic, but whose waters do not mingle with those of the surrounding sea. It is a salty river, saltier than the rest of the Atlantic. It has a mean depth of three thousand feet and an average width of sixty miles. In certain places its current travels at a speed of $2^{1}/_{2}$ knots. The quantity of water within it is greater than that of all the rivers on earth.

As Commander Maury discovered, the true source of the Gulf Stream, or if you will, its point of departure, is in the Bay of Biscay. There its waters, still cool and relatively colorless, begin to form. It then heads south, goes along Equatorial Africa, becomes warmed by the tropical sun, crosses the Atlantic, reaches Cape San Roque on the coast of Brazil and splits into two branches, one of which goes to the yet warmer water of the Caribbean. There, the Gulf Stream, whose job it is to re-establish the equilibrium of ocean temperatures and bring tropical waters to northern seas, begins its stabilizing role. Brought to a white heat in the Gulf of Mexico, it starts north along the coast of America up to Newfoundland, is deflected by the cold current coming through the Davis Straits and then heads out to sea. Toward the forty-third parallel, it divides into two branches, one of which, aided by the northeast trade winds, returns to the Bay of Biscay and the Azores, while the other, after warming the shores of

Ireland and Norway, goes beyond Spitsbergen where its temperature drops to below 40° and it empties into the Arctic Sea.

It was on this ocean river that the *Nautilus* was now sailing. Upon leaving the Florida Straits, in a channel thirty miles wide and over a thousand feet deep, the Gulf Stream travels at a rate of five miles an hour. It slows up slightly as it travels north, but only slightly, for if its speed and direction altered seriously, the climate of Europe would undergo changes of incalculable consequences.

Toward noon, I was on the platform with Conseil. I told him about the Gulf Stream, and when I was through with my explanation, I asked him to put his hand in the water.

Conseil obeyed and was astonished to find it felt neither hot nor cold.

"That's because the waters of the Gulf Stream, as they come out of the Gulf of Mexico," I said, "are at almost the same temperature as that of the human body. This current is a vast heating apparatus which permits the coasts of Europe to be continually decked in green. And if Maury's calculations are correct, the amount of heat it contains would be enough to melt a river of iron the size of the Amazon and the Missouri put together."

Where we were then, the Gulf Stream was traveling at a rate of slightly more than seven feet per second. Its current is so different from the surrounding sea that its waters are compressed and rise slightly higher than the colder water of the rest of the ocean. It is very rich in salts, and its deep indigo color is easily distinguishable from the green of the surrounding sea. Its line of demarcation is so clear that off the Carolinas the *Nautilus* had its spur within the Gulf Stream while its propeller was still churning the waters of the Atlantic.

This current carried with it a whole world of living beings. Argonauts, so common in the Mediterranean, were to be found here in large groups. Among cartilaginous fish we saw, the most remarkable were rays, whose long thin tails formed about a third of their bodies and who were shaped like a huge diamond twenty-five feet across. There were also small sharks with a three-foot-long body seemingly covered with scales, a large head, short rounded muzzle and sharp teeth arranged in several rows.

Among bony fish, I noted some gray wrasse, found only in these waters; a certain kind of gilthead, whose eye shone like fire; croakers three feet long, who had a large mouth full of little teeth, and who would let out a soft cry; black centronotae, which I have already mentioned; a kind of dolphin whose blue body is speckled with gold and silver; parrot fish, veritable seagoing rainbows which can rival the most beautiful tropical birds in color; blennies with their triangular heads; bluish garfishes without scales; toadfishes decorated with a yellow stripe in the shape of a Greek *T;* masses of little gobies with brown spots on their bodies; dipterodons with a silver head and yellow tail; various members of the salmon family; gray mullets with a slender body and soft sheen; and finally a lovely fish, the American horseman, covered with decorations and ribbons, which frequents the shores of that great nation where decorations and ribbons are held in such little esteem.

I must add that during the night, the phosphorescent waters of the Gulf Stream rivaled the electric light from the *Nautilus,* especially in the stormy weather which frequently threatened us.

By the eighth of May, we were off Cape Hatteras, on a parallel with North Carolina. There the Gulf Stream is seventy-five miles wide and seven hundred feet deep. The *Nautilus* continued to cruise about aimlessly. All surveillance on board seemed to have ceased. I had to admit that under such conditions it would have been easy to escape. The coast was not only inhabited, but dotted with safe harbors. The sea was constantly crisscrossed by steamers plying between New York or Boston and the Gulf of Mexico, and by schooners carrying on coastal trade between various other points along the shore. There would be reasonable hope of being picked up. It therefore seemed like a good opportunity, in spite of the thirty miles separating the *Nautilus* from the coast of the United States.

But one unfortunate circumstance put a complete stop to the Canadian's plans. The weather was very bad. We were getting near a region where storms are frequent, an area of waterspouts and cyclones fostered by the Gulf Stream itself. To brave a raging sea in a frail dinghy was to run the risk of almost certain drowning. Even Ned Land admitted this. But he was chafing at the bit; his violent homesickness could be cured by nothing but escape.

"Monsieur," he said to me one day, "this has got to come to an end. Things have to be cleared up. Your Captain Nemo is going out toward the open sea and heading north. But let me tell you that I had enough at the South Pole—I won't follow him to the North Pole."

"But what can we do, Ned, since we can't escape now?"

"We can do what I said before—talk to the captain. You didn't say a word when we were near your country, but now that we're near mine, I want to talk to him. When I think that in several days the *Nautilus* will be off Nova Scotia, and that between there and Newfoundland there's a large bay into which the St. Lawrence empties, and that the St. Lawrence is my river, the river that goes past Quebec, my home town—when I think of all this, I get so mad I almost go out of my mind! No, Monsieur, I'd rather jump into the sea than stay here! I can't stand it any more!"

The Canadian had obviously come to the end of his tether. His energetic personality could not take this prolonged imprisonment. His face was changing day by day, and his character becoming more somber. I could sympathize with him, for I too began to feel homesick. Almost seven months had passed by without our receiving the slightest news from land. Moreover, Captain Nemo's isolation, his altered mood, especially since the fight with the squid, made me see things in a different light. I no longer felt the enthusiasm I had once experienced. One had to be Belgian like Conseil to accept living in a part of the world inhabited only by whales and other creatures of the deep. Truly, I think that if this worthy fellow had gills instead of lungs, he would have made a splendid fish!

"Well, Monsieur?" said Ned Land, seeing that I did not answer.

"Well, Ned, do you want me to ask Captain Nemo what he intends to do with us?"

"Yes, Monsieur."

"Even though he's already as much as told us?"

"Yes. I want to know once and for all. Speak for me alone, if you want."

"But I see him very rarely. He even avoids me now."

"All the more reason to go and see him."

"I'll ask him, Ned."

"When?" insisted the Canadian.

"When I see him."

"Monsieur Aronnax, do you want me to go find him myself?"

"No, let me do it. Tomorrow . . ."

"Today," said Ned Land.

"All right, I'll see him today," I replied to the Canadian, who would certainly have ruined all our chances by doing it himself.

I remained alone. Once it had been decided to ask the captain, I resolved to do it at once. I like to get things over with.

I went to my room. From there I could hear someone walking about in the captain's cabin. I could not pass up this chance of seeing him. I knocked on the door. No answer. I knocked again, then turned the knob. The door opened.

I entered. The captain was bent over his work table. He had not heard me enter. I resolved not to leave without having questioned him. I drew nearer. He suddenly looked up, frowned and said in a rather rude tone of voice: "What are you doing here? What do you want?"

"I want to talk to you, Captain."

"But I'm busy, Monsieur; I'm working. You have the right to be alone on my ship; why can't I have the same right?"

This reception was not very encouraging. But I had made up my mind to stick it out no matter what he said.

"Monsieur," I said coolly, "I have to talk to you about something which cannot wait."

"And what is that, Monsieur?" he replied sarcastically. "Have you discovered something which has escaped my attention? Has the sea revealed some new secret to you?"

We were still at loggerheads. Before I could answer, he showed me a manuscript lying open on the table and said in a serious tone of voice: "Here, Monsieur Aronnax, is a manuscript written in several languages. It contains all my studies on the sea, and with God's help, it will not perish with me. This manuscript, signed with my name and containing also the history of my life, will be enclosed in a small unsinkable box. The last one of us to survive aboard the

Nautilus will throw this box into the sea, and it will drift wherever the wind and currents take it."

Signed with his own name! His life's story told by himself! Would this man's secret one day come to light? But to me at that moment, this statement gave me a way of leading the conversation around to the topic I wanted to discuss.

"Captain," I replied, "I can only approve of your idea. The fruit of all your studies must not be lost. But the means you intend to employ seem primitive. Who knows what winds will guide this box, or into whose hands it will fall? Might there not be some better way? Couldn't you, or one of your men perhaps . . . ?"

"Never, Monsieur," said the captain, cutting me short.

"But I and my companions would be willing to keep this manuscript for you, and if you gave us our freedom . . ."

"Your freedom!" exclaimed Captain Nemo, getting up.

"Yes, Monsieur, and this was precisely the subject I wanted to discuss with you. For seven months we have been on board your ship, and now I want to ask you, in the name of my companions and myself, if you intend to keep us here forever."

"Monsieur Aronnax," said Captain Nemo, "I will say now what I said seven months ago: whoever enters the *Nautilus* must never leave it again."

"But that's slavery!"

"You can call it whatever you like."

"But everywhere slaves have the right to recover their freedom! And by any means that present themselves!"

"But who has denied you this right?" replied Captain Nemo. "Have I ever bound you by any oath?"

The captain looked at me and crossed his arms.

"Monsieur," I said, "it is pleasant neither for you nor for me to go over this subject a second time, but since we've begun, let's finish with it. I repeat that it is not only a question of myself. For me study is a relief, a strong diversion, a lure and passion which can make me forget everything. Like you, I am a man who can live ignored and unknown, with the fragile hope of some day bequeathing to the future the results of my work, by means of a box entrusted to the hazards of wind and water. In a word, I can admire you and, without displeasure, follow you in a life which I partially understand; but there are other aspects of your life that are surrounded in a complexity and mystery in which my companions and I have no part. But then, even when our hearts were able to go out to you, touched by your sorrows or stirred by your acts of genius or courage, we were forced to suppress even the smallest tokens of sympathy or admiration. It is the feeling that we are foreign to whatever concerns you that makes our position unacceptable and impossible not only for me, but especially for Ned Land. Every man, merely by dint of being a man, is worth considering. Have you ever asked yourself what a love of liberty and hatred of slavery in a nature like Ned Land's means? To what plans of revenge it could lead him, what it could make him think, try or attempt? . . ."

I stopped. Captain Nemo got up. "Ned Land can think, try or attempt whatever he wants; it makes no difference to me! I didn't go looking for him! It isn't for my pleasure that I keep him on board! But as for you, Monsieur Aronnax, you are an intelligent man, one capable of understanding even silence. I have nothing more to say. This is the first time you have broached this subject with me, and I hope it will be the last, for if you bring it up again I shall not even be able to listen."

I withdrew. From that day on our situation was very tense. I reported this conversation to my two companions.

"Now we know we can expect nothing from him," said Ned Land. "The *Nautilus* is approaching Long Island. We'll escape whatever the weather's like."

But the sky became more and more threatening. We began to see signs of an oncoming hurricane. The sky became white and milky. Cirrus clouds were followed on the horizon by layers of cumulo-nimbus. Other low clouds sped by. The sea welled up in long waves. All birds disappeared except for the stormy petrel. The barometer dropped considerably, and the mixture in the storm glass decomposed under the influence of the electricity saturating the atmosphere. A struggle of the elements would soon be upon us.

The storm broke during the day of May 18, just as the *Nautilus* was off Long Island several miles from the entrance to New York Harbor. I am able to describe this struggle of the elements, for instead of diving to the ocean depths in order to avoid it, Captain Nemo, for some unknown reason, decided to remain on the surface.

The wind was blowing from the southwest at gale force, that is, at thirty-five miles an hour, and by three in the afternoon it had reached fifty-five miles an hour. This was now storm weather.

The captain, seemingly unaffected by the strong gusts of wind, had taken up a station on the platform. He had had himself tied around the waist as a precaution against the huge waves breaking over the ship. I hoisted myself out on deck and also had myself tied, dividing my admiration between the storm and this incomparable man observing it.

The raging sea was swept by large tattered bits of cloud soaking themselves in the water. I no longer saw any of those smaller waves which usually form in the hollow of big ones. There was nothing but long, murky undulations, so compact that their crests never broke. Their height was increasing. They seemed to stir each other on. The *Nautilus* rolled and pitched horribly, sometimes lying on its side and sometimes standing up as straight as a mast.

Toward five o'clock a torrential rain began to fall, but it calmed neither the air nor the water. The wind was now blowing in gusts up to a hundred miles an hour. It is under such conditions that houses are knocked over, that roofing tiles are driven through wooden doors, that iron grillwork is broken and that twenty-four-pound cannon are displaced. And yet the *Nautilus* in the midst of the storm merely proved the saying of nautical engineers that "a well-built hull can defy any storm." It was more than just a rock—for waves can destroy rocks; it was rather an iron spindle without masts or rigging, obedient and mobile, which could travel unharmed amid the sea's fury.

Meanwhile, I carefully examined the raging waves. They measured as much as fifty feet in height, between five and six hundred feet in breadth and were traveling at about a third the speed of the wind, or in other words at thirty-five miles per hour. Their size and force increased with the depth of the ocean. I then understood the role waves play, imprisoning air in their flanks and forcing it down to the bottom of the sea, where its oxygen brings life. Their pressure has been calculated to go up to 6500 pounds per square foot on any surface against which they strike. It was such waves which, in the Hebrides, moved a block of stone weighing 84,000 pounds, and which in the storm of December 23, 1864, after destroying part of Tokyo, traveled across the Pacific at 450 miles an hour to break that same day against the shores of America.

The violence of the storm increased as night came on. As it did at Réunion Island in 1860 during a cyclone, the barometer fell to twenty-eight inches. At twilight I saw a large ship pass by, struggling painfully along the horizon. It was lying to, at reduced speed, trying to stay afloat. It must have been a steamer from one of the lines plying between New York and Liverpool or Le Havre. It soon disappeared into the darkness.

By ten at night, the sky was on fire. The heavens were crisscrossed by lightning. It was too bright for me, but Captain Nemo looked straight at it and seemed to breathe in the soul of the tempest. The air was filled with a loud, confused noise coming partly from the crashing waves, partly from the roaring wind and partly from the thunderclaps. The wind seemed to come from all directions. The hurricane was whirling counterclockwise, as opposed to storms in the southern hemisphere, whose winds travel clockwise.

The Gulf Stream! It would be better to call it the King of Tempests! For it breeds these formidable hurricanes through the difference in temperature between its currents and the surrounding air.

The rain was followed by a shower of fire. The drops of water changed into sparks. One would have thought that Captain Nemo, wishing a death worthy of himself, was seeking to be struck by lightning. With a terrifying pitching motion, the *Nautilus* would lift its steel spur into the air, like the tip of a lightning rod, and I could see it give off long fingers of electricity.

I felt crushed and at the end of my strength. I crawled on my stomach toward the hatch, opened it and went back down into the lounge. The storm then reached its greatest violence. It was impossible to stand up inside the *Nautilus*.

Captain Nemo came back in at about midnight. I heard the reservoirs fill little by little, and the *Nautilus* gently sank beneath the surface.

Through the open panels in the lounge I saw large, frightened fish pass by like ghosts in the fiery water. Some were struck dead by lightning before my eyes!

The *Nautilus* kept on going down. I thought it would find calm water at a depth of fifty feet. But no, the upper layers of the sea were thrashing about too violently. We had to go down to a hundred and fifty feet, into the bowels of the ocean, before we could find peace.

But once there, what tranquillity, what silence, what calm! Who could have known that a terrible hurricane was raging on the surface of the sea?

CHAPTER XLIV
47° 24' North Latitude and 17° 28' West Longitude

We had been driven eastward by the storm. All hope of escaping in the region of New York or the St. Lawrence disappeared. Poor Ned, in a state of despair, shut himself up like Captain Nemo. Conseil and I no longer left each other's side.

I said that the *Nautilus* had been driven to the east. It would have been more accurate to say to the northeast. For several days it wandered about in the midst of one of those fogs so dangerous for sailors, sometimes sailing on the surface, sometimes under water. Such fogs are principally due to melting ice which fills the air with moisture. How many ships have been lost in these waters when they were almost within sight of the dim lights on the coast! How many wrecks these thick mists have caused! How many vessels have gone aground on reefs whose warning eddies were drowned out by the wind! How many boats have collided with one another, in spite of their riding lights and the warnings of their foghorns and alarm bells!

As a result, the bottom of the ocean in this area looked like a battlefield where all those ships conquered by the sea still lay. Some were already old and encrusted; others, still young, reflected the glare of our searchlight on their ironwork and the copper of their hulls. How many of these boats had gone down with all hands, including the crew and whole groups of immigrants, near those points marked as dangerous on charts: Cape Race, St. Paul Island, Belle Isle Strait and the mouth of the St. Lawrence! And in just the past few years how many victims have been entered in the grim annals of the Royal Mail, Inman and Montreal lines: the *Solway*, the *Isis*, the *Paramatta*, the *Hungarian*, the *Canadian*, the *Anglo-Saxon*, the *Humboldt* and the *United States*, all run aground; the *Arctic* and the *Lyonnais*, sunk in collisions; the *President*, the *Pacific* and the *City of Glasgow*, whose fate was never known! And the *Nautilus* cruised through this somber wreckage as if passing the dead in review!

By May 15 we were at the southern tip of the Grand Banks. This area is a product of marine deposits, a huge mass of organic debris brought either from the equator by the Gulf Stream or from the North Pole by the counter-current of cold water which runs along the coast of North America. It also contains piles of rocks dropped by the breaking up of the ice. In addition, it is a vast boneyard of fish, mollusks and zoophytes which die there by the millions.

The sea is not very deep over the Grand Banks, no more than several hundred fathoms. But toward the south there is an abrupt depression, a pit going down to ten thousand feet. There the waters of the Gulf Stream spread out, losing their speed and heat, but becoming an ocean.

Among the fish the *Nautilus* frightened away as it passed by, I will cite the three-foot lumpfish with a blackish back and orange stomach, which gives other fish a fine but little-heeded example of marital fidelity; a large unernack—a kind of emerald moray excellent to eat; karraks with big eyes and a head looking somewhat like that of a dog; blennies, which produce their eggs like a reptile; black gobies or groundlings three-quarters of an inch long; grenadiers with their long tails and brilliant silver sheen—fast fish who had wandered far from the Arctic Sea.

The nets also brought in a tough, brave and powerful fish, one with strong muscles and with spines on its head and fins, a veritable scorpion seven to ten feet long and the deadly enemy of blennies, gadoids and salmon. It was the bull-head of northern waters, with a gnarled body entirely brown except for the red on its fins. The sailors on the *Nautilus* had some difficulty with this fish, which, thanks to special gill covers, can keep its lungs from drying out in the air and can live for some time out of water.

Merely as a reminder, I will cite bosquians, little fish which often accompany ships for a long time in northern waters; sharp-snouted bleaks, found only in the North Atlantic; hogfish; and gadoids, represented by their principal species, the cod, which I was able to see in its favorite waters, the Grand Banks of Newfoundland.

One might say that cod are mountain fish, for Newfoundland is no more than an underwater mountain. As the *Nautilus* made its way through their close-pressed ranks, Conseil could not refrain from saying: "Are those cod? But I thought cod were flat like flounder or sole!"

"You simpleton!" I cried. "Cod are only flat in a grocery store, where they've been opened and spread out. But in the water they're as round and slender as mullets, and they're perfectly built for swimming."

"Since Monsieur says so, I'll believe it," replied Conseil. "But what an enormous number of them there are!"

"Yes, my friend, and there would be even more if not for their enemies, the hogfish and man! Do you know how many eggs have been counted in a single female cod?"

"Let's pick a good number," replied Conseil. "Five hundred thousand."

"Eleven million, my friend."

"Eleven million! I won't believe that until I count them myself."

"Go ahead and count them, Conseil. But it would be easier and quicker to just believe what I say. Besides the French, English, Americans, Danes and Norwegians catch them by the thousands. Prodigious quantities of them are consumed each year, and if it weren't for their amazing fertility, the seas would soon be empty of cod. Why, in England and America alone five thousand ships manned by seventy-five thousand sailors are used in codfishing. Each boat brings back at least forty thousand fish, which makes a total catch of twenty million. The figures from Norway are about the same."

"All right," said Conseil. "I'll take Monsieur's word for it; I won't count them."

"What?"

"The eleven million eggs. But just let me say one thing."

"What's that?"

"That if every egg hatched, you'd only need four cod to feed all of England, America and Norway."

While we skimmed over the bottom of the Grand Banks, I could clearly see the long lines armed with two hundred fishhooks which each boat puts out by the dozen. The lines were held down at one end by a little grappling anchor and held up at the other end by a cork buoy. The *Nautilus* had to maneuver skillfully through this underwater network.

But it did not stay long in waters containing so many fishing boats. It went up to 42° N. Lat., off St. John and Heart's Content, which was where the transatlantic cable ended.

Instead of continuing north, the *Nautilus* headed east as if it wanted to follow the underwater plateau on which the cable rests.

It was on May 17, about five hundred miles out from Heart's Content and at a depth of nine thousand feet, that I first saw the cable lying on the ocean floor. Conseil, whom I had not forewarned, thought it was some gigantic sea serpent and was about to classify it as he usually did in such situations. But I set him right, and in order to console him for having made such a mistake, I told him various facts about the laying of the cable.

The first cable was put down from 1857 to 1858; but after transmitting four hundred telegrams, it ceased functioning. In 1863, engineers constructed a new cable 2100 miles long and weighing 4500 tons, which was put aboard the *Great Eastern*. This attempt also failed.

Now, on May 25, the *Nautilus,* cruising at a depth of 12,585 feet, sailed over the exact spot where the break in this cable had occurred. It had happened 638 miles from the coast of Ireland and had ruined the entire project. At two in the afternoon it was noticed that communications with Europe had been interrupted. The electricians on board decided to cut the cable before fishing it back up, and by eleven at night they had brought up the part which had caused the trouble. It was repaired, spliced together again and then put back in the water. Two days later it broke again, but this time it could not be brought back up from the ocean depths.

But the Americans did not despair. Cyrus Field, the daring man who had promoted the enterprise and risked his entire fortune in it, issued a new set of bonds which were immediately bought up. Another stronger cable was manufactured.

Its bundle of electric wires was insulated inside a covering made of a rubberlike substance called gutta-percha, which in turn was protected by layers of different kinds of cloth and all placed inside a metal casing. The *Great Eastern* once more set out to sea on July 13, 1866.

This time they succeeded. Nevertheless a strange thing occurred. Several times as they were unrolling the cable, the electricians noticed that nails had been driven into it in order to corrode its core. Captain Anderson conferred with the officers and engineers; finally they put up a notice stating that if the guilty party were discovered on board, he would be thrown into the sea without even a trial. From then on, this criminal act was not repeated.

On July 23, when the *Great Eastern* was only five hundred miles from Newfoundland, it received a telegraphic message from Ireland saying that an armistice had been signed between Prussia and Austria after the battle of Königgrätz. On the twenty-seventh, it sighted the port of Heart's Content through the fog. They had finally succeeded, and the first message young America sent to old Europe contained those wise words so rarely understood. "Glory to God in the highest, and on earth peace, good will toward men."

I knew the electric cable would not be in its original state, looking as if it had just come out of the factory. And in fact this long snake was covered with bits of shell, encrusted with foraminifera and embedded into a mass of rocky matter that protected it against whatever mollusks might have been able to bore holes in it. It was resting calmly, protected from ocean currents and lying beneath a pressure which actually favors the transmission of that electric spark which goes from America to Europe in $32/100$ of a second. This cable will probably last indefinitely, for it has been remarked that its covering of gutta-percha is improved by being beneath the ocean.

Moreover, on this well-chosen underwater plateau the cable never lies at depths which might cause it to break. The *Nautilus* followed it to its lowest point, situated at a depth of 14,537 feet, and there it rested without any strain or traction. Then we drew near the spot where the accident had taken place in 1863.

There the ocean floor formed a wide valley seventy-five miles across, within which one could have placed Mont Blanc without having its peak emerge above the surface. The valley is closed off to the east by a vertical wall 6500 feet high. We arrived there on May 28, and the *Nautilus* was then no more than a hundred miles from Ireland.

Was Captain Nemo going to continue north toward the British Isles? No, to my great surprise he turned south toward continental waters. As we went around the Emerald Isle, for a moment I could make out Cape Clear and the lighthouse of Fasnet Rock which lights the way for thousands of ships leaving Glasgow and Liverpool.

An important question then crossed my mind. Would the *Nautilus* dare venture into the English Channel? Ned, who had reappeared since we had drawn near land, asked me continual questions about our course. But how could I know? Captain Nemo remained out of sight. After giving the Canadian a glimpse of the shores of America, did he now intend to show me the coast of France?

Nevertheless, the *Nautilus* continued heading south. On May 30 it passed within sight of Land's End, cruising between this tip of England and the Scilly Isles.

If he intended to enter the English Channel, he now had to turn sharply to the east. But he did not.

During the day of May 31, the *Nautilus* went around and around in a circular course that intrigued me greatly. It seemed to be looking for a certain spot, but having difficulty finding it. At noon Captain Nemo himself came up on deck to take our position. He didn't say a word to me. He seemed more somber than ever. What was making him so sad? Was it the proximity of European shores? Did he still feel pangs of homesickness for the country he had left? If not, what did he feel? Remorse, or regret? These thoughts occupied my mind for a long time, and I had a kind of presentiment that fate would soon betray the captain's secrets to me.

On the next day, June 1, the *Nautilus* continued the same maneuvers. It was obviously trying to find some precise spot in the ocean. Captain Nemo came on deck to shoot the sun as he had the day before. The sea was calm, the sky clear. Eight miles to the east a large steamship was outlined against the horizon. It was flying no colors, so I could not tell its nationality.

Several minutes before the sun passed its zenith, Captain Nemo took his sextant and looked through it with great care. The complete calm of the ocean made this operation much easier. The *Nautilus* lay immobile, neither rolling nor pitching. I was on the platform watching. When he had finished, the captain said: "It's here!"

Then he went back down the hatch. Had he seen the ship which had altered its course and seemed to be bearing down on us? I could not say.

I returned to the lounge. The hatch closed and I could hear the whistling noise of water entering the reservoirs. The *Nautilus* began to sink straight down, for its propeller was not turning.

Several minutes later it stopped at a depth of 2733 feet.

The lights went out in the lounge, the panels opened and through the window I could see the ocean brilliantly lit within a radius of half a mile by the light on top of the submarine.

I looked out to port and saw only a vast expanse of calm water.

To starboard, there was a large object sticking up from the ocean floor which attracted my attention. It looked like some ruin buried beneath a snowlike blanket of whitish shells. As I examined this object carefully, I thought I could make out the form of a rather large, demasted ship which had sunk bow first. It must have been a very old wreck. In order to be that encrusted with marine life, it must have already spent many years at the bottom of the ocean.

What ship was it? Why did the *Nautilus* come to visit this grave? Was it something more than a mere storm which had dragged this ship beneath the waves?

I did not know what to think. Then suddenly, next to me, I could hear Captain Nemo saying slowly: "This ship used to be called the *Marseillais*. It was launched in 1762 and carried seventy-four guns. On August 13, 1778, under the command of La Poype-Vertrieux, it fought bravely against the *Preston*. On July 4, 1779, it assisted in the capture of Grenada, along with Admiral d'Estaing's squadron. On September 5, 1781, it took part with the Count of Grasse in the Battle of Chesapeake Bay. In 1794, the French Republic changed the ship's name. On April 16 of the same year, it went to Brest to join Villaret-Joyeuse' squadron which had been ordered to escort a convoy of wheat coming from America under the command of Admiral Van Stabel. On May 30 and 31 this squadron met up with English ships. Today, Monsieur, is the first of June, 1868. Seventy-four years ago to the very day and on this exact spot, at 47° 24' N. Lat. and 17° 28' W. Long., this ship, after a heroic struggle, completely demasted, its hold filling with water and a third of its crew out of action, preferred to go down with its three hundred and fifty-six sailors rather than surrender. A flag was nailed onto its stern flagpost and then it disappeared beneath the surface, with all of its men shouting, 'Long live the Republic!'"

"The *Revenge*!" I cried.

"That's right, Monsieur. The *Revenge*. What a lovely name!" Captain Nemo murmured as he crossed his arms.

CHAPTER XLV
A Hecatomb

This strange way of talking, the unexpectedness of seeing such a wreck, the story of a patriotic ship told at first in a cold way but then building up to a strong emotion in the final words, and this name of the *Revenge*—the significance of which did not escape me—all these things made a deep impression on me. I did not take my eyes off the captain. He had stretched his arms out toward the sea and was looking at the glorious wreck with a glowing expression on his face. Perhaps I would never know who he was, where he came from or where he was going, but more and more I began to see the man in him as distinct from the scientist. It was not an ordinary hatred of his fellow men which had made him and his crew shut themselves up inside the *Nautilus,* but one that was so monstrous or sublime that time could never weaken it.

Was this hatred still seeking revenge? I would soon know.

Meanwhile the *Nautilus* was slowly climbing back up to the surface and the vague form of the *Revenge* slowly faded from sight. Soon a light rolling told me we had surfaced.

Just then I heard a dull explosion. I looked at the captain. He did not move. "What's that?" I asked.

The captain did not answer. I left him and went up on the platform. Conseil and the Canadian were already there.

"What was that explosion?" I asked.

"They're firing," replied Ned Land.

I looked in the direction of the ship I had noticed before. It was drawing nearer the *Nautilus* and one could see it was traveling at full speed. It was now only six miles away from us.

"What kind of a ship is it, Ned?"

"By its rigging and the heights of its lower masts," replied the Canadian, "I'd guess it was a warship. I hope it comes and sinks this cursed *Nautilus*!"

"What harm can it do to the *Nautilus?*" said Conseil. "Can it go and attack it under water? Can it shoot at it on the ocean floor?"

"Tell me, Ned," I asked, "can you see what country it belongs to?"

The Canadian knitted his eyebrows, squinted and for several moments trained his marvelous eyes on the ship.

"No, Monsieur," he replied. "I can't tell what country it belongs to. Its flag isn't up. But it's a warship all right, for there's a long pennant on the tip of its mainmast."

For a quarter of an hour, we stayed there observing the ship bearing down on

us. It seemed impossible, however, that it could have sighted the *Nautilus* from
that distance, much less known that it was a submarine.

Soon the Canadian announced that it was a large armored two-decker
with a ram on its prow. Thick black smoke rose from its two funnels. Its sails
were furled over the yards. It was flying no flag, and it was still too far away to
make out the colors of its pennant, which was floating in the wind like a thin
ribbon.

It was advancing rapidly. If Captain Nemo allowed it to get near, we might
have a chance to escape.

"Monsieur," said Ned Land, "if this ship comes within a mile of us, I'm
going to jump into the water, and I'd advise you to do the same."

I did not answer, but merely kept looking at the ship looming larger and larger
on the horizon. Whether it was English, French, American or Russian, it would
certainly welcome us on board.

"I would like to remind Monsieur," said Conseil, "that we are reasonably
experienced swimmers. So I will take the responsibility of helping Monsieur get
to the ship, if he intends to follow Ned Land."

I was about to reply when a puff of white smoke appeared near the bow of
the warship. Several seconds later there was a big splash of some heavy object
landing to the rear of the *Nautilus*. Soon the sound of a detonation reached my ears.

"What? Are they firing at us?" I cried.

"Good work, fellows!" murmured the Canadian.

"So they don't take us for shipwrecked men hanging on to the remains of
their boat!"

"If Monsieur doesn't . . . Goodness!" exclaimed Conseil, shaking off the
water another shell had splashed on him. "If Monsieur doesn't mind my saying
so, they've sighted the narwhal and are firing on it."

"But they must have seen there are men on it," I cried.

"Maybe that's why they're firing!" replied Ned Land, looking at me.

All of a sudden everything became clear. Undoubtedly people now knew what
this so-called monster really was. In its collision with the *Abraham Lincoln*, when
Ned Land had struck it with his harpoon, Commander Farragut had probably

"Almighty God! Enough! Enough!"

seen that the narwhal was a submarine, and therefore even more dangerous than a monstrous whale.

Yes, this was probably the case. And now, throughout the world's oceans, people were undoubtedly pursuing this terrible weapon of destruction!

And terrible it indeed would have been if Captain Nemo, as one might have supposed, had decided to use the *Nautilus* as an instrument of revenge! And hadn't it attacked some ship during that night we were locked in the cell, in the middle of the Indian Ocean? That man now buried in the coral cemetery, hadn't he been a victim of a collision brought on by the *Nautilus*? Yes, there was no other explanation. Part of Captain Nemo's mysterious life was becoming clear.

And even though his identity was unknown, at least now the nations which had joined up against him were no longer chasing a phantom, but a man who had vowed an everlasting hatred against them!

All this extraordinary past rose up before my eyes. And now, instead of finding friends on the ship approaching us, I knew we could only find pitiless enemies.

Meanwhile more and more shells began to land around us. Some of them would strike the surface of the water and ricochet into the distance. But none hit the *Nautilus*.

The armored vessel was now less than three miles away. In spite of its violent cannonade which, with a direct hit, might have proved fatal to the *Nautilus*, Captain Nemo did not come up on deck. Just then the Canadian said: "Monsieur, we must do whatever we can to get out of this situation. Let's signal them! Then, by God, maybe they'll understand we're friends!"

Ned Land took out his handkerchief to wave it in the air. But he had scarcely unfolded it when, in spite of his great strength, he was struck down by a hand of iron.

"You fool!" cried the captain, "do you want me to nail you to the prow of the *Nautilus* before it rams that ship!"

However terrible Captain Nemo may have been to hear, he was even more terrible to see. In his excitement his heart must have ceased beating for an instant, for his face was pale. The pupils of his eyes were fearfully contracted. He was leaning forward, twisting Ned's shoulders with his hands.

He then let him go and, turning toward the warship raining shells around him, he shouted in a powerful voice: "Do you know who I am, O ship of an accursed nation! I do not need to see your colors to recognize you! Look! Here are mine!"

And Captain Nemo unfurled on the front part of the platform a black flag similar to the one he had planted at the South Pole.

Just then a shell struck the hull of the *Nautilus,* but instead of penetrating, it ricocheted off near the captain and flew off to spend itself in the sea.

Captain Nemo shrugged his shoulders. Then, turning to me, he said in a curt tone of voice: "Go below, you and your friends."

"Captain," I cried, "are you going to attack this ship?"

"Monsieur, I'm going to sink it."

"You wouldn't do that!"

"I certainly would," Captain Nemo answered coldly. "And don't take it into your head to judge me, Monsieur. Fate has shown you what you should never have seen. They have attacked; the counterattack will be terrible. Go below."

"What ship is it?"

"You don't know? So much the better! Then at least its nationality will remain a secret for you. Go below."

Ned, Conseil and I could do little but obey. Captain Nemo was surrounded by fifteen or so sailors looking with implacable hatred at the vessel bearing down on them. The same need for revenge seemed to animate every one of their souls.

Just as I was going below, I felt another shell graze the hull of the *Nautilus* and I heard the captain shout: "Strike, mad ship! Waste your shells! You won't escape the *Nautilus'* spur. But you shall not perish here! I don't want your wreckage mixed with that of the *Revenge!*"

I went to my cabin. The captain and the first mate had remained on the platform. The propeller started turning. The *Nautilus* sped off and was soon beyond reach of the shells. But the chase continued, and Captain Nemo merely kept his distance.

Toward four in the afternoon I could no longer contain my impatience and anxiety, and I went back to the central companionway. The hatch was still open. I ventured out onto the platform. The captain was still there, pacing nervously up and down. He would occasionally stop and look at the ship, which was now five or six miles to leeward. The *Nautilus* was stalking around it like a wild beast, leading it on to the east and allowing itself to be pursued. Nevertheless, the captain did not attack. Had he not yet made up his mind?

I wanted to make one last attempt to prevent the oncoming disaster. But I had scarcely started in when Captain Nemo silenced me by saying: "I am the law and justice! I am the oppressed, and there is the oppressor! It is through him I lost everything I ever loved, cherished or worshiped—my country, wife, children, father, mother! I saw them all perish! Everything I hate is there! Now shut your mouth!"

I took one last look at the warship pushing forward at full steam. Then I went back to rejoin Ned and Conseil.

"We must escape!" I cried.

"Good!" said Ned. "What ship is it?"

"I don't know. But whatever ship it is, it will be sunk before nightfall. All the same it will be better to go down with her than be accomplices to a reprisal whose fairness we have no way of judging."

"I agree with you," replied Ned Land coolly. "Let's wait for nighttime."

Night came. A deep silence reigned on board. The compass showed that the *Nautilus* had not altered its course. I could hear its propeller churning the water in a regular rhythm. It stayed on the surface and rolled gently from side to side.

My companions and I had resolved to escape as soon as the ship was close enough either to hear or see us, for the moon, three days short of being full, was shining brightly. Once aboard the other ship, although we could not prevent the danger threatening it, we could at least do everything the circumstances would allow. Several times I thought the *Nautilus* was getting into position for an attack. But it was merely content to let its adversary draw near and then resume its flight.

Part of the night passed without incident. We waited for our chance. We were too excited to talk very much. Ned Land wanted to jump into the sea then and there. But I made him wait. My theory was that the *Nautilus* would attack this two-decker on the surface, which would make escape not only possible but easy.

At three in the morning I went out on deck, full of anxiety. Captain Nemo was still there. He was standing in the bow near his flag, which a light breeze was unfurling over his head. His eyes did not leave the warship. The intensity with which he looked at it seemed to draw it on, hold it spellbound, and make it follow in the *Nautilus'* wake more surely than if it were being towed!

The moon was then just passing its zenith. Jupiter was rising in the east. In the midst of this peaceful scene, with the sky and water rivaling each other in tranquillity, the sea offered night's planet the most beautiful mirror that had ever reflected its image.

The ship was two miles away from us. It had drawn nearer, always making for the glow that told it where the *Nautilus* was. I could see its green and red riding lights and its white navigation light hanging from the forestays. A dim glow lit up the rigging, indicating that its fires had been stoked to their utmost. Showers of sparks and burning cinders escaped from the funnels, looking like stars in the night.

I stayed there till six in the morning, without Captain Nemo's seeming to notice my presence. The ship remained a mile and a half away, and with the first gleam of dawn, its cannonade began again. The moment could not be far off now when the *Nautilus* would attack its adversary and my companions and I would leave forever this man I dared not judge.

I was about to go below and tell them to get ready, when the first mate, accompanied by several sailors, appeared on the platform. Captain Nemo either did not see them or did not choose to notice them. Certain operations were carried out which might have been the *Nautilus'* version of "clearing the decks for action." They could not have been simpler. First the jackstay which formed the railing around the platform was lowered. Then the helmsman's compartment and that containing the searchlight were let down into the hull until they were flush with the top of the submarine. Now the surface of this long steel-plated cigar had nothing whatever protruding which might have inhibited its movements.

I returned to the lounge. The *Nautilus* was still on the surface. Several streaks of morning light filtered down through the water. When the waves took on certain specific shapes, the glass panels would be lit up by a red glow from the rising sun. This terrible day of June 2 was beginning.

At seven o'clock the log showed that the *Nautilus* was reducing its speed. I realized it was letting the other ship draw nearer. Now the sound of detonations was considerably louder. Shells churned up the surrounding water and spun into the depths with a strange hissing noise.

"My friends," I said, "the time has come. Let's shake hands. May God preserve us!"

Ned Land was resolute, Conseil calm and I so nervous I was scarcely able to contain myself.

We entered the library. But just as I opened the door leading to the central companionway, I heard the hatch close sharply overhead.

The Canadian rushed for the stairs, but I held him back. A well-known whistling noise told me that water was entering the reservoirs. And in fact the *Nautilus* had soon submerged a short way below the surface.

I now realized what was going to happen, but it was too late for us to do anything about it. The *Nautilus* was not going to ram the two-decker along its waterline where it was protected by impenetrable armor plate, but below where its planks were no longer shielded by a metal covering.

We were once more imprisoned; we were forced to witness the grim drama about to take place. But we scarcely had time to think. We had taken refuge in my room, and we just sat there looking at one another without saying a word. I fell into a kind of daze; my mind stopped working. I was in the painful state of someone awaiting a horrible explosion. I waited and listened; I lived only through my sense of hearing!

Meanwhile, the *Nautilus'* speed had increased considerably. It was getting up momentum. Its entire hull trembled.

Suddenly I let out a cry. I felt a blow, but a relatively light one. I could feel the steel spur penetrating. I heard chafing and scraping sounds. But the *Nautilus,* impelled by its powerful engines, went right through the hull of the ship like a sailmaker's needle through cloth.

I could stand it no longer. I rushed out of my cabin and into the lounge, half out of my mind.

Captain Nemo was standing there, looking out of the port panel—mute, somber and implacable.

A huge object was sinking below the surface, and in order to miss no details of its death struggle, the *Nautilus* was following it down into the abyss. Thirty feet away I could see its pierced hull, into which water was rushing with a thunderous noise, then the double line of its guns and gunwales. The deck was covered with black shadows flitting about.

The water was rising. The poor victims rushed up the shrouds, hung on to masts and writhed about in the water. It was like a human anthill suddenly invaded by the sea! I was immobile, paralyzed with horror. My hair was standing on end, my eyes were wide open. I was without breath, unable to speak. For I too was looking! I was irresistibly drawn to the glass panel!

The huge ship sank slowly. The *Nautilus* followed it, observing its every movement. Suddenly there was an explosion. The air compressed inside the hull had blown the decks up in the air as if the ship's powder magazine had caught fire. The *Nautilus* swerved beneath the force of the explosion.

Then the unfortunate ship started sinking faster. First appeared its crow's-nests filled with victims, then its crosstrees, bending beneath the weight of all the men hanging on them, and finally the top of its mainmast. Soon its dark form disappeared, along with a whole crew of corpses sucked down by the swirling water. . . .

I turned toward Captain Nemo. This terrible dispenser of justice, veritable archangel of hatred, was still watching. When it was all over, he went toward the door of his cabin, opened it and entered. I followed him with my eyes.

On the opposite wall of his room, beneath the paintings of his heroes, I saw the portrait of a young woman and two small children. After gazing at it for several moments, Captain Nemo stretched out his arms toward the picture, sank to his knees and burst into deep sobs.

CHAPTER XLVI
Captain Nemo's Last Words

The panels had closed, shutting out this terrifying spectacle, but the lights in the lounge had not yet been turned back on. The inside of the *Nautilus* was all darkness and silence. A hundred feet beneath the surface the submarine started up again, and left this scene of desolation at a prodigious speed. Where was it going? North or south? Where would this man flee after such a horrible revenge?

I went back to my room where Ned and Conseil were sitting in silence. I experienced an insurmountable feeling of horror toward Captain Nemo. No matter how much he had suffered at the hands of men, he had no right to punish them like this. And moreover he had made me, if not an accomplice, at least a witness to his vengeance. It was too much!

At eleven o'clock the lights were turned back on. I went back to the lounge. It was empty. I looked at the various instruments. The *Nautilus* was fleeing north at twenty-five knots, sometimes on the surface and sometimes at a depth of thirty feet.

Once our position had been marked on the chart, I realized we were now entering the English Channel and were heading north at an incredible speed.

We were traveling so rapidly that I could only get a fleeting glimpse of the fish in these waters. There were long-nosed sharks, hammerheads and spotted dogfish common to these waters, large eagle rays, swarms of sea horses looking like so many knights in a game of chess, eels writhing about like squibs in fire-works, armies of crabs fleeing sideways with their pincers crossed over their shells, and finally schools of porpoises struggling to keep up with the *Nautilus*. But observing, studying and classifying were now out of the question.

By that evening we had traveled four hundred miles through the Atlantic, and the sea was covered in darkness until the moon came up.

I went to my cabin. But I could not sleep. I was troubled by nightmares. The horrible scene of destruction kept reappearing before my eyes.

From now on who could say into what part of the north Atlantic basin the *Nautilus* would take us? And always traveling at such speeds through these northern mists! Would we go to Spitsbergen or Novaya Zemlya? Would we sail through the unknown waters of the White Sea, the Kara Sea, Ob Bay, visit the Liakhov Islands and the unexplored northern coasts of Asia? I had no way of knowing. I could no longer calculate the passage of time, for the clocks on board had stopped. It seemed as if night and day, as happens in polar regions, no longer followed each other in their normal order. I felt myself entering a strange world in which Edgar Allan Poe would have felt at home. Any moment I expected to see, like the fabulous Gordon Pym, "a shrouded human figure, very far larger in its proportions than any dweller among men, lying athwart the cataract which bars all access to the North Pole!"

I estimated—but I could be wrong—that the *Nautilus* went on sailing like this for fifteen or twenty days, and I do not know how long this part of our journey would have lasted had it not ended in catastrophe. I no longer saw anything of Captain Nemo or of his first mate. Not even a single member of the crew was seen. The *Nautilus* cruised almost continually under water. When it surfaced in order to renew its air supply, the hatches would open and close automatically. Our position was no longer marked on the chart. I did not even know where we were.

I must say too that the Canadian had reached the end of his strength and patience, and he too no longer put in an appearance. Conseil could not get a single word out of him, and he was afraid that in a fit of madness or homesickness he might commit suicide. He therefore showed his devotion by never leaving his side.

But as one can see, our situation had become impossible.

One morning—of what day I could not say—I had finally dozed off in the early hours toward dawn, but my sleep was troubled and unhealthy. When I awoke, I saw Ned Land leaning over me, and he said in a low voice: "This is our chance!"

I sat up. "When?" I asked.

"Tonight. All surveillance on board seems to have disappeared. The whole ship is in a kind of daze. Will you be ready to go, Monsieur?"

"Yes. Where are we?"

"Within sight of some land I made out through the fog this morning about twenty miles to the east."

"What country is it?"

"I don't know, but whatever country it is, we're going to take refuge there."

"Good, Ned. We'll go tonight, even if the sea swallows us up!"

"The sea's bad and the wind's blowing strong, but the idea of doing twenty miles in the *Nautilus'* light dinghy doesn't worry me. I've been able to store some food and several bottles of water on it without the crew's seeing me."

"I'm with you, Ned."

"But let me tell you," added the Canadian, "that if we're caught, I'm going to defend myself even if I die doing it."

"We'll die together, Ned my friend."

I had made up my mind to risk everything. Ned Land left my cabin. I went out on the platform, where I could scarcely stand up for the waves beating against the ship. The sky looked menacing, but since there was land off there in the thick fog, we had to try to escape, and with no further delay.

I went down to the lounge half fearing and yet half desiring to meet Captain Nemo. What would I have said to him? Would I have been able to hide the involuntary horror I felt for him? No! It was best to avoid him, to forget him! and yet . . .

How long that day seemed, the last I was to spend on board the *Nautilus*! I remained alone. Ned Land and Conseil avoided speaking to me out of fear of betraying our project.

I dined at six, but I was not hungry. However, I forced myself to eat in order to conserve my strength.

At six-thirty Ned Land entered my cabin and said: "We won't see each other again before we leave. At ten o'clock the moon won't be up yet. We'll be able to take advantage of the darkness. You come to the dinghy; Conseil and I will be waiting for you there."

Then the Canadian left without giving me time to answer.

I wanted to check the *Nautilus'* direction. I went into the lounge. We were heading north-northeast very fast at a depth of 160 feet.

I took one last look at the wonders of nature and the masterpieces of art brought together in this museum, at this unrivaled collection destined one day to perish at the bottom of the sea along with the man who had gathered it together. I stayed there for an hour, bathed in the light emanating from the electrically illuminated ceiling, going over the treasures gleaming in their showcases. Then I went back to my room.

I got dressed in thick sea clothes. I got my notes together and tucked them carefully inside my jacket. My heart was beating fast and I was unable to calm my nerves. My excitement and uneasiness would certainly have betrayed me to Captain Nemo.

What was he doing at that moment? I listened at the door of his room. I could hear footsteps. Captain Nemo was there. He had not yet gone to bed. I thought that at any moment he would appear and ask me why I wanted to escape! I was continually startled by false alarms which were mainly small noises magnified by my imagination. This frame of mind got so bad that I thought it would be best to enter the captain's cabin, see him face to face and weather the storm of his look!

But this was the idea of a madman. Luckily I restrained myself and stretched out on my bed to try and relax. My nerves calmed down a bit, but in my still overstimulated mind I thought back over my whole life aboard the *Nautilus,* all the fortunate and unfortunate incidents which had taken place, from the disappearance of the *Abraham Lincoln* to the underwater hunting expedition, Torres Strait, the savages of New Guinea, the running aground, the coral cemetery, the passage beneath Suez, Santorin Island, the Cretan diver, Vigo Bay, Atlantis, the Great Ice Barrier, the South Pole, the imprisonment in the ice, the fight with the squid, the storm in the Gulf Stream, the *Revenge* and the grisly scene of the ship sunk with all hands . . . ! All these events passed before my eyes like one of those moving backdrops in a theater. Then, in this strange setting, Captain Nemo seemed to grow tremendously in stature. His good qualities became accentuated and he took on superhuman proportions. He was no longer an ordinary man like me, but the Man of the Sea, the Spirit of the Waters.

It was then nine-thirty. I held my head in my hands in order to prevent it from bursting open. I closed my eyes. I did not want to think anymore. Another half hour to go! A half an hour of nightmares which would drive me mad!

Just then I heard vague chords from the organ, sad harmonies with an undefinable melody, the wails of a soul which wanted to break its ties with the earth. I listened with all five senses, scarcely breathing, and my soul joined Captain Nemo's in this musical ecstasy drawing him into another world.

Then suddenly a terrifying thought struck me. Captain Nemo had left his room. He was in the lounge, through which I had to pass in order to escape. I could not avoid meeting him one last time. He would see me and perhaps talk to me! He might annihilate me with a single gesture, or bind me to his ship with a single word!

It was now almost ten. The time had come to leave my room and rejoin my companions.

I could not hesitate, even if Captain Nemo barred my way. I opened the door carefully, yet its hinges seemed to creak fearfully. But perhaps this noise only existed in my imagination!

I crept forward along the dark gangways of the *Nautilus*, stopping at every step to try and calm my pounding heart.

I reached the door leading into the lounge. I opened it quietly. The lounge was plunged in darkness. Soft strains from the organ filled the room. Captain Nemo was there. He did not see me. But he seemed so absorbed in his ecstasy that even with the lights full on he probably would not have seen me.

I crept across the carpet, trying not to make the slightest sound which would betray my presence. It took me five minutes to reach the library door on the other side of the room.

I was about to open it when a sigh from Captain Nemo rooted me to the spot. I realized he was getting up. I could even make him out in the few rays of light entering from the library. He came silently toward me with his arms crossed; he was gliding like a ghost rather than walking. His chest was heaving with sobs. I heard him murmur these words—the last I ever heard from him: "Almighty God! Enough! Enough!"

Was it remorse escaping from this man's conscience . . . ?

I rushed into the library in a state of desperation. I climbed the central companionway, went along the upper gangway and arrived at the dinghy. I climbed through the hatch and found my two companions already inside.

"Let's go! Let's go!" I cried.

"We're ready!" replied the Canadian.

Ned Land had brought along a wrench, and first he closed and bolted the hatch in the hull of the *Nautilus*. Then, after shutting the other hatch in the dinghy, the Canadian started to unfasten the bolts still holding us to the submarine.

Suddenly we heard a noise inside the *Nautilus*. There were voices talking excitedly. What was it? Had somebody discovered our escape? I felt Ned Land slip a dagger into my hand.

"Don't worry," I murmured, "we'll know how to die!"

The Canadian had stopped undoing the bolts. But one word, twenty times repeated, told me what was causing all the disturbance aboard the *Nautilus*. It was not us causing the excitement among the crew!

"The Maelstrom! The Maelstrom!" they cried.

The Maelstrom! In the midst of our terrifying situation, could a more frightening word have reached our ears? Were we in those dangerous waters off the coast of Norway? Was the *Nautilus* being dragged down into this abyss just as our dinghy was about to float free from its flanks?

As is well known, during ebb tide the waters rush out between the Lofoten and Faerö Islands with tremendous violence. There, they form a whirlpool from which no ship has ever been able to escape. Monstrous waves converge from all points of the horizon. They form this chasm so justly called "the Navel of the Ocean." It can pull things in from a distance of ten miles, and drag down not only ships and whales, but even polar bears from farther north.

And the *Nautilus* unintentionally—or perhaps even intentionally—had gotten into this whirlpool. It started spinning around in smaller and smaller circles. And the dinghy, still fastened to the hull, was carried around with it at breakneck speed. I could feel us whirling around and it made me dizzy and sick to my stomach. We were in a state of terror that cannot be imagined; our circulation stopped, our nerves became dead, and our bodies broke out in a cold sweat as if we were at death's door! And what a din there was around our frail dinghy! What roars echoed back from a distance of several miles! What a noise the water made as it was dashed against the sharp rocks on the ocean floor, there where the hardest objects are shattered and tree trunks are worn down until they "look like fur," as the Norwegians put it!

What a predicament! We were being horribly tossed about. The *Nautilus* was struggling as if it were a human being fighting for its life. Its muscles of steel cracked. Sometimes it would stand up straight on end, and us with it!

"We have to hold on," said Ned, "and screw the bolts back down! Our only chance is to stay attached to the *Nautilus* . . ."

He had scarcely finished his sentence when we heard a loud cracking noise. The bolts had given way. The dinghy was torn from its socket and thrown out into the middle of the whirlpool like a stone hurled from a sling.

My head hit an iron rib, and with this violent blow I lost consciousness.

CHAPTER XLVII

Conclusion

Thus ended this voyage beneath the seas. What happened that night, how the dinghy escaped the powerful currents of the Maelstrom, and how Ned Land, Conseil and I came out of that chasm alive, I cannot say. But when I regained consciousness, I was lying in a fisherman's cottage on one of the Lofoten Islands. My two companions, safe and sound, were sitting next to me holding me by the hand. We embraced each other with great emotion.

For the moment it is impossible to get back to France. Means of transportation between northern Norway and the south are scarce. I have to wait for the steamboat which sails twice a month from North Cape.

It is here, therefore, among these good people who took us in, that I have gone over the story of our adventures. I have told this story accurately. Nothing has been omitted, nothing exaggerated. It is a faithful account of our unlikely journey beneath an element till now inaccessible to man, but which progress will undoubtedly one day reveal to him.

Will people believe me? I do not know. But it makes little difference. No one, at least, can deny me the right to talk about these seas beneath which, in less than ten months, I have traveled twenty thousand leagues, or to describe the many wonders I have seen in the Pacific Ocean, the Indian Ocean, the Red Sea, the Mediterranean, the Atlantic, the Antarctic and northern waters!

But what happened to the *Nautilus*? Did it escape the powerful grip of the Maelstrom? Is Captain Nemo still alive? Is he continuing his terrible work of revenge, or did he stop after his last slaughter? Will the seas one day wash up the manuscript containing his life story? Will I ever find out this man's name? Will the nationality of the ship he sank give me a clue to his own nationality?

I hope so. I also hope that his powerful vessel conquered the sea in its most terrible of chasms, and that the *Nautilus* has survived where so many ships have perished! If it has and if Captain Nemo still inhabits the ocean—the country of his adoption—then may the hatred be appeased in his savage heart! May the contemplation of so many wonders extinguish in him the spirit of revenge! May the judge disappear and the scientist continue his peaceful exploration of the seas! However strange his destiny may be, it is also sublime! I myself have understood that much. Did I not also live this unnatural life for ten months? Thus, to that question asked six thousand years ago by Ecclesiastes, "That which is far off, and exceeding deep, who can find it out?" only two men now have the right to answer: Captain Nemo and myself.

Afterword

Ingenious, inspired, prophetic—these are the qualities most often ascribed to Jules Verne. And in *20,000 Leagues Under the Sea* Verne does indeed seem to predict some of today's marvels. But it is not this ability to envision the future that has made this book so enduring and successful. Rather it is Verne's powerful imagery and forceful characterizations that have captured the imagination of generation after generation of readers.

Born in France in 1828, Jules Verne is considered by many to be the "father" of science fiction. In such books as *From the Earth to the Moon, Journey to the Center of the Earth, The Mysterious Island, Around the World in Eighty Days,* and—of course—*20,000 Leagues Under the Sea,* he seems to foresee many of the technological advances and inventions of the past century. Such inventions as the automobile, telephone, helicopter, and nuclear submarine, as well as atomic power and travel to the moon by rocket, are all in some part predicted in the writings of Jules Verne. Yet throughout his writings, it is not science and technology that are the heroes, but the remarkable men who master them.

Captain Nemo is certainly such a man. And few characters in literature are as powerfully unforgettable and frustratingly enigmatic as the master of the *Nautilus.* Observing Nemo only through the often timid eyes of Professor Aronnax, we readers never learn the captain's nationality or age, nor do we learn much of his past. He is shrouded in mystery, yet always in indisputable command of his own private kingdom under the waves. One thing we do learn is that his life has been shaped by tragedy (the death of his beloved wife and children) and a burning passion to help the oppressed people of the world. Nemo is a romantic figure—passionately in love with the sea, fighting to bring freedom to the enslaved; an artist and engineer, a musician and a tyrant. He is the embodiment of the Renaissance man.

Nemo's three guests, or prisoners, are quite different. Each represents a different aspect of man's nature. Professor Aronnax is the erudite intellectual—an acute observer who attempts to classify and categorize all he witnesses. Conseil represents both humor and duty. Like Passepartout in *Around the World in Eighty Days*, Conseil is always conscious of his responsibility as a gentleman's gentleman. Ned Land the harpooner is the man of action. Ned is ready to take on risks and charge ahead to right what he perceives as wrong and to secure an escape for himself and his two fellow captives.

Interestingly, there were aspects of all four of these characters in Jules Verne. Like Aronnax, Verne was a quiet man with a detailed interest in science. Conseil's life of propriety and his strict adherence to rules of conduct were abandoned by Verne when, despite his law degree, he chose to be a writer and not to practice the law—thus breaking with family tradition (his father, grandfather, and brother were all lawyers). And certainly Ned Land and Captain Nemo, who ironically share a passion for the sea, freedom, and a romantic urge to wander, represent the vital and passionate side of Verne himself.

Verne was a great admirer of other writers. Among his favorite books were *Robinson Crusoe* by Daniel Defoe and *The Swiss Family Robinson* by Johann Wyss. In both these books can be seen the fierce struggles against nature that figure in many of the most perilous moments of the *Nautilus'* journey. Another major influence on Verne was the American writer Edgar Allan Poe. Certainly Nemo's steel-edged brilliance and moments of passion bordering on madness can be seen in two of Poe's most famous characters: C. Auguste Dupin (of *The Murders in the Rue Morgue* and *The Purloined Letter*) and Roderick Usher (of *The Fall of the House of Usher*).

Verne also enjoyed the friendship of several famous writers, including Alexandre Dumas and George Sand. Sand was especially encouraging to Verne and may even have given him the idea of writing *20,000 Leagues*. Verne sent her his first two books and a letter describing some of his future plans. "I have only one regret," she wrote back on July 25, 1865, "that I have finished them and have not another ten volumes to read. I hope you will take us soon into the depths of the sea and that you will make your characters travel in one of those submersible boats which your imagination and knowledge will be able to make perfect."

Though Verne began work on *20,000 Leagues* in August 1865, he put it aside for most of 1866 through early 1868 to finish *The Illustrated Geography of France and Its Colonies,* a project that was begun for his publisher by another author but taken over by Verne when the original author became ill.

Nonetheless, Verne seemed to recognize early on that *20,000 Leagues* was something very special. In a letter to his publisher, M. Hetzel, in the spring of 1868 he wrote: "I'm working furiously. I've had a good idea that emerges nicely from the subject. This unknown man must no longer have any contact with humanity. . . . The sea must provide him with everything. . . . Were the continents and islands to vanish in a new Flood, he'd live the same way, and I beg you to believe that his *ark* will be a bit better equipped than Noah's ever was. . . . Oh, my dear Hetzel, if I don't pull this book off, I'll be inconsolable. I've never held a better thing in my hands."

He wrote to his father about the novel around the same time: "I'm working on it with tremendous pleasure. . . . In three or four months, when I have the proofs, I'll try to send you and Paul [Verne's brother] the first volume, so that you can hunt out all the mistakes and imperfections. I very much want this machine to be as perfect as possible."

In yet another letter he wrote: "What is difficult is to make things that are very implausible seem very plausible, but I hope I've succeeded." And still later he wrote: "The hardest job is to make all that seem so plausible that everyone will want to go there. Well, we'll see." And again to his publisher he wrote: "Oh the perfect subject, my dear Hetzel, the perfect subject!"

Verne was right. *20,000 Leagues Under the Sea* was a huge success when published in 1869. Considered by many to be his greatest work, it has never been out of print in French or in English. First filmed as a silent movie in 1916, it was later remade as the now-classic film in 1954 starring James Mason as Captain Nemo.

For this new edition of *20,000 Leagues Under the Sea,* Leo and Diane Dillon, two-time Caldecott Medalists, have created a suite of fantastic illustrations. As an inspired touch, they have captured the feel of nineteenth-century engravings in their first few illustrations, which depict episodes preceding the arrival of Professor Aronnax, Conseil, and Ned on the *Nautilus.* But once these three are aboard the futuristic submarine, the Dillons' paintings are filled with colors and light, incredible underwater flora and fauna, and breathtaking visions of lost civilizations and the mighty *Nautilus* itself.

Serving to frame these wondrous images is an inspired frame of metal gears, rods, and other bits of machinery, created by the Dillons' son, sculptor and artist Lee Dillon. Together, these three artists have captured the remarkable world of Captain Nemo and the *Nautilus*, simultaneously giving freedom to the imagination and grounding their vision solidly in reality.

In this way, the Dillons' illustrations echo the very foundation of what makes *20,000 Leagues Under the Sea* so successful. As Verne himself wrote, to "make things that are very implausible seem very plausible" is extremely difficult. And yet both Verne and the Dillons have succeeded brilliantly—creating a book that will delight readers of all ages for years to come.

—Peter Glassman

BOOKS OF WONDER CLASSICS

DELUXE GIFT EDITIONS OF TIMELESS STORIES,
LAVISHLY ILLUSTRATED WITH FULL-COLOR PLATES AND BLACK-AND-WHITE DRAWINGS

THE ARABIAN NIGHTS
retold by Brian Alderson
illustrated by Michael Foreman

THE SECRET GARDEN
by Frances Hodgson Burnett
illustrated by S. Saelig Gallagher

ALICE'S ADVENTURES IN WONDERLAND
by Lewis Carroll
illustrated by John Tenniel

THROUGH THE LOOKING-GLASS
by Lewis Carroll
illustrated by John Tenniel

THE TROJAN WAR AND
THE ADVENTURES OF ODYSSEUS
by Padraic Colum
illustrated by Barry Moser

A CHRISTMAS CAROL
by Charles Dickens
illustrated by Carter Goodrich

OLIVER TWIST
by Charles Dickens
illustrated by Don Freeman

THE ADVENTURES OF SHERLOCK HOLMES
by Sir Arthur Conan Doyle
illustrated by Barry Moser

THE WHITE COMPANY
by Sir Arthur Conan Doyle
illustrated by N. C. Wyeth

THE THREE MUSKETEERS
by Alexandre Dumas
illustrated by Tom Kidd

THE MAGICAL LAND OF NOOM
written and illustrated by Johnny Gruelle

THE GIFT OF THE MAGI
by O. Henry
illustrated by Michael Dooling

THE LEGEND OF SLEEPY HOLLOW
by Washington Irving
illustrated by Arthur Rackham

RIP VAN WINKLE
by Washington Irving
illustrated by N. C. Wyeth

THE WATER-BABIES
by Charles Kingsley
illustrated by Jessie Willcox Smith

THE JUNGLE BOOK
by Rudyard Kipling
illustrated by Jerry Pinkney

JUST SO STORIES
by Rudyard Kipling
illustrated by Barry Moser

THE RAINBOW FAIRY BOOK
by Andrew Lang
illustrated by Michael Hague

THE STORY OF DOCTOR DOLITTLE
by Hugh Lofting
illustrated by Michael Hague

AT THE BACK OF THE NORTH WIND
by George MacDonald
illustrated by Jessie Willcox Smith

THE PRINCESS AND THE GOBLIN
by George MacDonald
illustrated by Jessie Willcox Smith

GREAT GHOST STORIES
selected and illustrated by Barry Moser

THE ENCHANTED CASTLE
by E. Nesbit
illustrated by Paul O. Zelinsky

FIVE CHILDREN AND IT
by E. Nesbit
illustrated by Paul O. Zelinsky

TALES OF EDGAR ALLAN POE
by Edgar Allan Poe
illustrated by Barry Moser

BLACK BEAUTY
by Anna Sewell
illustrated by Lucy Kemp-Welch

HEIDI
by Johanna Spyri
illustrated by Jessie Willcox Smith

A CHILD'S GARDEN OF VERSES
by Robert Louis Stevenson
illustrated by Diane Goode

DRACULA
by Bram Stoker
illustrated by Barry Moser

THE ADVENTURES OF HUCKLEBERRY FINN
by Mark Twain
illustrated by Steven Kellogg

THE ADVENTURES OF TOM SAWYER
by Mark Twain
illustrated by Barry Moser

A CONNECTICUT YANKEE
IN KING ARTHUR'S COURT
by Mark Twain
illustrated by Trina Schart Hyman

AROUND THE WORLD IN EIGHTY DAYS
by Jules Verne
illustrated by Barry Moser

20,000 LEAGUES UNDER THE SEA
by Jules Verne
illustrated by Leo and Diane Dillon

REBECCA OF SUNNYBROOK FARM
by Kate Douglas Wiggin
illustrated by Helen Mason Grose

THE HAPPY PRINCE AND OTHER STORIES
by Oscar Wilde
illustrated by Charles Robinson

OZ TITLES IN THE BOOKS OF WONDER SERIES

THE WONDERFUL WIZARD OF OZ
100th Anniversary Edition
by L. Frank Baum
with 24 full-color plates and over 130 two-color illustrations
by W. W. Denslow

THE MARVELOUS LAND OF OZ
by L. Frank Baum
with 16 full-color plates and over 125 black-and-white illustrations
by John R. Neill

OZMA OF OZ
by L. Frank Baum
with 42 full-color and over 21 two-color illustrations
by John R. Neill

DOROTHY AND THE WIZARD IN OZ
by L. Frank Baum
with 16 full-color plates and over 50 black-and-white illustrations
by John R. Neill

THE ROAD TO OZ
by L. Frank Baum
with 126 black-and-white illustrations on multicolored paper
by John R. Neill

THE EMERALD CITY OF OZ
by L. Frank Baum
with 16 full-color plates and over 90 black-and-white illustrations
by John R. Neill

THE PATCHWORK GIRL OF OZ
by L. Frank Baum
with 51 full-color and over 80 black-and-white illustrations
by John R. Neill

TIK-TOK OF OZ

by L. Frank Baum
with 12 full-color plates and over 78 black-and-white illustrations
by John R. Neill

THE SCARECROW OF OZ

by L. Frank Baum
with 12 full-color plates and over 104 black-and-white illustrations
by John R. Neill

RINKITINK IN OZ

by L. Frank Baum
with 12 full-color plates and over 104 black-and-white illustrations
by John R. Neill

THE LOST PRINCESS OF OZ

by L. Frank Baum
with 12 full-color plates and over 92 black-and-white illustrations
by John R. Neill

THE TIN WOODMAN OF OZ

by L. Frank Baum
with 12 full-color plates and over 92 black-and-white illustrations
by John R. Neill

THE MAGIC OF OZ

by L. Frank Baum
with 12 full-color plates and over 104 black-and-white illustrations
by John R. Neill

GLINDA OF OZ

by L. Frank Baum
with 12 full-color plates and over 91 black-and-white illustrations
by John R. Neill

LITTLE WIZARD STORIES OF OZ

by L. Frank Baum
with 45 full-color illustrations
by John R. Neill

DOROTHY OF OZ
by Roger S. Baum
with full-color frontispiece and 50 black-and-white illustrations
by Elizabeth Miles

OZ: THE HUNDREDTH ANNIVERSARY CELEBRATION
edited by Peter Glassman
with art and text in appreciation of Oz
by thirty favorite artists and writers

If you enjoy the Oz books and want to know more about Oz, you may be interested in The Royal Club of Oz. Devoted to America's favorite fairyland, it is a club for everyone who loves the Oz books. For free information, please send a first-class stamp to:

THE ROYAL CLUB OF OZ
P.O. Box 714
New York, New York 10011
or call toll free: (800) 207-6968

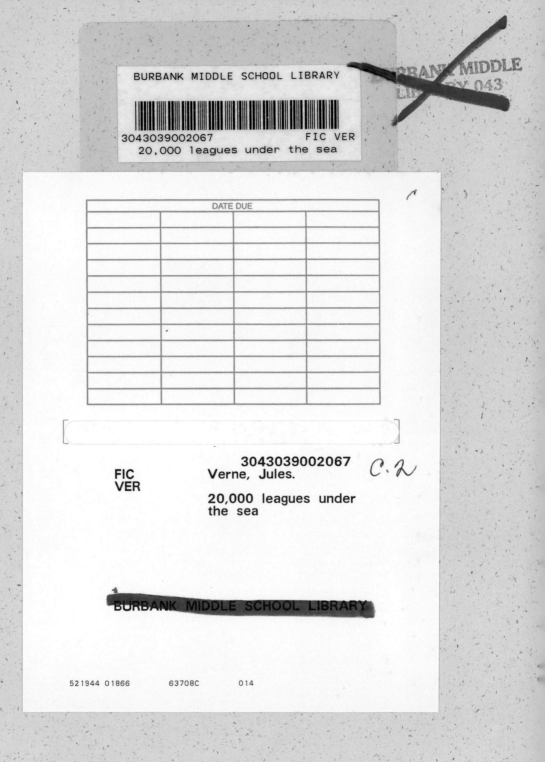

DATE DUE			